The Insubordination of Photography

Reframing Media, Technology, and Culture in Latin/o America

THE INSUBORDINATION OF PHOTOGRAPHY

Documentary Practices under Chile's Dictatorship

Ángeles Donoso Macaya

UNIVERSITY OF FLORIDA PRESS
Gainesville

Publication of this paperback edition made possible by a Sustaining the Humanities through the American Rescue Plan grant from the National Endowment for the Humanities.

Published in the United States of America

First cloth printing, 2020
First paperback printing, 2023

28 27 26 25 24 23 6 5 4 3 2 1

The Library of Congress has cataloged the printed edition as follows:
Names: Donoso Macaya, Ángeles, author.
Title: The insubordination of photography : documentary practices under Chile's dictatorship / Ángeles Donoso Macaya.
Description: Gainesville : University of Florida Press, 2020. | Series: Reframing media, technology, and culture in Latin/o America | Includes bibliographical references and index. |
Identifiers: LCCN 2019015137 (print) | LCCN 2019019192 (ebook) | ISBN 9781683401223 (ePDF) | ISBN 9781683401117 (cloth) | ISBN 9781683403548 (pbk.)
Subjects: LCSH: Documentary photography—Chile—History. | Authoritarianism—Chile—History. | Chile—History. | Collective memory—Chile. | Politics and culture—Chile—History.
Classification: LCC TR820.5 (ebook) | LCC TR820.5 .D66 2020 (print) | DDC 770.983—dc23
LC record available at https://lccn.loc.gov/2019015137

University of Florida Press
2046 NE Waldo Road
Suite 2100
Gainesville, FL 32609
http://upress.ufl.edu

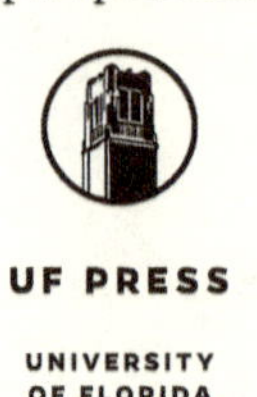

UF PRESS
UNIVERSITY
OF FLORIDA

CONTENTS

FIGURES

ACKNOWLEDGMENTS

In a passage from *The Arcades Project*, Walter Benjamin describes writing as a laborious climbing of narrow rungs. The writer steps on each narrow rung one by one, very carefully, "as one who climbs dangerous heights" and never allows herself "a moment to look around, not only for fear of becoming dizzy," but also because she "would save for the end the full force of the panorama opening out to her." That's how I felt when I started working on this project in late 2011. There it was, the vast photographic field, and here I was, planning to write it from a seemingly immeasurable distance. I thought that I would be climbing stairs for an eternity, that I would never reach a point at which I could turn my head to appreciate "the full panorama opening out" to me. However, during my very first research trip to Chile, I stopped feeling that way: I soon realized that Benjamin's suggestive image did not account for the collectivity that cares for the writer and enables writing. Benjamin, the writer, climbs the step ladder alone. While it is true that writing is filled with such moments—so many hours, days, and weeks spent sitting in front of a computer screen, surrounded by documents, notes, and books—writing is not an experience of the one, the singular. At least writing was not that for me. This book was nourished not only by readings and documents but by conversations I had with many people in encounters that sparked new friendships both here and over there: *acá* and *allá*, concepts in a state (pun intended) of constant change. I reside in two spaces that I call *here* (*acá*), and two that I call *over there* (*allá*), spaces that speak to me as much about the reality of civil insubordination and subversion under a brutally repressive regime as the archives that contain the photographic documentation of the protests, art actions, and publications studied here (and over there). This project was shaped, and in many respects transformed, by so many meaningful interactions. Because of these encounters, I was able to see and appreciate the objects that I study here from a different perspective and adopt a different orientation. Continuing, thus, with the Benjaminian metaphor: if I have reached the last rung, and I can turn around to look at the full panorama that this book opens out, it is because I did not climb this staircase alone. So many people have accompanied and helped me in different ways over the years; they have all contributed to my being able to complete this book. I am so happy to finally have this opportunity to acknowledge them.

I want to begin by thanking the photographers. To Luis Weinstein, my deepest gratitude, for various reasons. Lucho, thank you for believing in this project from the very beginning, for letting me browse your amazing archive of photo books, for helping me get access to and reproduce the archival materials that I needed; *gracias* for the delicious lunches and the wonderful welcome gifts; many thanks also for introducing me to all the other photographers, for granting me permission to use your photographs, and for your friendship. I am also extremely grateful to Paz Errázuriz, Helen Hughes, Kena Lorenzini, Luis Navarro Vega, and Claudio Pérez for welcoming me into their homes and generously sharing their time with me, answering my many questions over the years, and granting me permission to use their photographs. Thank you for your trust, dear Lucho, and for sharing difficult and painful memories with me. Dear Paz, thank you for the long conversations at your house, which I often have recalled while reviewing the manuscript and which have also motivated future projects. Dear Kena, I am forever indebted to you because it was one of your photographs that first triggered my critical reflection. Thank you for answering my questions, even up to the very last minute, about the "Pico" photograph.

I am indebted to Leonora Vicuña for visiting and discussing the exhibition *Chile desde adentro* with me, as well as to Mario Fonseca, Felipe Riobó, and Óscar Wittke, whom I thank for the illuminating conversations in which we engaged. Dear Susan Meiselas, thank you very much for receiving me at your studio in New York to research the *Chile from within* project file, and for answering my many questions. I also wish to thank Héctor López, Marcelo Montecino, Óscar Navarro, and Mauricio Valenzuela for answering my questions and granting me permission to reproduce your photographs.

I am particularly thankful to Hernán Parada. Hernán, I appreciate your trust: thank you for sharing the story of the arrest and ulterior disappearance of your brother, Alejandro; for telling me evocative memories and informative details about the project "Obrabierta A;" for granting me permission to reproduce photographic documentation of this meaningful project, and for allowing me to use one of these touching portraits—Alejandro's photocopied mask—as my book cover. I want to express my gratitude to visual artist Eugenio Dittborn, who told me I did not need his permission and that I could do whatever I wanted with his images. Eugenio: *muy agradecida* for the spread of your *Fallo fotográfico* that I have reproduced in the Introduction of this book and for the enlightening conversation we had about your artistic practice and about Ronald Kay's writings.

Archival objects, photographs, and documents not found in traditional archives are also protagonists of this story. I feel so lucky to have had the opportunity to meet all the magnificent people who have helped me out in significant ways in Chile and abroad. I cannot but say *gracias totales* to my superb collaborators in Chile. Dear Andrea Jösch, I am thankful for your unconditional complicity, your infinite hospitality (I am always looking forward to our next dinner), and for your outstanding (and so necessary!) curatorial and editorial work. José Pablo Concha, thank you very much for your notes on a preliminary draft of chapter 3, for sharing with me all your copies of *Punto de Vista,* and for inviting me to present part of this project at the Segundo Coloquio de Fotografía of the Instituto de Estética at the Pontificia Universidad Católica de Chile in 2013. Jorge Gronemeyer, you provided me high-quality copies of so many images in record time, and for that I will be forever grateful. Thank you also for our conversations about the exhibition *Chile desde adentro*. I am thankful to Sebastián Moreno, director of *La ciudad de los fotógrafos* and to Human Rights lawyer Francisco Ugás for answering countless questions. I also thank visual artist Elías Adasme for receiving me at his home in San Juan, Puerto Rico, and sharing with me valuable archival material; Jenny Holmgren, for granting me permission to use the photographs from Luz Donoso's archive; Paulina Varas, for introducing me to the work of Luz Donoso, prolific artist, documentarian, and *archivista delicada* (delicate archivist). I also want to recognize Justice Marianela Cifuentes of the Court of Appeals of San Miguel, Santiago, for granting me full access to the Lonquén case file. I extend my gratitude to her assistant, Cristián Vargas Albornoz, for aiding me during my research visit. Many thanks also to María Paz Vergara Low, Executive Secretary of the Fundación de Documentación y Archivo Vicaría de la Solidaridad, who helped me obtain the images I needed from the Vicaría's iconographic archive and granted me permission to reproduce them.

I am fortunate to have brilliant friends and colleagues from various latitudes who share my love of photography, documents, and archives. I am thankful to them for meaningful conversations and collaborations that have enriched my reflection on photography, the documentary mode, and the archive. I cannot begin to articulate how much Silvia Spitta means to me. My dear and much-admired Silvia, my adoptive mentor: thank you for having read me with such attention, for your lucid comments and suggestions, for believing that I was writing a book long before I realized it, and for always inviting me to collaborate with you (¡*sigamos*!). I would also like to commemorate here Andrea Noble, a remarkable scholar and a beautiful, generous human being, whom I was lucky to have met and whom I miss greatly. I am grateful to Andrea for having invited me to participate at the Photography and its Public Symposium, held at the Monash University Prato Centre, Italy, in April 2014, where I presented parts of this project, and for having introduced me to colleagues Thy Phu and Iván Ruiz, whom I admire and to whom I am also grateful. I started to work on this project several years ago. I would like to thank Lucía Guerra, who invited me to participate in a Symposium at the University of California at Irvine on the topic of urban Chile in 2011. Lucía asked me if I could talk about the relationship between the city and photography under dictatorship. Those were the first pages I wrote about the expanding photographic field. Thank you also to Mane Adaro, Margarita Alvarado, María Berrios, Matt Busch, Valeria De Los Ríos, Sebastián Díaz, Catalina Donoso, Rita Ferrer, Carl Fischer, Natalia Fortuny, Melissa Miles, Carla Möller, José Miguel Palacios, Leandro Villaro, and Edward Welsch.

The image of writing as the slow climbing of narrow rungs underscores the effort and labor intrinsic to this (at times solitary) activity. Yes, writing is work. It takes effort, costs time, and also depends on the work, the effort, and the collaboration of others to be done amid some tranquility. Kudos to César for his delicious cooking, for keeping me hydrated, and for taking care of all the domestic chores in the last stretch (wages for housework!). Marcial, *querido vecino*, you cannot imagine how meaningful were your suggestions and your unconditional support; also, thanks for the treats that made the revision process more joyful and fruitful! Xandra, *gracias* for urging me to buy a better chair (thanks to you I did not wreck my hips and my back). At the Borough of Manhattan Community College, CUNY, special thanks to my department chair, Maria Enrico, for the unwavering support throughout the years, to Margaret Carson, for the camaraderie, and to all the colleagues in the Modern Languages Department with whom I work. I am also grateful to my union (yes, I am a proud union member!), the Professional Staff Congress of the City of New York (PSC-CUNY), for having negotiated as part of the contract reassigned time for full-time faculty in tenure-track positions, so they are able to pursue research endeavors. (I feel extremely privileged to have a full-time position and will continue fighting to improve the labor conditions of my part-time colleagues.) Simply put, I would have not finished this book had it not been for these precious reassigned hours. The reassigned time meant I taught fewer courses, which allowed me to complete several drafts of my manuscript between 2013 and 2017. I also wish to acknowledge the support I received in the form of grants. A Fondo Nacional de las Artes (FONDART) grant, awarded by the Chilean National Council for the Arts and Culture (CNCA), allowed me to fund this project from July 2012 to July 2014. Support for this project was also provided by two PSC-CUNY Awards, jointly funded by The Professional Staff Congress and The City University of New York (from July 2014 to July 2015, and from July 2017 to July 2018), and by a CUNY Book Completion Award (from May 2018 to April 2019).

I reviewed the last draft of my manuscript while teaching a seminar at the PhD Program in Latin American, Iberian, and Latino Cultures (LAILAC) at The Graduate Center, CUNY. I am particularly indebted to my students from the seminar *Del espacio de acá:* Photographic Discourses and Practices in/about Latin America. Our discussions helped me to reformulate ideas in chapters 1 and 2. I am also very grateful to my colleagues from the PhD Program, Magdalena Perkowska, Fernando De Giovanni, and José Del Valle, for inviting me to present this research in 2014 and to teach in Fall 2018. I am thankful to Karrin Wilks, current Interim President at BMCC, for supporting this opportunity.

At the University of Florida Press, I am grateful to the series editors, Juan Carlos Rodríguez and Héctor Fernández, for having seen the potential in this project very early on and for the extensive feedback they gave me at different stages of the process. Special thanks go to external readers Antonio J. Traverso and Alessandro Fornazzari, whose detailed feedback and suggestions made the revisions process fruitful and almost painless. I was lucky to fall into the hands of Stephanye Hunter, my acquisitions editor, who guided me and helped me throughout the process. I am grateful to everyone at the University of Florida Press who made this book tangible, and beautiful, and to my copyeditor and indexer extraordinaire, Omar Al Jamal (*¡gracias Omar!*).

In late 2017, I became involved with the New Sanctuary Coalition of New York City (NSC), an organization that fights every day in defense of the rights of undocumented immigrants. As an immigrant myself, the experience of accompanying friends to immigration courts and ICE check-ins, along with the work we do in the NSC Pro Se clinic every week (we fill out different immigration and legal forms, write letters, and draft habeas corpus petitions on behalf of friends currently detained in jails indefinitely, without a date scheduled for a court hearing), instigated me to establish significant connections between my current present *here* (in the U.S.) and the past *over there* (Chile under dictatorship). Thanks to the NSC, I came to see and think of the work done by the Vicaría de la Solidaridad during the dictatorship in a different light. I want to thank the entire New Sanctuary Coalition (and Sara Gozalo in particular) for teaching me to believe in the power of community, for reminding me every day how important and necessary it is to fight collectively to build a more just society.

It is time to thank my family and friends. It fills me with joy to thank my parents, Lya and Enrique. I am grateful for your unreserved love, for your constant support, for your encouragement, and for pampering me whenever I visit you. I love you. And to my friends, I am deeply grateful. Some have always been there, and others have accompanied me at key moments of this process (reading parts of the manuscript, helping me with ideas for the title, for the cover, etc.). Thank you Daniela Aguirre, Manuel Carrión, Antonio Catrileo, Rosario Etcheverry, Marcela Fuentes, Germán Garrido, Marcial Godoy, Melissa González, Xandra Ibarra, Yolie Medina, Deyanira Rojas-Sosa, Laura Torres-Rodríguez, Rosario Valenzuela, Klara Waisz, Catrileo+Carrión, and COLACiones. Special thanks to Sergio Andrade, Jorge Araya, Natalia Grez, Alejandra Prieto, Pepa San Martín, Iván Smirnow, and Silvana Veto because every time we are together I feel extremely joyful, and also to Iván: I am infinitely thankful to you for your generosity and for your constant presence. I feel so fortunate to have you in my life.

I shall conclude by thanking time and time again César, my lover, my friend, my cook, my co-conspirator, and my home. *Compa* César, I cannot thank you enough for being the way you are with me: I admire you, I trust you, and I love you. *Gracias* for taking such good care of me; for buying me chocolates, wine, *maní confitado*, and for cooking everything else; for always listening to me; for teaching me how to play guitar; for being such a good talker; for being such a demanding editor, and loyal reader. Thank you, always, for your unwavering support and infinite patience. How many times did I read to you aloud the pages and pages of this manuscript, sometimes with little variation, over and over and over again? Happily, here it is: *The Insubordination of Photography* is for you.

INTRODUCTION

Adjusting the Depth of Field

> The subject of human rights abuses has sharply marked all Chilean narrative about the national body with images of human remains: of bodies that have not been found, bodies that have not been laid to rest. This lack of burial is the image—without recovery—of a historical mourning process, one that never completely assimilates the sense of loss, but rather conserves it in an unfinished, transitional version. It is also the metaphorical condition of an unsealed temporality: inconclusive, and therefore open to re-exploration in many new directions by our memory, increasingly active and dissatisfied.
>
> —Nelly Richard, *The Insubordination of Signs*

On May 1, 1984, thousands of people gathered at O'Higgins Park in downtown Santiago to celebrate International Worker's Day and to commemorate the anniversary of the First National Strike held to protest the dictatorship.[1] The attendance—between eighty thousand and one hundred thousand people according to officialist media, and up to two hundred and fifty thousand people according to opposition media—surprised even the Comando Nacional de Trabajadores (CNT) (National Workers Front), organizers of the event. They had reason to be surprised: this demonstration, authorized just a week earlier by the regime, was the largest in the history of May 1 celebrations held in Chile (to that date). The celebration happened amid a climate of heightened military and police repression, and as journalist María Olivia Mönckeberg highlights in a chronicle published in the opposition magazine *Análisis*, the "censorship and the manipulation of information [. . .] obstructed communications" about the event.[2]

Photographer Kena Lorenzini also attended this protest. She was there as a graphic reporter for *Análisis*. A photo she took—a wide shot that shows thousands of people, most of them young, with their arms raised—was published along Mönckeberg's chronicle. Lorenzini took many other photos that day. For Lorenzini, a member of the collective Mujeres por la Vida (Women for Life) and of the Asociación de Fotógrafos Independientes (AFI) (Independent Photographers Association), documenting this historic demonstration was important. One particular photo, which I have looked at countless times since I started writing this book, captures one of the many demonstrators in the foreground (see fig. I.1). This photo was not published in *Análisis*, and I for one did not see it until many years later, but I know that it was seen by many pedestrians in the late eighties, because Lorenzini walked around Paseo Ahumada (a pedestrian walk in the heart of downtown Santiago) with a large reproduction of the photo hanging from her shoulders. I learned of this original form of public display through another photo, which I also encountered many years later (see fig. I.5).[3]

Lorenzini's "Pico" photo always makes me smile. Always. I love its audacity, its humor. I know Lorenzini laughed too that day at O'Higgins Park when she noticed this guy amidst the crowd. How could she not? The man's T-shirt is so irreverent, yet so precise. In regular Spanish, *pico* means "beak;" in *chileno*, it also means "dick," as well as "fuck it" and "fuck this," which is the best translation in this case. Sometimes, looking at the picture, I consider the closeness between Lorenzini and her subject. Other times, I admire the agility with which the photographer adjusted the camera settings to take the photo (at demonstrations, everything changes quickly and the risk of police repression is always looming, so photographers have little time to prepare their cameras, adjust their lenses, focus, and take the photo). Over the years, I have written different short descriptive notes about this photo. One time, I wrote: "The photo frames a man. I don't know who this man is. He seems to be looking up, but I don't know what he is looking at. His gaze is somewhat defiant; I can see he is not afraid, or at least he doesn't seem afraid. There are other people around him, most of them out of focus. Some of them carry posters and banners. Some people look up. What are they looking at? I don't know. The message on the man's T-shirt is hilarious, but also very telling: *Pico. Pico*: this four-letter word condenses, in a way, the sentiment shared by the demonstrators."

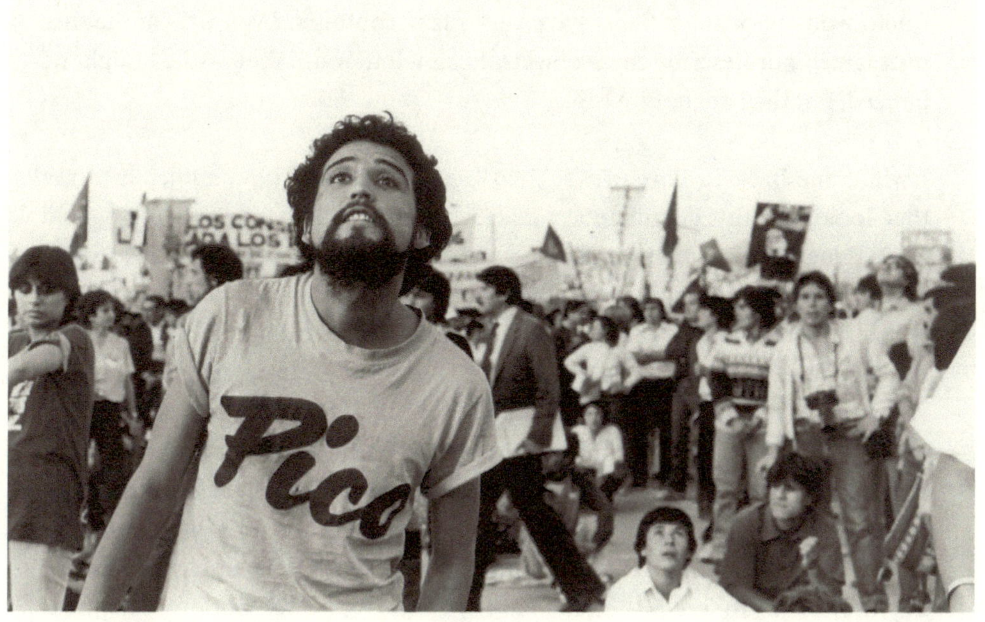

Figure I.1. First Rally, O'Higgins Park, Santiago de Chile, May 1, 1984. Credit: Kena Lorenzini. Black and white. Kena Lorenzini's personal archive.

Reading this note now, many years later, I realize I barely took notice then of other elements (people, posters, banners) also visible in the photo—all my attention was on the man's T-shirt, I guess. Yet, if I adjust my gaze, I can easily focus on these other elements, most of them blurred in the background. I can take notice, for example, of a man who carries some documents under his arm and seems to be hurrying along. He wears a suit and a tie. Considering that this was a rally held on a national holiday day, the presence of this man is intriguing. Where was he heading in such a hurry? What were those documents he was carrying? Why was he wearing a suit and a tie? I also take note of a man with a camera hanging from his neck—I say to myself, another photographer like Lorenzini, working on International Workers Day to document this important demonstration. If I readjust my gaze once more, I can turn my attention to the woman located to the left side of the frame: she seems to look at her arm insistently. I can also recognize, in one of the posters far in the background, Salvador Allende's face (the trace of a trace). With my eyes still on the photo, I can take in one important detail: most of the objects appearing farther in the background (men, women, posters, flags) have very fuzzy contours. Even if I can neither distinguish nor describe these objects, I can tell they are there—they might be blurred, but they are not invisible.

I will come back to Lorenzini's "Pico" photo later. For now, suffice it to say that, looking at this documentary image, I started to consider its depth of field more dynamically, which in turn led me to formulate depth of field as a critical concept to explore the expanding field of photography. In case the reader is not familiar with the concept, I shall offer a brief explanation: depth of field is a measure that designates the relative sharpness of an image. This relative sharpness is measured by the distance between the focused objects appearing in the foreground, middle ground, and background of an image: those photographs in which all elements have clear, sharp contours are said to have a great depth of field; in contrast, when the elements in the foreground or those in the background appear blurred, the photograph is said to have a shallow depth of field.[4] In *The Insubordination of Photography,* the notion of depth of field is concomitant to the notion of expanding field. Because of this link, both notions and their respective meanings get carried away, so to speak—not unlike photographs—in the play of metonymy and imagination. Thus, if depth of field commonly refers to the area of acceptable sharpness of a photograph, in the pages that follow the term evokes what is discernible, intelligible, or visible within the expanding field of photography. By adjusting the focus of the camera lens, objects or practices previously undefined or blurred can become visible or sharper in the frame and vice versa: this readjustment (among other aspects) allows for a greater depth of field. Likewise, by readjusting the view over the photographic field, objects not available or not previously considered can become visible, come to light.

And this brings me to the heart of my book: despite the relentless tactics devised by the civic-military dictatorship to control the visual field and adjust the depth of field, photography became a paramount documentary tool to denounce, protest, and challenge the dictatorship. In *The Insubordination of Photography*, I analyze the documentary practices of photography devised by different collectives (relatives of the detained-disappeared, visual artists, and photographers), organizations, and independent media that resisted, defied, and participated in the downfall of the Chilean dictatorial regime. I formulate the objects I study as documentary pratices of photography because I focus not only on *photographs* as evidence or testimonies of horror, but rather on photography as a *documentary practice*—a democratic "civil practice," to borrow Ariella Azoulay's formulation, one that opened up a political space of resistance based on collaboration, creation, sanctuary, solidarity, accompaniment, play, and even humor.[5]

The Military's Depth of Field

There is little doubt that photography was profusely used by the dictatorship. The military junta and officialist media not only shaped the visual field since the very first day of the coup, but also adjusted the depth of field through the production of documentary traces. Some events were displayed in the very foreground to terrorize and intimidate; other events were framed in convoluted narratives and complex backgrounds, just like those photographs with a deep depth of field, where a lot of elements are seen, at a distance, but it is sometimes difficult to distinguish them. Indeed, not long after the Hawker Hunter jets began to bombard La Moneda Presidential Palace on September 11, 1973, the military junta and pro-military media outlets gained almost absolute control over the depth of field.[6] The first photo reproduced on the front cover of *La Tercera*—one of the two newspapers that circulated two days after the coup—showed La Moneda in flames, behind a big headline that read: "Gigantic 'Clean-up' Operation of Extremists: Military Junta Took Control."[7] A caption printed over the photo indicated: "Thus fell La Moneda." An arrow points to La Moneda hidden behind the orange smoke in the background of the photo. The interior pages also included numerous photos. Some of them were out of focus because they were made in the middle of it all, in the hours (and minutes) prior to the bombardment (see fig. I.2). The photos showed tanks, soldiers in position pointing their weapons, people running with their hands up, and La Moneda Palace burning. The headings published alongside these images didn't offer much information: "Junta threatened to kill all extremists in resistance," "All bank accounts are frozen," and, amazingly, "The situation across the country is normal." Shaky, frenzied documentary footage of downtown Santiago and of La Moneda besieged by military tanks, obtained with handheld cameras, was also broadcast on Televisión Nacional the very day of the coup.

Officialist media outlets, led by media mogul Agustín Edwards—owner of *El Mercurio* and of the media conglomerate that, as is well documented, played

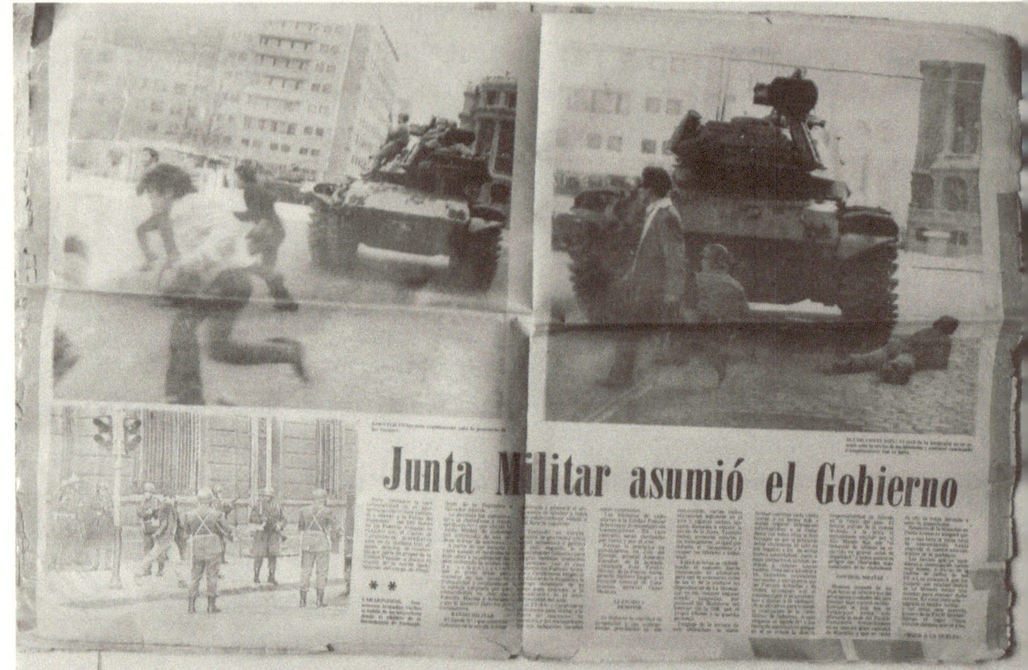
Junta Militar asumió el Gobierno

Figure I.2. *La Tercera* spread with large photos of military repression taken the day of the coup. September 13, 1973. Black and white. Elías Adasme's personal archive.

an instrumental role in the military coup—would soon give to these images and to the bombardment of La Moneda itself a framework, a (cover-up) story, and a deeper depth of field.[8] To be clear, this was not the first demonstration of military defiance, and the fabrication of fake news and propaganda did not begin with the civic-military coup either.[9] Indeed, this was the continuation of an ideological warfare partly financed by the U.S. government, first conceived and implemented in the context of the 1964 elections.[10] What changed after the coup, however, was that any expression of dissent or opposition to the military junta became forbidden and severely repressed. For nonofficialist national media, attempts to report or broadcast what was going on were considered forms of dissent, threats to the country's national security, and against the efforts of "reconstruction."

According to news specials that proliferated in the weeks that followed the coup, the bombardment had been in response to an alleged "auto coup" planned by president Salvador Allende to establish a "dictatorship of the proletariat." According to *El Mercurio* and *Las Últimas Noticias*—the latter also part of Edwards's conglomerate—a plan supposedly financed and concocted with the aid of Cuba and the Soviet Union aimed at the "physical elimination" of military leadership and Allende's opponents, including journalists and professionals. Not only did the Unidad Popular (UP) government already have in its possession "thousands" of firearms—alleged the newspapers—but also "thousands" of Cuban *guerrilleros* would help UP supporters to execute the attack. This "auto coup" would have taken place on September 17, 1973, had it not been for the timely, providential even, sacrifice and patriotism of the Armed Forces and the military that, assisted by God, intervened to save the country from its internal and external enemies. This paranoid story was based on a mysterious document titled "Plan Z," allegedly found inside a safe in the Ministry of the Interior's office, and included in the *Libro Blanco del cambio de Gobierno en Chile* (White Book of the Change of Government in Chile) (1973) as "Documentary Appendix."[11]

Libro Blanco, published in November 1973 to counter the bad press that was already circulating abroad, began with an instructive note penned by the General Secretariat of the Government (the military junta): "The truth about the events in Chile has been deliberately distorted before the world. Those who, from within, dragged the country to economic, social, and institutional ruin [. . .] and those who, from outside of Chile, actively collaborated in the catastrophe, have conspired to hide and falsify that truth."[12] The *actual* truth that *Libro Blanco* established—constructed—was thus carefully supported by documents. In addition to "Plan Z," the main appendix of the book included photocopies of maps, diagrams, minutes, and letters, lists of all kinds, deposits, and more, all compiled under the heading "Secret Documents." More important for my discussion, the book included *photographs*. The first photograph is a shot of the military junta at work; the following ten photos, all reproduced in consecutive pages in the first part of the book, depict different, related, scenes: a "*cubano* in *guerrillero* apparel" training Allende to use artillery; heavy and light weaponry allegedly found at Allende's private residence and at other places (there were four of these photos); parts of armored vehicles; stacks of banknotes corresponding to money supposedly stolen by the "hierarchs of the regime" ("hundreds of *escudos* and hundreds of thousands of dollars"); and even a pistol muffler focused in a close-up, "a typical gangsters' accessory," as the caption opines. *Libro Blanco*, as its title suggests, presented itself as a clean—and truthful—slate: it said, look, these are unequivocal facts, and here are the documents and the visual evidence to corroborate them.

Like *Libro Blanco*, other books comprised mostly of photographs were promptly published in late 1973 to clean the image of the military junta abroad and to strengthen anti-Allende, anti-Marxist, and anti-Soviet sentiment within Chile, including *La experiencia socialista chilena: Anatomía de un fracaso* (The Chilean Socialist Experience: Anatomy of a Failure) and a trilingual edition titled *The New Awakening. Three Years of Destruction* (published in Spanish, English, and French).[13] In 1974, the Psychology Department of the Human Relations Division of the General Secretary of the Government prepared a document detailing a "plan of massive psychological penetration" (an eloquent name, no doubt). The proposed plan's objective was "to destroy the Marxist doctrine." The main recommendation was to deploy very simple, straightforward forms of communication to convey the following: "Marxism = violence = scarcity = scandal = anguish = danger of death [. . .] Military Junta = therapeutic factor = welfare = solution to problems = progress = homeland."[14]

Perhaps there is no book as eye-catching (and as blatant) in the creation of this polarization ("us Chileans" versus "them Marxists") as *Chile Ayer Hoy* (Chile Yesterday Today) (1975). To formulate this antagonism as clearly as possible, *Chile Ayer Hoy* also crafts the narrative through photographs. The book displays photos of "yesterday" and photos of "today," reproduced on opposite pages and framed by captions that aim to convey contrasting ideas: violence/peace, evil/good, communism/morality, scarcity/abundance, terrorism/normality, chaos/order, protesters/students, communist activists/youth, extremist/citizen, and so on and so forth. "Yesterday" imagery is reproduced on the left side over black background; "today" photos appear on the right side over white background. The oppositional message conveyed by the photos is reinforced (or directed) by the captions, all written in Spanish, English, and French. This clear-cut composition suggests that the book's author(s)—most likely personnel of the Dirección Nacional de Comunicación Social (DINACOS) (Directorate of Social Communications)—attempted to apply verbatim the recommendations of the plan of massive psychological penetration.[15]

Chile Ayer Hoy's overarching theme was that "yesterday," Chileans lived under Soviet influence, communist demonstrations were recurrent, students didn't study, and people had nothing to buy because all businesses were closed; "today," people are happy, students study, people can shop, workers work, and the city is calm (the countryside is conspicuously absent from the narrative) (see fig.

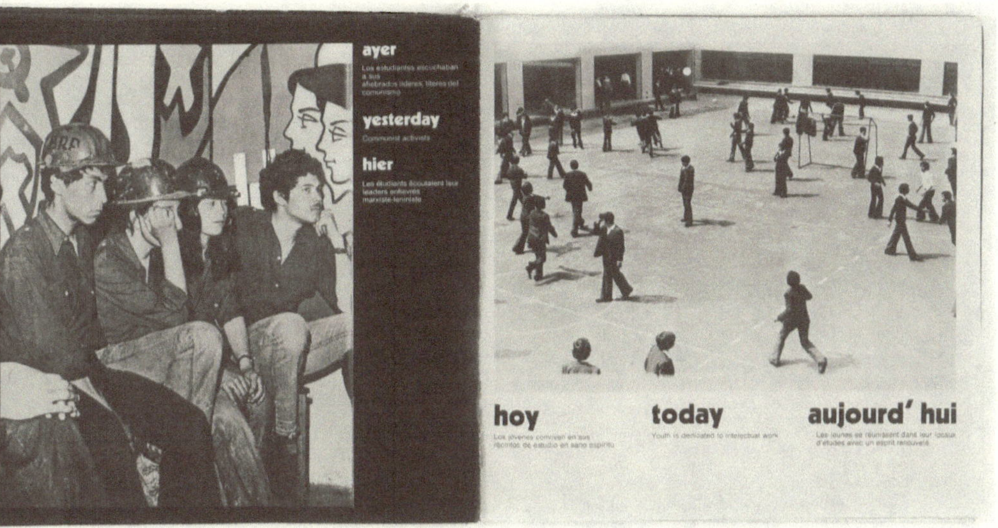

Figure I.3. *Chile Ayer Hoy* spread, two images of youth of "yesterday" (activists) and "today" (students). Black and white. Editora Nacional Gabriela Mistral (now defunct). Jorge Gronemeyer's personal archive (Taller Gronefot).

I.3). The imagery used to reinforce this dual portrayal was rather limited. This becomes apparent in the last section of the book. Here, close-ups of all kinds of firearms (pistols, rifles, cannons) are reproduced on both sides of the page to convey the idea of communist violence, as in *Libro Blanco.* These photos, all arranged over the same black background, are framed by captions such as "Guns to indoctrinate," "Guns to destroy Chile," "Guns sent from Moscow for Chileans to kill Chileans" (see fig. I.4). This "gun menace" is a predominant theme in *Libro Blanco*, *New Awakening*, and *Chile Ayer Hoy*. Paradoxically, while all three books insist on this matter—using the exact same photos, as a matter of fact—never in Chilean history were so many weapons displayed and used in the city and countryside as there were at that present moment ("today") that *Chile Ayer Hoy* celebrates.

Besides producing sophisticated publications to spread anti-Marxist propaganda and pro-military sentiment, Pinochet's regime was relentless in its effort to discredit denunciation and condemnation efforts, and its regime attempted, from very early on and by *all* means possible, to render invisible and annul legal claims about its resort to illegal arrests, torture, and abductions through its sol-

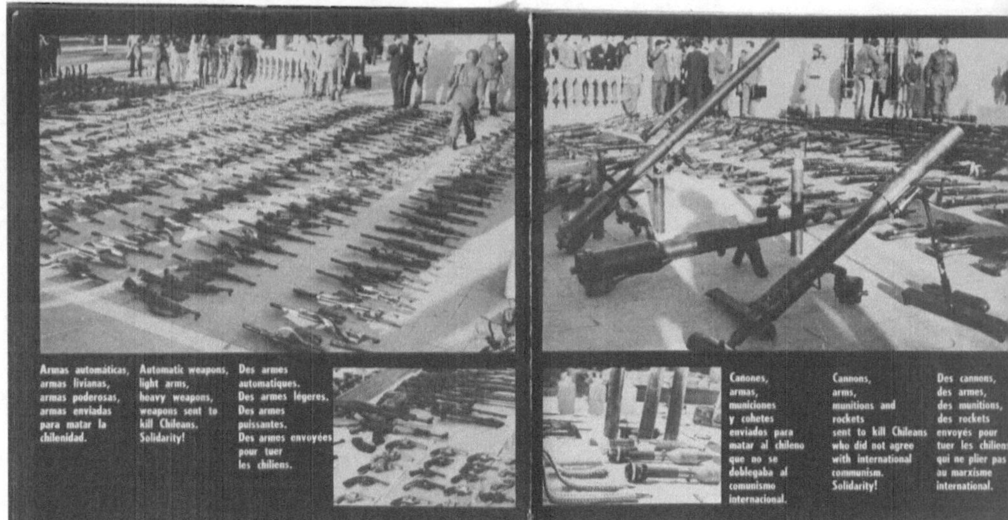

Figure I.4. *Chile Ayer Hoy* spread, four images showing arms. Black and white. Editora Nacional Gabriela Mistral (now defunct). Jorge Gronemeyer's personal archive (Taller Gronefot).

diers, the (secret) police, and secret intelligence services. These infamous cover-ups, or *montajes*, have been well documented and studied.[16] A paradigmatic one was Operación Colombo, the convoluted cover-up story devised by the notorious Dirección de Inteligencia Nacional (DINA) (Directorate of National Intelligence) in 1974–1975 to discredit the denunciations of forced disappearances. This international cover-up story proffered the idea that 119 disappeared people, most of them *miristas*, had not been forcefully disappeared; rather, according to the officialist media, some had killed each other in internal confrontations, and others had been killed in Argentina.[17]

Given this milieu saturated by disinformation and cover-ups of all kinds and restricted by repression and censorship, how does one demand and make visible the truth about the (denied) crime of forced disappearances? At a moment when resistance was gaining more space on the streets and on the independent media, how could one ensure the safety of independent photographers and challenge censorship? How does one convey denunciation when images are prohibited? The objects I study emerged as answers to these pressing questions. Different documentary practices of photography were devised to make visible the crime of forced disappearances in the public space (chapter 1), to produce a credible visual record of forensic evidence in a paramount legal case (chapter 2), to denounce and resist precarity and protect the work of independent photographers and reporters (chapter 3), and to challenge—and ridicule—censorship and the limitations imposed on freedom of the press (chapter 4). These practices not only changed the depth of field, which the dictatorship attempted by all means to control, but also, and perhaps more importantly, strengthened the ideology and the public space of the opposition and kept expanding the photographic field.

The Expanding Field of the Practices of Photography

Throughout this book, I speak of the *expanding field* of photographic practices instead of resorting to the most commonly used concept of *expanded field*.[18] The past participle form denotes completion; it suggests the idea of an already expanded field.[19] But the field of photographic practices is always expanding. It is an always-incomplete field; its persistent expansion is concomitant to the character of photographs—finite objects that work in a supplementary way. Meanwhile, photographic practice is not synonymous with photography or with photograph. This is not about resorting to a more attractive word to designate the same object. Pierre Bourdieu introduced the notion of photographic practice in 1965 in his well-known study about the social uses of photography.[20] In *Touching Photographs*, Margaret Olin builds on Bourdieu's notion to describe different actions linked to photography, including taking, posing for, and looking at photographs, as "photographic practices that inform the expectations people have of photographs, how they act in taking them or posing for them, and how photographs acquire their meaning or do their jobs."[21] For Olin, photography is first and foremost a material object, a visual presence that exists in the world; consequently, she is concerned above all with how people use, interact with, and are moved by photographs (thus the double meaning implied in the title of the book, *Touching Photographs*).[22]

My formulation of photographic practice builds on Olin's but is not restricted to the consideration of photographs only, because—as I hope to show—the materiality and the formal aspects of photographs do not completely determine their documentary weight. Does a photocopied photograph have the same documentary weight as a photograph? The profuse dissemination of photocopied portraits in the public space suggests that yes, it does. Can an empty square have documentary weight? Yes, it can: the display of empty frames in censored media was grounded in the performative referentiality of photography and rendered censorship palpable, visible.

A photocopied photo, an empty square, and a photograph can hold similar documentary weight because the expanding field of photographic practices that this book formulates and explores is defined neither by an individual (the photographer) or apparatus (the camera) nor by a format (photographs).[23] This expanding field necessarily engages the different individuals that used and produced photographs during this period (the relatives of the victims, photographers, visual artists, and photojournalists, lawyers and judges, photography critics, journalists, etc.); the processes related to photography and all photography-derived materials; the organizations and institutions that used, archived, and displayed photographs and other documents; and the different conceptualizations of photography and of photographs considered as documentary traces.

The critical gestures of exploring a number of objects—photographic practices—together with the field they constitute, depends on the perspective—the focus or view one has of/in the field—as well as on the availability of these same objects within said field. As many visual scholars have argued, there is a close connection between the notion of field and the gaze.[24] Sometimes the connection is explicit: consider the terms "visible field," "field of vision," and "visual field," as well as several denotations of the word "field" emphasizing aspects linked to visibility.[25] Here, I would like to follow a reflection developed in queer theory that considers the link between field and the gaze in terms of availability (of objects or actions) and reproducibility (of gestures, preferences, or practices). In *The Psychic Life of Power*, Judith Butler explains how heterosexuality is induced from very early on: it starts with the available objects that children find around them and to which they relate. Heterosexuality as "induced behavior" depends not only on the apparent availability of certain "heterosexual objects," but also on the renunciation of homosexuality as a possibility.[26] In Butler's words, this renunciation entails a "foreclosure, which produces a field of heterosexual objects at the same time as it produces a domain of those whom it would be impossible to love."[27] The renunciation, then, is at the same time facilitated and induced by/in the field of available heterosexual objects. In *Queer Phenomenology*, Sara Ahmed revisits this image of "a field of heterosexual objects" and considers the significance of the term "field" in Butler's formulation. In Ahmed's reading of Butler, this "field of objects would refer to how certain objects are made available by clearing, through the delimitation of space as a space for some things rather than others, where 'things' might include actions ('doing things')."[28]

The idea of field as a space that determines the availability—that is, visibility—of certain objects and also induces, based on this availability, certain behaviors (in the case of Butler and Ahmed, a field of heterosexual objects) informs my own formulations of the notions of depth of field and expanding field. Drawing from Ahmed's formulation, the word "objects" refers here to the constellation of photographic practices. The invisibility of certain objects in the Chilean cultural field, invisibility that resulted from specific acts of clearing (including censorship), as well as the delimitation of the dictatorship's cultural field as a space that welcomed certain objects and not others, determined and even constricted the field of practices of photography. The distribution of the available (visible) photographs was also determined by such acts of clearing—that is, by the series of critical, aesthetic, and political delineations that assigned certain photographs to certain spaces (artistic, civic, mediatic, forensic, etc.) for their use and circulation.

The Documentary Matters

In formulating the objects I study as "documentary" practices, I necessarily engage with a long theoretical discussion concerning the documentary genre, photojournalism, and the discursive spaces of documentary photography.[29] At the same time, because I attempt to think with and through—in other words, to let myself be oriented by—the documentary practices of photography that flourished in the seventies and eighties in Chile, my analysis departs from the orientation set by poststructuralist approaches about documentary photography and photojournalism.[30] My analysis also reconsiders critical formulations that emerged in the Chilean cultural field in the mid-seventies and that were inspired by the incorporation of photography in the artistic practices.

Much has been written and said about the documentary mode and about the ethics, politics, and aesthetics of photojournalism—a practice closely related to documentary photography. Olivier Lugon notes that the word *documentary* "has always encompassed varying images and attitudes and given rise to contradictory definitions [. . .] No one has ever known with certainty what the word 'documentary' actually entails."[31] This kind of argument seems like an easy way out: certainly, documentary photography has had different critical formulations, histories, and genealogies.[32] However, most of these critical formulations, genealogies, and histories refer us to the political or cultural contexts of some Western European countries (mainly England, France, and Germany) or of the United States, which complicates things further—at least for me.[33]

In the seventies and eighties, U.S. poststructuralist theorists decried documentary photography for being too paternalistic and photojournalism for rendering (and reproducing) horror and violence as spectacle. The dismissal of documentary photography by these theorists has even prompted one scholar to ask, "Why do photography critics hate photography?"[34] But the problem wasn't simply that they distrusted photojournalism or hated documentary photography. The problem had to do also with the geopolitics implicit in most of these critical approaches. Lest we forget: the photographs that theorists and critics such as Susan Sontag, Allan Sekula, and Martha Rosler, among others, were referring to had mostly been taken outside of the United States, in the hot spots of the Cold War and disseminated in U.S. print media.[35]

Those critical approaches that have considered the problem of geopolitics in addressing the practice of photojournalism don't always provide adequate explanations regarding local or regional photographic practices. For example, commenting on the development of photojournalism in Latin America in the seventies and eighties, Mary Panzer explains: "Much of the memorable reporting was done by outsiders, like Susan Meiselas, who were able to publish their work in Europe and the United States. For those who stayed, publication was often impossible or required brave and creative remedies—as in 1988 when one group of Chilean photographers made themselves into a 'living newspaper,' demonstrating against General Pinochet by carrying their work through the streets."[36] While Panzer acknowledges the bravery and creativity of Chilean photographers, the suggestion that "much of the memorable" photographic reporting was done "by outsiders" is inadequate—and unfortunate. As I show in this book, independent photographers in Chile were devoted to the important tasks of denouncing the repression and expanding the space of protest and resistance, and in doing so produced *memorable, iconic photographs*—Lorenzini's photograph is one of many examples—that they published and disseminated in independent magazines and photocopied photo books and displayed in countless exhibits.[37] This is why I claim that photojournalism flourished in Chile under the dictatorship—as Susan Meiselas herself was able to observe (see this volume's epilogue). Last, it must be said: while it is true that publishing high-quality photographic books was difficult for local independent photographers—not for the military regime, as we have seen—high-quality photo books are not the only

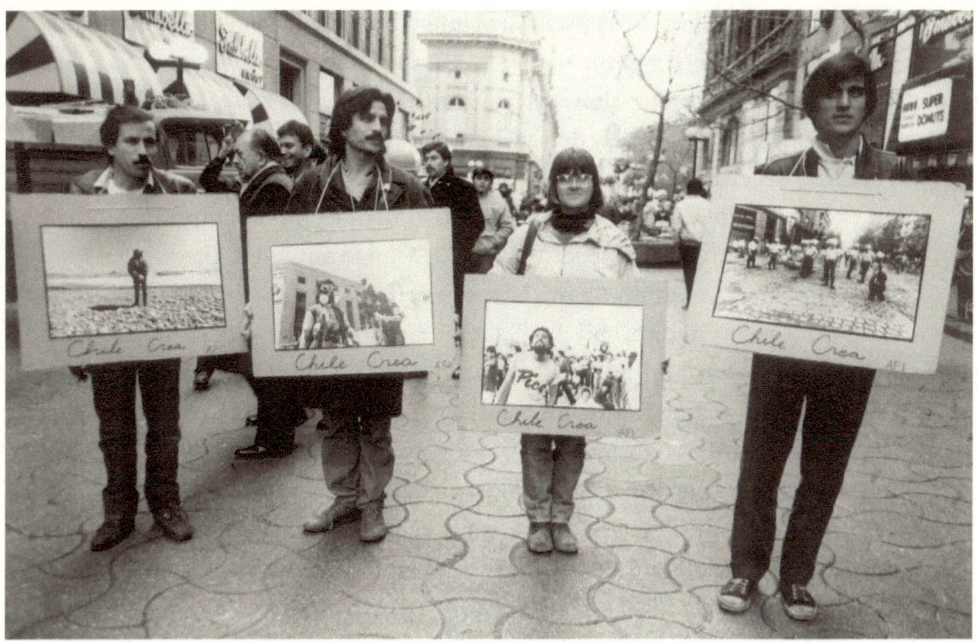

Figure I.5. "We the Photographers Protesting at Paseo Ahumada (taken by a colleague with my camera), Santiago, 1988." Black and white. Kena Lorenzini's personal archive.

way to disseminate photographic work. The 1988 demonstration mentioned by Panzer, and which I evoked in passing in my reading of Lorenzini's photo, is one example (see fig. I.5). The demonstration was in fact a street photo exhibition part of *Chile crea* (Chile Creates), an international solidarity event held in July 1988 that comprised art, science, and culture. One of Lorenzini's colleagues took a photo of the exhibit using her camera. The photo shows AFI photographers José "Pepe" Moreno, Álvaro Hoppe, Alejandro Hoppe, and Lorenzini, all smiling, proudly exhibiting their documentary work.[38]

A prevailing and oft-cited formulation of documentary photography defines it as an extension of the state, as a capture device that produces, at the same time, disciplinary forms of control and surveillance (the photo ID, for example) and ideological forms of identification. This is John Tagg's main argument in *The Disciplinary Frame.* Drawing from Michel Foucault's ideas about the relationship between documentation techniques, disciplinary practices, and the construction of subjectivity, Tagg emphasizes the underlying populism of the documentary genre as it flourished in the 1930s in the United States as well as its "fundamental and inescapable" relation to the state.[39] It is undeniable that photographs, as Tagg claims, "capture meaning." However, the machinery of the state, regardless of its influence, does not completely determine photographic meanings—even when it attempts by every means possible to do so. Not every performance of the document is necessarily disciplinary; not all documentary photographs reproduce paternalistic or populist perspectives. This is why throughout *The Insubordination of Photography,* I underscore Thomas Keenan's idea of the document as an operation, as performance, and Ariella Azoulay's formulation of photography as a civil practice.[40] According to Azoulay, "the invention of photography added a new way of regarding the visible, one that previously did not exist or that, at least, existed in a different manner."[41] Azoulay calls this way of regarding, "the civil gaze:" the civil gaze, which exists "always and only within a plurality [. . .] doesn't seek to control the visible, but neither can it bear another's control over the visible."[42] The different groups, collectives, and individuals opposing the regime not only persistently demanded the truth, but also strived to establish it and disseminate it by different means. The civil gaze, critical in contexts in which the state acts repressively against citizens, oriented and grounded the work of the opposition in the expanding photographic field. The documentary practices of photography gave different forms and materialities to this work; photography also allowed for the reproduction, display, and dissemination of different kinds of documents (including photographic documents) that were central in the mobilization of the collective power of insubordination.

The unofficial artistic practices that emerged under dictatorship also instigated important critical debates concerning the political significance of photography. The practices that different critical texts commented on did not establish a mechanical or illustrative association between photography and reality, but the concept of photography as a document and a trace became a significant theoretical notion to consider them.[43] Ronald Kay and Nelly Richard became two of the most influential theorists within the artistic field.[44] Kay's groundbreaking *Del espacio de acá* (On the Space Over Here), a collection of essays published in 1980, offered enlightening theoretical formulations about photography, ranging from the medium's phenomenology and ontology to its sudden arrival at the "New World." Inspired by Eugenio Dittborn's use of salvaged and altered documents, old photographs that framed forgotten and marginal subjects, Kay posited the image as a complex sign marked by constant struggles: the display of certain photos implied the invisibility of others; the same photos could be used for various purposes; the visible elements on the photo's surface led the viewer—Kay—to think of what remained hidden, invisible, off the frame:

> In every image, because of the practice in which it is embedded, antagonistic collective energies struggle; in each image, because of the concrete place it occupies in a contingency and in a given context, the triumphs, the coercions, the adulterations, the defeats, the attempts, the extortions of fighting forces are marked. Behind every image lies the trace, still fresh, of the exclusion of other images as well as the imminence of it being supplanted by new ones.[45]

Always conversing with the documentary images that populated Dittborn's practice, Kay also formulated photography's irruption into the Latin American subcontinent as a paradoxical event that while forcing indigenous people to be defined and represented by a modern technology—one that did not correspond with their lives and histories—also created the conditions for the emergence of a specific "Latin American gaze."[46]

Richard's *Márgenes e Instituciones* (Margins and Institutions) (1986) formulated a framework for a set of artistic practices that emerged in the mid-seventies. In this noteworthy book, Richard posited "unofficial" artistic practices as an *Escena de avanzada* (avant-garde scene). Regardless of the appropriateness of the term and the demarcations she produced, Richard compellingly showed the extent to which photography transformed the artistic field under dictatorship.[47] She recognized three moments regarding photographic uses in the artistic field: the year of 1977, when the resort to photography became systematic; the late seventies, when a group of "young artists" (Elías Adasme, Víctor Hugo Codocedo, Luz Donoso, Alfredo Jaar, and Hernán Parada, among others) made the use of photography more generalized; and "after 1980, [when] photography began to function as the unpretentious record of art actions and performances, fulfilling the task (along with video footage) of being the documentary support of performances and urban interventions whose ephemeral passage required this supplement of memory."[48]

Regarding the first moment, Richard considered a double sequence of exhibitions held at the galleries Cromo and Época. The artists who participated in these exhibitions (Eugenio Dittborn, Catalina Parra, Francisco Smythe, Roser Bru, Carlos Altamirano, and Carlos Leppe), not only incorporated photographic materials—found photos, photocopies, photographed contact sheets, newspa-

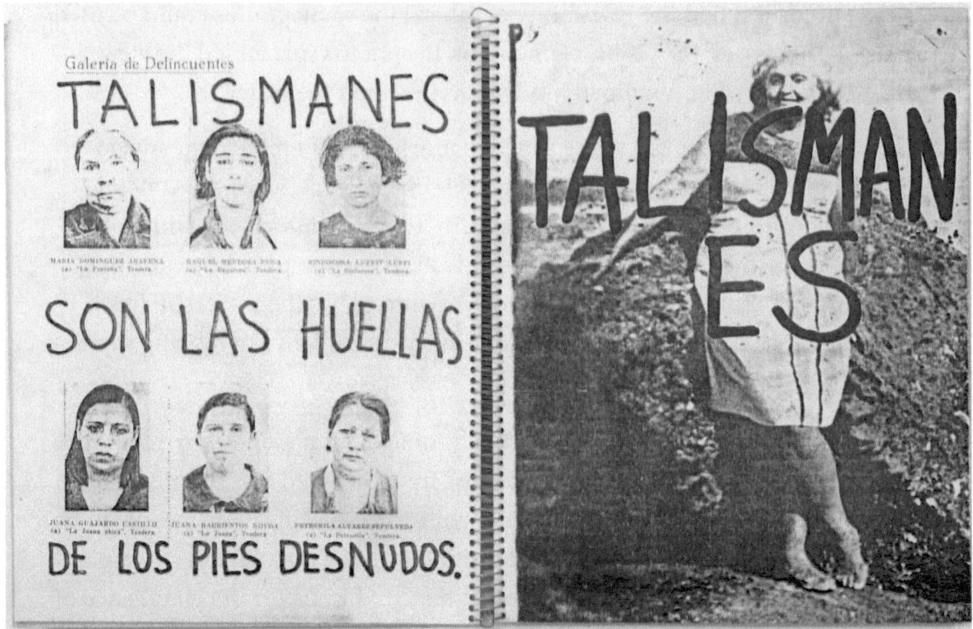

Figure I.6. Eugenio Dittborn's *Fallo fotográfico* spread, "A Gallery of Criminals." Photocopied mug shots and text. Credit: Eugenio Dittborn. Black and white. Jorge Gronemeyer's personal archive (Taller Gronefot).

per and magazines clippings, and negatives—but also altered these materials through collage, screen printing, staining, photocopying, dyeing, drawing, and sketching. For these artists, argued Richard, photography became an effective means to dismantle the academicism of fine arts, countering the traditional aestheticism of painting and, more importantly, commenting on the immediate political context.[49] Like Kay, Richard paid special attention to the political significance of photographic documents in Dittborn's work, which she read as collective "guardians of memory" (see fig. I.6): "In a country like Chile, this collective memory is suppressed by an official apparatus, which conceals the past and historically expropriates the signs of national or popular identity. Resurrecting these documents is equivalent to unearthing what was censored in the news in the past and then transferring it to the present as a confrontation."[50]

The incorporation of photographic documents into the artwork, which Richard and other critics posited as a reflexive use of the photographic image, was formulated in opposition to the testimonial use of photography in other arenas. Richard's description of photographic documentations of art actions and performances (a predominant documentary practice after 1980) as "unpretentious records," was related to this approach to photography. Indeed, there was a tendency to see documentary production either as a form of objective/testimonial practice or as form of photographic conventionalized subjectivism.[51] This opposition between the reflexive and the nonreflexive (or testimonial) uses of photography surfaces more prominently in Richard's *The Insubordination of Signs* (1994). Performing a Benjaminian reading of artistic practices under dictatorship, Richard conceptualizes two types of art: a contestatory art and what she calls a refractory art. The latter operated according to a logic of negation and deviation; it was unassimilable to traditional forms of cultural production and also rejected the frames of representation coopted by the "fraudulent language" of the dominant power. Militant or contestatory art, meanwhile, produced works that "were merely *contrary* to the dominant point of view," without challenging the military regime's language or its frameworks of representation.[52] Militant artistic practices served both the political parties of the left and the discourses of the social sciences, but "neither of these two languages was sufficiently sensitive to the turmoil of signs that had shaken the very machine of social representation."[53] I want to reconsider here both the clear-cut language Richard uses to formulate the distinction between these two artistic tendencies and the metaphor she uses to describe militant or contestatory art:

> It is true that the predominant tendency of Chilean contestatory art utilized by the traditional left sought above all to take revenge on the dictatorial offense by plotting—in *its symmetrical inverse*—an epic of resistance that would be *the photographic negative* of the official "take." But, on the flanks of that heroic and monumental art, new creative works battled—works that refused to attend to the merely figurative contingency of the "NO," without simultaneously critiquing the entire discursive regime responsible for transforming the dogmatic rigidity of "YES" versus "NO" into an imprisoning paradigm.[54]

The formulation of contestatory art as the symmetrical inverse of the narrative of the regime prompts the metaphor of this art as "the photographic negative of the official 'take.'" The photographic negative signifies here the exact opposite of the system of visibility of the dictatorship—pure reversed reflection without mediation. This metaphor can be read as a symptom of Richard's conceptualization of photography itself. Given the way in which Richard describes contestatory art, the metaphor indirectly posits photography as a mechanical apparatus. For instance, Richard describes the camera as "as a visual instrument unrivaled for showing" to emphasize that "the [art]works with the greatest reflexive density were those that led photographic documentation and pictorial representation to alternate and collate their critical-visual languages in the interior of the image itself."[55] Her consideration of different artistic refractory practices, including the documentary work of photographer Paz Errázuriz, and that of Dittborn—a visual artist who used and altered ID photographs in his work—is coherent with this conceptualization. It all comes back to the same idea: photography is an apparatus that needs artistic practices in order to articulate differently, in order to represent or signify in a reflexive way. However, as I will extensively develop throughout this book, the practice of photography always extends well beyond the camera and the photograph.

The idea that photography operates by default within given frames of representation, unless it is incorporated reflexively in the artistic practices, needs to be reconsidered because it is clear that there were documentary practices that did not emerge within the field of art and that revealed or suggested, reflexively, the loss of reference and the rupture of meaning in the face of catastrophe. One significant example is the seven-volume book *¿Dónde están?* published by the Vicaría, which I analyze in my first chapter. A second example is the Lonquén photographs, which I consider in chapter 2: a set of seemingly unassuming photos taken to give a precise account of the site where a heinous crime was committed. These photos were continuously used to evoke and point to that which the photos could not reveal, questioning the official frame of representation and adding further meanings to each public display. While these photos circulated profusely from 1979 onward, Richard suggests that "the Lonquén massacre [. . .] came to light and public knowledge thanks to the way in which Gonzalo Díaz's work effectively 'poked art's fingers into the sore spots of politics,'" in 1988 (ten years after the macabre finding).[56] Díaz's *Lonquén 10 años* (Lonquén 10 Years) (1989) was a touching performance and installation which, as Richard observes, revealed the present as "a disjunctive knot, capable of making recollection not a return to the past (a regression that buries history in the recesses of yesterday), but rather a coming and going along the winding turns of a memory that does not stop at fixed points."[57] While the artist did not use photographs of the mine's furnaces in the installation, the catalogue reproduced on the cover a somewhat altered copy of a well-known photograph taken from the top of the chimney (made by Helen Hughes). This documentary image was published in both *Solidaridad* and in the book *Lonquén*. This photograph was recognizable, and more importantly, referred everyone to the well-known, traumatic event that had occurred ten years earlier. Díaz himself hinted in the catalogue to the significance and latency of these photographs: in his words, he could confront this macabre event "only after ten years of metabolic retention, of looking at what those half-point photographic fauces concealed."[58]

I have dedicated so much space to Richard's formulations because her conceptualization of the refractory is significant and remains current, and above all because the turmoil of signs she so persuasively expounds in *The Insubordination of Signs* also affected the documentary practices of photography. If, as Richard suggests, refractory art arose out of the necessity of "having to name fragments of experience that were no longer speakable in the language that had survived the catastrophe of meaning" and in order "to escape military authoritarianism and the censorship administered by the official culture," then the documentary practices of photography I study here were undoubtedly refractory.[59] Furthermore, in the passage quoted in the epigraph, Richard postulates the impossibility of burial as "the image—without recovery—of a historical mourning process," and also as "the metaphorical condition of an unsealed temporality: inconclusive, and therefore open to re-exploration in many new directions by our memory, increasingly active and dissatisfied."[60] My venture into the photographic practices that emerged under dictatorship as a response to the issues to which Richard refers (human rights abuses and bodies not being found or not being laid to rest) is but a manifestation of this metaphorical condition.

To analyze the different forms and materialities these practices acquired under dictatorship, and consider their various meanings and importance, I look at the expanding field of photography. In proposing this approach, I am not simply arguing that photography was used to reproduce and disseminate more images and thus expand the space of the resistance—although this is, in and of itself, an important matter: countless photographs were taken and disseminated in different media and spaces (magazines, documentary films, catalogues, street murals, pamphlets, banners, etc.). I am arguing that the practice of photography instigated and facilitated the alteration and transformation of photographs into something else. Instances of what Azoulay calls "the civil imagination," these different practices—devised by people, collectives, organizations, and media opposing the regime—expanded and supplemented what photographs and documents were, meant, and did. Photographed portraits were amended, photocopied, and used as documentary and iconic traces of disappearance; "obvious" and unassuming forensic photographs became dense and evocative metonymies of the repression; even news photos were replaced with empty frames to challenge censorship. These documentary practices, I aim to show, were not the photographic negative of the official "take." They exploited the performative dimension of photography to keep denouncing, resisting, documenting, and persevering. They did not have to wait for art to happen. They were already working in a refractory mode, with all its density and multiplicity of meaning.

These documentary practices are "of photography" not only because they were products or byproducts of photographic techniques but, even more importantly, because they activated the performative referentiality of photography. The dissemination of the portraits of the disappeared in photocopies, the construction of forensic evidence by means of its documentation and photographic "fixing," the expansion of photographic and documentary activity through different media, and the use of linguistic supplements to make news photographs "speak" despite being censored, illuminate this referential performance of photography. These practices gained different meanings while they acquired different forms and materialities. Meanwhile, they are "documentary," because even though an array of visual objects (including documentary photographs) were reproduced, altered, created, and disseminated, the displays and framings of these objects bestowed on them a documentary weight. It is the persistence of these documentary practices that makes apparent the central role photography had in the collective struggle for the truth.

I, the Viewer

Documentary images, regardless of their materiality, exist to be viewed (even watched, claims Azoulay) and the ways they address, affect, or touch the viewer are concomitant to the viewer's own life experiences, her familiarity with the events/people portrayed, her ideas, beliefs, political stances, and so on. Likewise, the critical gestures of exploring, describing, or considering a number of objects—in this case, documentary photographic practices—in relation to the field that encompasses them depends on the perspective—the focus/view one has of/over the field—as well as on the availability of these same objects within said field. Since I explore an array of photographic practices in the expanding field, acknowledging my own perspective as both observer and researcher is key from the outset. I belong to the postmemory generation, to evoke Marianne Hirsch's notion; this implies, among other things, that my understanding of and connection to the events that occurred during the seventies and eighties in Chile are already mediated by archival objects, discursive practices, and documentary artifacts—photographs, films, literary texts, *testimonios* (testimonies).[61] However, not only does my linkage to "the events themselves" come mediated, but my relation with the photographs that emerged and circulated during this period is also traversed by mediations, marked both by closeness and distance.

This dual linkage has much to do with my own biography. I was born in Santiago, Chile, in 1980, so I am a contemporary, in the most literal sense of the word, of the expanding photographic field this book explores. I grew up listening to stories about the events that frame the photographic practices I study here and many of the places portrayed in the photographs—the Paseo Ahumada in downtown Santiago, the General Cemetery, Alameda Avenue, various public squares, and different streets—are places I have visited and with which I am familiar. Some of the photographs I study exude an *urgent* quality: they were taken to denounce the violence and repression perpetrated by military and police forces or to document the increasing acts of resistance against the dictatorship. Although many of these photographs were published and circulated in a number of magazines during the eighties, because I was a child, I was not aware of their existence until much later. Besides the fact that my first encounter with many of these photos occurred at a time far removed—many years after the end of the dictatorship—it also happened, so to speak, out of place, via a different medium—not photography itself, but cinema. So, at the same time that a strong cultural and affective bond brings me closer to the practices I study here—and also because I have come to know most of the people involved in this field—unavoidable displacements keep moving me away from them.

Not surprisingly, this oscillation between closeness and distance has become central to my critical approach. The successive temporal, spatial, and media displacements have enriched and nuanced my perspective on the photographic field, instigating critical reflection about the distance that mediates between this field and my position as both spectator and researcher in the present. Depth of field evokes precisely this twofold perspective: sometimes, taking a closer look at a specific photograph or series of photographs allows me to consider specific aspects—the elements portrayed, what remains hidden on the surface of the image, a recurring theme—in more depth. Other times, it is the distance that allows me to consider different relationships and processes regarding the photographic practices in the expanding field. In each case, I find it necessary to readjust my lens and focus.

The first time I learned about some of the photographic practices I study here was in the documentary film *La ciudad de los fotógrafos* (The City of Photographers) (2006). This documentary draws attention to the significant, albeit forgotten and ignored, role that a group of photographers played during the dictatorship. The film insists on the marginality of this field in the historiography of the period. In one of the first sequences, the documentary director Sebastián Moreno asks, What has become of these photographers? Why does nobody seem to know their stories? These questions guide the documentary. The film assumes the task of revisiting and showing this ignored photographic history. Moreno interviews several photographers on camera and asks them about their photographs, all now considered emblematic images of this period. The film elucidates the significance not only of photography as a political practice, but also of the photographers themselves, who, in addition to having worked in dangerous and precarious conditions, played an important role in the consolidation of the photographic field (most of the photographers interviewed, including Moreno's father, were AFI members).

The distance that separates me from this constellation of photographs became manifest the first time I watched Moreno's documentary. Although the vast majority of the photographs evoked (and reproduced) in the documentary circulated in different media opposing the military regime or were exhibited at different venues in artistic and cultural events during the 1980s and 1990s (both in Chile and abroad), I was seeing them for the first time in a documentary—that is, not in print—more than twenty years later. In other words, my first encounter with these images—audiovisual traces of photographic traces—was neither via the medium in which they had been produced (the photograph) nor via the media in which they had been reproduced (magazines, newspapers, gallery walls, and catalogues). Moreover, my first encounter with them was through a film that happened to touch upon *oblivion*—another form of distance, of effacement—the oblivion to which these photographs and their authors had been relegated despite the significant role the photos had played as tools of denunciation and despite also the crucial work these photographers did throughout the eighties.

La ciudad de los fotógrafos's composition is grounded in the concept of the photo as a documentary trace. The film incorporates a series of still images—

photographs—and sets them in motion. These traces of photographic traces—forgotten, ignored, and displaced traces revisited and reactivated in/by Moreno's documentary—are the starting point (but not the origin) of this book. It was the experience of seeing these displaced, reproduced, and transformed documentary photographs that first prompted me to investigate the notion of photography as an expanding field of practices—a field that not only remains, up to now, unexplored, but that also has not been outlined and considered in these terms. The experience of displacement and transformation of the photographs in Moreno's documentary (from laminated paper to digital image, from media illustration or archival object to filmic material) invited me to think about the materiality of what we commonly designate or identify as photographs and also about the variety of platforms where these photographs circulate or are disseminated.

If Moreno's documentary prompted me to think about photographic displacement, Lorenzini's "Pico" photograph inspired my formulation of depth of field as a critical concept. The perspective or point of view I adopt when looking at a photograph depends, at least in part, on the focus, framing, and depth of field of the photo. As I have already described, the first time I saw the "Pico" photo, I focused almost exclusively on the man's defiant look and on his T-shirt, barely noticing the people, posters, and banners in the background. In a way, it was the particular depth of field of this photograph—a shallow depth of field—that oriented my gaze in those early encounters. Orientations, in Sara Ahmed's expressive formulation, refer to the lines or directions that bodies follow in a given space or field and to the relationships that bodies, because of these orientations, establish with the objects deemed available in such a space or field. Bodies neither choose nor decide which orientations to follow; on the contrary, "'orientations' depend on taking points of view *as given*."[62] The notion of orientations resonates with ideas I already developed regarding the visibility of objects—photographic practices—in the expanding field. Thinking about photography in terms of orientations has further implications: it means that photographs themselves can operate as orientations, that is, as points of view already given that orient the field of the visible or, as Ahmed would say, as lines that help us find the way.[63] Thinking about photography in terms of orientations implicates also how historical events are inscribed and represented.[64] To state that photographs orient the visual field or that events can be inscribed photographically does not imply that photographs as lines or orientations indicate the "right" or "true" way, or even the only way: as Ahmed insists, orientations can certainly disorient us (to follow a line, an orientation, or a direction implies excluding everything that remains outside that line, from the outset).[65]

The Matters of This Book

Books like *Libro Blanco* (1973) and *Chile Ayer Hoy* (1975) and cover-up stories such as Plan Z and Operación Colombo reveal the significant role photography played in the manufacturing, validation, and dissemination of the narratives devised by the dictatorial power.[66] The logic is a familiar one: the more (visual, textual) documents we provide, the more evidentiary weight the alleged events acquire.[67] However, despite the different attempts by the military's repressive apparatuses to obscure and blur denunciations of killings, torture, and forced disappearances, by 1976, the civic-military regime's "free hand for memory work and propaganda inside Chile" weakened.[68] The people, collectives, and organizations whose documentary photographic practices I study here played a paramount role in this weakening.

The first coordinated effort to fight the human rights violations perpetrated by the military came from the relatives of the victims and from *parroquias* and local houses of worship, where people went to seek help. In October 1973, religious leaders from various denominations formed the Comité Pro Paz (Committee for Peace), an ecumenical organization in which priests, pastors, and vicars worked alongside lawyers and social workers, collecting the information people brought.[69] In 1974, relatives who were working with the Comité formed the Agrupación de Familiares de Detenidos Desaparecidos (AFDD) (Association of Family Members of the Detained-Disappeared).[70] The Comité began to file habeas corpus petitions on behalf of the detained-disappeared; due to the relentless pressure Pinochet and the military junta placed on the Comité, it was forced to dissolve in November 1975.[71] After the dissolution of the the Comité, Archbishop Raúl Silva Henríquez instituted the Vicaría de la Solidaridad (Vicariate of Solidarity) to continue and expand the work of the Comité.

An important part of the work done by both the Comité Pro Paz and by the Vicaría in defense of human rights was to document and create a counter-archive. The first Americas Watch Report about the Vicaría and its predecessor was published in 1987 in the United States.[72] Notably, each chapter is introduced by a documentary photograph. Indeed, the Vicaría produced, reproduced, catalogued, and disseminated countless photographs. The Vicaría used these photographs in its different legal, social, documentation, and communication endeavors. The first two chapters shed light on the important part this organization played adjusting the depth of field and expanding the field of photographic practices.

My first chapter underscores the counter-archival work carried out by the Vicaría in the composition of the photographic archive of the detained-disappeared; the chapter also considers the different transformations, displacements, and disseminations endured by the portraits of the detained-disappeared. ID portraits can be thought of as a documentary photographic practice produced by the state to control, discipline, surveil, and classify—as I explain in the first part of the chapter, this is in fact how they have been commonly theorized. However, because the civil imagination always excedes and is not bound by the logic of the state, there is a civil documentary photographic practice focused on ID portraits too. The civic-military state systematically negated that it was abducting and killing individuals. The relatives of the detained-disappeared responded by flooding the public space with portraits of the latter. This collective and public practice of photographic display divulged: "they are not presumed dead, they are not presumed disappeared—they are detained-disappeared." Indeed, I claim that the public display of photographic portraits of the detained-disappeared was critical to giving the crime of forced disappearance an image, a visual representation. People began this practice very early on outside police stations and imprisonment camps, to locate their loved ones who had been at very least detained (not neccesarily disappeared). The relatives of the disappeared also brought ID photos, portraits, and family snapshots taken from private family albums to the Vicaría's office for inclusion in habeas corpus petitions and case files. Since most of these photos were in very bad shape, they were rephotographed and even manually improved.

The analysis contemplates both the composition of the photographic archive of the portraits and the archive's dissemination in the public space. Vicaría photographers Helen Hughes and Luis Navarro, and visual artists Luz Donoso and Hernán Parada played a critical role in both of these matters. Hughes and Navarro worked with the photos the relatives brought to the Vicaría; they obtained better copies, which were used for different legal endeavors and also catalogued at the Vicaría with the victim's files. Donoso and Parada assisted members of the Agrupación by rephotographing, photocopying, and enlarging the photos the relatives used in streets demonstrations, vigils, and rallies; both artists included these enlarged photocopied images in their own artistic practices. I consider the Vicaría's publications *Solidaridad* (a biweekly newsletter), *Separata Solidaridad* (a special issue that focused on particular matters also considered in *Solidaridad*), and the seven-volume book series *¿Dónde están?* (1978–1979). I suggest that the visual representation of the crime of forced disappearances, which took shape with the public display of the portraits, was consolidated in these Vicaría publications, above all in *¿Dónde están?* I also study artistic photographic practices devised to display and disseminate these photographic portraits in the public space. The chapter begins and ends with a consideration of Parada's action "Obrabierta A" (1974–present), in particular one of its iterations in which the artist uses a photocopied mask of his brother, Alejandro Parada, detained and disappeared since July 1974.

It has been argued that the iconicity of the portraits threatens to cancel their political meaning, as if the political meaning resided in the images, as if politics was condensed on the photo's surface. I propose that it is not the portraits that carry political meaning, but rather that the political emerges and becomes apparent in the public display of the portraits. The relatives who began the documentary photographic practice of displaying these portraits in the public space inaugurated this political space. This spontaneous photographic practice instigated the successive reproductions of the small portraits. The portraits were repaired and reproduced so that they could continue to operate in the public space, so that they could persist as iconic traces of the disappeared and as visual evidence of the existence of the crime of forced disappearance. In this effort to consolidate and expand the visibility of this denied act of violence and repression, a counter-archive was created: the Vicaría's photographic archive of the detained-disappeared. This insubordinate act of photography involved different processes of transformation and displacement of the portraits of the disappeared: rephotographing and photocopying, archiving, and disseminating. My reading seeks to illuminate the mutable materiality of these persistent iconic portraits. To that end, I follow—or let myself be oriented by—their performative documentary traces.

In November 1975, Sergio Diez, Chile's representative to the United Nations, presented to the members of that official body a report prepared by the Legal Medical Institute that listed as "deceased" sixty-four individuals claimed as disappeared. This official report included the dates and times of each death, even autopsy protocols. Strangely, the bodies of seven men who had been listed as "dead" since 1973 appeared in Lonquén in 1978. Diez further indicated in his speech that there were 153 individuals, also claimed as disappeared, who were *entes presuntos* (plausible beings). These plausible (or fictional) beings had no official identification—no "legal existence"—according to Chilean military-government records.[73] One of them was Sergio Adrián Maureira Lillo, whose remains were also found in Lonquén. "How could he be denied legal existence," his widow Purísima Elena Muñoz would say later, "if I was married to him."[74] The Lonquén case, as it is known (the case has been widely studied), was the first case that confirmed, once and for all, the denied existence of the detained-disappeared. Besides establishing that fifteen men who had been detained on October 7, 1973, had been thrown (probably alive) into the furnace of an abandoned mine, buried, and left there, the forensic analysis and the inspecting judge's investigation also revealed that the depositions given by the policemen involved in the crime were completely false. The Lonquén case, in sum, helped to dismantle the deceitful explanations and complex cover-ups devised by the dictatorship to deny the existence of the crime of disappearances—and even of those individuals whom the dictatorship had made disappear.

Despite the prominence of the Lonquén case, little attention has been placed on the documentary photographs that served to *secure* and present the physical remains found *as* forensic evidence. In this sense, if the first chapter explains how a visual concept was created for a crime for which there was no evidence—the iconic image of the detained-disappeared was shaped and sedimented in the public space, through its countless reproductions, displacements, and displays—the second chapter investigates how the forensic documentary record that helped prove the crime of forced disappearance was produced and disseminated.

Instead of revisiting the histories of photographic evidence or problematizing the notion of photographic truth to explain how "did we get here"—Chile, December 1978—in this chapter I operate synchronously. I explore how photographs operated as documents and as forensic evidence at a particular historical juncture. With regards to the Lonquén case, this orientation allows me to consider the role the photographs had in the production of the forensic evidence. While the evidentiary weight of the Lonquén photos is undeniable, evidence is understood here "not in the sense of proof but rather in the more forensic sense of making something evident, presenting it to a public, calling for a judgment."[75] In other words, there is nothing obvious or definitive about the Lonquén photos, however simple they may seem. Their meanings were transformed and displaced in each of their iterations, due to the specific relationships photographs establish with their contexts and the different media through which they transit.

I consider two sets of photographs taken by Vicaría photographers Helen Hughes and Luis Navarro at the abandoned mine during the first days of December 1978, immediately after the findings. The photographers' presence at the site was due to the Vicaría's involvement in the case. Hughes took thirty-three photos on a first reconnaissance visit; some photos were taken at the site, and others were done at the Vicaría offices (the delegation that participated in the first reconnaissance visit considered necessary taking back with them a skull and a few bones in case CNI agents—the regime's secret police—found out about the site before they were able to file a legal claim and collect further evidence).[76] Hughes's photos were added to the Lonquén case file six weeks later—in late January 1979. On the first day of the exhumations at the site, Navarro was named the photography expert for the case. All the photographs Navarro took as photography expert (over a hundred) were submitted to the case file at the end of each exhumation day, and therefore had never been published before.

Taking as a point of departure the photos done by Hughes and by Navarro, I consider the problem of referentiality in the context of repression and forced disappearances. The problem of referentiality is important, not only because most of the photos that were disseminated revealed no physical evidence, but also because the physical evidence found was questioned again and again by pro-regime media and authorities—unsurprisingly, officialist media tried to discredit the findings and divert the discussion to other issues. Thus, the discovery of human remains in Lonquén, I argue, neither solved nor halted the problem of referentiality, but rather activated it. My analysis centers on the photos that were disseminated publicly and also considers how the unpublished photos (the vast majority) were discussed in the media. Amid a context of uncertainty and complete denial, the unpublished Lonquén photographs began to function as supplementary visual evidence of the material evidence. Producing this supplementary corpus was imperative to prevent potential cover-ups. Indeed, their mere existence allowed the judge to deny—although only partially—misinformation about possible mishaps or cover-ups in the investigation.

Regarding the published photos, I pay special attention to a set of photos disseminated alongside the first article *Solidaridad* published about the Lonquén findings, which questioned in large letters: "Who are *these dead*?" These photos are by Hughes. I underscore the matter of authorship here because Hughes's photographs have remained unaccredited for forty years. As I argue, even her presence at the site has not been accounted for. I was able to confirm which photos were hers by reading the Lonquén case file, of which I make extensive use in the chapter. This file only came into the public domain in July 2018, after the case was finally closed. Reading the depositions and looking at the photos organized inside one of the many heavy and thick volumes that comprise the Lonquén case file (there are dozens of them), I realized that the photos that have become iconic were taken by Hughes—and not by Navarro, as I had previously assumed. Hughes's photo of the furnace's mouth would continue to surface, as a metonym of disappearance, as a visual sign that evokes that which can't be shown. For this reason, the chapter ends with a brief consideration of Lonquén's documentary echoes—*No Olvidar* (Not to Forget) (1982) by Ignacio Agüero and Grupo Memoria, and *La ciudad de los fotógrafos* by Sebastián Moreno, two documentary films in which the traces of Lonquén continue emerging.

The starting point of the third chapter, which explores the discursive emergence of the photographic field, is the arrest of Luis Navarro on March 11, 1981, while attempting to take photographs at one of the events organized to celebrate the taking into effect of the new Chilean Constitution. Inspired by the intersection of these two events—the arrest of a photographer and the establishement of a new Constitution that paradoxically gave Pinochet absolute powers—I elucidate the connections between the discursive emergence of the photographic field and the state of emergency installed on the same day the new Constitution took effect. The arrest of Luis Navarro was a traumatic event for the photographer and revealed, once again, the brutal instruments used by the Central Nacional de Informaciones (CNI) (National Information Center) to torture civilians: Navarro was held for five days incommunicado; he was tortured and drugged.

Navarro's arrest was also significant at a collective level: it instigated, among other things, the formation of the AFI in June 1981. After the formation of the AFI, the photographic field underwent an unprecedented expansion. My analysis considers how this expansion took place in the middle of the most severe economic crisis (which reached a climax in 1982), and also how the prevailing precariousness determined both the discourses about the photographic field that was beginning to consolidate, as well as the materiality, themes, and formal aspects of the different initiatives designed to consolidate the photographic field. I argue that two concomitant tendencies with respect to the photographic field emerged: one surfaced amid the contingency and alongside various photographic initiatives emphasizing the day-to day-challenges, shortcomings, and achievements. I consider the texts published in AFI's magazine *Punto de Vista*

(1981–1990) and the two *Anuarios fotográficos* edited by the AFI in 1981 and 1982 as instances of this tendency. I underscore that the *Anuarios* were also significant because they attempted to reactivate discussion and appreciation of Chilean documentary photography. The second perspective about the field surfaced in two important critical texts that appeared at the end of the eighties, a curatorial text written by Mario Fonseca in 1987 and an essay by Claudia Donoso published in 1990.

In this chapter, I also analyze two collaborative photographic projects. One is *Ediciones económicas de la fotografía chilena* (Affordable Editions of Chilean Photography) (1983), an initiative devised by photographer Felipe Riobó to disseminate works by Chilean photographers using photocopied photobooks. I propose that the use of this minor format—the photocopy—instigated graphic and linguistic experimentation and activated meaningful crossovers between photography, literature, and photography criticism. The second is *El pan nuestro de cada día* (Our Daily Bread) (1986), a book edited collectively by photographers Óscar Navarro, Claudio Pérez, Paulo Slachevsky, and Carlos Tobar. Both projects reflected on—and can be considered manifestations of—the precarity that hampered the practices of photography and their milieu. Thus, the different photographic practices and critical texts I consider recentered and underscored the political consequence of the practice of photography: they opened up a critical forum that not only facilitated the circulation of and discussion about Chilean photography, but also called attention to matters related to photography, such as the place of visuality in the cultural field and the problem of censorship in media and the museum.

In the last chapter, I consider how independent magazines resisted and even mocked censorship. Around the same time that the Vicaría was established, a number of independent magazines began to appear: *Análisis* (1976), *Apsi* (1976), and *Hoy* (1977). While these magazines were not authorized to circulate on a daily basis and were subject to varying and various restrictions, they prompted a debate about the inexistence of real freedom of speech and, more importantly, became instrumental in denouncing human rights violations in the public space. In the early eighties, these magazines, along with *Cauce* (established in 1983) and the newspaper *Fortín Mapocho* (reestablished in 1984), began to focus more on national issues—the establishment of the Constitution in 1981, the 1982 economic crisis and its backlash, the national protests and general strike days that became recurrent in 1983—and to publish more and more photos. Whenever these publications became too blatant in their criticism of the dictatorship, DINACOS responded with stricter forms of censorship, including a total ban on images in 1984—only a few months after the May 1 demonstration at O'Higgins Park called by the CNT.[77] This ban and the responses it instigated underscored that the photographs published in the media were not unimportant illustrations.

The 1984 ban, which affected the magazines *Análisis*, *Apsi*, and *Cauce* and the newspaper *Fortín Mapocho*, prompted editors to devise ways not only to convey what the censored, absent images would have depicted, but also to make visible the violence intrinsic in the ban itself. Even though they did remove the actual photographs, they kept referring to them as if they were visible on the surface of the page. The empty rectangles that replaced the actual photographs, sometimes decorated with doodles or signs, became the visual marker of censorship—a marker that was both iconic (it was the visual rendering of the ban) and indexical (it was the inscription, the trace, of dictatorial power on the printed page). Indeed, the new meanings of these new "insubordinate photos" quickly expanded: they "showed" the situations or subjects described in the photo captions, evoked the protests that had prompted the ban in the first place, and became a symbolic way of protesting repression and censorship. Furthermore, photography began to be evoked to talk about democracy, freedom of the press, and freedom of expression. This is why I frame this as a matter of photography and its limits—a theoretical matter that does not concern only the artistic practices that use photography. I consider the limits imposed by the dictatorial regime on the freedom of the press, the limits of photographic truth, and the limits of photography itself—what the medium allegedly can or can't do. My analysis reveals how the independent media, using a language grounded on the referentiality of the photograph, produced an image that was visually striking, poetic, and carried evidentiary weight. My analysis also illuminates how as an effect of external administrative limitations, the photographic field was transformed. The censored magazines operated refractively: they not only circumvented censorship but also transgressed the alleged limits of press photographs (usually posited as informational, plain, unambiguous visual objects). The limitations imposed on press photography not only transformed the way censored magazines communicated and documented, but also instigated the displacement of protest photographs to other exhibition spaces.

The documentary practices of photography I study in the chapters that follow were not based exclusively on the indexical bond between the photograph and its referent; they resulted from different ways of creating and reproducing images, as well as from interactions between images and text. Indeed, photographs are never fixed identities: not even the documentary photographs that *Chile Ayer Hoy* so deliberately contextualizes can be defined once and for all. These images, like any photo, inevitably supplement their meanings: to begin with, they all carry the ghostly traces of Quimantú, the printing press founded by Allende, confiscated by the military after the coup and put to the service of the dictatorship's ideological consolidation. Quimantú was renamed Editora Nacional Gabriela Mistral and started to publish books like *Chile Ayer Hoy*.[78] The same ink, the same paper, even the same photographs—many of the photos published in *Chile Ayer Hoy* (framing scenes both of "yesterday" and "today") were appropriated from the archives of Quimantú.[79]

The Insubordination of Photography ends with an epilogue about the 2015 exhibition *Chile desde adentro*, one of the latest iterations of *Chile from Within*, a book edited by Susan Meiselas in collaboration with a group of AFI photographers in 1988 and published in New York in 1990. I conclude my exploration in the present not only to show how these documentary photographs keep expanding their meanings, but also because to fight for the truth, demand justice, promote solidarity and sanctuary, and generate collaborative alliances—key political efforts undertaken by the opposition—remain critical tasks today. Finally, *The Insubordination of Photography* claims that one can't think about the history of the resistance to the dictatorship, nor of the history of political struggle throughout this period, without considering the political space that the documentary practices of photography opened up.

1

PERSISTENCE OF THE PORTRAIT

It is no accident that the portrait is central to early photography. In the cult of remembrance of dead or absent loved ones, the cult value of the image finds its last refuge. In the fleeting expression of a human face, the aura beckons from the early photographs for the last time. This is what gives them their melancholy and incomparable beauty.

—Walter Benjamin, "The Work of Art in the Age of Its Technological Reproducibility"

Not having a family photograph is tantamount to not being a part of humankind.

—Ana González González[1]

In the days that followed the civil-military coup, family photos and unassuming ID photos acquired noteworthy political weight. This influence first materialized with an act of protest as simple as it was significant: the practice of publicly displaying portraits or snapshots of a detained loved one whose whereabouts are unknown. It would be impossible to determine the precise moment this practice began, but this does not matter; in fact, the meaning of this collective photographic practice resided not in its singularity or originality, but in its repetition and persistence. We do know that this civil practice of photography began just a few days after the coup, outside of the spaces temporarily repurposed by the military to detain and torture Chilean citizens. One such space was the emblematic National Stadium, used as a concentration camp from September 13 to November 9, 1973. Thousands of people were detained in this sports arena-turned-imprisonment, torture, and execution camp.[2] Outside of the National Stadium, family members of the prisoners began to congregate hoping to receive news about their missing loved ones. These family members, the majority of whom were mothers, wives, and sisters, did not know for certain if their missing loved ones were being detained in the repurposed stadium. It is not hard to imagine the scene: hundreds of anguished, scared people gathered along the perimeter of the stadium, clutching photographs—photos torn from old albums, family portraits, snapshots, copies of ID photos—and asking the few potentially sympathetic people who were able to enter and leave the stadium (Red Cross representatives, a few journalists and photographers, and a few recently released detainees), "Do you recognize this person?" or "Have you seen this person inside?"[3]

This spontaneous photographic practice is the point of departure for this chapter about the composition and dissemination of the photographic archive of the detained-disappeared. My exploration seeks to shed light on the paramount role the Vicaría de la Solidaridad (Vicariate of Solidarity) played in the composition and dissemination of this archive and thus in the devising and consolidation of the iconic representation of the victims of the crime of abduction. The analysis I develop here underscores how the Vicaría and the relatives of the victims of the military's repressive campaign, through their work in the Agrupación de Familiares de Detenidos Desaparecidos (AFDD) (Association of Family Members of the Detained-Disappeared) gave the crime of disappearances a visible form. The portraits of the disappeared were the main source for this visual rendering. At the Vicaría offices, photographers Luis Navarro and Helen Hughes devoted part of their time to making copies of the photographs submitted by family members soliciting legal aid. They reproduced and enhanced hundreds of portraits.[4] The new portraits facilitated the detainees' recognition and formed part of the legal records gathered by the Vicaría in order to prepare appropriate legal actions. Visual artists Hernán Parada and Luz Donoso also played important roles in the organization and reproduction of photographic portraits of the detained-disappeared. These artists began to work with the Agrupación in 1974: they received the few photographs obtained from relatives by the Agrupación, produced new camera shots, and finally developed the negatives and enlarged them at the Taller de Artes Visuales (TAV) (Visual Arts Workshop).[5] Donoso and Parada, working sometimes in collaboration with artists Elías Adasme, Víctor Hugo Codocedo, and Patricia Saavedra, incorporated these rephotographed and blown-up portraits into their practices, disseminating the photographic archive of the detained-disappeared even further.

This chapter develops, then, two interconnected threads: one investigates the role the Vicaría had in the composition and the dissemination of the portraits of the disappeared; the other analyzes and considers the displacements and the various material transformations the photographic portraits endured—displacements and transformations that were necessary to continue denouncing and protesting the military repression. My analysis reveals that the history of the composition of the photographic archive of the detained-disappeared was concomitant to the dissemination and the transformation of the portraits that constituted this archive. As we shall see, at the same time that the photographic archive of the detained-disappeared was taking form, its objects—copies of ID photos, rephotographed photos, contact-sheets, photocopies, and so on—were being altered, reproduced, displaced, and circulated through different media. The public display of photographic portraits was critical in putting *a face*—that is a visual representation—to the crime of forced disappearances.

The chapter first begins with a brief revision of Walter Benjamin's and Allan Sekula's formulations regarding the technical transformations endured by the photographic portrait since the mid–nineteenth century. The photographic portraits of the detained-disappeared have stirred important critical debates in the Southern Cone in the last few decades. My own reading builds on and expands the existing scholarship about the uses of the portraits of the disappeared. In the second part of the chapter, I explore the debates that emerged in the early nineties (and continue to this day) in the Southern Cone, regarding the display and uses of these portraits. I reconsider the predominance that critical studies have given to the photographic trace in determining the documentary value of the portraits, and I also interrogate the wariness with which these studies consider or address the intrinsic iconicity of the portraits. Taking as a point of departure the principle that the photographic portrait is a complex visual sign—simultaneously an index, icon, and symbol—my claim is that the documentary weight of the portraits of the disappeared resides as much in their iconic aspects as in the fact that they are luminous inscriptions (traces) of disappeared persons. The rephotographed and photocopied portraits I study performed as documents in the archive, in printed media (books and magazines), and in different public interventions, acquiring further symbolic meanings through these public performances. The different kinds of materiality and formal features the portraits had in these public performances defy the common view of the photograph as mainly an index or a trace.

The third part of the chapter begins by contextualizing the vital documentary and counter-archival work carried out by the Vicaría.[6] I propose the notion of the *photo-copy rationale* to consider how the visual representation of the disappeared was composed and how the Vicaría's photographic archive took shape. I analyze three key publications produced by the Communications Unit of the Vicaría: the magazines *Solidaridad* and *Separata Solidaridad*, as well as *¿Dónde están?* (Where Are They?), a seven-volume book series published from late 1978 to 1979. The visual representation of the crime of forced disappearances, which began to take shape in the practice of publicly displaying portraits outside concentration camps, was further disseminated and consolidated in these publications.

In the last part of the chapter, I analyze photographs of actions and interventions in which portraits were displayed, used, and *embodied*. Many interventions and public demonstrations were made, so to speak, for the camera. These public demonstrations did not last long—some lasted a few seconds, others a few minutes; it depended on how long it took for the police to arrive and dissolve the protest—so it was important to record them. The photographic and audiovisual records of these demonstrations became key in further amplifying the protest, through different media (for example, in articles or chronicles that reported on these demonstrations). Visual artists resorted to this strategy, and so did the relatives of the victims of the repression.[7]

In order to fully take stock of the composition and dissemination of this performative photographic archive, we must follow its echoes across space and time. Spatially, these echoes will take us from outside the National Stadium to the offices of the Vicaría, to the TAV, and from there to the various emblematic public spaces in the city—the Supreme Court building, the Veterinary School of the University of Chile, the Plaza de Armas, and the Estación Central, among others. Chronologically, the disseminations of this archive will take us from the days right after the coup to 1978, and from 1984 to 2015, the year I found a worn-out but meaningful contact-sheet at the Vicaría's photographic archive. I am getting ahead of myself . . . because before encountering this contact sheet (a photographic source that was also, in and of itself, a copy), I encountered and was deeply moved by a series of peculiar photographic portraits. In these portraits, the photographed subject wears a mask (see fig. 1.1). Also remarkable, the mask the individual wears is clearly a photocopied portrait. The masked individual performs different gestures in front of the camera, using his own hands: in one photograph he covers his eyes, in another his mouth, and in a third, his ears. With

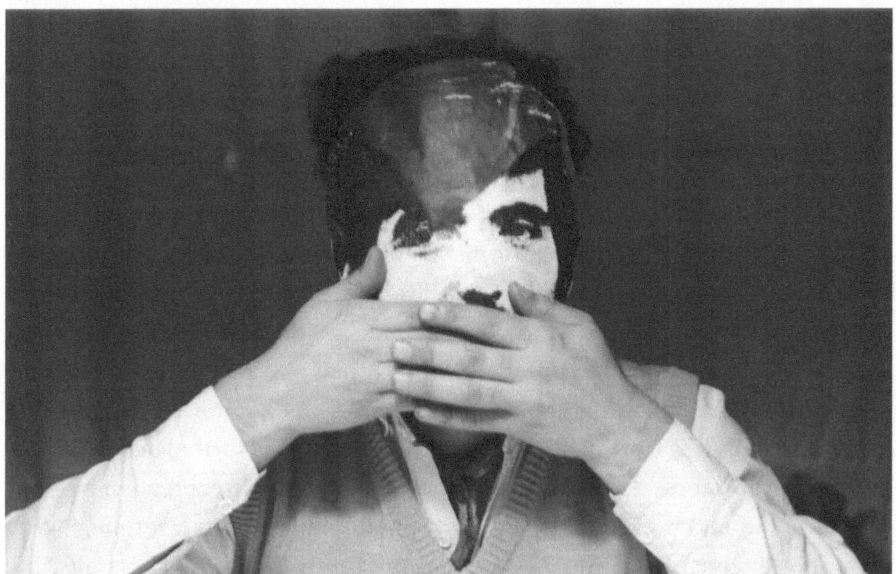

Figure 1.1. "Obrabierta A" (1974–present). Hernán Parada poses with Alejandro's mask on; he can't speak. July 1985. Credit: Adriana Silva. Black and white. Hernán Parada's personal archive.

these gestures, the masked man seeks to convey, to tell me, his spectator, that he can't see, he can't speak, and he can't hear. Why can't he see, speak, or hear? Who is the masked individual and to whom does the photocopied mask belong?

I shall finish this introduction by stating that what motivates the following reflections is, in many senses, *evident*. The portraits of the detained-disappeared seem so evident. So obvious to the eye—and to the mind.[8] Most of them are so simple: black-and-white, frontal shots cut over the shoulders. In some iterations, these austere portraits, somber icons, are displayed accompanied by the question *¿Dónde están?* (Where are they?). Some are wary of their iconicity: icons tend to be associated with pure images, with surfaces devoid of "depth."[9] There are different variations of these formulations in critical discourses—I will come back to this later. However, as some critics have also argued, reflecting on the evocative and mobilizing force of the portraits and on the visual strategies that allowed for, amplified, and sustained their persistent presence in the public sphere is imperative.[10] These matters are not disconnected from the question about the portraits' emergence—which flourished collectively: it began as a *disseminated* practice—the question about their consolidation, and the (not so) evident question regarding the composition of the crime of disappearance both as a legal concept and as an image.

(De)Constructing the Photographic Portrait

Which representational mechanisms and instances of identification, commemoration, control, and denunciation are at play in the photographic portrait? Which visual strategies, technical qualities, and uses are enabled in/by these instances? How—in light of what notions or ideas—does one address the reminiscent and haunting powers of a rephotographed and photocopied portrait? To elucidate these questions about the processes that underlie the composition of the portraits, it is worthwhile to begin evoking an idea formulated by Walter Benjamin and reproduced as an epigraph: "In the fleeting expression of a human face, the aura beckons from the early photographs for the last time."[11] Why early photographs? Benjamin feels a strong proximity to these old portraits. The persons depicted in these pictures seem more genuine and closer to him due to the natural lighting that surrounds them. In the ephemeral facial expressions of those old portraits the aura takes last refuge, as he explains. The presence of the aura in old portraits and its subsequent loss with the advent of studio portraiture, Benjamin claims, has a technical explanation. The long exposure time required for the lens to capture as much light as possible enabled, in the first decades of photography, the more "natural" apparition of the subject portrayed. As Benjamin put it in his "Little History of Photography:" "The procedure itself caused the subject to focus his life on the moment rather than hurrying on past it; during the considerable period of the exposure, the subject (as it were) grew into the picture."[12] Benjamin, who writes his "Little History" from the perspective of a fascinated viewer of photographs, talks at length about how these anonymous, distant faces, move him.[13] This dialectical tension between proximity and distance, which is commonly experienced when looking at photographs, is core in the notion of the Benjaminian aura.[14]

According to Benjamin, both the decay of photography and the loss of its aura took place toward the end of the nineteenth century, when "photographers made it their business to simulate the aura which had been banished from the picture with the suppression of darkness through faster lenses, exactly as it was being banished from reality by the deepening degeneration of the imperialist bourgeoisie."[15] The creation of faster lenses allowed photographers to work inside their studios, but the suppression of darkness and extreme sharpness of the new photographs were such that photographers had to "simulate" the aura by means of various retouching techniques:

> These pictures were made in rooms where every client was confronted, in the person of the photographer, with a technician of the latest school; whereas the photographer was confronted, in the person of every client, with a member of a rising class equipped with an aura that had seeped into the very folds of the man's frock coat or floppy cravat. For this aura was by no means the mere product of a primitive camera. Rather, in this early period, subject and technique were as exactly congruent as they become incongruent in the period of decline that immediately followed.[16]

Benjamin establishes thus a significant affinity between industrialization processes, the commercialization of photography—specifically of the studio portrait—and the contrived quality of the photographic portrait.

In relation to the historical conditions that determined the emergence of the photographic portrait, Allan Sekula's genealogy is also illuminating. Since the mid-nineteenth century, and particularly since the 1880s, photography functioned within a complex system of compilation, cataloguing, and information analysis whose most important artifact, according to Sekula, was not the camera but the filing cabinet. Still, Sekula suggests, "[This] archival promise was frustrated [. . .] both by the messy contingency of the photograph and by the sheer quantity of images."[17] Countering the more monolithic tenets about nineteenth-century photographic realism and its mimetic ideology, Sekula nuances the role of photography in the creation of police archives and denaturalizes certain fairly generalized ideas related to the photographic registers created by the police—from which the ID photo derives. Alphonse Bertillon, a member of the Paris police force at the end of the nineteenth century, attempted to organize the chaotic and enormous photographic archive of the institution—comprising more than one hundred thousand photographs by 1891—by creating the first effective system of criminal identification. In order to prevent ambiguity in the photographs, Bertillon insisted on the importance of a standardized focal distance, consistent, even use of light, and maintenance of a fixed distance between the camera and the subject.[18] These strategies were nevertheless insufficient for cataloguing subjects, so Bertillon created a file in which he included, besides the photographic portrait, an anthropometric description and a series of abbreviated and standardized notes.

We typically think of the ID photo as an almost exclusively denotative object, a sign of the purest visual empiricism. Benjamin's and Sekula's accounts, however, shed light on the sociohistorical conditions that gave form to the standardization of the studio portrait and the criminal mug shot; these accounts emphasize the mediated character of this photographic representation. Sekula illustrates how during an era in which the mimetic ideology prevailed—and consequently the notion that the photographic image was true because it was the exact reproduction of its referent—criminal record photography depended on a whole system of mediations. At the same time, it must be noted that Sekula's influential study falls short in one crucial matter. As Deborah Poole compellingly argues, "missing from Sekula's account [. . .] is any mention of either colonialism and its racial ideology or the thousands of native and colonial *cartes de visite* that joined—and indeed anticipated—criminal photography in delimiting what Sekula aptly refers to as the 'terrain of the *other*.'"[19] Indeed, as Poole demonstrates, the colonial visual archive participated "in specific ways in the consolidation, dissemination, and popularization of [the] logic of comparability and equivalency." This logic of comparability and equivalency precedes the emergence of the archive and nurtures archival rationale.

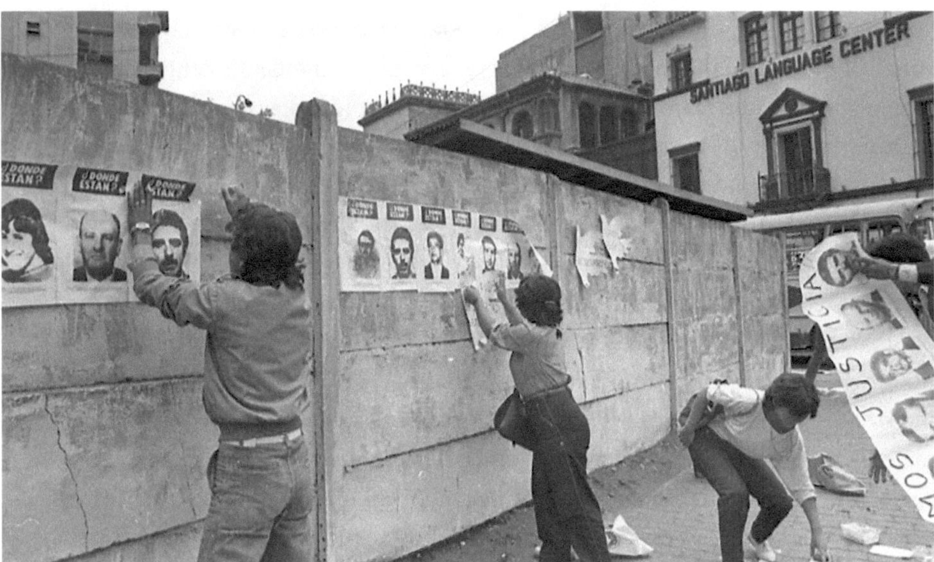

Figure 1.2. Members of the Association of Family Members of the Detained-Disappeared (AFDD) put posters on walls (January 1985). Credit: P.V. Black and white. Fundación de Documentación y Archivo de la Vicaría de la Solidaridad.

The Portraits of the Detained-Disappeared: Traces, Icons, and Symbols of the Repression

The display of family snapshots and ID photos became a widespread practice in the public rallies, marches, vigils, and hunger strikes organized to protest the repressive apparatuses of the dictatorship. Amid a context of complete silence—and denial—on the part of the militaries regarding the whereabouts of hundreds of persons who had been illegally detained or abducted (hence the use of the word *desaparecidos* by their relatives and by the organizations that advocated for them), photographic portraits of the victims of the repression began to surface everywhere. They appeared pinned to the clothes of the victims' relatives; enlarged photocopies of the portraits were made to be used as posters or banners in rallies and demonstrations (see fig. 1.2); ID photos and family portraits were disseminated in printed media; on occasions, group photographs were cropped, altered, and even enhanced to single out or highlight the particular features of the missing person. These diverse forms of photographic display, accompanied by the persistent enunciation of *¿Dónde están?* (Where are they?), sought to render visible and materialize in the public space what the regime was trying to hide, erase, and silence—the existence of the detained-disappeared. Without disregarding the fact that the photographs displayed referred to *real people* who were disappeared by state apparatuses, in what follows I investigate the tension between the evidentiary value of these images and their iconic status. This critical discussion will allow me to better elucidate in the following sections the technical and formal strategies used to compose and disseminate the portraits of the disappeared—iconic representations that continue being displayed to this day.

In *La ciudad de los fotógrafos*, Agrupación member Ana González relates that the only family portrait she has with her husband and children, all of them detained-disappeared, was taken by a street photographer who showed up at their house offering his services. Even though they barely had money to eat, they decided to pose for him and pay him for the photograph. This photograph would become a treasured memento for González. While it is true that some photographs were taken in exceptional circumstances such as this, in most cases, and leaving aside copied ID photos, the portraits and snapshots consigned in the photographic archive of the detained-disappeared came from the private sphere and were produced in everyday situations and family events (e.g., birthdays, family reunions, first day of school). The quotidian and intimate contexts of production of these snapshots ask us to see the photos as candid records, as if they were devoid of artifice or were not coded. Not only do these family photos compel a gaze that is affiliative and "identificatory" and seem "instantly familiar," as Andrea Noble argues, but also their public display "in the context of human rights activism in Argentina and indeed across a range of Latin American countries" has become familiar.[20] This apparent familiarity is connected to the iconicity of these portraits—an aspect that Noble also considers in her study of the public display of portraits of the victims of the repression during the Argentinean military dictatorship. Commenting on the media dissemination of portraits made for or in front of the camera, Noble draws attention to "the ubiquity of photographic icons of forced disappearances" and asserts, "as a mode of photographic performance and endlessly repeated gesture staged precisely for the camera, such images have achieved iconic status."[21] Ludmila Da Silva Catela, also studying the Argentinean case, further argues that the portraits of the disappeared "not only succeeded in representing the disappearance, but also [. . .] created a strong iconic referent for denouncing [such disappearances] [. . .] A black and white photo used in a march, pinned to the body of a mother, hanging in a square, stamped on an Argentine flag, rarely deserves the question, 'Who are they? What does it mean?'"[22]

These assertions are indisputable, but they raise questions: How did this happen? How did these portraits succeed in representing the disappearance? How did they become iconic referents for denouncing the military's repressive tactics? To answer these questions, we need to move the camera a little to the west and also readjust the focus. Why? Because we need to take a closer look at the Chilean case, which has not received as much critical attention as the Argentinean case has with regards to the portraits of the disappeared. The symbolisms the portraits have acquired over time, their strong iconicity, and their persistent displacements, are effects of these earlier efforts of reproduction, composition, and dissemination. In fact, one aspect that tends to be disregarded in critical studies about visual representations of the disappeared is that their photographic portraits were composed in different stages, that they were the result of several processes of manipulation and reproduction (cropping, enhancement, etc.).

Several critics have commented on the complexities and the paradoxes that frustrate critical consideration of the *desaparecidos* in the Southern Cone, particularly those that arise regarding their textual and visual representations—including, of course, the photographic portraits.[23] As already stated, the repressive contexts amid which these portraits emerged can't be disregarded. Given these contexts, it seems difficult not to accept the portraits at face value—that is, as they are *presented* to us, as the most direct and immediate sign of the person they *represent*. At the same time, as Diana Taylor reminds us in her influential *Disappearing Acts*:

> the *desaparecidos* (the disappeared), are, by definition, always already the object of representation. The flesh-and-blood victims, forcefully absented from the sociopolitical crisis that created them, left no bodies. Those disappeared. The victim reemerged as *icons*, either as "subversives" (for the military government) or as the "disappeared" (for the Madres and other human rights activists)—powerful, conflicting images that reintroduced the missing into the public sphere as pure representation.[24]

Undeniable as this assertion is, it does not resolve the complexity that arises in the attempt to critically consider the portraits—and Taylor does not fail to acknowledge this. About the photographic portraits displayed by the Madres de Plaza de Mayo, she reasons:

> These photos, like magic fetishes, keep the dead and brutalized bodies forever "alive." They tempt us to see them as "natural" and transparent manifestations of the "real." Thus it seems treasonous to resist that view by insisting on the iconic quality of these photographs [. . .] The political exigencies seem to beg for the uncritical acceptance of the object as the thing itself.[25]

The uses the relatives gave to the portraits of their disappeared loved ones incited art critics and theorists in Chile to reflect on the documentary qualities of the photograph, to ponder what specific traits made of photographs incontestable proof of those lives that were forcefully erased. In several writings, the photographic trace appears as the determining evidentiary attribute of the photograph. This is apparent in Jean-Louis Déotte's study about the "art in the epoch of disappearance," formulation that builds on and expands art critic Nelly Richard's ideas concerning the Chilean artistic practices' turn toward the medium of photography in the late seventies.[26] The sororal community formed around the relatives who looked for their disappeared loved ones, argues Déotte, needs to understand that the bodies have been "really swallowed, subtracted. This knowledge requires—but the paradox is only apparent—a return to the certainty that they really existed. Thus, the extreme importance of the photograph: minimum proof of existence against an uncertainty that increases."[27] According to Déotte, the artistic practices that resisted the military repression, just like the sororal community formed around the relatives, could not be disentangled from "a cognitive element, empiric even, that has to give the assurance that an existence had in fact, taken place. This element becomes the core idea of the work [. . .] The art in the age of disappearance requires the photograph and, more generally, the traces of an impression."[28]

Roland Barthes's formulation of the photograph as a physical "emanation of the referent," in his *Camera Lucida*, greatly influenced the critical debates that emerged in Chile in the late seventies;[29] so did Susan Sontag's definition of the photograph as a *memento mori* in her *On Photography*.[30] A passage from an oft-cited essay by Nelly Richard illustrates these critical orientations:

> If the device of the photograph contains in itself the temporal ambiguity of that which still is and of that which no longer is (of that which remains suspended between life and death, between appearing and disappearing), such ambiguity is over-dramatized in the case of the photographic portraits of disappeared people. This is why the portraits that the detainees' relatives carry pinned to their breasts have become the *densest symbol* in the crusade of memory conducted by the victims to remember and make us remember the past.[31]

Richard's argument brings attention to a separate issue that complicates even further the critical consideration of these photographs: strictly speaking, these are not portraits *of disappeared* people. The photos, obviously, were taken before the subjects portrayed in them became disappeared.[32] Richard connects eloquently the ambiguity that characterizes the photograph in general to the suspended temporality that frames the photographed subjects, neither alive nor dead, but disappeared. Richard's passage also allows us to appreciate the extent to which the portraits of the disappeared functioned as emblems or symbols as much as they did as certificates or traces. In suggesting that the portraits have become the *densest symbol* in the crusade of memory, Richard gives account of the photographic portrait as complex visual object: here is an iconic representation of an individual (just like a painted portrait can be an iconic representation), which carries also the individual's luminous trace (and in this respect it differs from the painted portrait), and which because of specific circumstances, can become a symbol—or many symbols. Indeed, the portraits are tokens of the repression and symbols of the resistance to the repression, to the crime of abduction; moreover, these symbols mourn loss and death and envisage love and the work of memory, and more.

The central idea advanced by different critical approaches is that in photography's civil political space (I evoke here Ariella Azoulay's formulation of a civil political space imagined day after day by people who use photography), the portraits of the disappeared were (and continue to be) displayed and used as visual proofs to attest to the existence of particular individuals, to claim (irreparable) damages, to demand justice, and to keep the memory of the victims of the repression alive. The incorporation of these portraits into artistic practices, besides connoting the ideas just stated, also conveyed the idea of disappearance as the sign of an epoch. Thus, the small, worn-out photographic portraits that began to emerge in the streets to denounce forced disappearances soon began to be supplemented with other meanings and functions: opposing the military regime, activating the work of memory, resisting forgetfulness.

However, that which twenty years ago was considered in terms of eloquence and performativity—the undeniable iconic and symbolic force of the portraits of the *desaparecidos*, their persistent presence in public spaces, and their eventual incorporation into artistic practices—is rendered in recent critical approaches an aspect that might not only objectify the portraits, but also stagnate the work of memory. Implicit in these claims is the idea that the very iconicity and reproducibility of the portraits ultimately fossilizes them. One critic, for instance, talks about the "pre-packaged" political meaning of the portraits of the disappeared and wonders whether "alternative or supplementary depictions of disappearance" can emerge.[33] The problem with this line of argumentation is that it considers only the incorporation of portraits of the disappeared in specific artistic practices, but fails to consider photography as a civil practice and thus disregards the political space opened up by these portraits in the public arena. I cannot help but wonder how the relatives of the *desaparecidos* would feel if they were told the portraits they display are fetishized fossils, objects with "pre-packaged" political meaning. Furthermore, if as Taylor justly reminds us, the *desaparecidos* are always already the objects of representation, what can their portraits be if not iconic supplementary representations? Can the rephotographed and photocopied portraits be considered something other than iconic supplements? I believe they cannot, but I don't see this as a limitation. Quite the contrary, I believe that it is precisely in their overwhelming iconicity that their evocative force resides.

The Vicaría and the Composition of the Photographic Corpus of the *Desaparecidos*

The Vicaría, which began to function on January 1, 1976, continued and expanded the work that the Comité Pro Paz had initiated in October 1973.[34] The creation of this organization within the Catholic Church was noteworthy: as

Vicaría's Executive Secretary Javier Luis Egaña Barahona suggests, "the only way to confront the military dictatorship was with a powerful institution, and it was very symbolic that the organization that defended human rights was located in the Archbishop's Palace, in the heart of the city."[35] The organization strived to disseminate the message about the importance of respecting and defending the

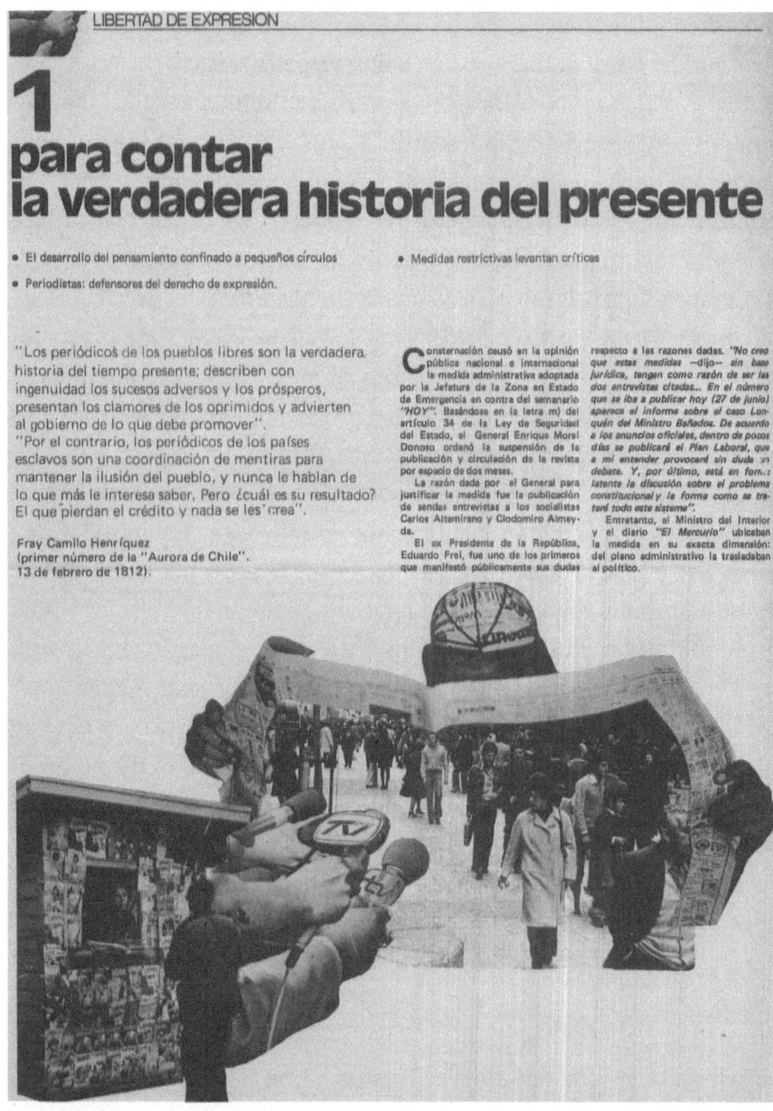

LIBERTAD DE EXPRESION

1 para contar la verdadera historia del presente

- El desarrollo del pensamiento confinado a pequeños círculos
- Periodistas: defensores del derecho de expresión.
- Medidas restrictivas levantan críticas

"Los periódicos de los pueblos libres son la verdadera historia del tiempo presente; describen con ingenuidad los sucesos adversos y los prósperos, presentan los clamores de los oprimidos y advierten al gobierno de lo que debe promover".
"Por el contrario, los periódicos de los países esclavos son una coordinación de mentiras para mantener la ilusión del pueblo, y nunca le hablan de lo que más le interesa saber. Pero ¿cuál es su resultado? El que pierdan el crédito y nada se les crea".

Fray Camilo Henríquez
(primer número de la "Aurora de Chile".
13 de febrero de 1812).

Consternación causó en la opinión pública nacional e internacional la medida administrativa adoptada por la Jefatura de la Zona en Estado de Emergencia en contra del semanario *"HOY"*. Basándose en la letra m) del artículo 34 de la Ley de Seguridad del Estado, el General Enrique Morel Donoso ordenó la suspensión de la publicación y circulación de la revista por espacio de dos meses.

La razón dada por el General para justificar la medida fue la publicación de sendas entrevistas a los socialistas Carlos Altamirano y Clodomiro Almeyda.

El ex Presidente de la República, Eduardo Frei, fue uno de los primeros que manifestó públicamente sus dudas respecto a las razones dadas. *"No creo que estas medidas* —dijo— *sin base jurídica, tengan como razón de ser las dos entrevistas citadas... En el número que se iba a publicar hoy (27 de junio) aparece el informe sobre el caso Lonquén del Ministro Bañados. De acuerdo a los anuncios oficiales, dentro de pocos días se publicará el Plan Laboral, que a mi entender provocará sin duda un debate. Y, por último, está en forma latente la discusión sobre el problema constitucional y la forma como se tratará todo este sistema".*

Entretanto, el Ministro del Interior y el diario *"El Mercurio"* ubicaban la medida en su exacta dimensión: del plano administrativo la trasladaban al político.

Figure 1.3. "Libertad de expresión." Interior page of *Solidaridad* 73 (1979). Black and white. Fundación de Documentación y Archivo de la Vicaría de la Solidaridad.

rights of *all* human beings and about loving and caring for the poor, and Vicaría's biweekly *Solidaridad* was an important medium to achieve this endeavor.[36] Since a good portion of its readership was only semi-literate, having an effective iconic language was key, and a Communications Unit was promptly established. This unit grew rapidly and attracted a number of professional journalists and photographers. The prevalence of the visual component is apparent in the spectacular design of the magazine (see fig. 1.3).[37] Thorough attention was paid to the way information was presented and conveyed, both in the covers and in the interior pages of the magazine.[38] So much so, that Helen Hughes recalls that when she applied for the second photographer position (Vicaría's first photographer was Luis Navarro), she was asked to submit a portfolio and also to complete different specific assignments—as if she were in a competition.[39] Navarro and Hughes did numerous photographic reportages for the magazine, and went on assignment to different parts of the city—and the country. Stunning collages were composed using their photographs. In many ways, the Vicaría also played a role in the promotion of visual literacy as well as in the development and dissemination of documentary photography.

One of the Vicaría's most important endeavors was fighting to establish the truth about the whereabouts of the disappeared. As some readers of this book may know, and as the *Report of the Chilean National Commission on Truth and Reconciliation* documents, during the first months following the military coup, thousands of people were detained. In most occasions, these detentions were not acknowledged; victims "were kept in clandestine detention, subjected to torture, and eventually summarily executed. Their bodies were disposed of in secret."[40] Disappearances were systematically applied during the first four years of military rule, but the *Report* notes that they were "not centrally coordinated" at the very beginning.[41] This changed in November 1973, when Augusto Pinochet established the DINA (National Intelligence Directorate), the infamous secret police headed by the merciless criminal Colonel Manuel Contreras. After the creation of this intelligence unit, "'disappearances' became a carefully organized method designed to exterminate opponents considered dangerous and to avoid accountability for such crimes."[42] After the military decided to close the last concentration camp that remained open in November 1977 (Tres Álamos), it became apparent to Vicaría workers that "there were many people for whom habeas corpus had achieved nothing. They had not returned home, they had not been released, or reported as expelled from the country, or taken to court. So, then we said: *we had to find a name for this situ-*

ation. That's how the Detained-Disappeared Unit was created."[43] As Vicaría lawyer Hector Contreras suggests, to be able to denounce and investigate the crime of disappearances, it was necessary to give it a name first—until that moment, the concept of detained-disappeared did not exist as such.

Vicaría staff devised a very efficient data-keeping-and-analyzing system that listed biometrical and biographical personal information, including political affiliation, union involvement, and the like, as well as details and facts regarding the time of the person's disappearance, particular physical traits, and relevant medical records (scars, teeth removals, etc.). This exceptional record-keeping system, which Vicaría staff called *la sábana* (the sheet) because of its large dimensions, permitted them to gather different kinds of information and present them in a way that facilitated its visualization.[44] *La sábana* allowed the Vicaría's lawyers, legal aids, and social workers to crosscheck data, compare records, and analyze information more effectively. This, in turn, allowed Vicaría lawyers to prepare more compelling legal claims and thus bring to justice hundreds of habeas corpus cases. The information compiled in this system became extremely relevant after a clandestine grave was discovered in the town of Lonquén (a documentary matter I study in the next chapter). As we shall see, the Vicaría devised very clever strategies to corroborate, secure, and make public physical and visual evidence that contested, for the very first time, the versions offered by the military regime and by the official media with regards to the detained-disappeared.

La sábana was a sophisticated and multilayered document, which was part of a much bigger archive, a counter-archive that was assembled, however precariously, on the run, its structure and internal logic evolving and changing according to the needs.[45] The main objective of this critical counter-archive was to keep track of, compile, organize, and analyze the dictatorship's distinct repressive methods. Remarkably, this counter-archive not only was contemporaneous to the repressive regime it resisted—the civic-military dictatorship—but was built right in front of the repressers' eyes. This counter-archive encompassed different kinds of publications—bulletins and internal reports prepared by the Church—and record-keeping systems, including the photographic archive of the detained-disappeared.

As González's story about her only family photo suggests, the relatives of the disappeared possessed few photographs and, in many cases, those in their possession were in such poor condition that it was necessary to mend, reproduce, and organize them. Navarro recalls that the number and condition of the photos brought by the relatives to the offices of the Vicaría made apparent the families' socioeconomic status. The poorest families possessed very few photos, and those they had were discolored and wrinkled. To obtain better-quality photographs of the already existing photos, a lens capable of focusing at a very close distance was needed. Since the lenses the photographers had in their possession lacked close-focus capabilities, it occurred to Navarro that turning the camera lens upside down and fastening it to the body of the camera with a tape would allow the photographer to produce higher-quality and sharper images of the old prints brought by the relatives. After making a satisfactory copy of the source photograph, Navarro printed it on matte paper and retouched it with a graphite pencil (as he saw fit). He then proceeded to rephotograph the improved portrait. In Navarro's own words, "we did not have the means, and these were things that were produced out of necessity."[46] After being cropped, mended, and rephotographed (and sometimes photocopied), the portraits were catalogued in the photographic archive and disseminated through printed media. This process, expectedly, produced a sort of standardization. The portraits, one next to the other, look quite similar. The resemblance is emphasized in the portraits' visual arrangement—the way they are displayed in the media, above all on the covers of the *¿Dónde están?* book series. These iconic covers suggest that the Vicaría not only composed the photographic archive, but also played a key role in the composition of the visual representation of the detained-disappeared.

The retouched and rephotographed portraits consigned in the photographic archive also appeared periodically in *Solidaridad*. Several portraits were disseminated in the sections detailing the habeas corpus presented by the Vicaría on behalf of the detainees (see fig. 1.4). Such is the case of Luis Mardones, Osvaldo Figueroa, William Zulueta, and Humberto Drouillas, whose portraits were reproduced in the section titled "Noticias Judiciales de la semana" (Legal News of the Week). Mardones, Figueroa, Zulueta, and Drouillas were abducted by DINA agents in May 1977. These four men, along with Eduardo de la Fuente and Jorge Troncoso, were charged, by means of forced confession under torture, with the kidnapping of minor Carlos Veloso. At the moment of the publication of number 19 of *Solidaridad*, it was known that they were detained at Cuatro Alamos, one of the clandestine torture centers set up by the DINA.[47]

The enlarged photographs reproduced in the pages of the magazine had, primarily, an illustrative function—by looking at the photographs, readers could identify the men. Their photographs were presented to complement the text that provided relevant information about the abductions: the moment at which each

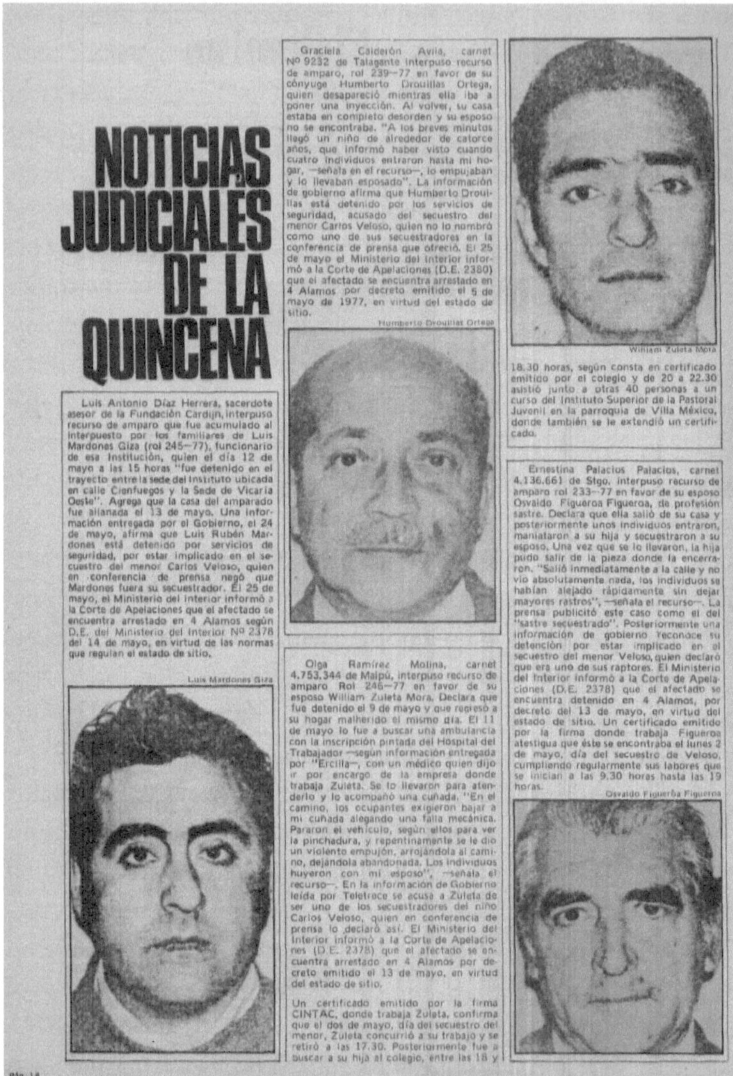

NOTICIAS JUDICIALES DE LA QUINCENA

Luis Antonio Díaz Herrera, sacerdote asesor de la Fundación Cardijn, interpuso recurso de amparo que fue acumulado al interpuesto por los familiares de Luis Mardones Giza (rol 245—77), funcionario de esa Institución, quien el día 12 de mayo a las 15 horas "fue detenido en el trayecto entre la sede del Instituto ubicada en calle Cienfuegos y la Sede de Vicaria Oeste". Agrega que la casa del amparado fue allanada el 13 de mayo. Una información entregada por el Gobierno, el 24 de mayo, afirma que Luis Rubén Mardones está detenido por servicios de seguridad, por estar implicado en el secuestro del menor Carlos Veloso, quien en conferencia de prensa negó que Mardones fuera su secuestrador. El 25 de mayo, el Ministerio del Interior informó a la Corte de Apelaciones que el afectado se encuentra arrestado en 4 Alamos según D.E. del Ministerio del Interior Nº 2378 del 14 de mayo, en virtud de las normas que regulan el estado de sitio.

Luis Mardones Giza

Graciela Calderón Avila, carnet Nº 9232 de Talagante interpuso recurso de amparo, rol 239—77 en favor de su cónyuge Humberto Drouillas Ortega, quien desapareció mientras ella iba a poner una inyección. Al volver, su casa estaba en completo desorden y su esposo no se encontraba. "A los breves minutos llegó un niño de alrededor de catorce años, que informó haber visto cuando cuatro individuos entraron hasta mi hogar, —señala en el recurso—, lo empujaban y lo llevaban esposado". La información de gobierno afirma que Humberto Drouillas está detenido por los servicios de seguridad, acusado del secuestro del menor Carlos Veloso, quien no lo nombró como uno de sus secuestradores en la conferencia de prensa que ofreció. El 25 de mayo el Ministerio del Interior informó a la Corte de Apelaciones (D.E. 2380) que el afectado se encuentra arrestado en 4 Alamos por decreto emitido el 5 de mayo de 1977, en virtud del estado de sitio.

Humberto Drouillas Ortega

Olga Ramírez Molina, carnet 4.753.344 de Maipú, interpuso recurso de amparo Rol 246—77 en favor de su esposo William Zuleta Mora. Declara que fue detenido el 9 de mayo y que regresó a su hogar malherido el mismo día. El 11 de mayo lo fue a buscar una ambulancia con la inscripción pintada del Hospital del Trabajador —según información entregada por "Ercilla—, con un médico quien dijo ir por encargo de la empresa donde trabaja Zuleta. Se lo llevaron para atenderlo y lo acompañó una cuñada. "En el camino, los ocupantes exigieron bajar a mi cuñada alegando una falla mecánica. Pararon el vehículo, según ellos para ver la pinchadura, y repentinamente se le dio un violento empujón, arrojándola al camino, dejándola abandonada. Los individuos huyeron con mi esposo", —señala el recurso—. En la información de Gobierno leída por Teletrece se acusa a Zuleta de ser uno de los secuestradores del niño Carlos Veloso, quien en conferencia de prensa lo declaró así. El Ministerio del Interior informó a la Corte de Apelaciones (D.E. 2378) que el afectado se encuentra arrestado en 4 Alamos por decreto emitido el 13 de mayo, en virtud del estado de sitio.

Un certificado emitido por la firma CINTAC, donde trabaja Zuleta, confirma que el dos de mayo, día del secuestro del menor, Zuleta concurrió a su trabajo y se retiró a las 17.30. Posteriormente fue a buscar a su hija al colegio, entre las 18 y 18.30 horas, según consta en certificado emitido por el colegio y de 20 a 22.30 asistió junto a otras 40 personas a un curso del Instituto Superior de la Pastoral Juvenil en la parroquia de Villa México, donde también se le extendió un certificado.

William Zuleta Mora

Ernestina Palacios Palacios, carnet 4.136.661 de Stgo. interpuso recurso de amparo rol 233—77 en favor de su esposo Osvaldo Figueroa Figueroa, de profesión sastre. Declara que ella salió de su casa y posteriormente unos individuos entraron, maniataron a su hija y secuestraron a su esposo. Una vez que se lo llevaron, la hija pudo salir de la pieza donde la encerraron. "Salió inmediatamente a la calle y no vio absolutamente nada, los individuos se habían alejado rápidamente sin dejar mayores rastros", —señala el recurso—. La prensa publicitó este caso como el del "sastre secuestrado". Posteriormente una información de gobierno reconoce su detención por estar implicado en el secuestro del menor Veloso, quien declaró que era uno de sus raptores. El Ministerio del Interior informó a la Corte de Apelaciones (D.E. 2378) que el afectado se encuentra detenido en 4 Alamos, por decreto del 13 de mayo, en virtud del estado de sitio. Un certificado emitido por la firma donde trabaja Figueroa atestigua que éste se encontraba el lunes 2 de mayo, día del secuestro de Veloso, cumpliendo regularmente sus labores que se inician a las 9.30 horas hasta las 19 horas.

Osvaldo Figuerba Figueroa

Figure 1.4. *Solidaridad* 19. Photographic portraits of four men detained, Luis Mardones, Osvaldo Figueroa, William Zulueta, and Humberto Drouillas. Black and white. Fundación de Documentación y Archivo de la Vicaría de la Solidaridad.

abduction took place (date, time, and place) and information about the habeas corpus as well as other relevant facts (testimonies of witnesses and information pointing to evidence of the detainees' innocence). Despite their illustrative function, the visual information offered by the images is limited; readers learned nothing about the height, body build, or other physical traits of the detainees.

The portraits showed only their faces in black and white. Furthermore, readers could not know for certain whether or not these were recent images. Yet, despite scarce and contingent visual information, these portraits were (and are) effective: the recognition and identification gesture is seemingly automatic. We cannot but stare at Drouillas's hopeful gaze, at Mardones's serious expression, or at the sadness projected by Zuleta's and Figueroa's gaze. The readers who saw these images in *Solidaridad* during that month of May knew that these men had been abducted and that, at the moment of the publication of the newsletter, they were detained in a concentration camp. Even today it is impossible to ignore this information while looking at these worn-out portraits.

What do these portraits show us? Mustaches, moles, wide eyebrows, and a full head of hair or baldness. More than an informative function, the portraits featured in these news sections have perhaps an affective role. The invocative power of these images lies in the countenance's emblematic authority. These gazes reclaim the viewer's attention; they interpellate us. If the Vicaría gave a name to the detained-disappeared, the portraits "put faces" to the name, augmenting the realness of these cases. In these portraits, the Barthesian division between *studium* and *punctum* becomes indistinct. Or, to put it a bit differently, these portraits illustrate that the distinction between these notions is always relative. Even though the photographic *punctum* is commonly described in terms of contiguity, uniqueness, and immediacy, Barthes himself suggests in *Camera Lucida* that the *punctum* carries within it a transformative force, that the *punctum* has a metonymic and expansive potential that allows for a certain latency.[48] This means not only that the single memory of an image can activate the *punctum*, but also that the photographic subject herself can multiply and differ. As Eduardo Cadava and Paola Cortés-Rocca explain in their reading of this essay: "What Barthes engages [. . .] is nothing less than what produces the difficulty of all contemporary reflections on photography: the absence of the subject. But, as he suggests—and here lies his strength and courage—this absence does not result from disappearance or effacement, but, on the contrary, from multiplication and proliferation."[49]

I think of this dialectical relationship between absence and proliferation as I watch a set of photographs published in *Separata Solidaridad* in November 1978 (see fig. 1.6). Photographic portraits not only appeared *along* texts in the informative sections, they also became photographic subjects, protagonists of other photographs disseminated in the Vicaría publications. In this issue of *Separata Solidaridad*, for instance, the portraits of the detainees coexist inside the photographs with other elements (the chains) and other subjects (the women who display the portraits pinned to their garments). *Solidaridad* readers did not need to read the text to know that the women had chained themselves as a form of protest and that the worn-out photographs they carried pinned to their clothes were of their disappeared relatives. They did not need to read this because women from the Agrupación persistently circulated in public with these portraits pinned to their clothes—portraits that, until then, had not left the private space. To this first instance of displacement and dissemination—the portrait leaves the album, the frame—a second instance of displacement is added in the rephotographing of the portrait, and further in the dissemination of the photo in the magazine. Navarro took these photographs at a public demonstration organized by the Agrupación. The women chained themselves to the main gates of the CEPAL building (the United Nations Economic Commission for Latin America and the Caribbean), carrying photographic portraits pinned to their clothes. The demonstration was to protest the regime's explanation regarding the figure of the "muerte presunta" (presumed death). Agrupación women rightfully refused to accept this legal figure, which allowed the military (by placing pressure on the justice system) to dismiss habeas corpus claims—a person declared "presumably dead" was not detained-disappeared, and thus the habeas corpus claim could be overruled.[50]

At the left of figure 1.5, two portraits have been rephotographed by Navarro. The portraits are of protestor Lucía Cantero's sister and uncle, both disappeared in 1976.[51] By cropping Cantero's face from the frame, the photographer prevents her from becoming the center of the picture. Instead, he places the small portraits at the center. With this gesture, the photographic representation points to the coincidence between the political gesture and the affective gesture. That the portraits may be in bad shape, or that they may be photocopies, is irrelevant; a woman, a protestor, carries these portraits pinned to her chest, and with this act she gives flesh to the expression "*te llevo en el corazón*" (I keep/carry you in my heart). Meanwhile, the lower photograph shown in figure 1.6 portrays a collective of eleven women of different ages. Because the framing cuts off the last woman in the row, it suggests that the row continues. The attitudes and poses of the women vary. The woman on the left appears tired, with a blank stare, as she leans against the fence. Some women look directly into the camera while others look off to the side; at least two appear to be smiling.

The structure, bounds, and contents of the Vicaría's counter-archive were continuously being transformed and expanded; these contents were also displaced

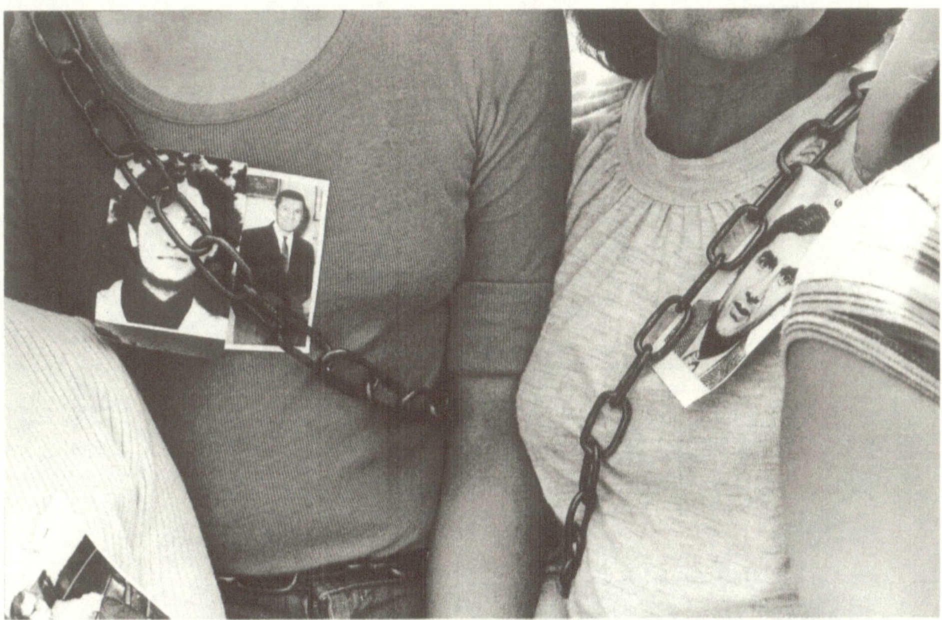

Figure 1.5. Detail of Association of Family Members of the Detained-Disappeared member and protestor Lucía Cantero, with portraits of her sister and uncle pinned to her chest. (November 1978). Credit: Luis Navarro Vega. Black and white. Luis Navarro Vega's personal archive.

and disseminated in the book series titled *¿Dónde están?*, whose seven volumes were published between November 1978 and May 1979. The series presented a compilation of all the documents gathered by the organization pertaining to the cases brought to the courts on behalf of 478 *desaparecidos*, all of them detained in different circumstances between 1973 and 1976. In the Introduction to the first volume, Episcopal Vicar Reverend Cristián Precht states:

> In the pages that follow, the reader will find the *exact reproduction* of the personal records delivered to the Ministry of the Interior, and which constitute a summary of *the compiled documentation and evidence* each family also possesses [. . .] The antecedents given are not new for either the Courts of Justice or the government: nor are they completely unknown to the public. They are a compilation of what the families of the *detenidos-desaparecidos* have been denouncing to the country, the courts of justice, the government, international organizations, in thousands of efforts made.[52]

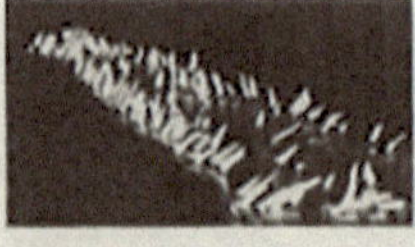

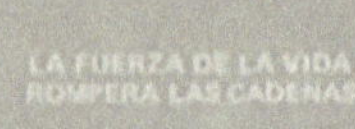

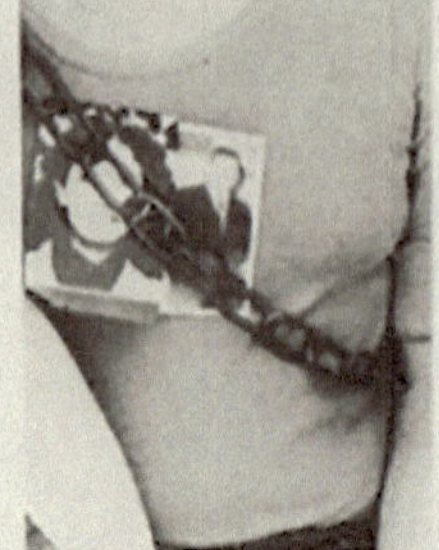

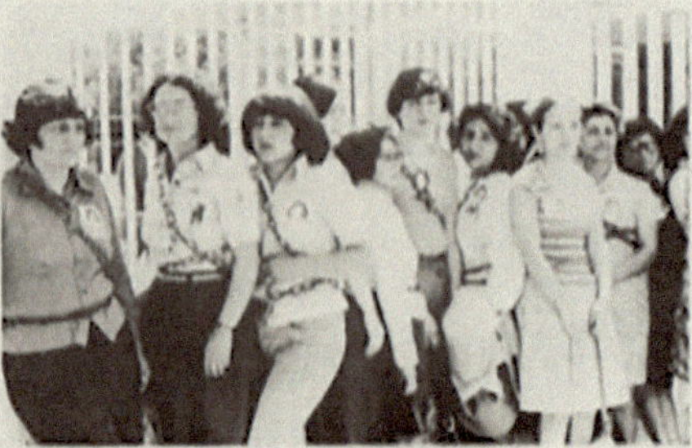

sucesos, no existe elemento alguno que lo inhiba del establecimiento de *"la verdad, nada más que la verdad y toda la verdad"* a lo que el país entero dice hoy que tienen derecho los familiares de las personas desaparecidas. No será así el Gobierno directamente quien lleve adelante la pesquisa y ordene la comparecencia de los testigos, sino que será un colaborador que ha comprometido anticipadamente su cooperación para que se aclare un problema en cuyo esclarecimiento anuncia solamente su interés específico. La naturaleza judicial que el problema tiene en sí mismo, por estar comprometidos en él los derechos más sensibles de nuestro ordenamiento jurídico, y que hace inexcusable la intervención de las instancias más calificadas del Poder Judicial, la admite el propio Gobierno al expresar el Sr. Ministro del Interior: **"Cualquiera sea la verdad concreta en cada situación, ella puede ser investigada por los tribunales de justicia".**

¿Será necesario añadir una sola palabra a lo que la Iglesia ha dicho en estos cinco años, a las expresiones antes citadas del Ministro del Interior, del Embajador de Chile ante las Naciones Unidas, del General Augusto Pinochet, de numerosos editoriales que reflejan el estado de la opinión pública en la materia, para afirmar ante V.E. que este drama nacional que provoca un público clamor constituye la *"alarma pública"* a que la ley alude para el nombramiento de un Ministro en Visita extraordinaria?. No parece posible imaginar que pueda provocarse mayor alarma pública que ante el hecho incontestable, hoy por todos reconocido y calificado de un drama nacional, del desaparecimiento inobjetable de 651 chilenos. ¡Pero se multiplica aún esta alarma pública si tal suceso trágico no queda definitivamente esclarecido! ¿No es alarmante para una sociedad el que no sólo un hecho así pueda ocurrir en ella sino que ni siquiera se pueda identificar cómo, en qué circunstancias, por quién, han desaparecido de la faz de la tierra centenares de sus miembros? Mientras el problema no se esclarezca habrá que sospechar que sus causantes tienen el poder de impedir tal esclarecimiento, con lo que, si ello es así, pende sobre nuestra sociedad la amenaza de su repetición. El carácter acentuado de alarma pública que una situación así cobra es innegable. En realidad, la única manera de lograr una seguridad en esta materia es comprobar que nuestra sociedad tiene el vigor y la salud vital para llevar a la luz pública su verdad y para condenarla. Hoy los causantes de este drama se ocultan en la penumbre y se solazan en su anonimato y en la ignorancia de la sociedad acerca de lo realmente ocurrido. ¿Si en tales circunstancias vuelven ellos, u otros, a forjar planes siniestros, serán ellos los únicos responsables de nuevos hechos dramáticos? Si se les da el espectáculo de

instituciones sociales débiles, ¿acaso no los estamos fortaleciendo? La debilidad de la ley es la fuerza de la ilegalidad. En cambio, si el país aprecia la conducta ejemplar de un Poder Judicial inclaudicable, que en su compromiso de justicia con la sociedad cumple con su mandato de esclarecer este drama de las personas desaparecidas, se eliminará la alarmante aprehensión sobre una eventual repetición de estos hechos por parte de los mismos o de diferentes grupos. Imposible cumplir con los anhelos históricos de nuestro país de caminar resueltamente hacia un futuro institucional si iniciamos nuestros pasos con tal fardo a nuestras espaldas.

POR TANTO:

Respetuosamente e invocando los derechos de protección a la vida, a la integridad física y a la libertad personal de las personas desaparecidas después de su detención y el derecho de sus familiares a obtener de la justicia el esclarecimiento definitivo de estas situaciones que los mantienen en la incertidumbre y los angustian solicitamos de este Alto Tribunal encargado por mandato constitucional de la suprema protección de los derechos fundamentales, la designación en visita extraordinaria de un Ministro de cada una de las Cortes de Apelaciones de Iquique, Antofagasta, Copiapó, Valparaíso, Santiago, Rancagua, Talca, Chillán, Concepción, Temuco, Valdivia para que en sus respectivas jurisdicciones, tomen a su cargo las investigaciones judiciales encaminadas a establecer las circunstancias de la detención, el o los lugares a que han sido conducidos después de practicadas las detenciones, el o los lugares en que han permanecido y actualmente permanecen privados ilegalmente de su libertad, su estado actual o la suerte corrida por las personas desaparecidas que se individualizan en las nóminas que por separado para cada una de las Cortes de Apelaciones antes indicadas, acompañamos en el primer otrosí.

PRIMER OTROSI:

Acompañamos nóminas que contienen los nombres de 651 personas detenidas desaparecidas, correspondientes a las diferentes Cortes de Apelaciones señaladas en lo principal, para la investigación de cuyas detenciones y suerte se solicita la designación de Ministros en Visita Extraordinaria.

Resuelta que sea esta petición, si procediere, acompañaremos duplicado de estas nóminas para ser remitidas a cada uno de los Señores Ministros designados.

Sírvase V.S. Excma. tener por acompañadas las nóminas.

SEGUNDO OTROSI:

Con motivo del compromiso contraído por el Sr. Ministro del Interior en su citado discurso del 15 de Junio del presente año por cadena nacional de radio y televisión, en orden a explorar **"cualquier camino serio que respecto de algún caso particular pueda presentársele"**, diversos señores Obispos de la Iglesia Católica han estado enviándole antecedentes de personas detenidas desaparecidas.

Acompañamos esos antecedentes ya enviados, que corresponden a 478 personas, haciendo presente a V.S. Excma. que resuelta que sea esta solicitud acompañaremos las correspondientes al resto de las personas incluidas en las nóminas, para que los señores Ministros que se designen cuenten desde el inicio de sus investigaciones con los antecedentes de todos los detenidos desaparecidos a los cuales ellas deben extenderse.

ENRIQUE ALVEAR URRUTIA
Obispo Auxiliar de Santiago
Vicario Episcopal Zona Oeste

JORGE HOURTON POISSON
Obispo Auxiliar de Stgo.
Vicario Episcopal Zona Norte

IGNACIO ORTUZAR ROJAS
Vicario General y
Vicario Episcopal
Zona Providencia
Las Condes

CRISTIAN PRECHT BAÑADOS
Vicario Episcopal para
la Solidaridad
Secretario de Pastoral
del Arzobispado

GUSTAVO FERRARIS
DEL CONTE, S.D.G.
Vicario Episcopal Zona Sur

SERGIO URIBE GUTIERREZ,
O.F.M.
Vicario Episcopal Zona Centro

MAURICIO VEILLETE
G., O. M. I.
Vicario Episcopal
Zona Avda. Matta

ALFONSO BAEZA DONOSO
Vicario Episcopal para la
la Pastoral Obrera

RENE VIO VALDIVIESO, SS.CC.
Vicario Episcopal Zona Rural – Costa

JUAN DE CASTRO REYES
Vicario Episcopal Zona Oriente

JAVIER MAC MAHON A., O.F.M.
Vicario Episcopal para Religiosas

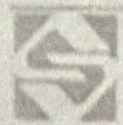

SEPARATA DE
SOLIDARIDAD: Publicación de la Vicaría de la Solidaridad del Arzobispado de Santiago – Chile
Director y Representante Legal: Vicario Episcopal Cristián Precht Bañados
Producción: Vicaría de la Solidaridad, Plaza de Armas 444, Casilla 30-D Santiago

Nº 23, NOVIEMBRE 78

Talleres Gráficos Corporación Ltda. - Fono 30645

Figure 1.6. *Separata Solidaridad* 23. "The force of life will break the chains." Frontal shot of Association of Family Members of the Detained-Disappeared members (all women) chained to the CEPAL November 1978. Credit: Luis Navarro Vega. Black and white. Fundación de Documentación y Archivo de la Vicaría de la Solidaridad.

This book series is presented as the "exact reproduction" of the compiled documentation and evidence brought by the Vicaría to the courts. In Precht's introductory note, I recognize what I call the photo-copy rationale of the Vicaría's counter-archive. The acts of reproducing, registering, certifying, compiling, and displaying both frame and enable this photo-copy rationale.[53] The photo-copy rationale—which I write purposefully with a hyphen to stress both elements—conveys the persistent and urgent practice of reproducing, rephotographing, and photocopying portraits and various types of documents, not only with the aim of generating and providing counternarratives, but also with the objective to understand how the repressive and intelligence apparatuses of the military operated. (Where were the clandestine torture centers? When and under what circumstances did detentions occur? Etc.). While Precht insists that the antecedents given are "not new," this compilation of portraits and documents was nothing short of an event. The event, here, is the devising of the systematic visual and textual corpus *¿Dónde están?* whose impetus was the likewise systematic disappearance of people. Notwithstanding the complete indifference of the authorities, Vicaría workers take on the task of documenting, recording, compiling, organizing, and displaying this corpus of disappearance *qua* disappearance (and not as "alleged" disappearance).

In *Archive Fever*, Jacques Derrida suggests that "the technical structure of the *archiving* archive also determines the structure of the *archivable* content even in its very coming into existence and in its relationship to the future. The archivization produces as much as it records the event."[54] What Derrida calls archivization produces the understanding of the crime of forced disappearance as a continued event and frames it as one that should not exist. This systematic corpus of disappearances is offered in the form of a pending question: *¿Dónde están?* (Where are they?). This question would continue to resonate, for, as Ann Laura Stoler observes regarding counter archival practices, "no matter how many documents are amassed as 'proof,' they might not be 'enough' for one [. . .] to be released from unspecified detention."[55] Precht insists indeed on the unresolved quality of their legal endeavors, despite the data amassed and presented: attempts to clarify the fate of the disappeared detainees "have not yielded until now any results;" "A clarifying response [. . .] has not yet arrived;" "Despite the quality of the documentation presented and the efforts deployed, we have not yet obtained any kind of response."[56]

Each personal file included detailed information of the disappeared person, testimonies of relatives and/or neighbors (information such as the date the person was last seen, what he/she was wearing, etc.) and, in most cases, a portrait photo. The elaborate display of these portraits, some of which had already acquired new appearances due to the careful work (cuts, enlargements, enhancements, etc.) of Vicaría photographers, urges us to consider this publication without disregarding its visual composition (see fig. 1.7). The technical structure of the archive (compilation, reproduction, serialization of photographic portraits, lists of names, and personal files) structures this pending corpus (*corpus pendiente*) comprised of absent bodies (*cuerpos ausentes*), deploying all of the available signs at the moment: photographic portraits (not always obtainable), personal information, witness accounts of the moment of the abduction or criminal detention, and legal and administrative actions undertaken in each case.

The tangible temporality denoted in the expression "available signs at the moment" must be emphasized here: this pending corpus of the disappearance, this compilation of documents, facts, and photographs, was composed *before* the findings of human remains at the Lonquén mine site in November 1978 (the macabre finding occurred just weeks after the publication of the first volume of *¿Dónde están?*). The forensic investigation would determine that the human remains found buried in the furnaces belonged to fifteen men who had been detained under different circumstances on October 7, 1973. Their names appeared on the list of detainees who remained disappeared as well as on the list of names published in the first volume of the *¿Dónde están?* series. Until the Lonquén findings, no institutional, governmental, or judicial framework had recognized the legal figure of the detained-disappeared. I quote again from Precht's Introduction to the first volume: "Government authorities, despite all the evidence, still talk about *presumed* missing persons;" "their arguments remain unclear because [. . .] they do not refer to people who are actually among the detained-disappeared."[57] Moreover, Reverend Father Gustavo Ferraris maintains in the fifth volume: "They even got to claim that because of the possible game of double identities, the disappeared were fictional characters."[58]

The arrangement of the portraits is also striking. Like the texts that state similar variations of the same information, the same data, over and over again, the covers and interior pages convey seriality, repetition, systematicity. These iconic portraits whisper, talk of something that was happening and that continued to happen over and over and over again. This visual montage is both simple and effective. Behind the austere display lies the accumulation of information compiled, the amassed documents (file cards, photos) that refer to other documents (in *la sábana*, for example), which reminds me of what Ariella Azoulay suggests

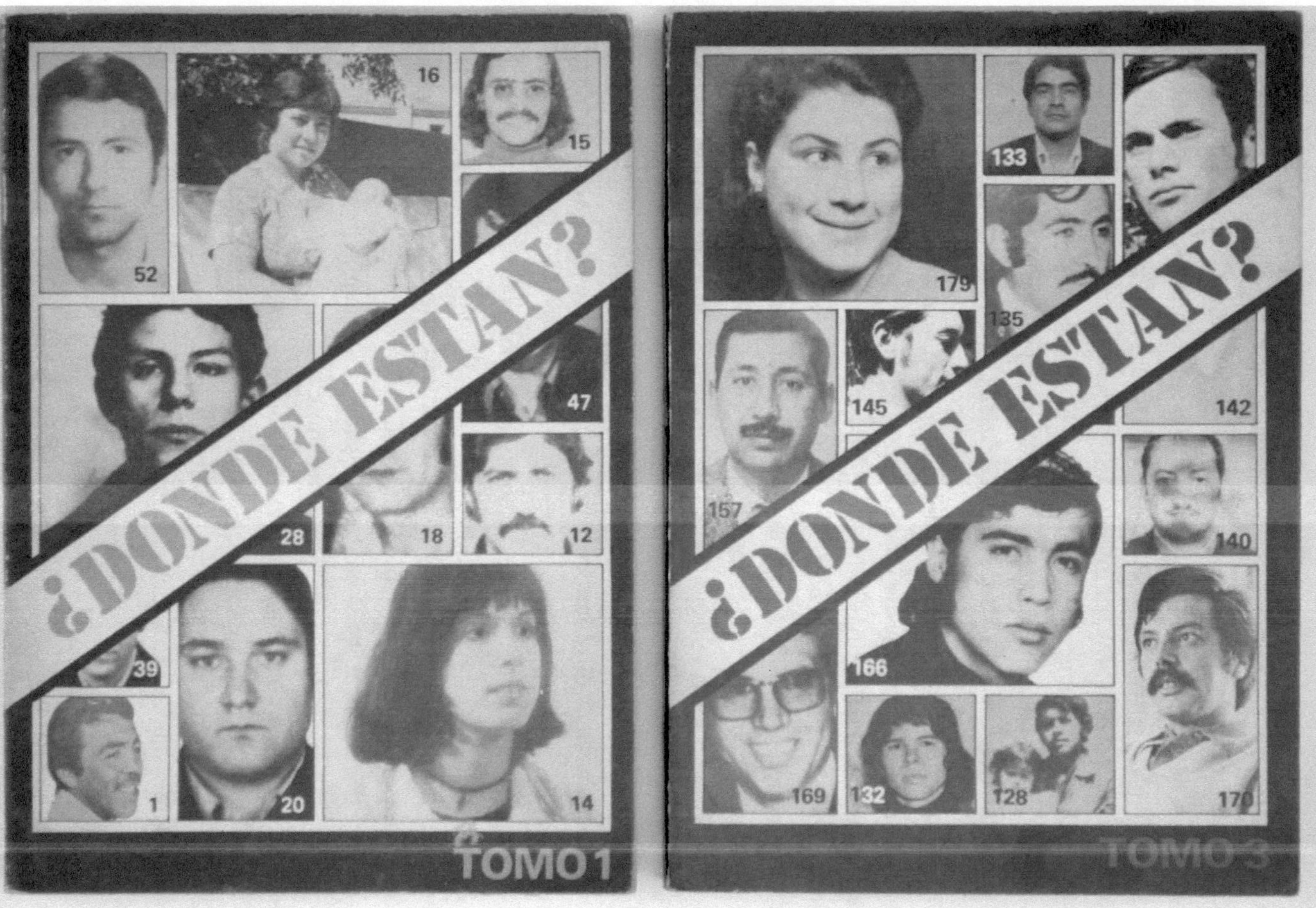

Figure 1.7. Volume 1 and 3 of *¿Dónde están?* (7 volumes). November 1978. Color. Fundación de Documentación y Archivo de la Vicaría de la Solidaridad.

regarding Derrida's notion of archive fever. As the critic cogently asserts, more should be said of this notion:

> Archive fever is not reducible to the claim to study documents. Archive fever is also the claim to revolutionize the archive; the claim to a different understanding of the documents it holds, of its supposed purpose, of the right to see them and to act accordingly; the claim to the forms and ways of categorizing, presenting, and using these documents. Archive fever challenges the norm that stands at the basis of how sovereign power defines archival documents: documents the writing of which the powers that be dictate, and later also order their hiding.[59]

¿Dónde están? does precisely this: it offers a different understanding of the documents the archive holds, the documents that were prepared, compiled, and presented to the legal authorities in hundreds of habeas corpus cases, all of which were disregarded. *¿Dónde están?* offers another way of categorizing (the individuals are presented as detained-disappeared, a category the legal authorities disavow) and invites its readers to scrutinize the documentation it presents, also differently. The legal illegibility of the detained-disappeared is inscribed—in order to be contested—in the *¿Dónde están?* book series. Official accounts, until that date, claimed that they didn't exist, that they were never born, that they were presumably dead, and even that they were fictional characters, among other false allegations.

This legal illegibility appears in the books as a problem that affects the visual and the textual references, and their correlation. On the one hand, this problem is made manifest in the avowed absence of clues or traces pertaining to the whereabouts of the disappeared. Most of the hundreds of personal files end in a similar way: "since that moment it has not been possible to locate him in any detention site;" "despite the efforts to find his whereabouts, everything has been useless;" "despite the innumerable efforts made, to date nothing has been known of him;" "it was not possible to locate the whereabouts of the detainee and to this date his fate remains ignored;" "currently, he remains missing;" "since then, nothing more has been known about him." Such observations are repeated over and over in the hundreds of personal files compiled in almost two thousand pages. On the other hand, the portraits published in *¿Dónde están?* appear without names and are not necessarily ordered numerically (see fig. 1.8); in some instances, a blank square framed in black suggests the absence of a portrait, but of whom?

The visual arrangement, the repetition and juxtaposition of rephotographed

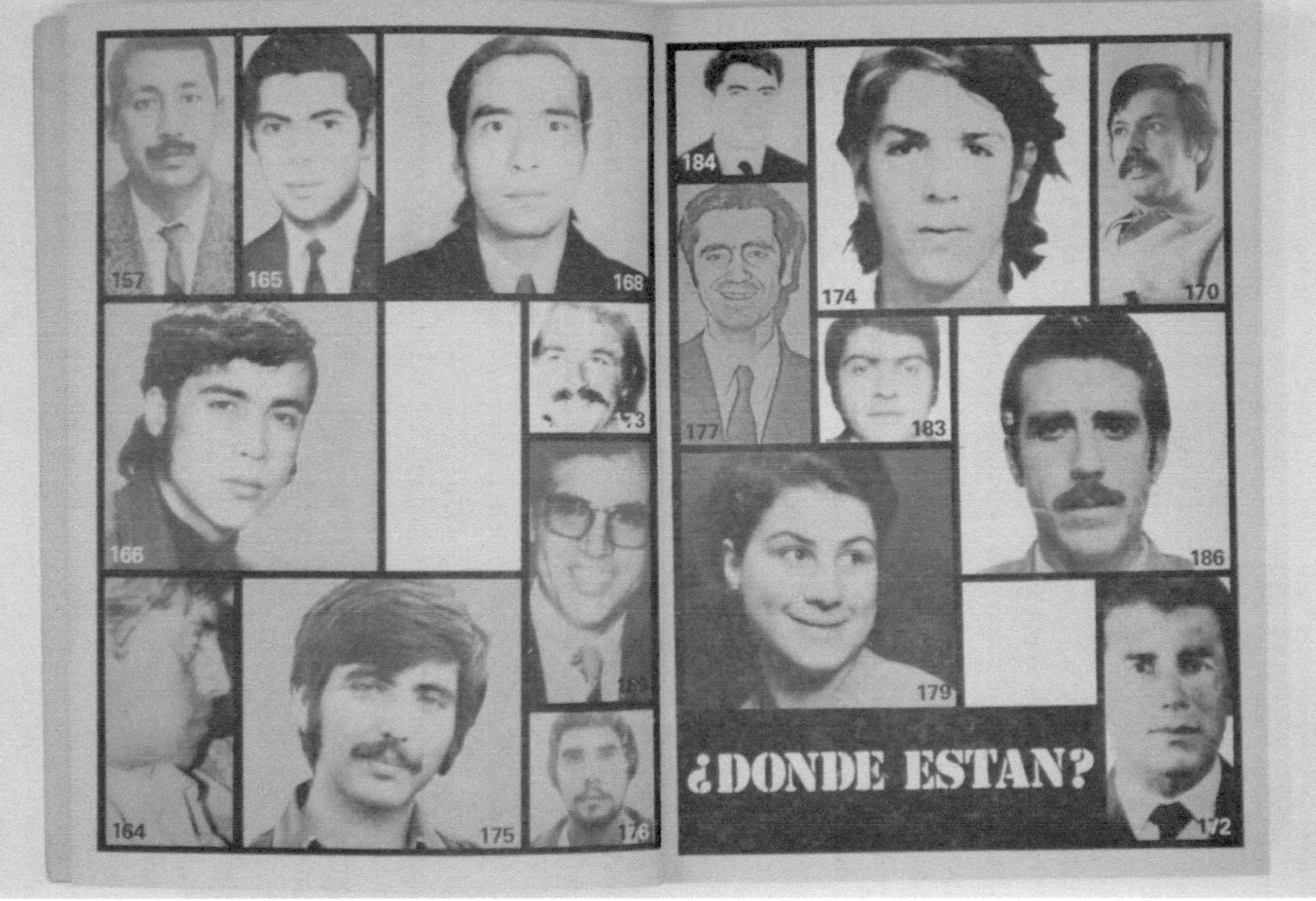

Figure 1.8. *¿Dónde están?* Spread (November 1978). Black and white. Fundación de Documentación y Archivo de la Vicaría de la Solidaridad.

photos (some of them extremely damaged, most of them numbered) and blank framed squares, provides a visualization of the corpus of disappearance, a *corpus* that searches bodies (*cuerpos*), a pending corpus that demands references. The small rephotographed portraits supplement the textual information with visual information. They supplement, that is to say, rather than complement. Because of their supplementary condition, these small portraits inevitably enter into a substitutive chain. This happens, if I may, at a meta level, where the reference is displaced again and again due to the separated arrangement of texts and images. While the decision to publish the portraits separately may have been dictated largely by economic factors (it is less expensive to print pages with text only than pages with text and images combined), the separation of names and personal files from portraits inevitably instigates the question about "the referent." The portraits (reproductions of photos in manifest poor condition, many of them altered to better resemble an ID photo or a portrait) appear juxtaposed on the covers of each volume and also on consecutive pages following lists of names, each of which is assigned a number corresponding to the detainee's file.

¿Dónde están? is a revealing instance of the portraits' displacements. Material objects, the portraits were displaced in different stages—from the family album to the streets, from the streets to the photographic archive, and from the archive back again to the streets, via signs, leaflets, magazines, and books. ID photos experienced further displacements in relation to their use value (from disciplinary to commemorative). The relatives of the victims reappropriated a visual document whose first and primary objective is to serve as proof of identification, bestowing ordinary ID photo portraits with an aura and a humanity lacking in their original form. There are also displacements of a different order involving subjects (both the subjects photographed and spectators), times (both past and present), spaces (both the space photographed as well as the space of publication or exhibition, both physical and virtual spaces), and materials (film, negatives, papers, etc.). Meanwhile, the photographed subjects also experienced material displacements (from flesh and bones to the negative, and from the negative to paper), as well as successive temporal and spatial displacements reactivated in each of the instances in which the portraits are watched, rephotographed, or photocopied. The different stages that comprise the photo-copy rationale—the many displacements the subjects photographed have endured both before and after the first photographic take, and the transformations of the "original" photos from which some of the portraits are made—seem to move the portraits, and the subjects, away from us. However, the evocative force of these portraits—

which is apparent both in the haunting power of the "fleeting expression of their human faces," as Benjamin might put it, and in the feeble physical marks that despite the amends, the rephotographing and the retouching, are still visible in these portraits—brings them closer, again.

Touching Photocopies

The portraits, which were displaced from family albums and ID cards into the streets, and from there into the archives, magazines, and a book series, were also integrated into artistic practices.[60] In this penultimate section, I continue developing the notion of the photo-copy rationale to illuminate further the performative dimension of the documentary practices of photography under the dictatorship. I consider, in particular, the collaborative practice of two artists, Luz Donoso and Hernán Parada, who endeavored to put the portraits of the *desaparecidos* back into circulation. The artists resorted to photocopying and rephotographing to disseminate, display, and activate the photographic archive of the detained-disappeared. A core motivation of their collaborative work was to influence and engage passersby on the streets. Needless to say, there are hundreds of photocopies for which no register remains, which cannot be seen, which have been lost (recording, visuality, and loss—all these notions are closely related to the photo-copy rationale). I am thinking here of those ephemeral objects that were never consigned to archives, those photocopies that were not made to remain, but to destabilize—albeit briefly—a besieged urban landscape. All that remains of the hundreds of posters pasted on walls and photocopied leaflets left on windshields and thrown into the air during rallies and marches is their audiovisual or photographic documentation.[61]

As stated earlier, Donoso and Parada were in charge of rephotographing, organizing, and classifying the portraits received from family members at the Agrupación. Donoso put herself to the task of making enlarged photocopies of the portraits. She began confectioning different tapes by attaching all the enlarged copies together. She created different variations of the tape, which she titled "Huincha sin fin. Hasta que nos digan dónde están" (Endless tape. Until we are told where they are). The title of the piece was not figurative. It aimed to convey the incommensurability of the project, its indefectible in-progress character: every day another relative came with news of a disappeared family member, every day another old ID picture or family album photo needed to be rephotographed, photocopied, enlarged. So the "Endless tape" kept growing and

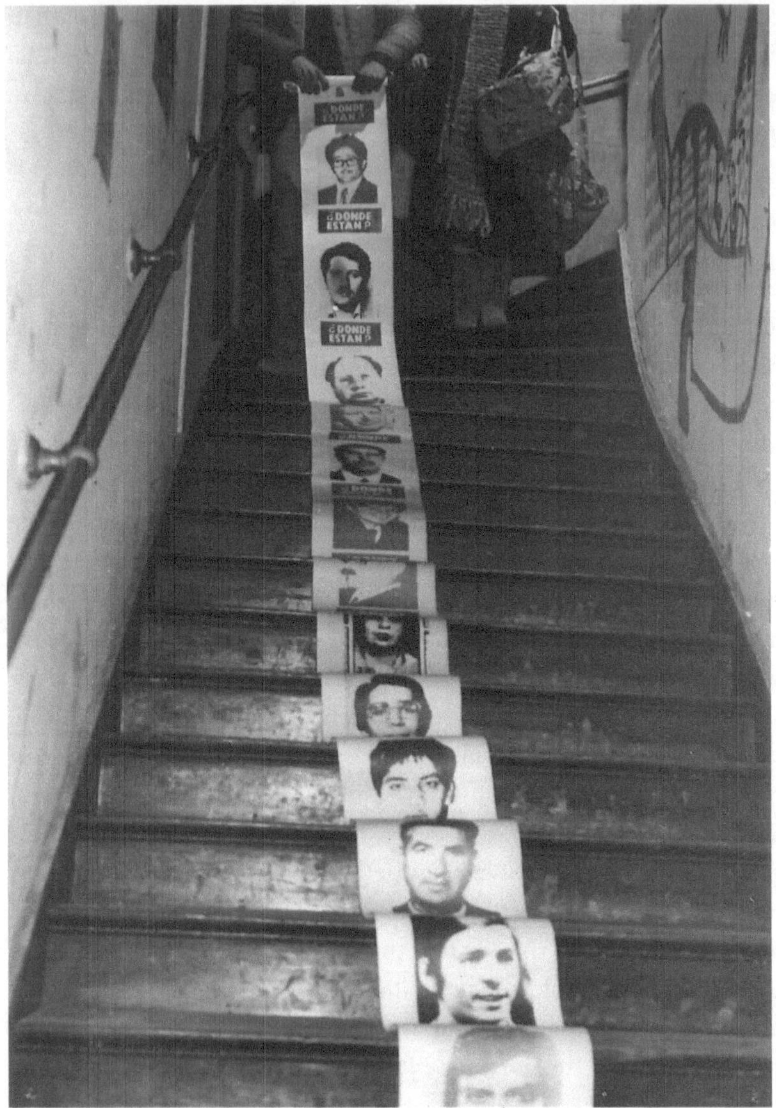

Figure 1.9. Photographic documentation of "Huincha sin fin." Black and white. Credit: Luz Donoso. Luz Donoso's archive (courtesy of Jenny Holmgren).

growing. The tapes had "papers, photos attached, pamphlets of marches, photocopies of newspapers depicting a piece that is multiplied, handwritten script."[62] As Paulina Varas explains, "Endless tape" was exhibited in art spaces and museums in Chile and abroad, but also, "and perhaps more insistently, in places of denunciation, in exhibits or spaces where family members of the detained-disappeared and human rights organizations gathered to protest, and on the street itself, emerging whenever it was possible to unravel it. Never in the same way, it appeared vitalized by the event that made it unfold."[63]

What remains of the "endless tape," for all of us to see, is a series of photographs. One of them depicts the tape extending the length of a staircase (see fig. 1.9). The photograph itself provides an example of the portraits' displacements and performativity. The photo expresses the impossibility of viewing the entire photographic archive simultaneously. Due to the incessant proliferation of portraits, the photograph of the action signals the nonclosure of the sequence and insists, as does the tape itself, on the incommensurability of state terrorism: *Hasta que nos digan dónde están*. The photographer cropped out of the frame the heads of the figures grabbing the "endless tape," showing only their bodies. As in the case of Navarro's portrait, this forces us to focus our attention on the rephotographed faces of those who seem to ask about their own bodies: "Where are they?" The only eyes that return our gaze, even if from afar, are those of the people whose ID photos have been photocopied: rephotographed, enlarged, printed, and photographed again.

In addition to creating several versions of "endless tape," Donoso collaborated with other artists at the TAV—Hernán Parada, Patricia Saavedra, and Elías Adasme, among others—in various art actions in which portraits played a central role. Such is the case of "Acciones de Apoyo: intervención de un sistema comercial" (Supporting Actions: intervention of a commercial system) (1979) and "Acciones de Apoyo: intervención fotográfica de un muro" (Supporting Actions: photographic intervention of a wall) (1982). In a brief statement featured in *Ruptura* (CADA's publication) in 1982, the artists point out that media "are the necessary nexus to materialize an action. Although they are indispensable in order to make-register-show and/or disseminate some action or theoretical material, they are not in themselves an artwork (although their influence exists), but rather elements/tools at the artwork's service."[64] The statement emphasizes the role of media—photography and video—as disseminating tools. Photographs are disseminated and help to disseminate further at the same time: some of the portraits used for these actions, and which through these actions were disseminated even further, were produced by copying and rephotographing portraits reproduced—that is, previously disseminated—in the *¿Dónde están?* series.

In "Supporting Actions: intervention of a commercial system," the portrait of a disappeared woman, whose name is Lila Valdenegro, interrupted for a few minutes the programmed sequence of images exhibited on the television screens

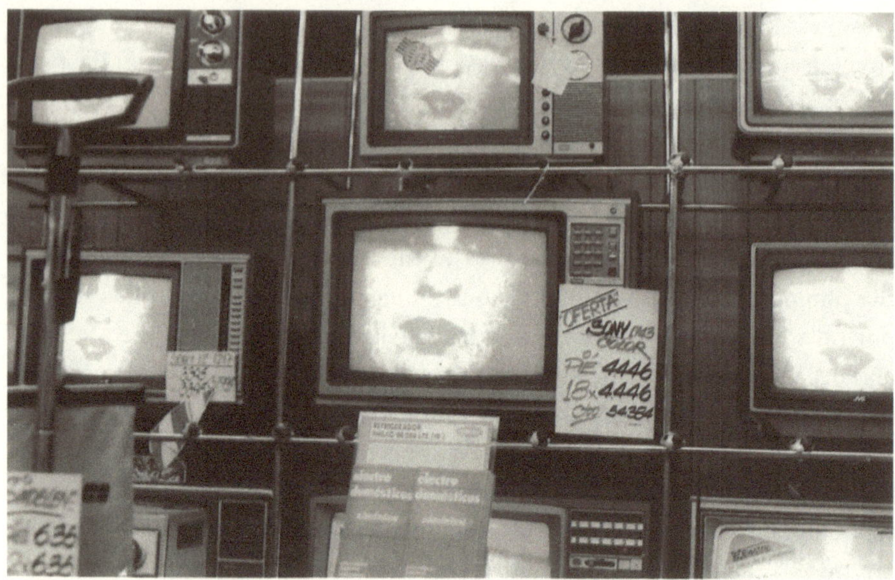

Figure 1.10. Photographic documentation of "Acciones de Apoyo: Intervención de un sistema comercial." 1979. Black and white. Credit: Luz Donoso. Luz Donoso's archive (courtesy of Jenny Holmgren).

in a store display in Paseo Ahumada, in downtown Santiago (see fig. 1.10).[65] The image of this face irrupted into an environment besieged by a system that tried to make precisely this type of image invisible.[66] In this action, television and photography are put "at the service of the artwork" as a means of dissemination. Photography also served as a means to document the action. As Parada recalls, "Talking to Patricia Saavedra, the idea came up to put photos of the detained-disappeared on televisions inside electronic stores. Patricia entered and negotiated with the clerks [. . .] and then we photographed the images appearing in the display windows. We had to act fast."[67] The photographic and sonorous documentation of these interventions was a key aspect of the work; many actions were performed for the camera. The photographic documentation of these actions intensifies the dissemination and proliferation of the portraits even further.

Photography has been described as a second skin, an apt metaphor when considering the photographic portrait. But what happens in this case? Where is that portrait? How did it get there? The supposed materiality of the photographic trace diffuses and multiplies in the very image that tries to bring to us, spectators, the face of a disappeared woman. If at the moment of the action some passerby had the opportunity to view the portrait—which, it goes without saying, is ultra-mediated as it is an image that has been rephotographed or photocopied, taped on video, projected on a TV screen, and exhibited in a display window—it comes to us mediated one more time through yet another lens, that of the camera capturing the action. It is worthwhile recalling here the idea of the portrait as the staging of a becoming, as a multiplying force rather than as a single reflection. Because, what is, after all, the referent of this photograph? Is it the woman's face on the screen, the TV sets, or that polishing machine that appears out of focus on the left side of the display window? Is the display window itself the referent? How many layers or "skins" mediate the spectator's view of the woman's face? The photo of the action displays a reflection—perhaps involuntarily—on the immaterial condition of the photographic trace. Further, it illustrates the "putting into crisis of a temporal order in which first there is an object and then later its representation."[68]

For the action "Supporting Actions: photographic intervention of a wall" (1982), the artists pasted the photocopied portrait of another disappeared person on a wall in downtown Santiago (see fig. 1.11). By directing our attention to the

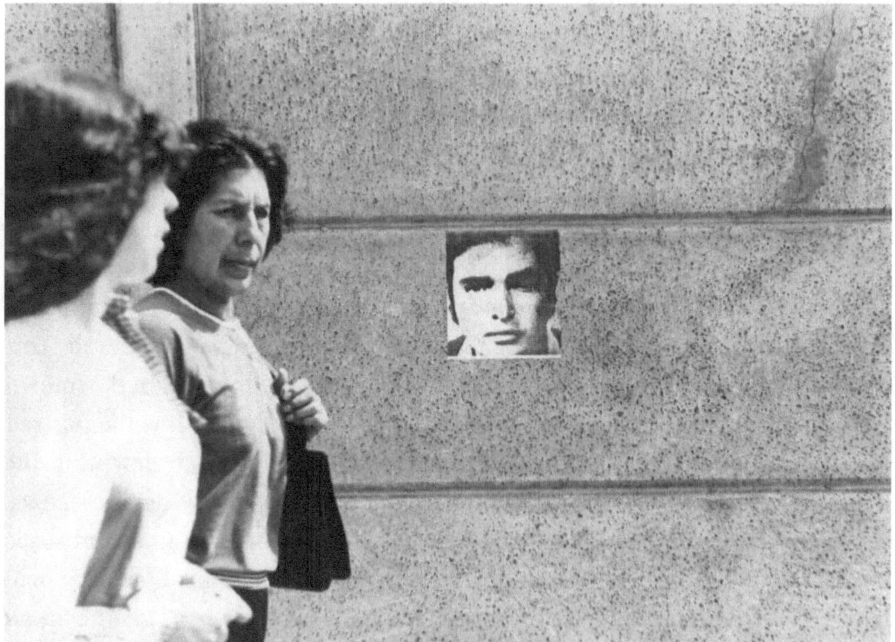

Figure 1.11. Photographic documentation of "Acciones de Apoyo: Intervención fotográfica de un muro." 1979. Black and white. Credit: Luz Donoso. Luz Donoso's archive (courtesy of Jenny Holmgren).

photographs that documented the action, it is possible to appreciate the many ways in which the portrait was displaced, activating memory and its political potentials. In its displacement, the photocopied portrait depicted in the photograph stimulated collective memory by interpellating the passerby directly, enabling the expansion of her consciousness, as Varas also argues.[69] We must also emphasize that in "Photographic intervention of a wall" the displacement operated not only at the spatial level—the portrait of the *desaparecido* appears where there should not be any image, that is, on the street wall—but also at a symbolic-referential level.

The permanence of the photocopied portrait was undetermined. Given the sociopolitical context, this photocopied portrait glued to a wall acquired a particular symbolic and political depth. While the passersby who were confronted by the photocopy on the wall (we can see some of them in the photographs) could not identify the person depicted in the portrait, the vast majority of them most likely (rightly) anticipated it belonged to one of the thousands who disappeared at the hands of the dictatorship. This sort of fundamental anticipation (which is also at play in the action discussed earlier) illustrates the imaginary and symbolic burden borne by these portraits. The portrait interpellated the passerby, who turned toward the image glued to the wall because of what it represented: the fact of abduction and disappearance. While the subject's identity remained unknown to the viewer, the acknowledgment of the subject's legal status—disappeared—enabled a transitory frame of reference.

In some photographs, the movement of out-of-focus passersby is juxtaposed with the complete steadiness of the small portrait that seems to almost disappear in the vastness of the wall. In this way the photographs express the coexistence of two temporalities: the temporality of everyday life that does not stop, which continues its course, and the suspended temporality of the portrait, manifestly expressed in the suspension of the photocopy in the middle of the wall. This photocopy, which (timidly) interrupts the continuity of the wall in downtown Santiago, is an illustrative instance of displacement. Although it is the portrait of a specific disappeared person, I cannot help but think, as I view it, of the hundreds of faces of disappeared people who appeared every day in leaflets, signs, and printed media. But this small portrait suspended in time and space moves me. The name of the man in the photocopied portrait is Francisco Juan González Ortiz. This individual was detained on September 9, 1976. I found his name, portrait, and personal file while examining volume two of *¿Dónde están?* in which he appears listed as detained-disappeared number 120. Despite this specificity, the portrait will not stop supplementing itself; it will not stop supplementing the act of disappearance either.

The final corpus of photographs I examine are photographic records of a sequence of actions within Hernán Parada's project "Obrabierta A" (Open Work A) (1974–present). These actions reactivate the iconic power of the photographic portrait, by embodying it. Alejandro Parada, Hernán Parada's brother, was detained and disappeared on July 31, 1974. In 1984, to commemorate the tenth anniversary of his brother's disappearance, Hernán devised a photocopied mask, which he obtained by *photocopying* a portrait of his brother. The production of the mask entailed various stages. About the overall project, Luz Donoso would say: "The pain gave Hernán Parada the lucidity to make a precious "Obrabierta A" that keeps incorporating what happens with the detained-disappeared, infinite variations that add up to a work that does not end, that remains in time, unfinished until he decides to end it, perhaps when he finds his brother."[70] The passage illustrates the affinities of Donoso's and Parada's practices: there is no doubt that "Obrabierta A" shared the impetus that also animated Donoso's "Endless tape."

Between July and December 1984, Parada performed at various emblematic public spaces with the mask on: the building of the Courts Justice, the Train Central Station, the Plaza de Armas, the School of Veterinary Medicine of the University of Chile. Luz Donoso and Víctor Hugo Codocedo accompanied Parada to document these ephemeral public appearances with audio recorders and cameras. Other locations included the TAV (November 1984), Parada's own house (December 1984), the Patio 29 of the General Cemetery (May 1985) (see fig. 1.12), the workshop of photographer Adriana Silva (July 1985), the Estación Mapocho Cultural Center (July 1985), and the residence of video artist Gloria Camiruaga (July 1986).[71] At Silva's workshop, Parada posed for the photos that I introduced at the beginning of the chapter, where Parada, always wearing Alejandro's mask, gestures in front of the camera that he can't hear, speak, or see (see fig 1.1). Nobody wants to talk or hear about the disappeared, no one sees what is going on, the masked man seems to be saying.[72] The photo also allows for a different reading: Alejandro, the disappeared, is the one who can't hear, speak, or see because he is in a sort of in-between, in an uncertain place, neither dead nor alive.

This is precisely what "Alejandro" shared in his different appearances. For instance, inside the main hall of the Courts of Justice building, he recited the following:

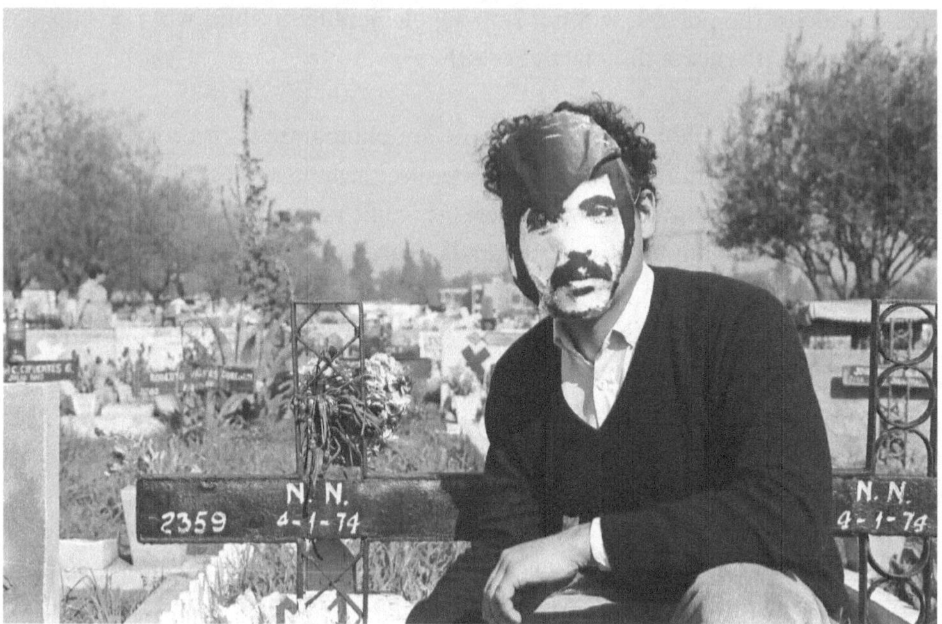

Figure 1.12. Photographic documentation of "Obrabierta A" (1974–present). Patio 29, General Cemetery. May 1985. Credit: Luz Donoso. Black and white. Hernán Parada's personal archive.

> Gentlemen of the Court, I am Alejandro Parada. I am a veterinary student. Today is the tenth anniversary of my detention and disappearance. I come here to ask that you not forget about us. We who have been detained and disappeared do not deserve to live in this situation. We are denied life, and we are denied death. We have the right to one thing: we want to know if we are dead or if we are alive. It is painful to live in uncertainty. Do not forget us.[73]

According to Parada, the intention behind going to the Courts of Justice with the mask on was that a disappeared person should ask others about people like himself. This shifted the locus of enunciation from a collective "¿Dónde están?" (Where are they?) to the first person "¿Dónde estoy?" (Where am I?). This shift in the locus of enunciation is significant because it calls attention to what Diana Taylor calls "percepticide" at a personal, subjective level. The displacement instigated both collective and individual awareness: if I do not know where I am—because I am disappeared—then, where are you, and where are we? "Dónde estás?" "¿Dónde estamos?" In other words, what country am I (are you/are we)

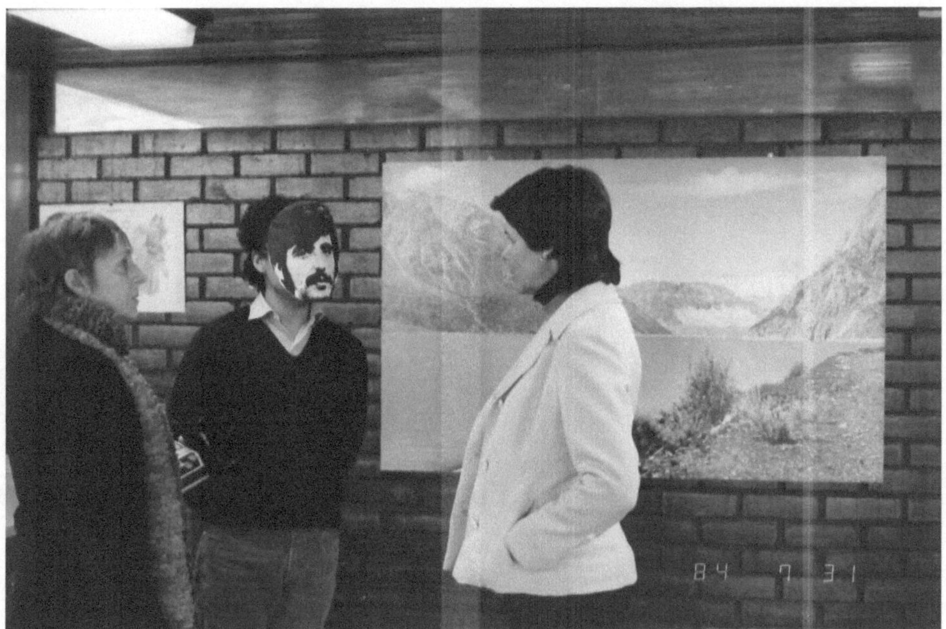

Figure 1.13. Photographic documentation of "Obrabierta A" (1974–present). Veterinary School, Universidad de Chile. July 1984. Credit: Victor Hugo Codocedo. Black and white. Hernán Parada's personal archive.

in that would inflict terrors such as that of disappearing its citizens and denying closure to loved ones of the deceased? Something similar occurred at the veterinary school where Alejandro Parada was a student until 1974 (he was, like many others, dismissed from school by the military). There, "Alejandro" talked and tried to engage staff and students (see fig. 1.13). He asked them for help to resolve "the uncertainty" in which he found himself.

Through these different actions, the identification between photographic portrait and subject—between Alejandro's mask and Alejandro as a person—is performed and embodied; the loving/photographic act entails, here, becoming other.[74] Indeed, "Obrabierta A" illuminates the idea of the photograph or, in this case, the photocopy—it does not matter—as a force of transformation at its purest: with the mask on, Hernán *becomes* Alejandro. Because not only the disappeared person mutates, but also the relative who searches for him. Hernán is transformed by giving body and voice to Alejandro, whose body has disappeared and whose voice has been silenced. The photographs that document

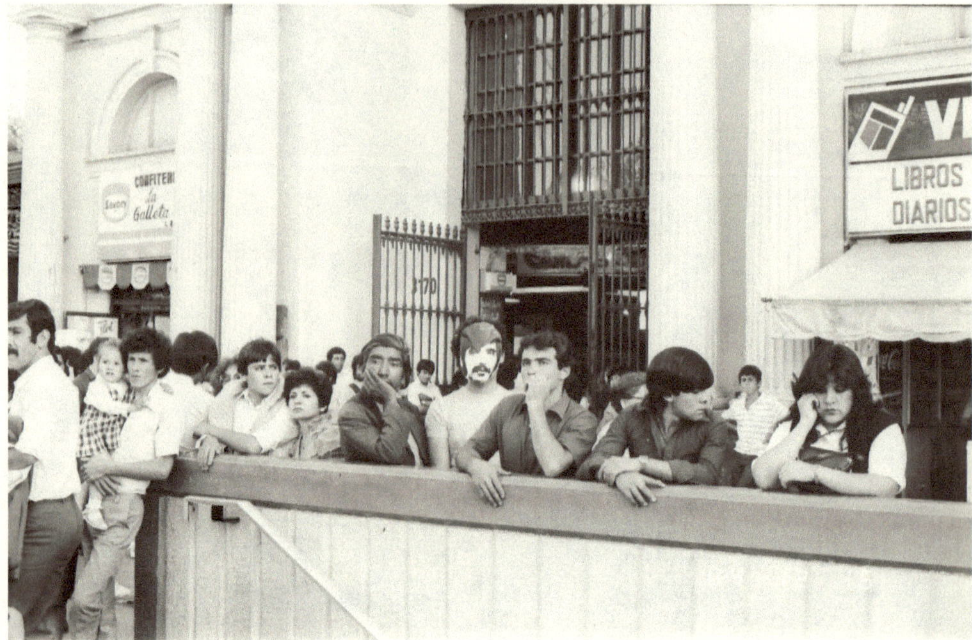

Figure 1.14. Photographic documentation of "Obrabierta A" (1974–present). Central Station. December 1984. Credit: Luz Donoso. Black and white. Hernán Parada's personal archive.

Hernán Parada's actions illustrate the irruption (in the most literal sense of the word) of photocopied portraits in the middle of urban everyday life.

Although this irruption can be appreciated in each photograph, it acquires a different depth in the photograph taken at the Central Train Station, where Parada, wearing Alejandro's mask, almost blends in with the other faces (see fig. 1.14). Notably, the people surrounding Parada seem not to notice the presence of this strange subject. Also, the mask is the only face "looking" at the camera. Indeed, I consider the photographic documentation of these different public appearances as portraits. Insubordinate portraits that inscribe the unexpected appearance of a disappeared person in the public space, these photographs also belong to the expanding photographic archive of the detained-disappeared. Parada, wearing Alejandro's mask, *poses* for the photographer (Luz Donoso).

These photographic registers of the action stage the question about identity differently than do the actions themselves. They make us think of that impossibility of recognizing oneself in the portrait, an idea contended by Benjamin and Barthes alike. The subject appears hidden; the photograph does not show him—it shows us only his mask. "[The] photograph is the advent of myself as other: a cunning dissociation of consciousness."[75] In the encounter between photographic portrait and mask, the photographs display the noncoincidence between a subject and their portrait. By entering the photographic space, the subject loses her identity.[76] This loss appears doubly displayed in the photographic images of Parada's action—doubly, because the portrayed subject wears a mask. At the same time, the photographic portrait—and this may appear paradoxical—seems to resist this dissolution: the mask returns our gaze.

These portraits of photocopied faces wandering about the city, in their crossing of alterity and the auratic, in their effacing of the photographic trace, in their subtle rendering of the ineffability of loss and of becoming other, avow that even when the photocopy of a portrait does not carry with it the trace of the subject, it still can acquire life by, paradoxically, becoming an iconic mask. In a brief but provocative essay entitled "El xenotafio de luz" (The light xenotaph), critic and philosopher Willy Thayer makes the following case regarding the reproduction of an image from a previous photograph:

> The artistic process that usually goes from the living light to the negative and from the negative to the photograph inverts itself. In this irregular case, it is the light already embalmed in a photograph that travels toward the negative, and from the latter toward its multiple reproduction. The negative derived from a photograph does not host, then, the light of a living face; it hosts, rather, the somber nature of an inert paper.[77]

Is it odd to include in (and conclude) a chapter about the composition of the photographic archive of the detained-disappeared, photographs that displace even further the rephotographed and photocopied portraits, photographs of photocopied masks, inert paper? Is it odd to feel moved by a photocopied mask? I ask these questions because, before Thayer's arguments, Alejandro's photocopied mask could be seen as a superfluous prop that makes an icon of a real, "flesh-and-blood" disappeared person. The photocopied mask and the photograph of the photocopied mask seem to take the "real subject"—Alejandro Parada—even further away from us; they seem to occlude his luminous trace.

The photocopied mask surely intensifies the iconic aspect of the photographic portrait; I say intensify because, as I have already emphasized, photographic portraits are *always* iconic. The link between referent and portrait is very strong in contexts of forced disappearance—these images move us, touch us. But this touch expands beyond the physical: memory and imagination are also intimately related to these portraits. "Imagination," as Georges Didi-Huberman observes, "is not a withdrawal to the mirages of a single reflection, as is too often thought. It is often a composition and a montage of various forms placed in correspondence with one another. This is why, far from being an artist's privilege or a purely subjectivist recognition, it is an integral part of knowledge in its most fertile, albeit most daring, movement."[78] Imagination is in fact a critical tool to become involved with these rephotographed and photocopied portraits. As Marianne Hirsch stresses, photographs enable us "in the present, not only to see and to touch that past, but also to try to reanimate it."[79] Hernán Parada pushes the evocative force of the portrait to the limit. With the mask on, he becomes his brother. The act enlivens the photocopied mask, a piece of inert paper: it transforms it into photocopied skin. Thus, despite Déotte's emphasis on the ethical dimension of the photographic trace (commented on earlier) and Thayer's suggestive claim regarding the inert quality of the photocopy, Alejandro's photocopied mask has much to teach us about the performativity and the persistence of the photographic portraits of the detained-disappeared. Although many of the portraits that continue to circulate originated in what Thayer refers to as "the somber nature of an inert paper"—in other words, despite the fact that these documents do not refer us directly toward a flesh-and-blood subject—the photocopied and rephotographed portraits kept (and continue to hold) their value as objects of living memory. The portraits of the detained-disappeared persisted by means of composition, duplication, and dislocation: they were enhanced, copied, classified, and consigned to the photographic archive, but they did not remain there, lightless and motionless. On the contrary, they continued circulating; they kept being disseminated and multiplied.

Alejandro's photocopied mask indeed oriented my exploration of the composition and dissemination of the photographic archive of the detained-disappeared from the start. This iconic photocopied mask and the history of its composition—which in a way condenses the histories of the successive reproductions, alterations, and displacements endured by so many portraits—inspired the critical reflection I have developed here. How could it be otherwise, if Alejandro's photocopied mask is intimately related to the contact-sheet I mentioned at the beginning of the chapter? While completing the research for this chapter, I e-mailed Parada. I expressed my interest in his resort to photocopying and asked him where he had obtained the source photo. I cannot but quote his reply in full:

> From September 1973 to March 1974, Alejandro Parada González hid in his sister-in-law's house, located in the Central Station neighborhood of Villa Francia, Santiago. In that house, the husband of his sister-in-law, who was a family photographer, took several photos of the couple, Alejandro and Angélica. Angélica submitted one of these photos to the Vicaría archive so it could be published in a number of little books about the disappeared, *¿Dónde están?*, which began to emerge in the late 1970s with the story of each *desaparecido*. Several books were published by the Vicaría. Eventually an edition came out with the information about my brother, Alejandro. I decided to take his photo [from the book]. Because the image was diagrammed in black and white dots, I was able to expand it better. First, I re-photographed the image and began to expand it, to play with it . . . This first enlargement of 22 by 27 inches was mounted on a piece of plywood. From that piece I obtained an image which I used in important places around the city in different actions focusing on Alejandro's face . . . After this first incursion with the enlarged image of Alejandro, the idea emerged to Xerox the photograph in regular size, in real scale [1:1]. Since I already had this image, I was captivated by the possibility of taking this further. I decided thus, intimately, fraternally, to lend my body to Alejandro. I would have to feel and think as my brother would, wearing a mask of his face. While wearing this mask, I would be Alejandro, conceptually. I talked about this idea with my friend, Luz Donoso, and she was as delighted as I was to do something with this new and so significant use of a photograph. We thought about going out, *along with Alejandro*.[80]

The portraits, no matter how displaced and transformed, carry within them a referential force. This referential force puts photos, referents, and us—the beholders—in motion. The performative force of Alejandro's mask led me from a number of photos documenting an artistic action, to a photo I found in Elías Adasme's personal archive (fig. 1.15). The photo depicts Adasme, Donoso, and Parada holding the plywood matrix of Alejandro's portrait that was used to make the first enlarged copies of Alejandro's portrait. This photo, in turn, led me to the high-contrast portrait reproduced in volume 3 of *¿Dónde están?* (see fig. 1.8) and, ultimately, to the photographic archive of the *Vicaría*.

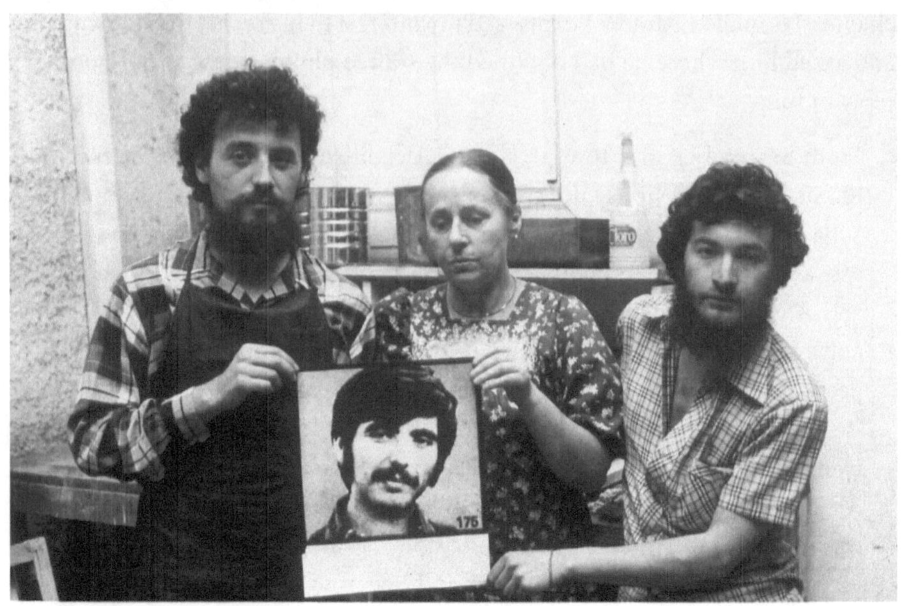

Figure 1.15. Hernán Parada, Luz Donoso, and Elías Adasme at Taller de Artes Visuales (TAV). Color. Elías Adasme's personal archive.

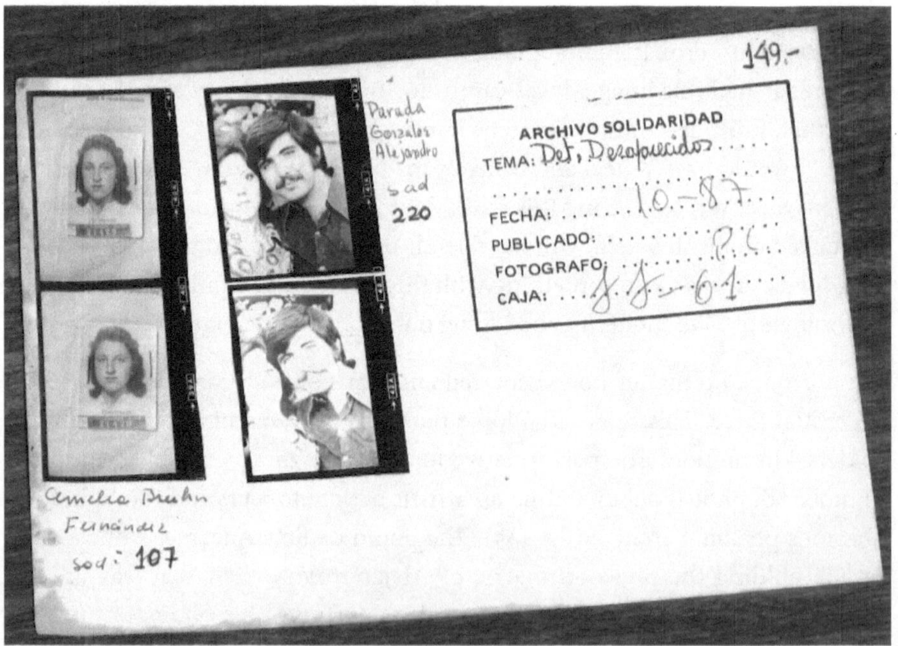

Figure 1.16. Alejandro Parada's photo identification card at the Fundación de Documentación y Archivo de la Vicaría de la Solidaridad. Color. Photograph: Ángeles Donoso Macaya.

I encountered Alejandro's card file at the Vicaría's photographic archive in 2015 (see fig. 1.16). The card had attached a contact sheet (the source photograph) consisting of two copies of a portrait of Alejandro and his girlfriend Angélica. Looking at this file card, I thought of this: a couple's portrait, taken as a memento, was rephotographed and cropped at the Vicaría offices to show only Alejandro's face in the style of a portrait, so that the disappeared person could be identified more easily; this new photo, which looked more like an ID photo, was consigned into archive and also published in *¿Dónde están?*; the published portrait (shown in reverse because it is a negative of the contact-sheet) was in turn rephotographed, enlarged, and further manipulated by a group of artists; the newly obtained image was transferred onto different canvases and later made into a photocopied mask; photographs of the artist wearing the photocopied mask were made—photographs that I observe today, in the present. I kept reminding myself of this sequence of transformations as I began to elucidate the composition of the expanding photographic archive of the detained-disappeared, as I explored the different materialities and formal qualities of these portraits—performative iconic traces with immense memorial force. By following the path of this displaced, performative trace, I was able to grasp the different materialities, spaces, individuals, affects, and senses (vision, tact, sound) implicated in the photographic practice.

Parada's embodiment of Alejandro's portrait invites us to think of all the portraits of the detained-disappeared as the staging of a becoming that, while appearing to direct our attention at a first moment toward that which *has been*, in fact opens the photographed subject to the potentiality of a time *to come* at the very same time it multiplies it. This loving/photographic act transforms not only the portrayed subject, but the beholder as well. In the context we are addressing, the logic of transformation and metamorphosis distinctive to the photographic becoming was even more significant in that it impacted the materiality of the source photographs without disturbing the affect. Spouses, lovers, siblings, children, and other relatives were cropped out of some photographs. New photocopied portraits emerged, which were in turn retouched, enlarged, enhanced. These new portraits were disseminated and continue traveling through both time and space via new photographs.

It would be absurd to negate the link between portrait and photographed subject. Nevertheless, in positing and considering this linkage, we ought to pay attention to the haunting and evocative powers of the photographed, rephotographed, photocopied, and enlarged portrait as well as to its materiality. I have attempted here to consider the truth-value of the photographic portrait in different forms and materialities, starting with the logic of its displacements and unraveling it from the theoretical constraints of the photographic trace. Thus, I shall conclude by underscoring the performativity of the photographic portraits of the disappeared. The different processes involved in the photo-copy rationale that instigate, structure, and keep nurturing the expanding photographic archive illuminate the referential performativity of the photograph. This performance of referentiality becomes apparent each time photos are displayed and presented as visual evidence. As I have argued, it was not "indexicality" that bestowed on these persistent portraits their evidentiary documentary value. The photocopies and the rephotographed photos do not bear the trace of the persons they represent—but they do resemble them, even conjure them. The performance of these iconic photographic portraits begins and concludes with their public display; this performance encompasses their composition, presentation, and recognition *qua* photographic portraits of the disappeared, their material and formal transformations, and their displacements inside and out of the photographic archive. This performance is also manifested then in the ability of photographs to move, migrate, and be transformed into something else (photocopies, for instance).

Visual and performance studies scholars have not failed to underscore the political aspect that underlies the public display of the portraits. Diana Taylor elucidates in *The Archive and the Repertoire* the ways in which the Madres used the portraits to interrupt and destabilize the hegemony of the official archive in Argentina: "Instead of the body in the archive associated with surveillance and police strategies, [the mothers] staged the archive in/on the body, affirming that embodied performance could make visible that which had been purged from the archive."[81] My analysis of the photographic archive composed by the Vicaría in Chile nuances the kind of exclusive assimilation Taylor formulates between archival and surveillance practices. The Vicaría's tasks of compiling, composing, and disseminating the photographic archive of the detained-disappeared was an effective and necessary counter-archival strategy to resist repression, challenge official versions regarding the disappeared, and formulate other narratives and explanations. By analyzing how private family snapshots, portraits, and ID photos became performative icons of the victims of the repression, I have recovered the simultaneously important politico-memorial and iconographic role of the Vicaría in the composition of the photographic archive of the portraits of the disappeared. Meanwhile, Andrea Noble studies the "mode of photographic display *qua* political tactic [. . .] across the subcontinent."[82] Her analysis underscores the public display that is performed for the camera as an effective strategy. My reading of the photographs that document the public demonstrations and artistic interventions in which the portraits were exhibited, used, and embodied builds on (and expands) Noble's key consideration of the performativity intrinsic to the photographic display. My analysis of these photographs enriches the prevailing understandings of the practice of photography as performance and as a form of protest. My reading attests to both the persistent presence of these portraits in the public space as well as to their intrinsic performativity. As we have seen, the iconicity, symbolism, and documentary value of these portraits triggered further displacements and disseminations in the public space. These displacements and disseminations, in turn, materialize the persistence of the portrait. Persistence is commonly defined as the sustained existence of something; it also refers to the firm continuance in a course of action in spite of difficulty or opposition. Regarding the portraits of the disappeared, their "continuance . . . in spite of" is precisely what is at stake. Even when political and economic circumstances conditioned and transformed the materiality of the source photos, the faces reproduced in photocopies and photographs of photographs—visual objects in which it would not be possible to trace any (photographic) trace—continued to be utilized to call attention to the paradoxical existence of the *desaparecidos* and to refute the official versions given by military officials who, in some cases, went so far as to deny the legal existence of some of the victims.

The display and embodiment of portraits in the public space promoted affective interactions, reactivated the work of individual and collective memory, and also enabled a transitory frame of reference at a time when all referential frames seemed to have been suspended. The displacements experienced by the persistent portraits studied here were of different orders—including spatial, temporal, material, and referential displacements. These displacements draw the contours of a dynamic visual archive comprising the portraits of disappeared individuals, documentation of artistic actions, and portraits of masked subjects—all images that activate our photographic memory and acquire new depths when read together. In this expanding archive comprised of rephotographed and photocopied photographs, and photocopied and rephotographed masks, there is no difference between living light and dead light. The only seemingly immutable phenomenon is the affective bond those distant faces establish with us in the present, luminous faces whose traits are repeated and accentuated on the iconic surfaces of the reproduced portraits. According to Benjamin, due to the long period of exposure required in early photography, "the subject (as it were) grew into the picture." In a way, the long, persistent display of the portraits of the disappeared in the public space makes (as it were) their iconic faces grow—it keeps them present, gives them light, and multiplies them.

2

FORENSIC MATTER

> The document is a truth-claim-making machine, an operational form, structured so that even if it's hollow it can and will go on functioning.
>
> —Thomas Keenan, "What Is a Document?"

In November 1978, an extravagant old man—he was wearing an explorer's hat, tall boots, and had a very long beard—arrived at the offices of the Vicaría.[1] He had something important and urgent to tell and wanted to do so under confession. He talked to priest Gonzalo Aguirre, who had been given a quiet office precisely to this end—to listen to the stories people came to share. The privacy of the office allowed individuals to "unload their fears."[2] The old man told Aguirre that he was a retired miner and working as a truck driver. He had been searching for some time for his disappeared son, who had been abducted by unknown agents. A tip about a clandestine cemetery led him to the mountains surrounding Talagante, a town about twenty-five miles from Santiago. Driving around that area, near the small town of Lonquén, he found an abandoned mine. Searching around the abandoned mine site, he spotted evidence of human remains at the base of one of the mine chimney's ovens. He believed that this could be a clandestine cemetery of disappeared people. He asked Aguirre if someone from the Vicaría could go to the mine site and verify what he had seen. He also asked him to keep his name secret.

A few representatives of the Vicaría traveled secretly to Lonquén to confirm the old man's finding. They saw what he had described: human remains protruding from the base of one of the mine's ovens. Upon their return, they checked their records and found that they had records of several disappearances from the surrounding area, Isla de Maipo.[3] This extraordinary revelation—the potential existence of a clandestine cemetery of disappeared people—coincided with the preparations of an international symposium on the topic of Human Rights, also organized and convened by the Vicaría. An array of international entities would be attending the symposium, including "prominent Church and human rights figures from sixteen countries and the Vatican."[4] Displayed on a giant banner outside the Cathedral in downtown Santiago, the symposium's motto read, "Every Man Has the Right to Be a Person," a message that was both sensitive and challenging. Cardinal Raúl Silva Henríquez and Vicaría's Vicar Cristián Precht feared that the military Junta would try to "discredit the symposium as a 'show' mounted to create an international scandal," or even worse, frame the Lonquén findings as leftist propaganda, if they disseminated the news during the days of the Symposium (November 22 to November 25).[5] Given the severity of the findings and because they wanted the Supreme Court to take the Vicaría's claim seriously, they decided to wait until after the symposium's closure to present their claim to justice authorities.

On November 30, 1978, a few days after the symposium was over, Cardinal Silva and Vicar Precht summoned an ad-hoc committee comprised of ecclesiastic, legal, and media entities to corroborate their finding before presenting the claim to the authorities. Besides Vicar Precht, the ad-hoc committee included Santiago's Auxiliary Bishop Enrique Alvear; Vicaría's Executive Secretary Javier Egaña; Vicaría's Chief Legal Representative Alejandro González; lawyer and Vice-President of the Chilean Human Rights Commission Máximo Pacheco; Vice-Director of *Hoy* magazine Abraham Santibáñez (besides *Solidaridad*, *Hoy* was the only independent biweekly magazine circulating in 1978); and the director of *Qué Pasa* magazine, Jaime Martínez (a manifestly right-wing, pro-regime magazine). The group convened on that same day at the Vicaría's offices and traveled together to Lonquén. Three younger priests (in case more force was needed to move heavy stones) and photographer Helen Hughes accompanied them.

Upon their arrival, they found two old tower-shaped ovens that appeared to have been abandoned. A layer of dirt, concrete, and stones covered the top of the first oven. They did some digging in the superior section of the wall only to hit a concrete slab and find nothing. They then proceeded to the other oven and dug in the inferior section, where the ashes rested at the mouth of the oven. There they found human remains, fragments of fabric, and stones with pieces of "organic material and human hair."[6] Vicar Precht and González excavated a hole large enough for one person to enter the oven. Meanwhile, priest Gonzalo

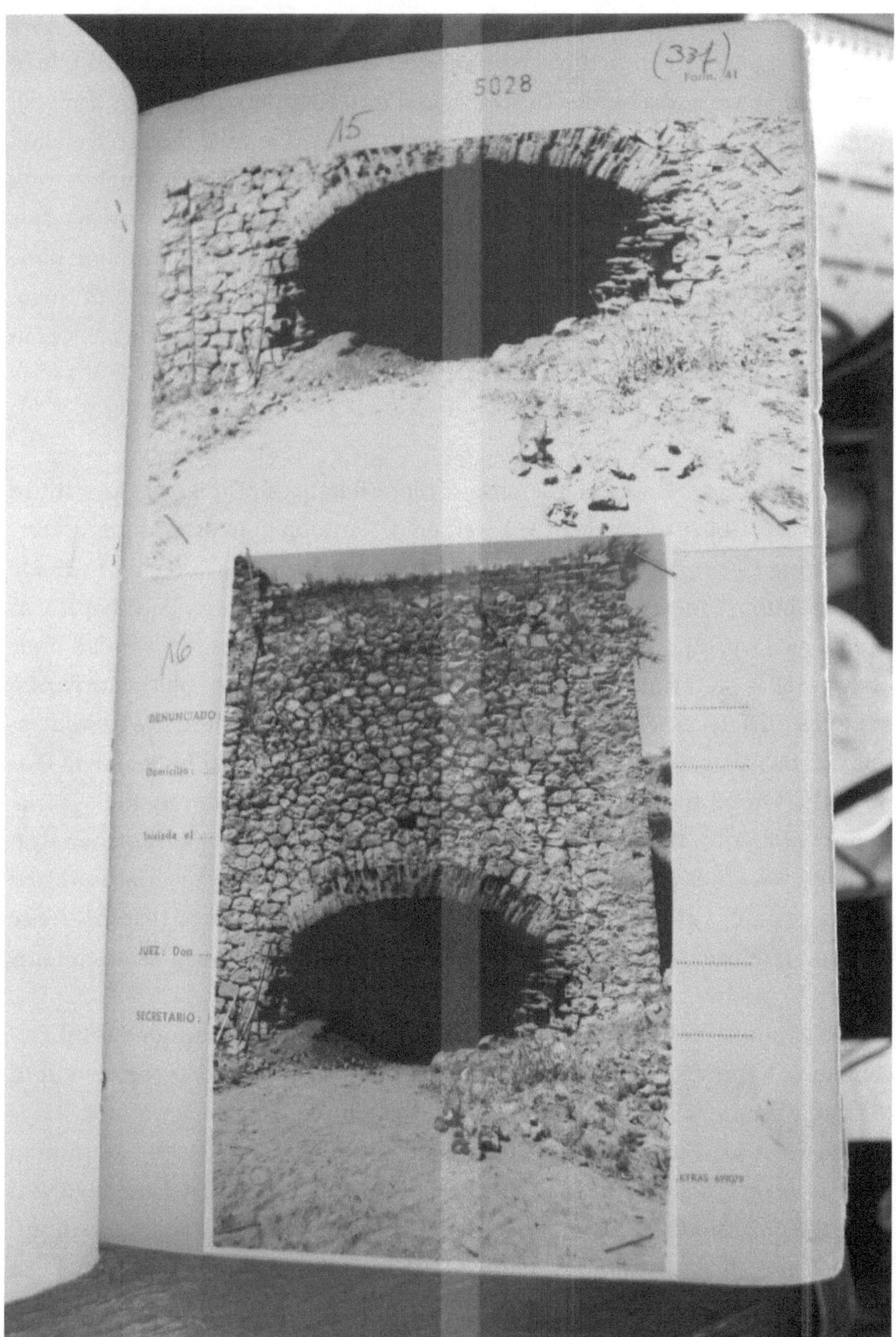

Figure 2.1. Frontal view of tower one of Lonquén furnaces. Credit: Helen Hughes. December 1978. Black and white. Lonquén case file, Vol. XI, Court of Appeals Legal Archive, Santiago. Photograph: Ángeles Donoso Macaya.

Aguirre excavated a hole on the top of the chimney. Taking turns, aided by improvised paper torches, those who entered the oven's ashtray found "a pile of interlaced bones and a human body covered by a very dark fabric."[7] A skull fell from the pile, braking into pieces. The group decided to take the broken skull and a few pieces of bones back to the Vicaría as evidence. Helen Hughes took frontal shots of the oven (see fig. 2.1); she also photographed the towers' exterior walls and the chimney from above. Back at the Vicaría, Hughes also took photographs of the broken skull and of the bones the group had taken with them. The material evidence and the photographs were stored at the Vicaría's offices in case further proof was required by legal authorities to corroborate the Vicaría's findings.

The next morning, Friday, December 1, representatives of the Vicaría went to the Supreme Court and presented a written declaration to Israel Bórquez, president of the Court. Bórquez manifested his weariness of the "inventions made by the Church," to which the representatives of the Vicaría replied that it was Bórquez's duty to present the claim to his peers in the Court.[8] Within an hour of this exchange, the plenary of the Supreme Court signed a resolution ordering the Judge of Talagante to be notified of the claim and to visit the site to confirm the Vicaría's allegations. The order fell on Talagante Criminal Judge Juana Godoy, who visited the site and confirmed the information given by the Vicaría. Representatives of the Vicaría were told to accompany Judge Godoy on her visit. Photographer Luis Navarro went along on this occasion. The Vicaría also hired a private company to complete the excavations. The group feared that the police or secret intelligence services would find out about the discovery, get to the site, and try to remove the bodies to get rid of the evidence.

The exhumations began on Saturday, December 2, and continued until December 6. Representatives of the Vicaría, including Navarro, were present until the end of these labors. On December 6, the Supreme Court appointed Judge Adolfo Bañados Cuadra, from the Santiago Appellate Court, as the examining magistrate investigating the case. The forensic evidence assembled and reviewed by Judge Bañados Cuadra would confirm that which the relatives of the disappeared, as well as the Vicaría, had been demanding to know (and had been fearing) for over five years.

Bañados Cuadra's investigation proved that fifteen "*presuntos desaparecidos*" (persons presumed disappeared) had in fact been disappeared. Although only one body would be officially identified at the time (that of Sergio Adrián Maureira Lillo), the evidence revealed that the bones found at the mine corresponded to fifteen men who had been detained on October 7, 1973, by a patrol comprising seven policemen who followed the instructions of Lieutenant Lautaro Castro Mendoza. Of the fifteen men, eleven were farmers who lived in that area and worked at the Fundo Naguayán; they had been detained at their homes (policeman Pablo Ñancupil, the officer who commanded the patrol, was an acquaintance of several of the victims) and listed as disappeared soon thereafter: Sergio Adrián Maureira Lillo (46) and his sons Sergio Miguel Maureira Muñoz (27), José Manuel Maureira Muñoz (26), Segundo Armando Maureira Muñoz (24), and Rodolfo Antonio Maureira Muñoz (22); brothers Carlos Segundo Hernández Flores (39), Nelson Hernández Flores (32), and Oscar Nibaldo Hernández Flores (30); Enrique René Astudillo Álvarez (51) and his sons Omar Enrique Astudillo Rojas (20) and Ramón Astudillo Rojas (27). Also on October 7, four young men had been detained by the same patrol at the central square of Isla de Maipo: Miguel Ángel Brant Bustamante (19), Iván Gerardo Ordóñez Lama (17), José Herrera Villegas (17), and Manuel Jesús Navarro Salinas (20). All these men had been beaten, thrown into the ovens, and buried.[9]

Notwithstanding the various efforts made by the military junta and their intelligence apparatuses to hide and obscure the evidence of the repression, the evidence started to appear, everywhere. The Lonquén case became emblematic in this regard: this was the first time since the beginning of Pinochet's dictatorship that factual and physical evidence brought to light the fact that authorities had lied all along about the existence of the disappeared. This chapter brings to the fore a pivotal documentary corpus, a set of photographs that gained status of supplementary forensic evidence and was used as the visual corroboration of the existence of the detained-disappeared. As forensic documents, these photographs were to offer an exhaustive visual record of the mine site—the ovens of the limestone mine and their surroundings—and of the physical evidence found there: human skeletal remains, bullet caps, remnants of clothing. Yet, given the atrocity, the magnitude of the situation they were meant to register, how exhaustive could these photographs be? What did the Lonquén photographs look like? What did they show, and what did they not show? When and how were they displayed to the public? What role have these photographs played in the public space, in what Thomas Keenan and Eyal Weizman call the forum? My analysis attempts to answer these questions by taking into consideration different domains in which these photographs have been displayed, used, or discussed.

A study of this documentary photographic corpus must begin by acknowledging the important role the Vicaría played in the Lonquén case. As historian Steve J. Stern argues, "the Vicaría acted astutely to prevent a cover-up."[10] In his argument, Stern mentions the inclusion of a conservative (Martínez) and a centrist (Santibañez) journalist in the ad-hoc committee that corroborated the information provided by the old man, the hiring of an excavation team to secure the remains, the divulging of all the documented disappearances by the Vicaría in that area, and the securing of relevant anthropomorphic information from the relatives of the victims.[11] However, another key procedure to avoid a potential cover-up was the production of forensic documentation. The Vicaría was also responsible for this task. Vicaría photographers Helen Hughes and Luis Navarro were both present at the site—Hughes during the first reconnaissance visit, and Navarro during the days of the exhumations.[12] They both took several photographs of the evidence found at the site. These two sets of photographs were swiftly incorporated into the Lonquén case file as supplementary forensic evidence. Besides having had a role in a major legal case, some of these photographs also circulated in the public space. Their dissemination in different media from early 1979 onward amplified and strengthened the discourse of the opposition. Used as denunciatory photography, the Lonquén photographs not only brought to the fore the worst features of military repression—illegal abductions, clandestine killings, and forced disappearances—but also became visual documentary matter—physical traces, icons, and symbols—of a horrible and unrepresentable crime.

Photos of the ovens and of the chimneys, taken by Hughes, were published in the magazine *Solidaridad* in January 1979, and in subsequent issues of the magazine. The image of the ovens and the detail of the oven's dark mouth became powerful visual metonymies of disappearance. A larger set of forensic photographs, some taken by Hughes at the Vicaría's offices and others by Navarro at the site, was reproduced in the book *Lonquén*, edited by attorney Máximo Pacheco and published in 1980 (the edition was censored, but it circulated among members of Editorial Aconcagua's readers' club; the book was republished in 1983). The publication of *Lonquén* made the forensic evidence and the written documents pertaining to the case available to the public for the first time. Further proof of the prominence of the Lonquén documentary photographic corpus are *No Olvidar* (Not to Forget) (1982), a film by Ignacio Agüero and Grupo Memoria, which disseminates related forensic documents and analyzes the media coverage of the case, and *La ciudad de los fotógrafos* (The City of Photographers) (2006), a film by Sebastián Moreno, in which the historical and symbolical significance of the Lonquén case and of the photographs taken at the site is revisited.

Forensic photographs materialize in the aesthetic domain—as any photograph does—and also transit through different spaces, overflowing them: the legal space, the forensic, and that of media.[13] To analyze and consider the Lonquén photographs in relation to these different domains, in the first part of the chapter I frame the photographic document and forensic evidence in light of recent critical formulations concerning the relation between the domain of forensics and the aesthetic domain. Regarding this linkage, Thomas Keenan and Eyal Weizman argue: "Aesthetics, as the *judgment* of the senses, is what rearranges the field of options and their perceived likelihood and cuts through probability's economy of calculations. The word *conviction* thus articulates the legal verdict with the subjective sensation of confirmed belief, of being convinced."[14] In their disseminations, the Lonquén photographs never appeared isolated: in *Solidaridad*, they were published in articles and news related to the case; in *Lonquén*, they were contextualized by other documents and framed by captions that gave them meaning as visual forensic evidence; in the documentary films, the photos were combined with other visual and sonorous signs in the sequences. The performance of the Lonquén photographs as forensic evidence and as denunciation photography entailed, then, both a transformation—from photographs into forensic documents and from forensic documents into icons and symbols—as well as a displacement—from the legal realm into the larger public space, via their dissemination in magazines, a book, and documentary films.

Despite the prominence these photographs have had in the public forum, they have been overlooked by historians and photography critics. Furthermore, the presence of both Hughes and Navarro at the site is rarely mentioned (an ironic rebuttal: Hughes's and Navarro's recollections have been key to countering some of the gaps and silences of the archive). It could seem odd that their photographs have not been studied. However, this critical inattention is not that surprising. Notwithstanding the unprecedented relevance acquired by the production and dissemination of photographic documents in the Chilean public sphere—a phenomenon that the Lonquén case made apparent—critical studies have tended to disregard documentary photographic production in its own right.[15] When photographs connected to the Lonquén case are included in critical studies, their presence tends to be illustrative.[16] But photographs are never mere illustrations.

In order to interpret the Lonquén photographs, in order to consider their many layers and depths, we need to elucidate their specific context of production, which was extremely precarious; we also need to address their different contexts of dissemination. My approach throughout this chapter can be described as a forensic methodology in its own terms. I make exhaustive use not only of the documents related to the case (many of them assembled in the book *Lonquén*), but also of the media coverage of the findings. To reconstruct the scene of the production of this photographic corpus, in the second part of the chapter I dig into the Lonquén case file, which in late 2018 was finally opened to the public (the case coming to a close only after forty years). In a few declarations and depositions (some of them published in *Lonquén*, and others available only in the case file), I found what I was searching for: the (overlooked) presence of the photographers and of their cameras at the site of the findings. The chapter's third part deals with the media frenzy instigated by the case. As we shall see, the existence of the photographs began to be mentioned and even discussed long before the public had access to them, before they could see the photos. Yet in a certain way, the mere existence of this corpus guaranteed the authenticity of the evidence. In the fourth part of the chapter, I analyze different forms of display of the Lonquén photographs in light of the idea of forensics as aesthetics: I consider how the photographs were framed and displayed as evidence in front of the public—the forum.

Some photographs evoke the fact of disappearance; these photos point to a crime scene that they could never fully reveal. I argue that the force of these photographs resides precisely in their incompleteness, in the impossibility of their showing it all. Other photos document and frame the evidence—skulls, a bullet cap, the oven—but the visual information is sometimes vague or opaque. Their public display, I maintain, sought not so much to *certify*—consider that by the time the larger set of forensic photographs was published and began to circulate, the case had already been closed by a military tribunal—but, rather, *rekindle* the forum. The public display of photographic documents, along with textual documents, was meant to keep Lonquén aflame: since justice *had not* been served, people had the right to decide for themselves, and also the right to remember, to not forget. In the chapter's concluding section, I consider Lonquén's persistence in the public forum, listening to its documentary echoes. Despite all efforts on the part of the military regime to obliterate Lonquén, it continues to manifest. In this final section I comment briefly on *No Olvidar* and *La ciudad de los fotógrafos* to show that the documentary traces of Lonquén—traces that I interpret as echoes—continue to resonate.

On Documents and Forensic Evidence

That photographs are not documents in and of themselves has been established by photography criticism.[17] Photographs perform as documents every time they are displayed, contextualized, or validated as visual evidence of something; they also gain the status of documents every time they are reproduced.[18] Paradoxically, and despite necessary reproductions and reframings, whenever photographs take on the role of documents, they become unnoticed as constructed visual objects. Because of the factual aspect of photographs as documents it would seem that there is nothing to say *about* them. Yet all photographs are complex visual signs: part indexes, part icons, and part symbols. Photographs are indexes in that they are physically connected to their referents; they are icons whenever they resemble the qualities of the object they represent; and they can also become symbols.[19] Because of these different attributes, the meanings of photographs as documents fluctuate with each public display.

Since what I am interested in exploring is the performance of the Lonquén photographs as forensic documents, I begin by reviewing some critical formulations about the document—what documents are and what they do—and about forensic evidence. Even though photographs have been used as visual evidence in courts since the mid-nineteenth century, they do not have an "intrinsic" probative value. The history of photographic evidence reveals that nothing is "evident" about photographs: the epistemological status of the photograph as visual evidence has varied significantly; its evidentiary weight depends on particular staging; and its meaning as evidence is always open to interpretation.[20] As legal scholar Jennifer L. Mnookin explains, there was a movement in the photograph, from illustration to proof: first, photographs served as illustrations of the claims made by oral eyewitnesses. This meant that oral eyewitnesses affirmed the demonstrative value of photographs—or, as Mnookin explains, human beings made the photographs speak.[21] Over time, photographs became independent forms of visual evidence. In both instances, though, the status of photographs as evidence is determined by different rhetorical procedures: "an ostentatious display, a heartfelt plea, a demonstrative gesture."[22] Therefore, just as nothing is definitive in the construction and presentation of evidence in the legal field, nothing is obvious or definitive about photographs used as visual evidence, however simple or straightforward the photographs may appear.

Just like utterances, photographs are linked to specific contexts of enunciation and of (re)presentation. These contexts can define the performance of photographs as documents. The importance of display, context, and framing in the formulation of any object whatsoever as a document is brought to the fore in Suzanne Briet's classic essay "What Is Documentation?" Briet asks: "Is a star a document? Is a pebble rolled by a torrent a document? Is a living animal a document? No. But the photographs and the catalogues of stars, the stones in a museum of mineralogy, and the animals that are catalogued and shown in a zoo, are documents."[23] Scholars who cite Briet's famous passage usually highlight the last idea: animals on display in a zoo are documents.[24] However, I believe the first part of the answer is more striking and also more pertinent for our discussion: "the photographs and catalogues of stars . . ." A photograph of a star has, in Briet's definition, the same documentary weight that a stone displayed in a museum has. From this formulation, it follows that a photograph of no matter what object is a document of that object. Yet, are photographs documents because they carry the luminous trace of the object(s) they depict? Are photographs documents because of their iconic aspects—that is, because they look like their referents? Or is it, perhaps, that photographs are documents because, like display cases in the museum or the cages in the zoo, they also are operational forms, hollow structures?

Even though Briet's definition seems to suggest, at first glance, a somewhat straightforward identification between physical objects (stars and stones) and photographic images, the fact that she places photographs alongside other presentational devices (display cases and zoo cages) underscores the performative aspect of all documents, or to evoke Thomas Keenan's formulation used as the epigraph of this chapter, the notion that the document is always a hollow structure, an operational form. Anything can become a document through an act of capture, enclosure, and display—stones, animals, and stars. Still, if the document is a hollow structure, an operational form or a "truth-claim-making machine," then something needs to happen—a transformation, a displacement—for a photograph to perform as a document.[25]

A brief consideration of the discursive space of the document will help us elucidate these transformations and displacements. The etymology of the word "document" traces back to the Latin word *docere*. As Keenan observes, this root suggests that the document retains some linkage to the idea of instruction, in the sense of warning. Because of this supplementary instructive (and even corrective) function, Keenan argues, "the event that is document(ed) does not fully coincide with itself or is doubled as an exemplum; it constitutes a trace, which is pedagogically oriented toward the future."[26] Little by little, the meaning of the word "document" moved from the realm of education and of exemplum to that of data, facts, and proofs. Although these spaces are not completely separate, this change of meaning of "document" sheds light on the document's temporal dimension. The notion of the document as proof or certification tends to refer us to the past, to the event or to the referent of which the document is proof or inscription; however, the idea of the document as an instructive operational form emphasizes the link between the document with the present and with the future.

If documents are oriented toward the future, if their display is meant to instruct about something, then documents do not halt the act of thinking, deliberating, or pondering, but rather prompt it. As Keenan observes, this is precisely what happens all the time in legal contexts: presentation of evidence never happens at the end of the trial; on the contrary, evidence is what prompts the trial. Both in trials and in political life, documents are presented, refuted, corroborated, "their meanings explored and contrasted. Interpreters gather around them in disagreement because they have something to teach."[27] This formulation decenters the issue of authenticity, which is not to say that the questions of whether the document is or is not a truthful inscription or of whether what the document shows is or is not actual are irrelevant. Rather, it means that emphasis is placed on the space opened up by the document due to its performance as exemplum: "The document retains a tie to 'what happened' by virtue of its specimen or exemplary status; it is ripped or doubled from what happens, but in order *to teach*, which means it's the lesson that somehow has primacy, rather than the event."[28]

Similar to the document, which is displayed with the intention of instructing about something, but the effect of its lesson can't be determined in advance, the display of forensic evidence in front of the forum also has no guaranteed outcome. Once forensic evidence is put up for consideration, everything is at stake and anything can happen: this is why the gestures of display, presentation, explanation, and contextualization of the evidence are pivotal. This is what Keenan and Weizman suggest in their discussion of the scientific and legal procedures established to determine the identity of Mengele's skull (discovered in 1985 in Sao Paulo, Brazil). The critics formulate the visual procedures and techniques deployed to corroborate the identification of Mengele's skull in terms of a forensic aesthetics. They argue, "Forensics is [. . .] not simply about science but about the presentation of scientific findings, about science as an art of persuasion. Derived from the Latin *forensis*, the word's root refers to the 'forum,' and thus to the practice and skill of making an argument before a professional, political, or legal gathering."[29] The display and the presentation of the evidence by a mediator opens up the space of the forum. This forum, moreover, "is not a given space, but it is produced through a series of entangled performances. Indeed, it does not always exist prior to the presentation of the evidence within it."[30] Because each of the components needed for the forum to materialize—the object, the mediator, and the forum itself—is dynamic, the discursive space of forensics is constantly crossing the boundaries of the legal realm.

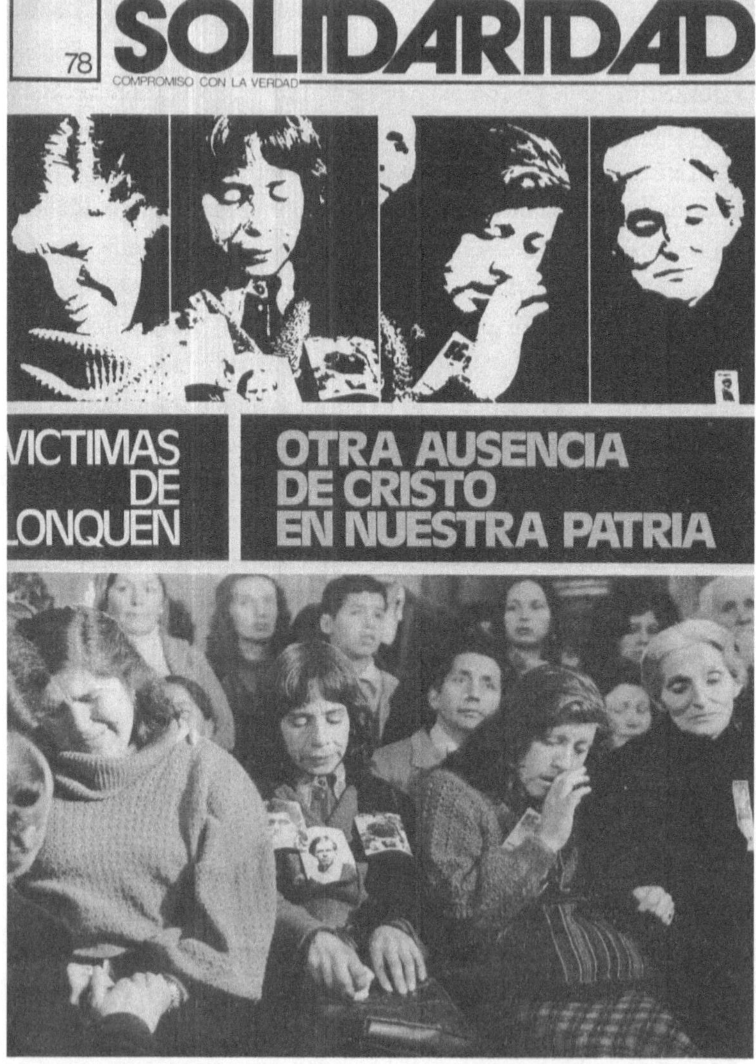

Figure 2.2. "Victims of Lonquén. Another Absence of Christ in Our Homeland." Cover of *Solidaridad* 78 (1979). Black and white. Fundación de Documentación y Archivo de la Vicaría de la Solidaridad.

The Lonquén case overflowed the levees of the juridico (legal) space since the very beginning (see fig. 2.2). The notion that the human remains found at the site could belong to people illegally detained by state agents materialized as soon as the old man confided his discovery to the Vicaría priest; this notion kept "haunting," so to speak, Bañados Cuadra's forensic probe. Although it was being investigated as a regular police case, the numerous public accusations about enforced and illegal disappearances, the particularities of the site—an abandoned and secluded mine—and the fact that several bodies had been buried and *hidden* there suggested that this had not been an ordinary crime. It did not help that officialist media responded with disparate accounts of the evidence found: there were as few as four or six and as many as fourteen or even twenty-five corpses; there were two women and one black person among the victims. Given the unavoidable speculations and considering the impact the investigation's results would have both on the military regime and on the relatives of the more than five hundred people listed as detained-disappeared to that date, it was imperative that the forensic probe be as exhaustive and precise as possible. After all, amidst a restricted political climate of intense public (and military) scrutiny, how does one make sure the physical evidence is not altered or destroyed? Moreover, how does one impede a cover-up and/or the dissemination of misinformation?

The (Photographic) Evidence

Let's now go back to the afternoon of December 2, 1978. Judge Juana Godoy, standing in front of the mine's ovens, understood pretty quickly the severity and significance of the discovery and expressed concerns about the military or the police potentially interfering in the forensic investigation. Indeed, all the people present on that day feared (and knew) that very soon members of secret intelligence services would be monitoring the site. Thus, protecting the site and the evidence there was pivotal. But this task was interpreted in different ways by the various entities involved. For the representatives of the Vicaría, it meant hiring a private contractor to complete the exhumation and their own photographer to record the evidence found at the site. For Judge Godoy, protecting the evidence also meant documenting the site and part of the evidence before the arrival of the police. It would have been counterintuitive, if not altogether foolish, for the judge to trust the Technical Police Laboratory, a state agency, with this endeavor.

Once the investigation started, however, protecting the evidence meant having Talagante's police officers patrolling the site day and night to keep the press and intruders at bay. Meanwhile, for the police, protecting the "Site of the Incident" (as they called it in legal documents) implied trusting neither in the way the exhumations were being conducted (their reason: the site had been manipulated prior to their arrival), nor in the unidentified individuals whom the police encountered at the site on December 2 (all representatives of the Vicaría). For Judge Bañados Cuadra, protecting the evidence meant assuring the relatives of the detained-disappeared, the representatives of the Vicaría, and the greater public that the forensic evidence would be handled properly, that all options would be thoroughly investigated, and that nothing would be taken for granted. The photographs Hughes and Navarro took at the site between November 30 and December 6 played a key role in all of these matters. Both Hughes's and Navarro's photographs would stand as *supplementary* visual evidence in case the material evidence was altered or destroyed.

A close reading of the legal reports and the depositions reveals how the evidence was exhumed, collected, and *photographed*. Some of these depositions are included in Pacheco's book *Lonquén*; others are available in only the case's legal file. (For security reasons, Pacheco did not include the statements given by Vicaría representatives or by those who participated in the first visit.) Unlike Navarro, Hughes did not play a formal role as a forensic photographer. However, her photos were also incorporated into the case file. This happened on January 18, 1979, the day the Vicaría's lawyer Alejandro González and Hughes herself gave their depositions to Judge Bañados Cuadra. In the case file, Hughes's photos are numbered one through thirty-three (1–33). In his deposition, González notes that the first photograph in the set "represents the inferior mouth of the oven just like we found it."[31] He explains that of the thirty-three photographs they would be submitting to the court that day, some had been "taken at the Site of the Incident, and others, in which a smooth background is appreciated, had been captured at our office in the Vicaría with better illumination."[32] In her deposition, Hughes corroborates this information: "I took the photographs of all the human remains that were secured on that day [. . .] Some photographs were captured at the site of the incident and others at an office in the Vicaría where the remains had been taken."[33]

In his deposition to Judge Bañados Cuadra, given on February 12, 1979, Navarro indicates: "My role was to photograph everything that the Magistrate indicated to me, as matter was being extracted from the interior of the oven and its surroundings [. . .] It is my understanding that before me there was a young female photographer who took some photos that were stored in the Vicaría, that no one had access to [the photos], [. . .] and that these were delivered to the Court."[34] According to Navarro's recollections of his first evening at the site, Judge Godoy did not know that the Vicaría had brought a photographer—she realized right there, at the site, that Navarro was a photographer. After this realization, she asked Navarro to take photographs of the site and of the evidence found there, before the arrival of the police. Before entering the oven, Judge Godoy asked Navarro to sign an agreement—Navarro was not an official forensic photographer, so this legal protocol was required. According to the agreement, all the photographs taken by Navarro would belong to the forensic investigation. Navarro would develop all the film at the end of each day and turn over the photographs and the developed film to Judge Godoy the following morning.[35]

In her written reports, Judge Godoy describes the official inspections carried out by her court on December 1, 5, and 6. All three reports chronicle the order to take photographs of the evidence found. The report written at the end of the second day indicates: "At 6:00 p.m., the Court put an end to the procedure, ordering the custody of the place to police personnel. It was also ordered that photographs be taken of the process carried out and added to the proceedings."[36] (Remarkably, this last order appears handwritten in the memo I found in the case file.) During the Court's third inspection, on December 6, a five-centimeter bullet cap was found. In her written report, the Judge details the finding and the order to "take photographs and add them to the proceedings."[37] That same day, the upper section of one of the ovens partially collapsed. Several remains of human skeletons with clothing and five human skulls fell to the ground at the bottom of the oven. Judge Godoy's report details, accordingly, that "photographs of the place and of the bones found were taken, and also ordered to be added to the case."[38] Judge Godoy's reports do not reveal the tension that reigned over the site while the exhumations were being carried out. They also fail to reveal the apprehensions and the fear felt by the individuals involved in this difficult task.

On top of the nature of the task at hand—exhumation of human remains—the presence of police and secret intelligence agents made the whole endeavor extremely stressful and nerve-racking. This becomes apparent in the declaration given by Hernán Cristi, the private contractor hired by the Vicaría to complete the exhumations. In his deposition, Cristi states that he learned about the nature of the work—the removal of corpses—only when he arrived at the mine site, and that if he decided to continue with the work the next day, it was because "he had contracted a certain commitment with the representatives of the Vicaría."[39] His statement gives an account of the physical and psychological exhaustion of his workers and of the overall tense environment in which the exhumations were carried out: "We were deeply disturbed and displeased by the work, which had demanded expending a lot of energy and which, in addition, had been the object of monitoring and control efforts that inspired considerable fear [. . .] Everyone tied the discovery that had been made with the involvement of the Vicaría to the issue of the disappeared, which is public knowledge."[40] Regarding the surveillance of the site, Cristi indicates that he did not see any kind of surveillance on Monday, December 4 (his first day of work). Yet, on Tuesday and Wednesday, both he and his workers noticed the presence of "armed civilians"; however, because nobody displayed their credentials, they could not determine which individuals were detectives or agents and which were from the intelligence services.

Cristi's statement says nothing of the work performed by Navarro at the site. However, two deputy commissioners of Talagante, Bille Martínez Pave and Hugo Espinoza Orellana (Deputy Chief Commissar), talk at length about Navarro in their joint deposition. Judging by the tone of their description, the presence of the photographer and of other members of the Vicaría at the "Site of the Incident" clearly took them by surprise. In their deposition, they offer a meticulous physical description of Navarro. It must be said that they don't describe anyone else with such level of detail. I quote the passage at length:

> [The] investigating officers mentioned above, verified, at the Site of the Incident [. . .] the presence of four individuals who did not belong to the Court, one of them calling attention for being a professional photographer with lots of work equipment; three cameras; a zoom lens, a wide angle lens, and a telephoto lens; electronic flash; this individual was around thirty-five years old, dark-skinned, thin, tall, slim face with prominent cheekbones, thick lips, black and frizzy hair; when asked to say his name, he refused to provide it; the same situation happened with the rest of his companions. While the photographer carried out his work for the Court, his colleagues went directly to the mouth of one of the ovens, which was covered with rocks of regular size, *confirming with this action, that the aforementioned Site of the Incident, had already been violated* [. . .] Despite the secrecy of the assignment, it was possible to verify through the conver-

> sations of the individuals, that they were representatives of the VICARÍA and that they were called by the names of LUCHO, HÉCTOR, MARIO, and GONZALO—the latter, apparently, a priest. This staff arrived at the site equipped with tools. Because of the precision in carrying out tasks, it was easy to deduce that these people had already been to the Site of the Incident [. . .][41]

For the deputy commissioners, the apparent familiarity with which the officials of the Vicaría, including Navarro, operated in the place, was proof that the site "had already been violated." Perhaps for this reason, they felt the need to also describe in detail the work carried out by Navarro on Saturday, both inside the mouth of the oven and in the surrounding areas. This part of their deposition renders a blurred image in our imaginations of the dirty work, the burden, Navarro undertook inside the oven. The deputy commissioners recount how after the other officials of the Vicaría had removed the stones with which they had covered the mouth of the furnace the previous day, "the photographer, protecting his nasal region with a handkerchief, introduced his head in dorsal decubitus and began taking several shots [*vistas fotográficas*]; later, he said that due to the effect of the flash, he had been able to observe the presence of around ten corpses inside the mouth of the oven."[42]

In my interviews with Navarro, the photographer recalled the physical and emotional strain involved in carrying out this work, emphasizing the unbearable panorama he had encountered when he went inside the oven on that Saturday. The orifice was very small, and he barely had room to move; the smell of rot was unbreathable (he had indeed covered his nose with a handkerchief). Because the interior was absolutely dark, he noticed the human remains around him only when his camera's flash illuminated this startling vision, macabre and momentary and forever recorded in his memory. In his deposition, Navarro takes notice of these photographs and explains what he sees as an "error in the distance:" "the views of Folios 17, 18, 19 (inferior photo), correspond precisely to what I saw when I first lay in the ash bed at the mouth of the oven and peered up into the shaft. In some photos there is an error in the distance, which happens because it was not possible for me to adjust the focus in circumstances that I did not have a mask and the environment was impregnated with a very penetrating smell."[43]

Reading Navarro's statement at the Court of Appeals Human Rights Division Archive, I think back to the officers' deposition, in particular the instance

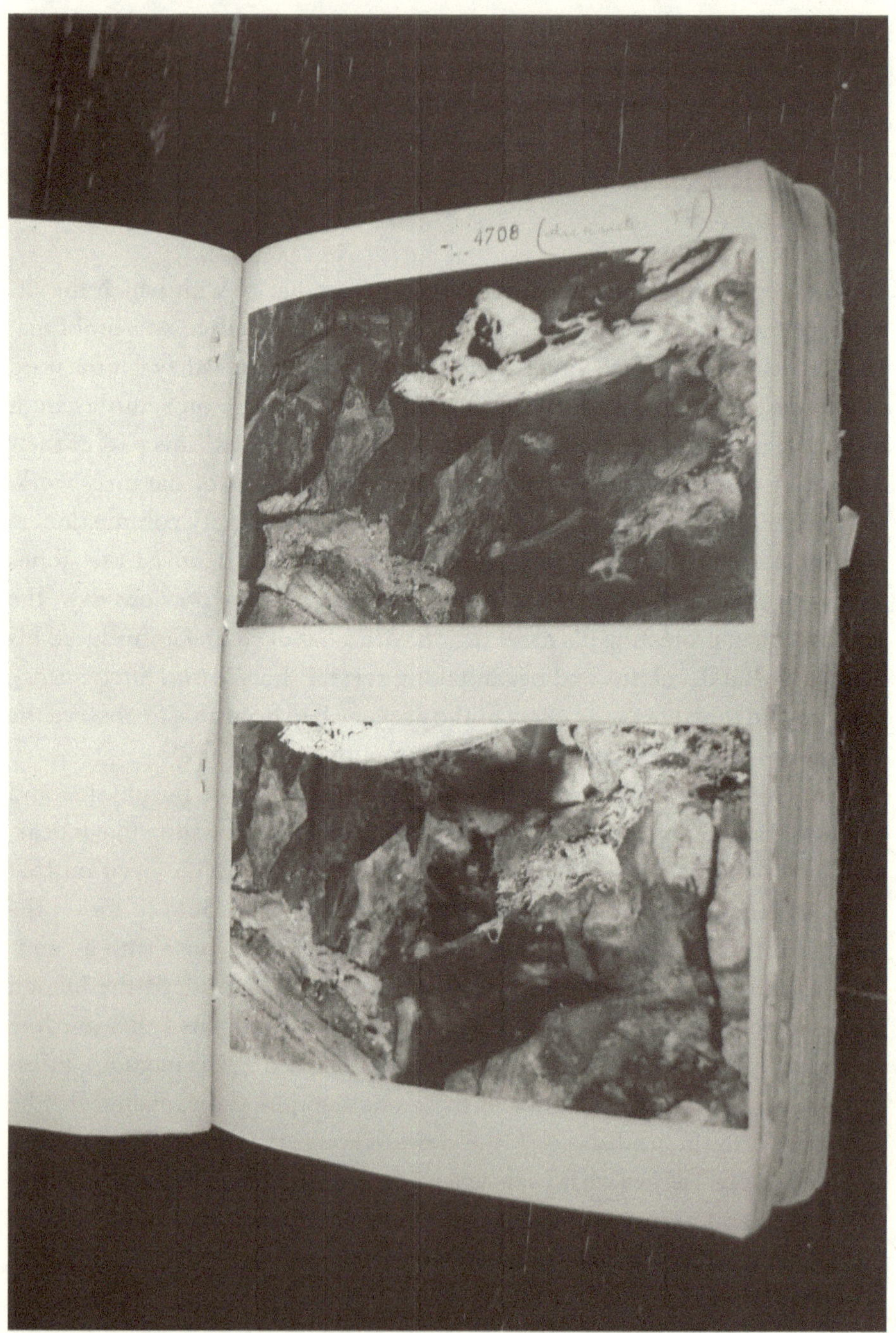

Figure 2.3. View inside the furnace's shaft at Lonquén. Credit: Luis Navarro Vega. December 1978. Black and white. Lonquén case file, Vol. XI, Court of Appeals Legal Archive, Santiago. Photograph: Ángeles Donoso Macaya.

in which they describe the photos that Navarro took inside the mouth of the furnace as "photographic views" or *vistas*. The photos Navarro took on his back in the mouth of the oven are not views—they don't offer a panoramic view of some serene landscape. Describing him as shooting a *vista* implies that Navarro and his camera maintained some kind of distance, that he could choose his position, his angle. It seems to suggest that Navarro was able to raise his camera, focus, and take the picture. This was not the case. With one hand on his camera and the other holding a handkerchief over his nose, Navarro lay flat on his back trying to orient himself and to adjust his eyes and his vision to the darkness inside the cave (see fig. 2.3). Lying there in the ashes of the corpses above him, Navarro enjoyed no cushion of distance from his subject. There is no depth of field in these photographs; rather, everything seems to be falling from above, crumbling—decaying shreds of clothing, layers of hair, cobwebs, rocks, and mineral sediment—collapsing. These photos are no panoramas, no ordinary stills; these photos display a disaster piled on like stones in a quarry, a *material* disaster composed of human bones, fabrics, and remains of hair—of horror—and smelling of confinement and death. Navarro's photograph evidenced a crime committed right there where he lay and exposed the matter of the detained-disappeared, raising the questions of how, when, and to whom this happened.

The photographs Navarro took inside the oven look almost like abstract paintings. They do not "show" much. The camera is so close to its subjects—pieces of fabric and tattered clothes amid layers of stones—it almost seems as if the fabrics were touching the lens. The camera's flash illuminates parts of the clothing in the foreground, but it is hard to tell what is fabric from what is stone in the background, where everything turns black. The darkness of the background allows us only to imagine the panorama these stones are covering, the fabrics intertwined with human remains in that darkness. Far from *vistas fotográficas*, these stills are documentary matter.

The Lonquén Forum Opens Up

The Lonquén findings and the investigation that ensued opened up an essential forum. The macabre discovery triggered, reasonably, a number of questions and speculations. Abraham Santibañez, one of the members of the ad-hoc committee that visited Lonquén on November 30, published a testimonial piece in *Hoy* by mid-December in which he asked:

> Who are these dead? Who eradicated them? Were they alive when they arrived, dying little by little [. . .]? And finally, the definite questions: Are these some of the hundreds of disappeared who have been tenaciously denounced and whose "supposed" existence has been denied in an equally tenacious manner? Do they correspond to the names and the ID cards of people from Talagante registered in the lists of the Vicaría de la Solidaridad, of which half a dozen were reported disappeared in October 1973? For now, there is no answer. None of us—the first witnesses—can provide it.[44]

Santibañez's telling account was published two weeks after the initial findings. While this does not seem like such a long time, and despite the secrecy with which the Lonquén affair had been handled since the very beginning—from the moment the old man confessed—the news of the discovery leaked very rapidly. What the Lonquén findings were and were not, soon became a public matter. Indeed, already on the second day of the exhumations—Tuesday December 5—workers saw reporters trying to access the site.

Different from the exhumation of Mengele's skull, which, as discussed by Keenan and Weizman, was done in front of the cameras for all to see, the exhumations at the Lonquén site were completed beyond the reach of media outlets.[45] In his deposition, Cristi indicates having noticed the presence of some journalists "loitering near the ovens" and speculates: "The news must have been known perhaps Monday night; it is possible that intruders arrived after we finished working [. . .], but police kept guard of all that sector from Tuesday onwards."[46] Although the presence of unidentified armed civilians was inevitable, Judge Godoy and, later, Judge Bañados Cuadra, made sure that the exhumations were carried out without the presence of media outlets. The policemen who guarded the place banned the passage of reporters and photographers. Besides Navarro, who arrived always accompanied by other representatives of the Vicaría, the second photographer who had access to the site from December 6 onward was the forensic expert Manuel Gutiérrez Muñoz.

During the first two weeks that followed the findings, the public read, listened, or was told about the mine site, not only about the evidence found there—human remains, bullet caps, and clothing in shreds—but also about the photographs that had documented (fixed) the evidence. But what did the public actually see? Did they see the skulls? No. Did they see the stones with hair attached, the pieces of fabric, the loose bones, or the bullet caps? No. Since the site was located in an uninhabited area, far from the main road, and was cordoned off by policemen, photojournalists and reporters could not get near the place of the exhumations. The news articles published in officialist newspapers indicated that the place was "practically inaccessible" or that journalists could only "talk to the judge once he leaves the site, as the entire place is surrounded by *carabineros*."[47] The restricted access to the site could be one reason why the vast majority of articles and notes published about the findings in *El Mercurio*, *La Segunda*, and *La Tercera*, among other newspapers, did not include photographs (those that did included small photographs of the site in which the towers of the ovens are seen from a significant distance). Without denying this fact—that media access was restricted—the absence of photographs can also be considered an editorial choice, an attempt on the part of these media outlets to diminish the significance of the discovery. One notable exception is an article published in *Las Últimas Noticias*, which was illustrated with large photographs. Because these photos were also taken from a distance, the editors decided to add black arrows over the images to point out Judge Bañados Cuadra and the pit from which human remains had been retrieved.

That access to the site was prohibited did not impede media outlets from spreading (mis)information about the discovery—newspapers, magazines, TV stations, and radio stations reported on the case.[48] How many cadavers had been found? When had these people died? Where was the mine located? What groups had access to that area? On December 6, while the exhumations were still in process (the second furnace had yet to be explored), media aligned with the military regime started to provide disparate versions. *El Mercurio* reported that four cadavers had been found in an abandoned mine, whereas *Las Últimas Noticias* reported six cadavers had been found. The next day, *La Tercera* declared, categorically: "DEFINITIVE: twenty-five cadavers, two women among them," and they added: "It transpired that the majority of the cadavers present bullet holes in their foreheads." Both claims would turn out to be incorrect. On December 8, a news article published in *El Mercurio* stated: "Exactly fourteen cadavers were rescued. This information, although classified, was given to *El Mercurio* to put an end to exaggerated reports." Granted, this information was closer to that which Judge Bañados Cuadra's investigation would end up establishing: according to the judge, fifteen men had been buried at the Lonquén mines. However, the same article sharing this "classified information" indicated that "among the dead, one person is of the black race."

Pro-regime media outlets speculated not only about the possible gender or race of the deceased whose remains were found, but also about the time passed since their burial—proffering two or three years or less than twenty-four months.[49] They even suggested that the abandoned mine and the surrounding areas had been used by *miristas* as a training site. These explanations and racist speculations sought to counteract, destabilize, or even weaken the notion that the human remains found at the Lonquén site were proof, confirmation, that ordinary people had been illegally detained and forcibly disappeared.[50] This line of argumentation was heightened a few weeks after the findings at Lonquén, when another discovery of human remains was made near the area of Cuesta Barriga (an area thirty miles west of Santiago and close to Talagante).

Statements issued by the Minister of the Interior on December 20 regarding this new finding indicated that the remains corresponded to "extremist elements." Officialist media became emphatic in their support of the regime's claims. An *El Mercurio* editorial argued on December 22 that people needed to grasp the fact that it was a context of "war" that led to these events, and that exposing them was detrimental to advancing on the new path of "reconciliation"; after all, these were events from "the past," and it was time to move forward. On December 23, a rather hostile news item published in *La Segunda* suggested that the discovery at the Barriga slope—also denounced by the Vicaría—was a mise-en-scène designed to destabilize the military regime and that behind the denunciations of these findings were twisted motives of revenge. In direct response to the Minister of the Interior's declarations and the *El Mercurio* editorial, the relatives of the victims—the claimants—would state in the legal suit: "The discovery of the [. . .] remains demonstrates, without any doubt of any kind, the reality and truth of the drama of the detained-disappeared, treated with unscrupulous lightness by some sectors interested in concealing their transcendence."[51]

As soon as he took the case, Judge Bañados Cuadra's immediate actions assured the public—the forum—that his investigation would be thorough. On December 7, he called his court into session at the very site of the incident to inspect the ovens firsthand. (He ordered that the second oven be investigated, a job that would continue for a few days; no human remains would be found). On December 8, he ordered a number of procedures that would be fundamental: the Legal Medical Service was ordered to perform autopsies and identify the corpses; the Technical Police Laboratory was commissioned to perform ballistic analysis of the few bullet caps found; the Technical Police Laboratory and the Homicide Brigade were also requested to turn over all photographs taken at the site, both of the objects and of the organic remains found; the Courts of

Melipilla, San Bernardo, and Talagante (the courts near the Lonquén area) were requested to hand over all the cases and reports involving missing persons or victims of alleged misfortunes after September 11. The judge requested the same of several Ministers of Justice, including the Court of Appeals of Santiago: that they provide all information and cases related to missing persons. He also asked the Vicaría first to submit all available information about cases related to missing persons, and second to prepare anthropometric cards of all people whose detention-disappearance the Vicaría had certified and registered. These cards were to include the physical characteristics and clothing worn by these persons at the time of arrest.[52] Last, Judge Bañados Cuadra requested that "the series of photographs that Luis Navarro was ordered to develop" be added to the Lonquén case file.[53]

One of the matters some pro-regime media outlets kept insisting on concerned the legitimacy of the evidence: What if not all the evidence collected at the site before Judge Bañados Cuadra began presiding over the case was in the file? What if the evidence had been altered? Whenever the judge answered questions about the case, he emphasized the professionalism with which the forensic analysis was being conducted and did not fail to mention the existence of the photographs. Thus, at the end of January, a headline in *La Tercera* would assert, "Human remains are photographed and will not be altered."[54] The article includes a few statements from Judge Bañados Cuadra, in which he explains that although it was not yet possible to determine the number of bodies, the Medical Legal Institute had given him "photographs of the skeletons inside the mines [i.e., the photos taken by Hughes and by Navarro], to be collated with the photographs of the bodies." The objective of this procedure "was to avoid allegations that the bones were changed or that they do not correspond exactly to those found in the limestone mine."[55]

The fact that state agencies—the Technical Police Laboratory or the Legal Medical Institute—could alter or eliminate evidence also troubled the relatives of the detained-disappeared. Indeed, they pressured to have international experts monitoring the probe and thus guaranteeing its regular course. In another interview, Judge Bañados Cuadra would address these requests and concerns explaining—by means of a visual metaphor—that State agents could not hide results without being "noticed" or alter the evidence because, "everyone had an eye on the case." He also added, to further support his opinion: "In addition, Judge Juana Godoy has acted from the beginning with a cautious sense, so that everything that has come out of the site *has been fixed through photographs*."[56]

We have considered at length the context of production of the Lonquén photographs: it is now time to consider their contexts of dissemination—where, how, and when they were published.

The Lonquén Photographs Enter the Forum

Viewing a photograph of the Holland House Library in London taken in 1940, just weeks after an aerial bombardment completely destroyed it, Eduardo Cadava asks, "How can we respond to the experiences commemorated, displaced, and cyphered by this image? [. . .] What can memory be when it seeks to remember the trauma of violence and loss? How can we respond to what is not presently visible, to what can never be seen within the image?"[57] I remind myself of these questions as I watch a set of photographs of the old and abandoned tower reproduced in issue 62 of *Solidaridad*, in January 1979. These were some of the photos taken by Hughes on November 30 and introduced to the case file on January 18—that is, after they were published in *Solidaridad*. The title of the very first article published by this magazine about the Lonquén case was "Lonquén: ¿Quiénes son estos muertos?" (Lonquén: Who Are These Dead?). The article's title echoed the questions posed by Santibañez a few weeks prior: "Who are these dead? Who eradicated them? Were they alive when they arrived, dying little by little?" The article featured five photos, including close-ups and mid-shots of the two ovens and their chimneys, along with a small portrait of Judge Bañados Cuadra (see fig. 2.4). The three photographs of the oven reproduced on the first page of the article in *Solidaridad* did not include captions, and the large photograph reproduced in the middle of the page was clearly oversaturated. Given that the article was being published over a month after the macabre findings had been made public—that is, the Lonquén site *itself* was not news material anymore—I cannot help but wonder about the photographs' purpose and their meanings. What did these photographs show, and how did they show it? Why the repetition? Would just one photograph of the oven not have sufficed? What was the function of the highly contrasted oven close-up reproduced in the middle of the first page? What about that which these photographs could not show?

Acknowledging the ostensible "insufficiency" of the photographs, the captions of the photographs published on the second page of the *Solidaridad* article underlined the existence of a previous time for which the photographs could not account—that is, the moment of the finding of the bodies: "Top image: exterior view of the ovens of the limestone mine, where the bodies were found. Bottom

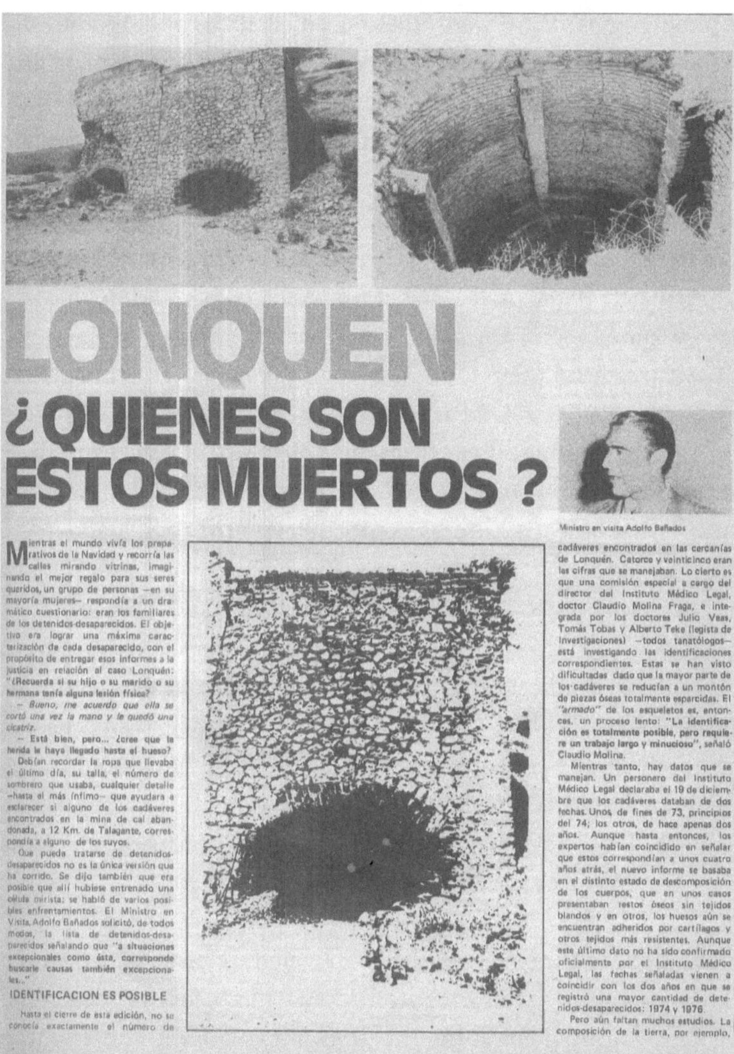

LONQUEN

¿QUIENES SON ESTOS MUERTOS?

Mientras el mundo vivía los preparativos de la Navidad y recorría las calles mirando vitrinas, imaginando el mejor regalo para sus seres queridos, un grupo de personas —en su mayoría mujeres— respondía a un dramático cuestionario: eran los familiares de los detenidos-desaparecidos. El objetivo era lograr una máxima caracterización de cada desaparecido, con el propósito de entregar esos informes a la justicia en relación al caso Lonquén: "¿Recuerda si su hijo o su marido o su hermana tenía alguna lesión física?

— *Bueno, me acuerdo que ella se cortó una vez la mano y le quedó una cicatriz.*

— **Está bien, pero... ¿cree que la herida le haya llegado hasta el hueso?**

Debían recordar la ropa que llevaba el último día, su talla, el número de sombrero que usaba, cualquier detalle —hasta el más ínfimo— que ayudara a esclarecer si alguno de los cadáveres encontrados en la mina de cal abandonada, a 12 Km. de Talagante, correspondía a alguno de los suyos.

Que pueda tratarse de detenidos-desaparecidos no es la única versión que ha corrido. Se dijo también que era posible que allí hubiese entrenado una célula mirista; se habló de varios posibles enfrentamientos. El Ministro en Visita, Adolfo Bañados solicitó, de todos modos, la lista de detenidos-desaparecidos señalando que **"a situaciones excepcionales como ésta, corresponde buscarle causas también excepcionales..."**

IDENTIFICACION ES POSIBLE

Hasta el cierre de esta edición, no se conocía exactamente el número de cadáveres encontrados en las cercanías de Lonquén. Catorce y veinticinco eran las cifras que se manejaban. Lo cierto es que una comisión especial a cargo del director del Instituto Médico Legal, doctor Claudio Molina Fraga, e integrada por los doctores Julio Veas, Tomás Tobas y Alberto Teke (legista de Investigaciones) —todos tanatólogos— está investigando las identificaciones correspondientes. Estas se han visto dificultadas dado que la mayor parte de los cadáveres se reducían a un montón de piezas óseas totalmente esparcidas. El *"armado"* de los esqueletos es, entonces, un proceso lento: **"La identificación es totalmente posible, pero requiere un trabajo largo y minucioso"**, señaló Claudio Molina.

Mientras tanto, hay datos que se manejan. Un personero del Instituto Médico Legal declaraba el 19 de diciembre que los cadáveres databan de dos fechas. Unos, de fines de 73, principios del 74; los otros, de hace apenas dos años. Aunque hasta entonces, los expertos habían coincidido en señalar que estos correspondían a unos cuatro años atrás, el nuevo informe se basaba en el distinto estado de descomposición de los cuerpos, que en unos casos presentaban restos óseos sin tejidos blandos y en otros, los huesos aún se encuentran adheridos por cartílagos y otros tejidos más resistentes. Aunque este último dato no ha sido confirmado oficialmente por el Instituto Médico Legal, las fechas señaladas vienen a coincidir con los dos años en que se registró una mayor cantidad de detenidos-desaparecidos: 1974 y 1976.

Pero aún faltan muchos estudios. La composición de la tierra, por ejemplo,

Ministro en visita Adolfo Bañados

Figure 2.4. "Lonquén: Who Are These Dead?" First article about Lonquén in *Solidaridad* 62 (January 1979). Photos by Helen Hughes. Black and white. Fundación de Documentación y Archivo de la Vicaría de la Solidaridad.

photograph: Chimney escape where the bodies were found under layers of concrete." If the captions seemed to suggest that photography had, in a way, arrived late to the "Site of the Incident"—as indicated earlier, the forensic investigation would determine that five years had passed since the fifteen men had been buried alive there—what can we say about the relationship between the title of the article and the photographs? Who were "these dead" that the photographs *did not show*? How can one begin to consider the relation between photograph and referent when the referent—"these dead"—cannot be photographed? In fact, can we designate as "referent" something that, as Cadava says, "can never be seen within the image?"

In *Images in Spite of All*, Georges Didi-Huberman observes that we tend to ask "too much or too little of the image."[58] When we ask too much of the images, they become immediately *inadequate*—"what we see [. . .] is still little in comparison to what we know"—and *inexact*.[59] When we ask too little of them, we either "immediately [relegate] them to the sphere of the *simulacrum* [. . .] [excluding] them from the historical field as such, or we demote them to the sphere of the *document* [. . .] [severing] them from their phenomenology, from their specificity, and from their very substance."[60] The photographs of the Lonquén ovens are strange visual objects; as forensic documents, they are inadequate: their informative content is scant, even rough. Let's take, for instance, one of the photographs depicting the top pit of the ovens, published with the article in *Solidaridad* and also in Pacheco's *Lonquén*. Their con*text*—the captions in both the article and the book—indicate that the image shows one of the chimneys, but it could just as well be showing a ravine, a well, the entrance to an artisanal mine, or a mushroom cloud.[61] The absolute blacks and whites produced by the shadows and lights are highly contrasted. Because the copy of this photograph is not completely focused, it is not possible to distinguish with clarity the elements at the bottom: are they rocks or dry bushes?

Those who were able to see the oven site up close recall the sinister aspect of the ovens and their dark mouths. Santibañez's testimonial piece, for one, described the macabre vision awaiting them at the site, beginning with the construction that enclosed the ovens, "impressive in and of itself: a tall tower of square stones, with a corner about to break loose, its naked gray appearance has something medieval. Below, at ground level, one next to the other, like sinister fauces, the wide-open black mouths of the ovens: from one of them the first human remains were vomited."[62] Hughes was also affected by this vision. The photographs she took of the site repeat shot after shot, from different angles and distances, visions of the ovens, their chimneys, and their dark mouths (described as "fauces" both by Santibañez and by Gonzalo Díaz ten years later).

The display of these photographs in *Solidaridad* heightened the ominous aspect of the ovens. This ominousness is emphasized in the frontal close-up of one of the ovens reproduced in high contrast at the center of the first page of the article. That large dark spot—the fauces—seems to be hiding something; it is a mystery. This darkness is repeated in different sizes in every photo. These frontal close-ups are penetrating. They are a powerful reflection of loss and ruin. The cavernous black holes that puncture each photograph conjure the (disavowed) actuality of forced disappearances. Indeed, the image of the black mouth of the oven will keep emerging, resonating as an echo in subsequent *Solidaridad* issues and also in the cover of Pacheco's *Lonquén*. Meanwhile, the name "Lonquén" would be evoked a few weeks later, after the remains at Cuesta Barriga were found, and also over six years later, when remains inside La Veleidosa mine in Tocopilla—a town located in the north of the country—were found (the case was referred to in the opposition media as "El Lonquén de la pampa").

The photograph of the ruin, Cadava suggests, points toward "'the ruin of ruin,' the emergence and survival of an image that, telling us it can no longer show anything, nevertheless shows and bears witness to what history has silenced, to what, no longer here, and arising from the darkest nights of memory, haunts us, and encourages us to remember the deaths and losses for which we remain, still today, responsible."[63] Trauma has been described many times as a break, a fissure, or a vacuum. I think of these notions as I ponder what the photographs display and do not display on their surfaces, and also as I consider the photographs' display in the article. The photographs of the Lonquén ovens have always called my attention for their overwhelming visual economy, their apparent simplicity. These photos have an undeniable iconic and symbolic power. This power is not despite but because of their apparent insufficiencies, something that becomes already apparent in the *Solidaridad* article—the photographs' first public display.

In a way, it is through the *repetition* of a series of photographs depicting the very same elements (oven, chimney, and dark mouth) where the Real pushes through. I am referring here to the Lacanian Real, to what is traumatic, what is repressed.[64] If the photographs of the ovens provoked and touched *Solidaridad*'s readers, calling their (and my) attention, they did so by means of insistence. The contrasts between blacks and whites, or lights and shadows, reveal on the surface of each image that element which must remain latent. By repeating the darkness emanating from these abandoned ovens—the sinister fauces at the center of these ruins of stone, ash, limestone, and death—the photographs published in *Solidaridad* told their readers (and also tell us) that they can't show anything, anything but darkness. In a way, the dark spots point toward that which cannot be shown: the remnants of fifteen men murdered by state organisms, which remained illegally buried for five years. In a sort of metaphoric displacement, the photographs continue to hide that which can only remain hidden, something that resists being revealed: an amalgam of human remains, ashes, and stones (see fig. 2.5).

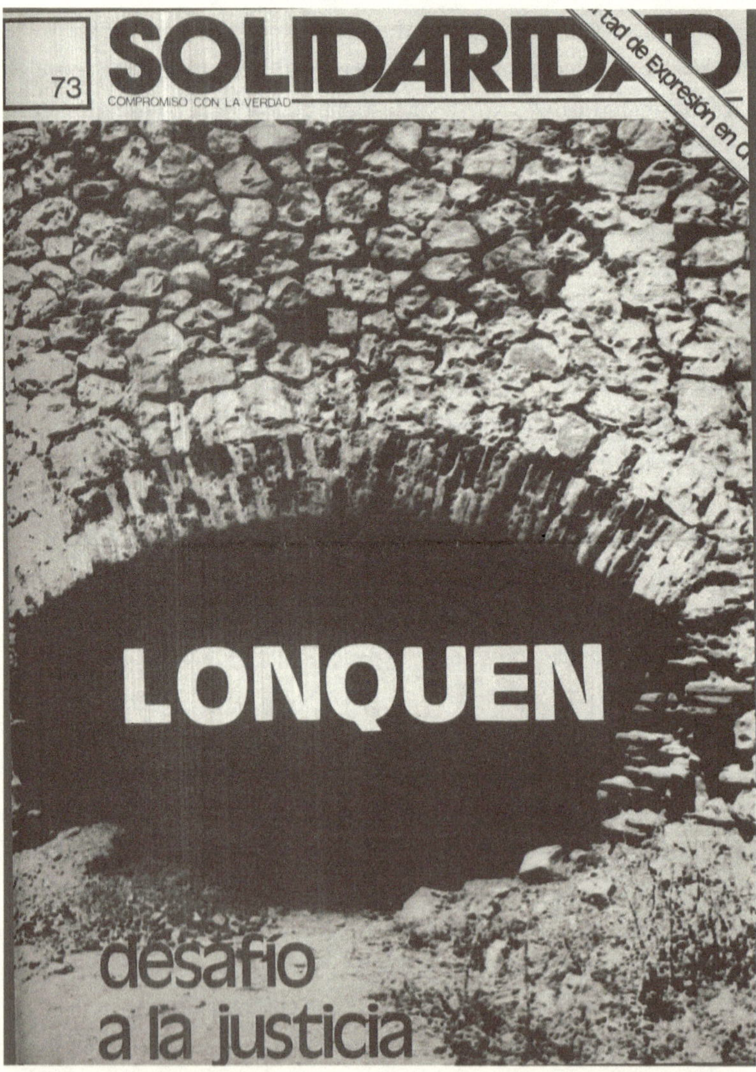

Figure 2.5. "Lonquén. A Challenge to Justice." Cover of *Solidaridad* 73 (1979). Black and white. Fundación de Documentación y Archivo de la Vicaría de la Solidaridad.

In April 1979, Judge Bañados Cuadra finished his investigation. After working four months under intense public scrutiny, the judge established the testimonies given by the policemen were false and that they were responsible for the deaths of the fifteen men they had detained on October 7, 1973. Since all the accused were policemen, the judge recused himself, and the case was taken over by a military court. In July, a military prosecutor ordered the incarceration of all the accused, but in August, a military court resorted to the 1978 Amnesty Laws—established by the military regime to protect itself—and acquitted the policemen responsible for the murders. A martial Court confirmed this ruling in October of the same year.

In late March 1980—months after the case had closed, and soon after the obliteration of the ovens—the attorney of Editorial Aconcagua, Claudio Orrego Vicuña, submitted a request to publish *Lonquén*, the book edited by Pacheco. In the Introduction, Pacheco stated that the book was "the *precise transcription* of the most important parts of the process"—a legal process whose file, as the author-editor also clarified, "comprises five volumes and 1850 folios."[65] This "precise transcription" included different kinds of texts: copies of the final reports submitted by Judge Godoy, Judge Bañados Cuadra, and the Military Tribunal; copies of the depositions made by those who participated in or saw the exhumations (some of which I reviewed earlier); copies of the depositions made by the policemen involved in the arrests, by relatives of people claimed as disappeared in the area of Talagante, by Lonquén neighbors, by one of the owners of Fundo Naguayán, and by different experts: transcriptions of the legal claim submitted by the plaintiffs (the victims' relatives) to Judge Bañados Cuadra. These copies of declarations, reports, depositions, and statements, referred, in turn, to other documents (folios, dentists' reports, minutes, letters, photographs, x-rays, etc.) not included—or rather, not transcribed, not copied, and not reproduced—in the book.

The request to publish *Lonquén* was promptly denied by the military. Brigadier General Humberto Gordon Rubio, in charge of making the initial decision regarding publication, stated in his prohibition that a book about a "case already known to the public [did] not contribute to the fraternal coexistence of Chileans."[66] Why prohibit the publication of *Lonquén* if the case was already closed and, as Gordon himself stated, it was "already known to the public"? After Gordon's decision, Pacheco and Genaro Arriagada (one of Editorial Aconcagua's directors) filed a *recurso de amparo* (appeal) with the Court of Appeals in Santiago. The appeal was also denied. In their ruling, the judges also considered the Director of DINACOS Jorge Fernández Parra's opinion. A few sentences of Fernández Parra's statement provide an answer as to why publishing the book was prohibited:

> The publication of the work LONQUÉN [. . .] refers to the discovery of human remains [. . .] in an abandoned mine [. . .] The work reproduces verbatim—as the author states—the documents involved in the process [. . .] The very serious issue here is that the work attempts to rekindle the case, *to make the public hold it in their memory*; the names of the localities stand out in it in capital letters in order to draw attention *and to mark the reader*. Furthermore, relevance is given only to the negative and not to the authorities' version of the case, with the evident purpose of implicitly blaming them for what happened.[67]

According to Fernández Parra, *Lonquén* was unpublishable not because it attempted to disseminate documents hitherto unknown to the public—as one could have expected—but rather due to the intended *effect* of publishing such a work. In Fernández Parra's own words, the book aimed to "mark" readers, to make them "hold the case in their memories." Needless to say, Fernández Parra's objections were well founded: Pacheco's explicit aim was to reopen the forum. As the author-editor states in the book's Introduction, "I believe that the facts investigated are of such gravity that it is indispensable to make them known, in an absolutely objective way, through their verbatim transcription [. . .] so that the public opinion knows about them and [people can] form their own judgments."[68]

If, as it has been argued, the document, as exemplum, never fully coincides with itself and is oriented toward the future, then *Lonquén* should be considered not only as a compilation of documents, but also a document in its own right. The condition of *Lonquén* as exemplum, as a document oriented toward the future, is already manifest in Fernández Parra's opinion. According to the DINACOS Director, *Lonquén* was not only the exact reproduction of documents pertaining to the case ("the work reproduces verbatim . . ."), but also, additionally, it operated as a catalyzer of the case ("the work attempts to rekindle the case"). This condition also becomes apparent in Pacheco's Introduction in the book, in which he asserts, "I trust that knowing what happened in Lonquén may serve, in some way, so that similar events do not happen again in Chile."[69] Both Pacheco's explanation for wanting to publish the book and Fernández Parra's motive for denying its publication offer eloquent formulations of what a document is, and above all, what a document does.

It must be said that the regime's attempt to stop the circulation of *Lonquén* was, to some extent, unsuccessful: a brief note published in *La Segunda* in 1981 stated that the first edition of the *Lonquén* book "had sold out anyway," despite the prohibition.[70] How was this possible? *Lonquén* was the first book in a series titled "Documents for the Truth," published by Editorial Aconcagua and the Chilean Human Rights Commission. Editorial Aconcagua had a reading club, which had 1,500 subscribers. The readers club system not only allowed independent publishers to keep operating at a time when bookstores struggled to remain open, but also—and perhaps more importantly—it fostered the circulation of books through informal channels that the dictatorship had failed to eliminate. The appeal of becoming a member of Aconcagua's reading club was to be able to have books that could not circulate in the formal market because they expressed views opposed to the military regime.[71]

Pacheco wanted to publish *Lonquén* so that the civil community could read, see, and judge for itself, so that the public could learn from this horrible crime. This intention would come to fruition in 1983, when *Lonquén* was republished. The second edition did circulate in the formal market. Besides the documents mentioned above, the second edition included the documents related to the prior censorship of the book. This supplementary frame—the documents pertaining to the book's ban were presented in the book's preface—added extra layers of meaning to the documents assembled for *Lonquén*'s first edition. In 1983, the average Chilean reader/spectator opened the book already knowing that inside were not only important legal documents—forbidden documents—but also memories.

A remarkable aspect of *Lonquén* was it showed photographs that had not been published before. The book included abundant visual evidence—mostly reproductions of the photos taken by Hughes during the first reconnaissance visit as well as a few photos taken by Navarro during the exhumations. Besides the photos of the ovens previously published in *Solidaridad*, the book included several photos of some of the evidence collected inside and outside the ovens: bones, skulls, stones and pieces of fabric with hair attached, and a bullet cap. These photos were displayed as full-page spreads ("to leave a trace in the reader's memory," the Director of DINACOS would opine) and organized in such a way that they coincide, in most cases, with the textual contents of the opposite page. For example, the photograph of the bullet cap appeared facing the transcript of the ballistic analysis conducted by the Police Technical Laboratory submitted to Judge Bañados Cuadra.

Pacheco states that *Lonquén* is "absolutely objective." As mentioned earlier, the texts included are described as the "precise transcription" of the documents located in the case file. What about the photographs? These images are meant to be precise visual transcriptions—visual records—of the evidence found, and the photographs' captions, in turn, precise transcriptions of the photographs. Indeed, the photographs' captions describe very matter-of-factly the location (of the mine and ovens) and the evidence found there (skulls, bullets, remains).

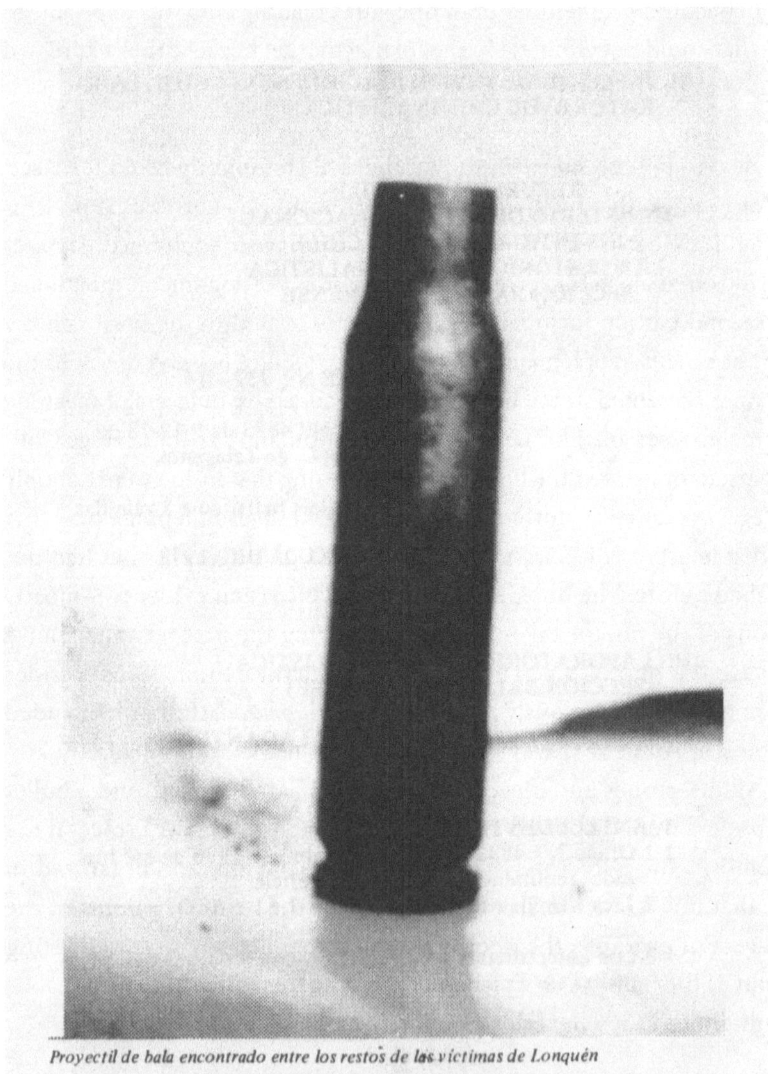

Figure 2.6. Bullet casing found at the Lonquén site. Credit: Luis Navarro Vega. December 1978. Black and white. Published in Máximo Pacheco's *Lonquén*.

These captions signal (or rather, attempt to signal) that which the photographs show, allegedly, in an unmistakable manner: "Bullet found among the remains of the victims of Lonquén;" "Skulls found in the limestone mine at Lonquén;" "Skull of a victim of Lonquén with remains of scalp;" "Remains found in the limestone mine of Lonquén;" "Superior cavity of the Lonquén ovens, blocked after the victims were buried."

In the captions' matter-of-factness, I recognize an intention—a forensic intention—of presenting the photograph as evidence, as "precise transcription." *Lonquén* constructs the photographs as visual evidence; or, to put it differently, the book and the captions make the photographs *evident*. The captions identify, single out what the photographs, supposedly in a "direct" and "simple" way, are showing us. One caption informs the spectator/reader that what appears depicted in the photograph is a bullet cap found among the victims. I look at the photographs. I know what I must be seeing because the caption is telling me what it is: this is a bullet; here you see the cave of the oven. Yet the photographs are ambiguous: the "bullet cap" seems to be standing in the middle of nowhere, in a sort of deserted landscape (see fig. 2.6). The photograph of the oven is also abstract, almost nonfigurative (see fig. 2.7). Further, because the photographs can't "show it all," the captions also tell the spectator/reader about other times, other actions, not visible on the surface of these photos: for example, the fact that the bullet *was found* among the victims' remains, or that the top furnace shaft *was blocked* after the victims were buried. These captions, in a somewhat paradoxical move, rather than asserting the transparency of the photograph as document—inasmuch as the photographic document performs a visual corroboration, as unequivocal proof—reveal that "the image is always itself an enigma, demanding that we articulate what it really shows."[72]

Because bones and things "do not speak for themselves," Keenan and Weizman suggest, "there is a need for a translation, mediation, or interpretation between the 'language of things' and that of the people."[73] Keenan and Weizman are referring here to the relation between the forensic scientist and the evidence she presents to the forum. It is she, as forensic expert, who makes the bones speak. Her status as expert is vital in that the "evidentiary value depends at least in part, on the authority (probability) of the expert who publicly deciphers it."[74] Even though Pacheco does not attempt to "translate" or "interpret" the evidence, to some extent, the book does so. *Lonquén* acts as a mediator between the language of things and the language of people. In the moment of the findings, the photographs served to protect and fixate the human remains. Meanwhile, in the

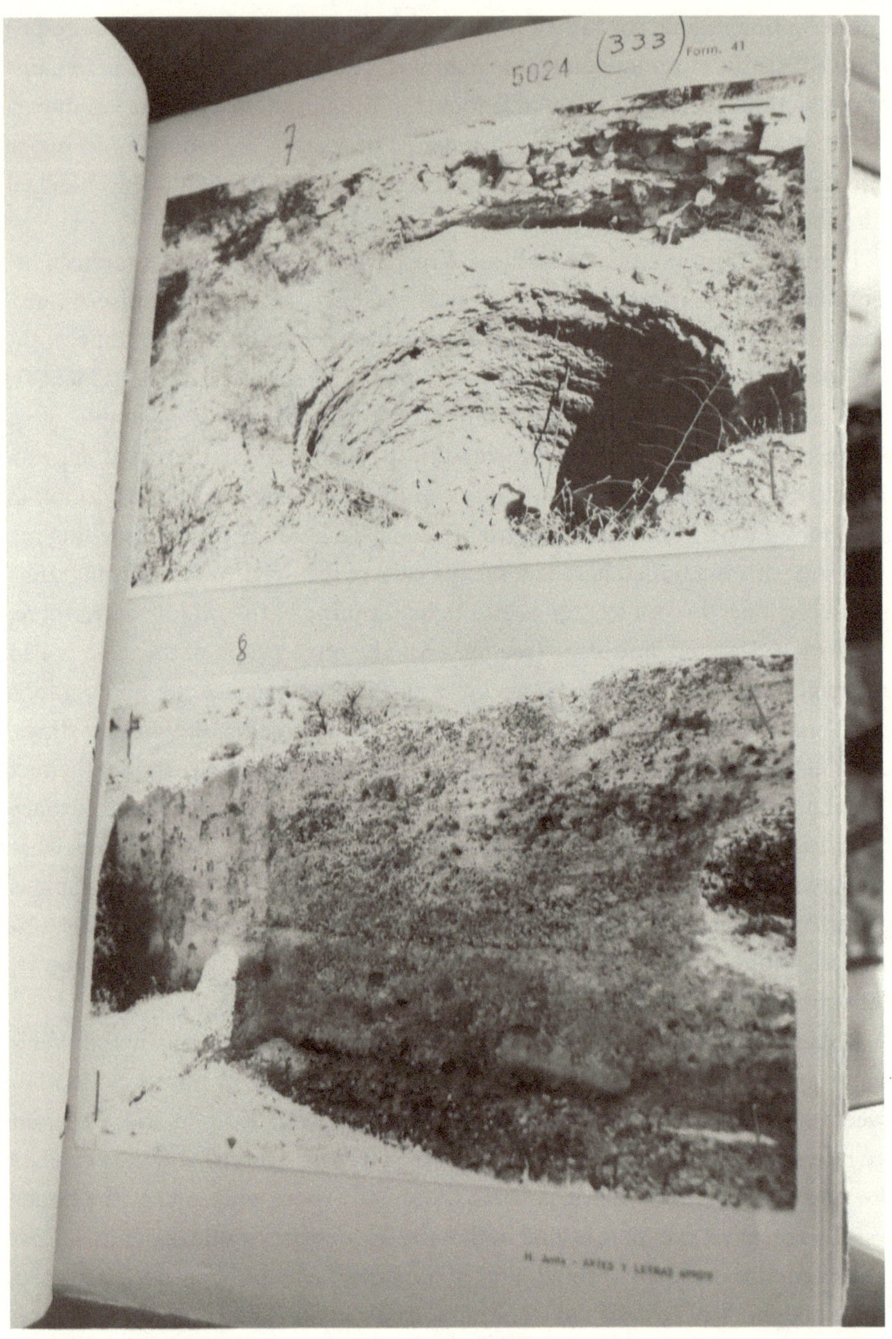

Figure 2.7. Top crater and sidewall of one of the Lonquén furnaces. Credit: Helen Hughes. December 1978. Black and white. Court of Appeals Legal Archive. Photograph: Ángeles Donoso Macaya. (Also published in Máximo Pacheco's *Lonquén*).

moment of the presentation and dissemination of the "evidence" to the forum, via photographs, it is the captions and *Lonquén* (the book as a whole) that fixate and secure—although never completely—the visual content of the photographs.

Documentary Echoes of Lonquén

Until November 1978, the Lonquén ovens held the memory of an infamous crime; a few months later, they became a sacred place—a site of mourning and commemoration. In February 1979, the Vicaría organized the first *romería* (pilgrimage) to the ovens. Carrying flowers, a procession of over 1,500 people walked three miles—from the church in the town of Lonquén to the site of the ovens—to commemorate and pay homage to the victims who had been killed and buried there. A massive wooden cross was placed atop the ovens. Vicar Cristián Precht gave a poignant homily and sanctified the site. The *romerías* became a destabilizing force for the military regime. So much so, that in September 1979, after the case had already been dismissed, a piece of land that included the ovens was transferred to a private mining company. The new owners set up a huge black gate locking the access road and even placed a guard so family members could no longer visit the site. Meanwhile, after enduring for over five years the excruciating process of searching and waiting for answers, and ultimately finding their loved ones dead, family members were denied the opportunity to give their relatives' remains proper burial. On September 11—of all days—the military court ordered the remains to be returned to the relatives. Two days later—on the night before the funeral services were to be held—this decision was reversed: the remains of the victims were to be taken from the Medical Legal Institute and thrown into a common grave in a cemetery in Isla de Maipo. On Friday, September 14, family members, together with 4,000 attendants, waited in vain at the Recoleta church for the coffins to arrive.[75]

In his study of Lonquén, Stern describes the whole affair in terms of a dynamic "memory knot." He argues, "what made the Lonquén affair so unsettling from an officialist viewpoint was not only its exposure of the truth of disappearances and their cover-up by the state. The Lonquén affair turned into an incredibly dynamic memory knot: it mobilized people and symbols in ways that threatened to escalate and escape control."[76] One of these symbols was the abandoned mine itself, with its tall towers and its dark-mouths ovens. Indeed, as if all of the measures to obliterate the Lonquén case from the public forum had not been enough—they weren't, as I hope to have shown in this chapter—in

March 1980, the Lonquén ovens were blasted, allegedly to begin a new mining development. Regarding the different oppressive measures devised by the military regime since the news of the finding became public, including the theft of the bodies and the complete destruction of the ovens, Stern argues: "By mid-1980, the memory box of Lonquén had been forcibly closed. Knots on the social body that might galvanize outrage had been largely destroyed: no more ovens, no more bodies, no more *romerías*."[77]

The *romerías* and the obliteration of the ovens are at the center of Ignacio Agüero and Grupo Memoria's *No Olvidar* (Not to Forget). In February 1979, when he was still studying film, Agüero heard about the pilgrimage to the Lonquén ovens organized by the Vicaría. He went there and was introduced to the Maureira family, who had lost five of its members. Purísima Elena Muñoz (Sergio Maureira's wife) told Agüero that they went every Sunday to put flowers at the ovens. Agüero imagined these ovens as Chile's giant *animita* [shrine]. As Agüero puts it: "I convinced the family and I filmed them walking. It was on a Sunday. A month after the film shoot ended, the ovens were blasted, I read it in a newspaper [. . .] I told myself, I had to make a film to be viewed and to linger. I filmed little by little, it took me over a year; my idea was to preserve the image of them walking."[78]

"This film is part of the memory of Chile. These images search out images that are beginning to blur," says a voiceover while a camera follows the Maureiras in their weekly procession toward the ovens. The documentary replicates the unhurried pace of the women's ritualistic walk. A solemnity and slowness infuse all of the sequences, even those in which the camera shows only forensic documents (diagrams, reports, and photographs). Indeed, *Not to Forget*, just like the photographs discussed in this chapter, takes us again and again to the site of the ovens, before and after their destruction. In the sequence that surveys the site after the implosion, the camera stays very close; we can almost touch the pile of rocks, feel the different shapes of the ruin. But *Not to Forget* does not end with the images of ruin. Rather, it opts to conclude with images taken prior, when the ovens were still in place and the Maureiras could still walk there to mourn their dead. In the closing sequence, in what can be described as an eloquent reflection on the materiality of the documentary image, we see the Maureiras looking at photographic slides of one of their last mourning rituals at the ovens.[79]

There is no doubt that the concerted measures to materially obliterate the site and the victims of the crime, and even the chance to publicly remember them, are as significant as they are horrendous—no doubt whatsoever. But, was "the memory box of Lonquén" ever really closed? As we have seen, the Lonquén case left a significant trail of documentary images, photographic traces that keep resonating and reverberating as if they were echoes. If we listen to and follow these documentary echoes, the visual and sonorous traces of Lonquén, we realize that the Lonquén memory box has never been closed, that, on the contrary, it keeps expanding and resonating. How could it not keep resonating if nearly thirty years passed between the discovery of human remains and their proper identification?[80] How could they not keep resonating if forty years went by before the policemen involved in the abduction and disappearance of fifteen men were finally convicted?[81]

I speak of documentary echoes, of sonorous and visual traces, because the first I learned of the Lonquén photographs and the ovens' destruction was in *La ciudad de los fotógrafos*. In one of the initial sequences of the film, the camera follows a man as he walks along a dirt road. When the man stops, he stares at what appears to be an empty field. But as the camera moves away from the subject to frame what he is looking at, I, the spectator, realize that in that empty field there used to be something. What was there? The montage, by means of a photograph, provides the answer. The man around whom this sequence revolves—Navarro—holds in his hands a large photograph he had taken at the site many years earlier. An overwhelming sense of loss haunts the entire sequence. "How everything changes," is the first thing Navarro says upon arriving at the empty site: one moment, I see the photographer walking, wandering almost, amidst some ruins; at another moment, I see him trying to find the exact position and angle from which he took the photo he carries in his hand. When he finally pinpoints the location, the photo slowly begins to fill the frame. When frame and photo finally coincide, a flash is accompanied by the sound of a camera shutter. Navarro's photo, retaken in the documentary's sequence, does not frame an empty field; on the contrary, I see many people in the scene (see fig. 2.8). Some people appear standing atop the ovens; others appear standing or seated at the bottom of the hill, facing the ovens.[82] The photograph's reframing reveals, in the sequence, the existence of different spectral layers that haunt this field—the ruin of the abandoned limestone mine and the traces of the horrible crime committed there. It was this photograph, with its doublings and reframings, that instigated the research for this chapter and that has guided my reading throughout. The photograph of the romería performs in the documentary as the visual trace of the stories that this (now empty) field conjures.

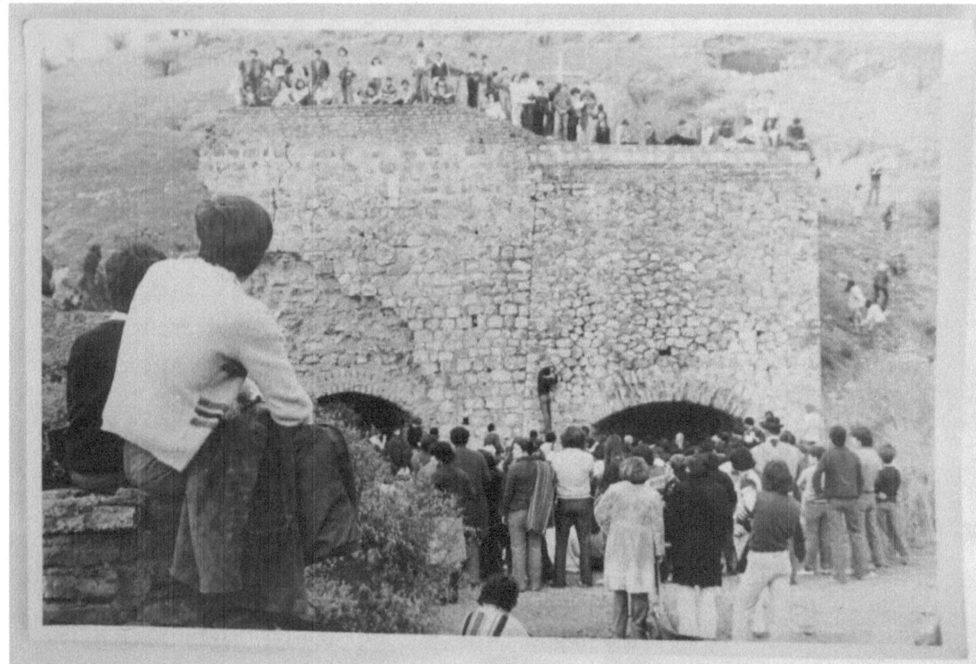

Figure 2.8. Lonquén's first *romería*. Credit: Luis Navarro Vega. February 1979. Black and white. Luis Navarro Vega's personal archive.

Because photographs are commonly used and conceived of as visual evidence in the legal realm, there is a depth of meaning in the forensic photographic archive that has not yet been explored. As we have seen, the photographs Hughes and Navarro took in Lonquén in late 1978 functioned from the very beginning as supplementary forensic evidence. Navarro was, in fact, ordered to produce a set of photographs that could stand as trustworthy visual witnesses of the human remains and objects found at the "Site of the Incident." Even though they were not immediately displayed, the existence of the photographs was enough to validate and protect the materials found as forensic evidence. An effect of their performance as forensic documents, the photographs came to substitute for the evidence: in the event that the actual, material, evidence was destroyed or altered, the photos would be there as alternates, as supplements.

The transformation of the photographs into forensic evidence becomes apparent once these images began to be disseminated. As I have shown, the human remains, the fabric with pieces of hair attached, the stones, the skulls, and the bullet cap were never presented before the public forum; what was presented and contextualized by other documents related to the case as visual forensic evidence were the *photographs* of the human remains, of the fabric with pieces of hair attached, of the skulls, and the bullet cap. Thus, once they materialized in the public forum, the documentary weight of these photos increased even more: in the pages of *Solidaridad* and of *Lonquén*, the photos became evidence. This transformation was the result of an aesthetic movement, the effect of their forensic display—the photographs were presented, constructed, as forensic evidence.

Used first as forensic documents, these photos became symbolic documentary traces of the crime of forced disappearances. The photos taken by Hughes at the entrance of the ovens, with their overwhelming visual economy, opened up a political space precisely because of what, in their insistence, in their repetition, they were unable to show. My reading of the photos of the ovens published in *Solidaridad* emphasizes both the serial arrangement of the photos on the page and the organization of the elements on the surface of the photos—the total blackness of the mouth hole, the lights and shadows—in the visual elaboration of the signifier "Lonquén" as a collective trauma.

The different forms of display and concurrent displacements and transformations sustained by the Lonquén photographs reveal that even though they are related to a unique (and macabre) event, their context of production does not determine their meanings once and for all. As Cadava suggests in his reading of Benjamin, the fact that photographs are historically marked, that they can be read as historical indexes, "does not mean that they 'belong to a specific time'—the time of the camera's click, for example—but that they only "enter into legibility [*Lesbarkeit*] at a specific time.""[83] The Lonquén photographs, we can say along with Benjamin, are not definitive traces of an already gone and completed past. The meanings of these photos are expanded and transformed every time they are shown, reframed, contextualized, or discussed. By contemplating the photographs and reflecting on what they (forcibly) leave out of frame, repeat tirelessly, or are unable to focus on, we can begin to respond to that which is not "presently visible in the image."

Echo is commonly invoked as that figure destined to repeat what she hears, with no possibility of variation (something similar could be said of documents, at least of photographic documents). Jacques Derrida, however, insists that in Echo's response one can hear "something other than what she seems to be saying. Although she repeats, without simulacrum, what she just heard, another simulacrum slips in to make her response something more than a mere reiteration."[84]

Everything in this famous scene, Derrida notes, "turns around a call *to come*."[85] Echo's response is a declaration of love that transforms a mere repetition into a correspondence. Echo's response, like the presentation of the evidence in front of the forum, is without guarantees. The documentary echoes of Lonquén repeat and insist, and they do so from a space located "at the intersection of repetition and the unforeseeable."[86] A retired miner—an extravagant old man—went to a priest and told him in confession that he had discovered an illegal cemetery. The priest asked him if he could breach the secrecy of confession and repeat what he had heard to his superiors. These first whispers triggered everything else: the discovery's corroboration, the conformation of an ad-hoc committee, the formal complaint, the exhumation, the forensic investigation, the unbearable wait of the victims' relatives, and the media frenzy. As in other cases that ensued—the illegal cemetery found at Lonquén would be the first of many others—the process of individuation and recognition of the human remains found put into circulation countless photographs, testimonies, objects, and documents of all kinds (dental x-rays, order detentions, letters, pieces of clothing, etc.). Many of these documents, including the photographs taken by Hughes and Navarro, started to itinerate as soon as the case began, and they continue to do so today.

3

EMERGENCE OF A FIELD

Because even if it's true that times are tough, this situation is not perpetual, and it is precisely what people do, all people together, that which determines the dynamics of situations. In this sense, we must start by what is ours, that which defines us as a group: the photographic activity.

—Luis Weinstein, *Punto de Vista*

New formations can "emerge" only when there are frames that establish the possibility of that emergence.

—Judith Butler, *Frames of War*

On March 11, 1981, agents of the Central Nacional de Informaciones (CNI) abducted photographer Luis Navarro while he was doing a photographic assignment for the Vicaría. This was not the first time a photographer was being arrested without reason—photographers began to be persecuted, abducted, tortured, and disappeared or killed in the weeks immediately following the coup.[1] What makes Navarro's arrest noteworthy is that it was concomitant to another significant event, one that changed the political, social, and cultural field for decades to come. On March 11, 1981, the new Chilean Constitution entered into effect, and General Augusto Pinochet assumed the presidency of the Republic. The alleged legality of all of this must be restated: a "majority" on an illegitimate referendum held, emblematically, on September 11, 1980, approved the Constitution. Moreover, the Constitution itself included a temporary and transitory legislation (*legislación de emergencia*) for the following eight years.[2] The last chapter of the Constitution included "Transitory Provisions" that stipulated that "the current President, Commander in Chief of the Army Augusto Pinochet Ugarte, will continue to serve as President of the Republic" for eight years. Despite Pinochet's new title, "President of the Republic," the civic-military regime would continue to be perceived by most people as eminently autocratic and repressive. Moreover, since the opposition knew the regime's "repressive legality [had emerged] from an 'urgent' (*emergencia*) or 'transitory' legislation," which the judicial power condoned, the mistrust and the rejection of government institutions also affected, though not in the same fashion, the judicial power.[3]

Navarro was supposed to cover the official events organized to celebrate this major event, including a special *Te Deum* held at Santiago's National Cathedral.[4] According to Navarro's recollections, he and his colleagues had come up with a cover for *Solidaridad* 110 (corresponding to the second half of March), consisting of a photograph of Pinochet entering La Moneda Palace, with the headline, "A constitution conceived turning its back on the people" (the photo would have shown Pinochet's back).[5] Navarro managed to take the photographs, but lost them all because the agents who arrested him confiscated his film.[6] Navarro was held incommunicado for five days; he was tortured and drugged. He was released on March 15, just a day before *Solidaridad* 110 was released. The cover of *Solidaridad* ended up being a photo of La Moneda Palace, but the photo looks like a snapshot, as if it had been made in haste. Considering how much dedication typically was put into these covers, the photo seems to suggest, or indicate, that something is off. La Moneda is not centered in the photo (a third of it is cut off the frame), and the scene also seems random: a few passersby, a police officer, and a big truck are captured inside the frame. Some of the people in the background appear to be looking up at the Palace, and others simply walk by. The headline reads, "Constitución y derechos humanos: ¿lo legal o lo justo?" (Constitution and Human Rights: What Is Legal or Just?).

The question posed on the cover began to introduce *Solidaridad* readers to Navarro's violent arrest. The very first segment in the magazine, dedicated to relevant issues occurred during the previous two weeks, was dedicated in full to the events of March 11. Under the headline "March 11: Guarantees suspended," the note explained that the transitory provisions that had come into effect with the new Constitution significantly circumscribed individual rights. The note underscored the "long interim provisions" and questioned the existence of "two simultaneous states of exception." Even more significant to our discussion, the note brought attention to the direct correlation between, and the paradox implied in, the coming into effect of the transitory provisions of the new Constitution and the arrest of the photographer:

> On the same day the transitory provisions came into effect [. . .] a staff of our Vicaría de la Solidaridad—photographer Luis Navarro—was arrested without it being clear under what legal provision his arrest [fell] [. . .] The officials gave conflicting versions. While some said that the transitory provision 24 had been applied, others argued that Article 4 of the Constitution, which referred to the state of siege, had been applied to this case.[7]

The note underscored that Navarro's arrest was the first to happen under the new Constitution. Using as case studies the photographer's arrest and that of Gerardo Espinoza at the Cementerio General (Espinoza had been Minister of the Interior during Allende's term), the note concluded: "Only these two commented measures—the cases of Navarro and Espinoza—allow us to ask ourselves to what extent civil, individual, and social rights are effectively guaranteed by the new Constitution." A statement signed by the Vicaría, included below this news segment, condemned the arbitrariness of it all—that is, the fact that Navarro had been arrested for no clear reason, held incommunicado, and finally released without charges. While the Vicaría's statement did not fail to acknowledge the fact that the arrest of its photographer was "part of a known history," it also underscored that this was "not just another case: Lucho was arrested the very day the new Constitution came into force and General Augusto Pinochet was sworn in as President of the Republic."

"Both the doing and the suffering of an epoch suppose their regime of light. Likewise, all that is thought in an epoch, all the ideas of an epoch, suppose their regime of statements," says Gilles Deleuze in his lectures about Michel Foucault.[8] What Deleuze calls "the regime of light" is another name for the visual field—the space that enables, determines, and organizes (in other words, that *orients*) both the visible and the invisible. This chapter explores the discursive emergence of the field of photography during the dictatorship. As we shall see, this process is unavoidably related to the political and economic policies implemented by the civic-military dictatorship, including the permanent state of emergency implemented on March 11, 1981. I will consider how the concept of photographic field materialized in the discourses and how it was expanded amid pervasive precariousness, censorship, and intensified repression. The notion of "emergence" signals "the process of coming into being" or "coming into view;" the verb "to emerge" means to "become apparent or noticeable"; both words, as well as the notion of emergency, come from the Latin *emergere*, "become known, come to light." I can't help but point out these luminous coincidences: photography means the act of writing or drawing with light (we know this all too well); photographic practices can be thought of as materializations of what Deleuze calls the regime of light of an epoch; in Chile, the notion of the photographic field emerged—came to light—during the dictatorship. While the notion of emergence might suggest the idea of an origin or a first occurrence ("the process of coming into being, coming into light"), I do not mean to suggest that it is the photographic field in and of itself that emerged for the first time in the 1980s. More than indicating here the process of coming into being of the field, emergence signals rather the "sudden irruption" (like lightning striking), and subsequent iterations of, the notion of "photographic field" in the discourses.[9]

The establishment of the Asociación de Fotógrafos Independientes (AFI) (Independent Photographers Association) in June 1981 was a landmark in this regard. One of the main reasons that led a number of freelance photographers and photojournalists to assemble and organize as a guild was Navarro's illegal detention earlier that year.[10] AFI's primary goal was to ensure the safety and integrity of its members. Notwithstanding this critical task, AFI photographers also took upon themselves the task of fostering the photographic activity and disseminating photographic works from different parts of the country, both in Chile and abroad.[11] On occasions collaborating with people not associated to the AFI (photographers, artists, critics), AFI photographers developed a number of initiatives and publishing endeavors. In their publications, AFI photographers celebrated the reemergence of photographic activity, considered the difficulties hindering the achievements of various photographic initiatives (repression and censorship, absence of photography criticism, and lack of interest), attempted different forms of critical reflection, and offered reviews of exhibitions not covered in other media. The photographers also expressed their views regarding the precarious status of "Chilean photography" and insisted on the absolute necessity of thinking about photography, both in the national and Latin American context. Hence, amid constant harassment by the police, censorship imposed by the military and, to a considerable extent, despite the indifference toward documentary photography sustained by critics and academic circles, the photographic field began to be conceived as such by the photographers.

Statements, as Deleuze reminds us in his reading of Foucault, should be understood in relation to what they make possible. Like visibilities, statements are "the conditions for the unfolding of an entire network of ideas"—what is said and what is silenced or remains muted, what is understood and what is seen, what is ignored and what is hidden.[12] The regime of statements does not refer us to a person or a sovereign subject as the author of the speech, but corresponds rather to that anonymous "it is said/ they say" that proliferates and circulates in every epoch.[13] While photographers (and a few critics) are main actors of the story I tell in this chapter, the statements contained in the texts they wrote interest me more as expressions of a historical regime—"what was said" about the photographic field or about photography during the dictatorship—than as their subjective opinions or personal perspectives. In fact, I also consider as statements a series of nonsubjective practices—composition techniques and editing processes—that too made possible the unfolding of new ideas concerning the dissemination of photographs and the critical writing about photography. Still, while I acknowledge that we must not identify in this "it is said" any kind of personhood or subjective agency, I also bear in mind that at specific historical convergences, political practices and political subjects do emerge.[14]

I say this because not all publications shared the same vision regarding photographic activity. A few publications that also celebrated the development of photography as a profession, as a form of "self-expression," and even as a "hobby," did so without touching on any political matter. This "apolitical" or "unideologized" (read: pro-military, conservative) celebration of photography is most apparent in *Fotogente* (1980), the first magazine dedicated to photography that appeared during the dictatorship.[15] In its first issue, a large graphic text titled "Photography is . . ." presented to the readers the different attributes and uses of photography. While it is undeniable that photography has in fact many, many uses, the disparity and randomness of the list made of the whole endeavor a mere game, celebratory and innocent. According to *Fotogente*, photography can be used not only "to investigate," "record," "show," "create," "craft," "falsify," "criticize," "print," "study," and "lie," but also "to do harm," "commemorate love," "search for beauty," and even "overcome a sexual complex." The playful list, in a way, invites me (the reader) to play along: looking at the list, I can't help but think of yet more (random) photographic uses.

Fotogente appeared at a moment when photography was acquiring a major role in the public sphere, both as a form of propaganda and as a tool for denunciation. The magazine even published articles and essays with such titles as

"Presence of Press Photography in 1979," "The Current State of Contemporary Photography," and "Photography as a Historic Document." However, *Fotogente* did not make even one reference to the most immediate context. This omission should come as no surprise: *Fotogente* was approved, even praised, by people belonging to the most select circles and higher ranks of the military. A letter signed by Admiral José Toribio Merino, published in its entirety in the magazine's second issue, is testimony to this:

> I deeply appreciate the kind gesture you have made in sending me the first two issues of *Fotogente*, a magazine that provides evidence that there is interest in perfecting and exchanging technical and professional knowledge among the many photography aficionados. I take this opportunity to congratulate you most warmly for the excellent edition of this magazine that has come to satisfy a need felt by all those of us aficionados of this art-hobby. Besides wishing you the best of success in successive publications, I am pleased to reiterate the acknowledgment of my highest consideration and esteem.[16]

Merino describes himself as a cultist and an aficionado of this "art-hobby," photography. The correspondence is noteworthy. Lest we forget: Admiral Merino was second in command after Pinochet. As a member of the governing military junta, he was in charge of the economic sector and presided over the Economic Committee of the Council of Ministers. Merino's interest in photography had a material impact on the ulterior development of the field. As Claudia Donoso pertinently observes:

> Curiously, the dictatorship, in such an extreme situation, generated an unprecedented movement of great critical potential, paradoxically sponsored by the triumphant free-market of the so-called economic boom and, more precisely, by Admiral José Toribio Merino [. . .] The admiral was especially concerned with eliminating customs tariffs for cameras and equipment—perhaps to promote photography as a hobby. The freedom of imports democratized photography in Chile and contributed to the emergence of many amateurs who, coming from different sectors and fields of generalized marginality and later connecting to opposition media, have documented part of these years.[17]

Although I will not claim here that the dictatorship "generated" this movement of great critical potential—the photographic field—Donoso's observation acutely points to the definite and paradoxical material relationship between the civic-military regime's economic policies and the development of the field. It is undeniable that these economic policies contributed to the democratization of photography (before these measures were implemented, cameras were considered luxury items). This is why *Fotogente*, in Merino's words, also came to satisfy a need: until then, there had been no magazines specializing in photography. At the same time, the same economic measures that allowed for cameras and photographic equipment to become more affordable (but not cheap) and that help explain the appearance of photography magazines such as *Fotogente*, led the country to a severe economic crisis in 1982. Remarkably, and despite the economic crisis, not long after the publication of the first issue of *Fotogente*, a number of publications dedicated to photography (exhibition catalogues, newsletters, and photography books) began to surface. Unlike *Fotogente*, these publications recentered and underscored the political consequence of the practice of photography.

I recognize two concomitant perspectives or tendencies with respect to the field of photography in these publications: one perspective, which I call the synchronous view, surfaced amid the contingency and alongside various photographic initiatives emphasizing the day-to day-challenges, shortcomings, and achievements. This perspective is most noticeable in AFI's newsletter-turned-magazine *Punto de Vista* (1981–1990) and in the *Anuarios fotográficos chilenos* (1981 and 1982), also edited by AFI photographers. In the first part of the chapter I consider these publications. In the second part, I analyze two collective photographic publications that reflected on, in addition to being manifestations of, the state of emergency and the precarity that hampered the practices of photography and their milieu: *Ediciones económicas de la fotografia chilena* (Affordable Editions of Chilean Photography) (1983) and *El pan nuestro de cada día* (Our Daily Bread) (1986). The background of these collaborative publications is the pervasive economic crisis that reached a climax in 1982.

The second perspective, which I consider in the last part of the chapter, surfaces in two important critical accounts written at the end of the eighties: a curatorial text by Mario Fonseca in 1987 and Claudia Donoso's essay, quoted earlier, published in 1990. I consider the retrospective stance assumed by these critical perspectives. Even though these texts attempted to assess the field and its development (or lack thereof) over time, I argue that they are also part of the field they attempted to survey and are also affected by the urgency (and emergency) that circumscribed the photographic field. This is why I identify this second perspective as *quasi*-retrospective. Both the concurrent and the quasi-retrospective perspectives acknowledge the existence of a photographic field, an existence deemed precarious. This precarious existence surfaced in all the discourses as a deficiency the photographic field had to overcome in order to become autonomous—as if the photographic field could exist autonomously. When analyzing these discourses, my interest is not in pointing out their flaws or shortcomings, but rather in illustrating how the material conditions of production, in conjunction with prevailing ideas about "Photography," oriented the discursive formulation of the photographic field itself as a precarious and emergent field. The discursive emergence of the photographic field, an element that consistently stands out when reading different publications, is one of the most significant (and lasting) effects of the practices of photography that flourished in this period.

The Photographic Field: An Emergent Issue

What "was said" about the photographic field during the dictatorship? It was said that this was an "emergent," "still developing" field. It was said that, despite the variety of photographic initiatives (exhibitions, magazines, etc.), photographic works rapidly disappeared or "dissolved" in a precarious environment, circumscribed by lack of knowledge, interest, resources, and support. It was even said that there was "no history of Chilean photography." A few introductory examples: in "Fotografía chilena: proyecto actual, proyecto posible" (Chilean Photography: A Current Project, a Possible Project), the author (a photographer) claims, "If the field does not become more solid and consistent, photographic achievements will continue to dissolve into mediocrity."[18] The uncertain place of photography as a profession within the cultural field is also a recurrent topic: "In a developing country like ours, with its culture still forming, photographers, whose professions still do not have precise contours, must know how to determine and defend their place within society. Some media have the tendency to underappreciate photography professionals."[19] This statement establishes a linkage between the country's economic development and the development of the cultural field, an idea that surfaces in a wide range of texts; more importantly, the statement underlines the photographers' marginal place within the cultural field. Some statements address the need to defend both the photographers' trade and photography's place within the cultural field; other, more positive, statements praise the fact that "Chilean photography continues to expand. The lack of space, exhibitions, and material and institutional support has not been able to stop this strong creative image-producer movement. The 80s generation persists in its activity and innovation."[20]

The notion of photographic field emerged in the early eighties, striking the discourses like a bolt of lightning. Let's stay for a moment with this image of lightning striking to examine the notion of emergency. The word "emergency," like the word "emergence," comes from the Latin *emergere*, but denotes the occurrence of something unexpected, serious, and often dangerous. The notion of emergency makes us think of something urgent, requiring immediate action; an emergency also evokes the idea of a disaster or a catastrophe. In the legal realm, a "state of emergency" is declared in moments of crisis and generally involves the suspension of the constitution, political institutions, and/or regular legal procedures. At the same time, the "exceptional measures" implemented under a state of emergency—a "lawless state"—are enforced *as though* they had a legal backing. This is why Giorgio Agamben claims the state of emergency is the paradoxical legal form of what cannot have legal form as it denies the state of law.[21] If the state of emergency is a paradox impossible to resolve from a constitutional point of view, then Pinochet's 1980 Constitution and its appended "provisional measures" quite clearly illustrate Agamben's propositions. As indicated earlier, this set of "provisional measures" bequeathed extraordinary attributions to Pinochet as President of the Republic and instituted a permanent state of emergency for the rest of Pinochet's tenure (eight years). This is why the state of emergency and the generalized condition of precarity under the military dictatorship must be considered together. As Judith Butler argues, "it is not the withdrawal or absence of law that produces precariousness, but the very effects of illegitimate legal coercion itself, or the exercise of state power freed from the constraints of all law."[22] The notion of emergency, in this sense, conveys both that which emerges in the discourses—the notion of photographic field—as well as that which determines the practices of photography that emerged amid the state of emergency, the catastrophe imposed by the military.

What happened in Chile at this particular historical juncture with regard to the photographic field? The civic-military state, human-rights organizations, civilians, and cultural actors began to engage with photography in a way that had not occurred before. As discussed in previous chapters, organizations such as the Vicaría de la Solidaridad and the Agrupación de Familiares de Detenidos Desaparecidos incorporated portraits of the detained-disappeared in cases brought to justice; the Vicaría and other organizations also used photography to substantiate related claims (existence of clandestine communal graves, physical evidence of torture among survivors of prison camps, etc.). The dictatorship, in turn, proved relentless in its effort to control the flow of information: through the DINACOS, the regime did not cease to monitor and censor the circulation and publication of photographs (see chapter 4). Despite the censorship, photographers and photojournalists kept documenting and exposing instances of violence and repression as well as acts of civilian resistance.

Regarding the artistic field, while traditional photography criticism struggled to define what constituted art in the context of photography in more traditional terms—distinguishing, for instance, documentary uses and creative uses—the medium of photography was being incorporated into artistic practices and theorized anew by art critics, philosophers, and writers. These critical texts (most notably those of Claudia Donoso, Mario Fonseca, Ronald Kay, Enrique Lihn, Justo Pastor Mellado, Pablo Oyarzún, Nelly Richard, and Adriana Valdés) developed different formulations regarding the aesthetic and political implications of photography's incorporation into artwork.[23] These debates flourished in a continuous dialogue with the practices of those visual artists (Elías Adasme, Carlos Altamirano, Roser Bru, Víctor Hugo Codocedo, Eugenio Dittborn, Luz Donoso, Virginia Errázuriz, Hernán Parada, Catalina Parra, Lotty Rosenfeld, and Francisco Smythe, among others) who began incorporating photographic materials, archival photos, and even portraits of the detained-disappeared into their practices as a way of exposing and commenting on the conflicting uses of photography in the public space (photography as both a disciplinary and memorial medium). The integration of photography with artwork, a matter widely studied, encouraged in the Chilean context a series of debates about the relationships between the artwork, its reproducibility, and the political arena, the opposing dialectics of inscription and representation, the ideologies of the gaze, and the undermining of the notions of authorship and craftmanship, among other matters—in sum, a wholesale formulation of "the photographic condition" of the visual arts, as Nelly Richard aptly described it.

Punto de Vista (1981–1990)

Despite being more overlooked, AFI photographers were critical actors in the discursive emergence of the photographic field.[24] They did not stop at denouncing the absence of photography criticism; they did photography criticism. They didn't just lament the lack of spaces to exhibit photography or the marginality of documentary photography within the cultural field; they devised different ways and forms of critical commentary, put together collective exhibitions and colloquia, circulated translated excerpts of texts published in other media, and wrote about the local documentary photographic tradition. Likewise, in order to compensate for what they saw as a shortage of photography books (photo books are costly to produce), they devised strategies to circulate photographs in more affordable ways. Indeed, soon after the formation of the guild, AFI photographers began publishing a newsletter that was distributed to all AFI members. The texts published in *Punto de Vista* covered an array of aspects specific to the professionalization of photography under dictatorship in Chile, from the dangers faced by freelance photographers working on the streets to questions regarding fees associated with photographic works. *Punto de Vista* also aimed at promoting and disseminating documentary photography: photographic monographs of AFI photographers, articles about Chilean and international documentary photographers, and notes about exhibitions or topics related to the documentary tradition were published. Some issues of the magazine also addressed the shortcomings of photography criticism, denounced the censorship imposed on their members' work, and offered brief reviews and commentaries about exhibitions not covered in other media (see fig. 3.1).

In a context in which the urgency to document and denounce became prevailing, one of the most urgent reflections was that of the role of the photograph as a social document. In a short text aptly titled "Absence of Criticism: A Commentary," AFI photographers claim: "In Latin America, photography is closely related to History, the Social Document, and the testimony of LIFE. Somehow, photography comes to supplement the lack of information and of recent history."[25] To be sure, it is easy to recognize two presumptions here: it is not "Photography" altogether, but rather certain styles or photographic modes which can be characterized by their manifest social, historical, or testimonial content; moreover, the testimonial function of photography is not necessarily characteristic or more important in Latin America than in any other continent or region. At the same time, if in this text the photograph is defined primarily as a social document it is because in this specific geopolitical context, the lack of information is deemed inversely proportional to the overabundance of misinformation. In this brief "Commentary," AFI photographers also explain the conclusions at which they arrived after a number of talks regarding the "Lack

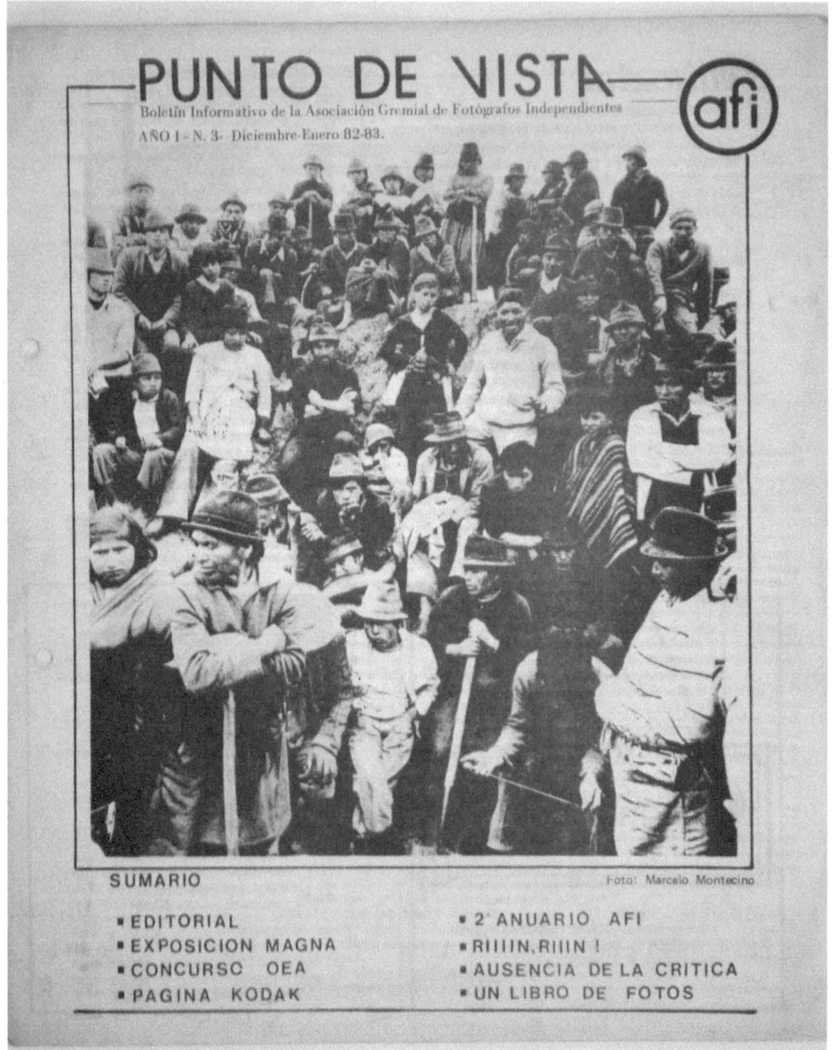

PUNTO DE VISTA
afi
Boletín Informativo de la Asociación Gremial de Fotógrafos Independientes
AÑO I - N. 3- Diciembre-Enero 82-83.

SUMARIO

Foto: Marcelo Montecino

- EDITORIAL
- EXPOSICION MAGNA
- CONCURSO OEA
- PAGINA KODAK
- 2° ANUARIO AFI
- RIIIIN.RIIIN !
- AUSENCIA DE LA CRITICA
- UN LIBRO DE FOTOS

Figure 3.1. Cover of *Punto de Vista* 3 (December 1982–January 1983; now defunct). Black and white. Luis Weinstein's personal archive.

of Criticism." Several questions were raised, including: "Is it possible for truthful criticism to exist within the prevailing system?," "To whom is this criticism actually addressed?," and "What is the function of criticism?" The problem was not that official media did not consider photographic works, nor that the space these media had intended for this kind of critical reflection was, to some extent, limited (although these were two issues of concern); the main issue was, rather, that the possibility of the existence of "real" criticism in the context of the dictatorship, "the prevailing system," was uncertain.

One pressing concern in this respect was censorship. Photography did not have an "official" space within the Museo Nacional de Bellas Artes (National Museum of Fine Arts), but the Foto Cine Club de Chile organized its annual *Salones de Fotografía*, which were held at the Museo. AFI photographers, at times, challenged the *Salones'* rules, charging that they were arbitrary, subjective, and, most importantly, conservative. When the *6° Salón de Verano de la Fotografía* (6th Photography Summer Salon) was held in December 1983, AFI photographers published a Commentary in *Punto de Vista* condemning the censorship of two photographs by Paz Errázuriz and another two photos by Jorge Brantmayer for allegedly being an affront to public morals. Given that Errázuriz's photographs had already been displayed at Galería Sur and one of Brantmayer's photos had been included and published in the *Segundo Anuario de Fotografía Chilena*, the *Salón*'s censorship was, to say the least, absurd. (Another incongruity was the fact that these banned photos, which were not displayed in the *Salón* as would have been expected, were listed in the catalogue—a *faux pas* emphasized not without sarcasm by the photographers.)[26]

The relationship among photography, artistic practices, and censorship was not the only theoretical concern tackled by *Punto de Vista*. AFI photographers also addressed the relationships between photography and media and photography and consumption. The inclusion of excerpts from Sontag's *On Photography* in the first issue of *Punto de Vista* illustrates this.[27] In the quotes selected, encapsulated in key words—consumerism, acquisition, and control—photography is defined as an "incomparable means to decipher behavior, to predict it, to infer it" and cameras are described as "both the antidote and the disease, a way of appropriating reality and making it obsolete." The quotes are not accompanied by a written commentary, but this does not mean that critical reflection is absent. Quite the contrary: critical reflection materializes in the selection of quotes itself, as well as in the organization and montage of quotes under different titles. There is a graphic, material relationship that unfolds between photography on the one hand, and the notions of consumerism, acquisition, and control on the other. Is it paradoxical that AFI photographers disseminated Sontag's formulations under such critical circumstances?[28] Not if one considers the photographers as critics. The aim of this note was to emphasize the concept of photographic uses and the notion that photography can be used both as a means of information and disinformation.

The precarity of the milieu is insinuated constantly in *Punto de Vista*. Most "Notas," "Comentarios," and "Anuncios" follow the same pattern: they underscore the potential condition of an initiative, just to signal the initiative's unavoidable limitations. An announcement regarding a potential "AFI Agency" is an example. While the idea was to underscore both the novelty of the initiative, the announcement also signaled the many challenges yet to be faced, some of them very concrete: "Our agency lacks infrastructure. We don't have an office or a telephone [. . .] In our country there are no photographic agencies. There is a dearth of private archives; they are small, disorganized, and incomplete. Usually they are constrained in terms of space and they are not up to date, so in no way could they satisfy a potential market."[29]

The precarity of the milieu also affected the continuity of this relatively marginal publication. Mindful of periodicity as one of the basic characteristics of a newsletter (and of a magazine), AFI photographers articulated the problem of *Punto de Vista*'s discontinuity in almost every issue and also expressed the hope that *Punto de Vista* might, at some point, be published periodically. I read these recurring references as a symptom of the pervasive economic crisis—a crisis that certainly affected the photographers' endeavors. Indeed, AFI photographers struggled to finance even *Punto de Vista*. As photographer and AFI president Jorge Ianiszewski recalls, "securing funds to continue the publication of *Punto de Vista* was not a gratifying experience; it was difficult to find businesses willing to engage with contents as contingent as ours."[30] This idea also surfaces in the editorial in the second issue of *Punto de Vista*: "The situation affecting our country entails a considerable deterioration in the activities of photographers. This becomes apparent in various ways, for example, in the high cost of equipment, in the rising prices of supplies, in fewer job opportunities, in the difficulty in receiving payment for work completed, etc."[31]

Given these various concerns—political, economic, aesthetic, communicational—it should come as no surprise that the most pressing issue, one that surfaces in most editorials, is the paradoxical condition of the photographic field: despite the critical role photography plays in different spaces and events, the field remains in a developing and precarious state. An editorial penned by Luis Weinstein illustrates this paradox:

> How difficult it is to be a photographer these days—even more, how complicated it is to be a good photographer these days—having an alert, mindful, expressive and incisive gaze capable of grasping what is going on

> and communicating this impression to a large audience. It suffices not to be blind to understand that this difficulty in expression is not limited to photographers and that threatening elements abound, from economic problems to blatant censorship. Nevertheless, it is important that despite these problems, we begin to build the foundations, even if they are shy and small, that shall allow us to develop the photographic field, so this activity, this form of expression, this subjective (and therefore real) way of interpreting reality transcends our walls and social circles. While it is true that times are tough, this is not an eternal situation, and it is precisely the people's doings, all the people together, that determine the dynamics of a situation. In this sense, we must begin by what is ours, by what defines us as a group: photographic activity. Let us begin, for example, by addressing a problem that is not at all new and unfortunately remains unresolved: I am talking about the necessity of laying the groundwork for a discussion about the existence of a CHILEAN PHOTOGRAPHY, or the possibility of the existence of a National Photography, understanding national photography as a set of images in which a considerable group of us (living in the same geopolitics) can recognize ourselves, understand ourselves, look at ourselves again, and reencounter ourselves—that is, communicate this, dialogue about this, discuss this, and respond to this.[32]

This editorial functions almost as a manifesto: the author summons his colleagues, even amid "difficult times," to keep thinking (and dialoguing and debating) about what concerned them most directly, "the photographic field." Thus, a photographer's work is twofold: on the one hand, they must understand what is going on and communicate it; on the other hand, they must think about "the photographic field" beyond the concrete situation in which they are living.

Even if the situation was "not eternal," as Weinstein said in reference to the dictatorship, as the crisis deepened, the demonstrations against the dictatorship became recurrent, and the repression against the demonstrators intensified. In 1985, a short edition of *Punto de Vista*, not numbered, was hurriedly produced. What triggered the publication was the violent arrest of AFI photographer Álvaro Hoppe, who was abducted while photographing the Jornadas por la Vida (Rallies for Life) in August in Lo Hermida, a poor neighborhood in the periphery of Santiago. The back cover depicted a "Declaration" signed by the AFI editorial/directorial board in which they condemned the violence used by policemen in their colleague's arrest and demanded his immediate release.[33] AFI photographers also denounced the strong censorship and repression prevailing since 1984.[34] In addition to this "Declaration" and a letter of repudiation signed by the workers of ECO (Educations and Communications), this four-page leaflet included a fragment of an article penned by Enrique Lihn about the censorship of photographs published originally in *Cauce* magazine; a call for submissions to an exhibition titled "La Juventud" (Youth), which stated, "There will be no censorship or restrictions of any kind; all formats and styles are accepted;" a separate call for the *II Encuentro Chileno de Fotógrafos* (2nd Chilean Symposium of Photographers) titled "Por el valor de la fotografía" (For the Value of Photography), which sought "to structure both organically and theoretically all aspects encompassing photographic activity;" and a commentary about the formation of the Agency FOTOBANCO. The urgency that prompted this edition is apparent both in the content of each text and in the "rushed" layout: the lines dividing the texts, the speech balloons used to announce the photo contest and a brief clarification regarding the "fragment of an article published in *Cauce* by Enrique Lihn" are handwritten—a "precarious style" that also characterizes the layout and edition of the *Ediciones económicas*, as we shall see later.

The dissemination of a number of initiatives (a photo contest, an exhibition, the creation of a photo agency, and a symposium) suggests that besides serving the more urgent purpose of condemning the repressive policies of the regime against a colleague, this unnumbered edition had another, albeit not unrelated, goal: to reassert AFI's existence. Amid a state of emergency that oppressed and restricted, the photographers took the time to publish this rushed issue, an editorial gesture that gave *Punto de Vista*—and the AFI—a continuity of sorts. Even if one were to argue that the photographers did not number this issue in order not to disrupt the thematic and editorial continuity of *Punto de Vista* (the sixth issue, published in December 1987, is similar to the fifth issue published in January 1984), the publication of this precarious item is significant. Amid precarity, there emerges a subject—let's call it "AFI photographers" or "AFI"—which, despite everything (precarity, repression, censorship, etc.), asserts its existence, proves its persistence:

> Our Association, like all of those representing a social sector, has gone through the usual ups and downs, which have been prompted both by the economic situation and by changes in intensity of the permanent "States of Exception" under which we have had to live for a long time now. How-

> ever, despite what some people have been divulging irresponsibly, we have never disappeared, much less died, as an organization. The many exhibits and activities that the AFI has promoted or in which we have participated stand as proof of this. [. . .] The driving force behind all of these activities, and the true "Alter Ego" of the AFI, has been the sector of "art" photographers [. . .] whose enduring and persistent activity gave birth to this group four years ago.[35]

AFI photographers insist on their collective existence ("we have never disappeared, much less died, as an organization") and remind their readers of the various photographic initiatives put forward thus far by the association, initiatives that stand here as confirmation of their existence and persistence ("stand as proof of this"). I recognize here, in this four-page leaflet, the same impetus at play in *Presencia del hombre*, which I discuss below. This marginal publication, unregistered (AFI photographers did not number it and scholars have not considered it) can be read as a minor certificate of presence of the photographic field—a field that, despite all, develops and persists.[36]

Anuarios fotográficos chilenos (1981 and 1982)

The discursive emergence of the photographic field surfaces most times in statements celebrating the renewal or reemergence of photographic activity. This reemergence was concomitant to the restitution of a specific tradition, the Chilean documentary photographic tradition of the fifties and sixties. This reconsideration of the testimonial function of photography became manifest in the selection for the first AFI collective exhibition, "La Fotografía como vocación y oficio" (Photography as a Vocation and an Occupation) as well as in the publication of *Presencia del hombre: Primer anuario fotográfico chileno* (Presence of Man: First Chilean Photo Yearbook) a few months later.[37] As the title suggests, the selection sheds light on the "presence of man," and it does so by focusing most exclusively on marginalized groups.[38] A photograph by Paz Errázuriz depicts a group of adult men laughing, most of their teeth missing. These men, like other people depicted in these photographs, appear to be wearing dirty, worn-out clothes, and they are seated on old sacks and crates along the sidewalk. Many photographs show children, whether posing for the camera or seemingly ignoring it. Most of these children are barefoot and wearing dirty clothes; their faces are also dirty. Some of the children photographed are lying down in the streets, which may suggest homelessness. Some are sad or have a suffering countenance (a photograph by Daniel Arnoff, for instance, depicts a sad-eyed child dressed as a clown, posing while eating what looks like a piece of bread); others, however, laugh and pose for the camera (as in a well-known photograph by Luis Navarro).

Several photographs focus on physical work: I see a group of traveling peasants standing in the back of a cart (photo by Ronnie Goldsmied); a shoeshiner, ready for a new customer, poses before the camera (photo by Pablo Adriasola); I see the hands and feet of a group of fishermen as they remove their catch from the nets (photo by Inés Leiva), and also what could be a family or a group of friends posing in front of their humble homes (photo by Lincoyán Parada). Some photos focus on popular places: domino clubs (photo by Luis Navarro), bars (photo by Leonora Vicuña), circuses, and asylums (photo by Paz Errázuriz). Not every photograph shows people. In some photos, the "presence of man" is suggested by "his" (and I must add "her"/"their") traces: I see shadows, footprints, remnants of buildings, and precarious constructions. A photo by Luis Weinstein (see fig. 3.2) depicts the shadows of pedestrians as they walk by a square; another by José Domingo Marinello shows a shaky roof zinc strip secured only with large stones; Michel Jones photographs the ruins of a wooden staircase that leads nowhere.

Presencia del hombre expresses in its very title the will to "be present" as an affirmation. The photographers included in the selection reclaim popular places in the city, the harbor, and the countryside. "The works [. . .] published show us a Chile of laughter and tears—stone and cotton—a country of madness and tenderness," underscore the editors in this elusive description, aimed at avoiding possible censorship, in the Editorial.[39] While the condition of precariousness is evoked or seems present in almost every photograph, in order to avoid censorship, the editors decided to leave photographic content deemed "too political" or too "ideological" off the frame, so to speak: there are no photographs depicting military repression or violence.[40] However, these unpretentious "simple" photographs of laughter, stone, tears, and cotton invite metaphorical or allegorical interpretations. Indeed, it is not difficult to imagine that the viewers who saw these bare photos back then also read them allegorically. How could one not see (or feel) the uncertainty evoked in the stairs photographed by Jones, a staircase to nowhere? How could the images not evoke the disappearances in the shadows without subjects, the silhouettes that seem to haunt Weinstein's photo?[41] How could one not be reminded of precarity while looking at Marinello's photo, in which rooftops are weighed down with stones? How not to think of the wide-

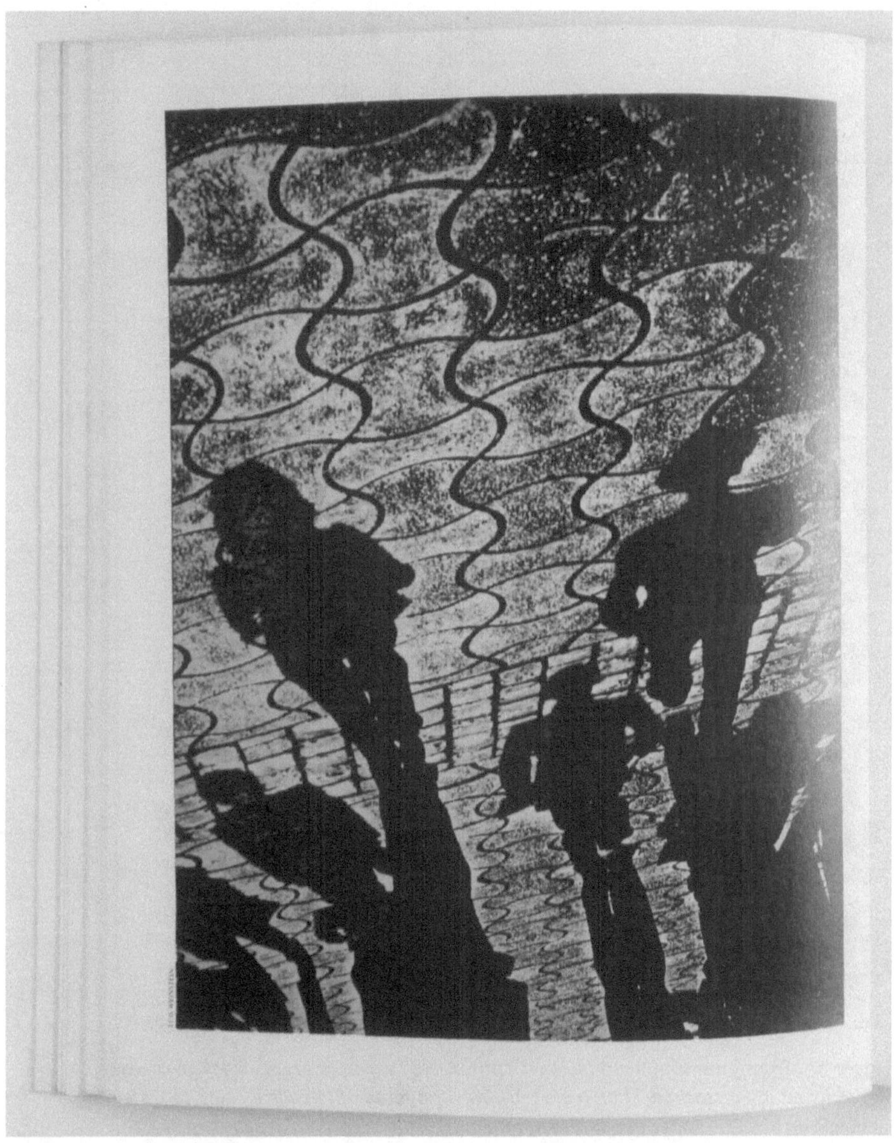

Figure 3.2. Shadows of pedestrians. Credit: Luis Weinstein. Black and white. Reproduced in *Presencia del hombre: Primer Anuario fotográfico chileno*. Luis Weinstein's personal archive.

spread abandonment and poverty that affected so many elderly people, just like those Errázuriz captured so movingly with her camera (see fig. 3.3)?

Perhaps the most allegorical image is one taken by Luis Navarro on September 18, 1980, during the *Te Deum* (see fig. 3.4). This photo suggests that the

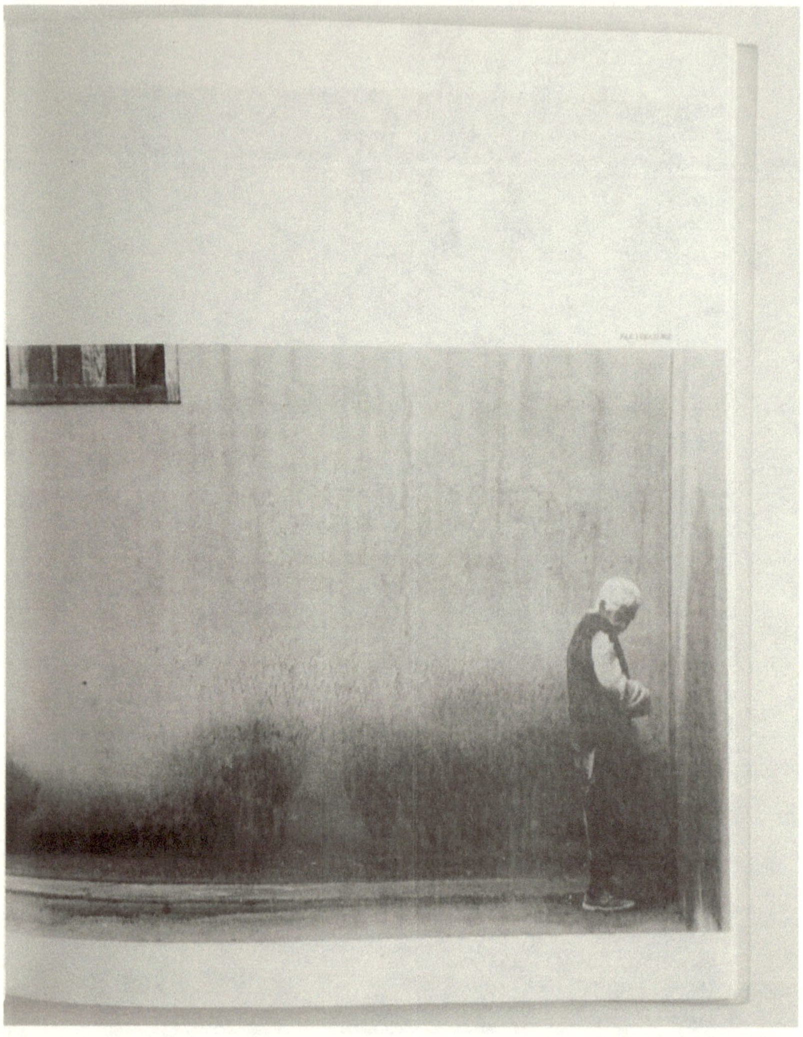

Figure 3.3. Elderly person standing on a corner. Credit: Paz Errázuriz. Black and white. Reproduced in *Presencia del hombre: Primer Anuario fotográfico chileno*. Luis Weinstein's personal archive.

mere presence of military forces in the public space has placed a great strain on society. This, one could say, is a more ominous depiction of the "presence of *men*" in the public space. In this iconic photograph, the contrast between a pigeon and the impeccable military formation is so strong that it is difficult not to spark the beholder's imagination. This unique, specific, unrepeatable pigeon,

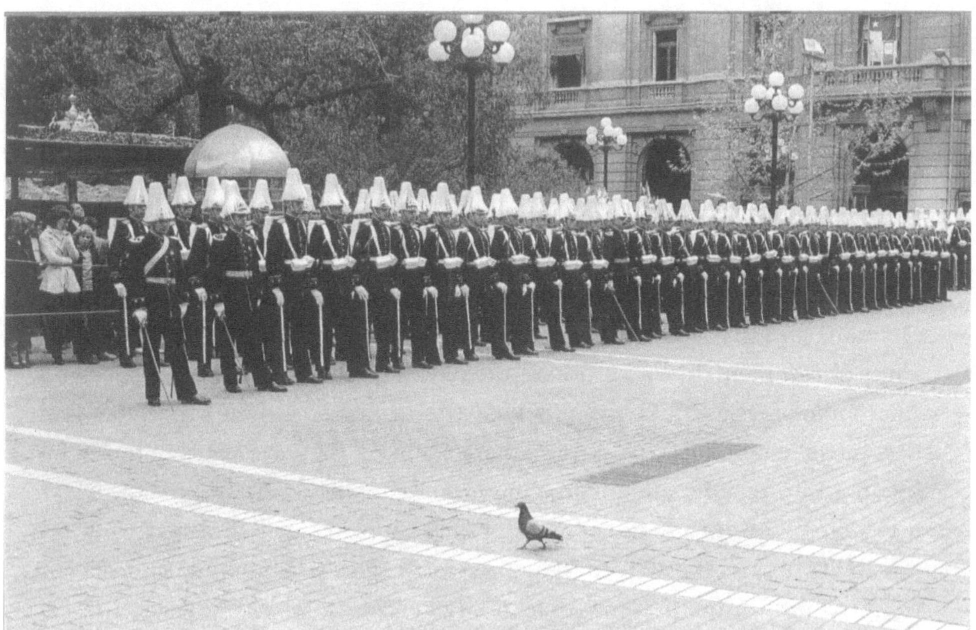

Figure 3.4. Te Deum at the Cathedral. Credit: Luis Navarro Vega. September 18, 1980. Black and white. Luis Navarro Vega's personal archive. (Also reproduced in *Presencia del hombre: Primer Anuario fotográfico chileno*).

photographed at that "decisive moment," as Henri Cartier Bresson might say, appears here captured, her movement arrested as if for a brief moment. This unassuming pigeon seems to evoke and to connote, or in other words, to put in motion, much more than the idea of "a pigeon." It seems difficult not to supplement the photograph, not to consider this pigeon allegorically. The pigeon as if it were the people; as if it were democracy; as if it were the political prisoners; as if it were the relatives of those political prisoners or of the thousands of *desaparecidos*—even as if it were the photographers themselves. The allegory is certainly powerful, and the movement of reference, unstoppable.[42]

The photographs that comprise *Presencia del hombre* certainly challenge the image of order and prosperity prevailing in officialist media—an image that was already shattering and that would become unsustainable after the '82 economic crisis. Still, I believe the relevance of *Presencia del hombre* lies not exclusively in the allusions to the political and social contexts that the photographs certainly evoke or depict, whether denotatively (poor men and children, toothless old men, precarious constructions) or allegorically (pigeons, sad kids dressed up as clowns, stairs that lead nowhere, shadows). Rather, *Presencia del hombre*'s relevance resides in the production and display of a corpus—a precarious corpus—and also in the change of perspective revealed by this corpus.[43] *Presencia del hombre's* Editorial hints toward this change in its description of the photographers as "people trained in this decade with a new style and a new focus, and a renewed communicating philosophy."[44]

The proposition of a "new style" and a "new focus" entails here a restitution, in the sense of a return, of the documentary photographic tradition that flourished in Chile in the fifties and sixties under the aegis of photographer Antonio Quintana and that was predominant in the early seventies during the Popular Unity government. The assertion of the return of a style as a "new style" and a "new focus" reveals the spacing (between one moment and the other) that renders possible iteration. The documentary tradition that reemerges in the eighties, in a way, renders the documentary photographic tradition possible anew; it is a repetition (or iteration) that not only supplements but also restores the possibility of this otherwise marginalized and neglected photographic tradition from the past in the present context.[45] *Presencia del hombre* reinstates documentary photography as the most essential—urgent and/or necessary—form of representation. Documentary photography conveys here, rather broadly, the mode of photography most suitable to attest to and expose different realities. This representational mode stands in opposition to "studio photography," the latter also a representational mode understood in very broad terms, associated with such notions as "artificiality" and "insensibility," as the editors suggest in the Introduction: "We think that this generation, the generation of the seventies, appears strengthened, balanced. It is a generation that rejects the artificial and the insensible."[46] If each iteration supplements in the affirmative, in the statement conveyed in the title *Presencia del hombre*, I also read the editors' attempt to show and substantiate the presence of documentary photography in the public sphere. *Presencia del hombre* documents, as best as it can, the presence of people in different regions of the country and, more broadly, hints toward the renewal or reemergence of photographic activity in the early eighties.[47] I am tempted to say that *Presencia del hombre* unfolds a "photographic logic" of sorts: I am referring here not to the photographs included in the book, but rather to the book itself as a precarious "certificate of presence" of the photographic field.

While the editors of *Presencia del hombre* did not fail to mention the difficulties entailed in accomplishing such an unprecedented initiative, the editors of the *Segundo anuario fotográfico chileno*, published a year later, focused mainly on the field's achievements. Whereas the *Primer anuario* included fifty photographs (all in black and white, all by AFI members), the *Segundo anuario* showcased 128 photographs, both in black and white and in color. Moreover, the open call resulted in a greater variety of themes and photographic styles, one of the major aims of the publication being to communicate the idea of photography as a medium that exists and functions in different spaces (arts, advertising, news, etc.). In the Introduction, the editors claimed:

> In 1981, for the first time in our field, we began to work on an *anuario fotográfico* [. . .] We talked back then of a nascent photographic movement whose roots went back to the 70s. We claimed it was necessary to clarify its foundations and guidelines, to strengthen it and make it palpable. The *Primer anuario* attempted to contribute to the realization of these objectives. We think that this book is a master achievement of photography as a social document [. . .] This year, we want to consolidate this movement, this search. The photographic debate has grown and become richer; there are talks, forums, and exhibitions. We have seen a number of articles and essays about photography in different media. We feel we are part of, and in a way, initiators of this movement.[48]

The editors had reason to be celebratory in their Introduction: because of the different initiatives put forward by the AFI in only a year—the first *Anuario* and numerous photo exhibits—photography had begun to be appreciated as a discipline and as an activity beyond "studio photography."[49] At the same time, it must be acknowledged that *Segundo Anuario* had an unfortunate ending. The editors had secured sponsorship from the Canadian Embassy in Chile, and it was agreed that the book would be published in Toronto. Although the book was completed, the printshop filed for bankruptcy shortly after production and never shipped the books to Chile, so most of the copies were lost. A photographer carried with him the few copies he was able to salvage from the publisher and accommodate in his luggage. Even knowing that not too many people read or saw the *Segundo Anuario*, I am putting forth an effort to rescue it precisely because the edition and its disastrous finale were both inscribed in the history of the photographic field that began to be written during these years.[50]

Affordable Photographic Initiatives for Precarious Times

The adoption of trade liberalization measures that eliminated import custom taxes in order to stimulate the influx of imported goods—including photography equipment—was one of the economic proposals of a group of technocrats and economists known as the Chicago Boys (among them Sergio de Castro, Minister of Finances between 1976 and 1982).[51] These proposals stemmed from a document known as *El ladrillo* (The Brick), a text drafted by the Chicago Boys in 1973 as an answer to "the disastrous economic policies initiated by the Government of the Unidad Popular."[52] The Chicago Boys' proposals aimed to privatize, deregulate, and significantly reduce social spending.[53] As a consequence of the irregularities (and scams) induced by the deregulation and liberalization of formal and informal markets, the financial sector experienced its first crisis in 1977 with the bankruptcy of several financial institutions. Indeed, as Naomi Klein persuasively argues in *The Shock Doctrine*, Chile's "period of steady growth that is held up as proof of its miraculous success did not begin until the mid-eighties [. . .] That's because in 1982, despite its strict adherence to Chicago doctrine, Chile's economy crashed: its debt exploded, it faced hyperinflation once again, and unemployment hit 30 percent—ten times higher than it was under Allende."[54] The economic crisis generated a widespread climate of opposition and resistance. Almost ten years after the coup, the banking businesses were almost broke, the unemployment rate was escalating, the new wealth was concentrated in the hands of a few individuals, and workers did not have the collective leverage and tools to exert pressure on their factory bosses—all the gains won in previous decades by popular movements and workers had been abolished.

The economic crisis did not stop photographers from creating and devising new ways to disseminate their work. Different photographic initiatives were devised to denounce and to protest, and also to consolidate the field and expand it. The practices of photography that emerged did so amid precarity: as precarious bodies, they not only made visible, but also materialized the precarity of the milieu within which they were surfacing. Some of them even transformed what was regularly understood as photographic work, producing a supplement or excess that, in turn expanded the field.

Ediciones económicas de la fotografía chilena (1983)

One remarkable case is that of *Ediciones económicas*, photographic monographs made from photocopied photos, copied on regular paper, and bound with staples.[55] Felipe Riobó, creator of the project, resorted to photocopying in order to stimulate the photographic field; the photocopy, an affordable means of reproduction, allowed him and the photographers involved in the initiative (Mauricio Valenzuela, Luis Weinstein, and Paz Errázuriz) to resolve the high cost of producing photography books:[56]

> The interest of this series of affordable photography lies in the ability, to the extent that this is possible, to rescue virtualities and then establish a space for the creation-circulation-dissemination of images and concepts in our medium *and according to our possibilities*. The inferior craftwork of these visions, in photocopy, and the texts associated to them, embody our most radical conviction: that today photography has arrived at a degree of existence that obliges it to recognize its own being.[57]

In the Presentation to the first issue, Riobó refers to the photocopy as an "inferior" medium, indeed, but one in "accordance with" the photographers' "possibilities." Through the formulation of a photocopy as a necessary albeit inferior means of reproduction, *Ediciones económicas* becomes an exemplary case within the expanding field of photographic practices. I interpret these books made of photocopied photos as both supplements and precarious bodies through and through. The term "supplement" is pertinent here because it not only conveys the idea that these photocopied books took the place of that which should have been—"proper," "real" photography books—had conditions been different or the photographic field been stronger and more well established, but also enriches (or supplements) our understanding of photography. Moreover, the physical photocopy supplements the photograph by adding material layers as well as layers of meaning.

These photocopied books are also precarious bodies because even if photography revokes the idea that there is something like an original photographic version, from the "vantage point" of photography, the photocopy of a photograph carries the stigma, so to speak, of being an imperfect copy. A photocopied photograph implies an inevitable deterioration in terms of lighting, color quality, saturation, gray scales, and other elements. This hierarchical relationship surfaces in Riobó's claim as well as in other photographers' views: photocopies are deteriorated versions of photographs—"inferior craftworks"—therefore the goal is to achieve the "best possible photocopies," as Errázuriz indicates.[58] But then again, although "inferior," a photocopy is nevertheless presented as the most suitable way to disseminate Chilean photography. In brief, the creator of the whole initiative seems to be saying: the choice is between these precarious objects, these photocopied photographs, or nothing.

The photocopying mechanism ("a Ricoh machine, less expensive and better

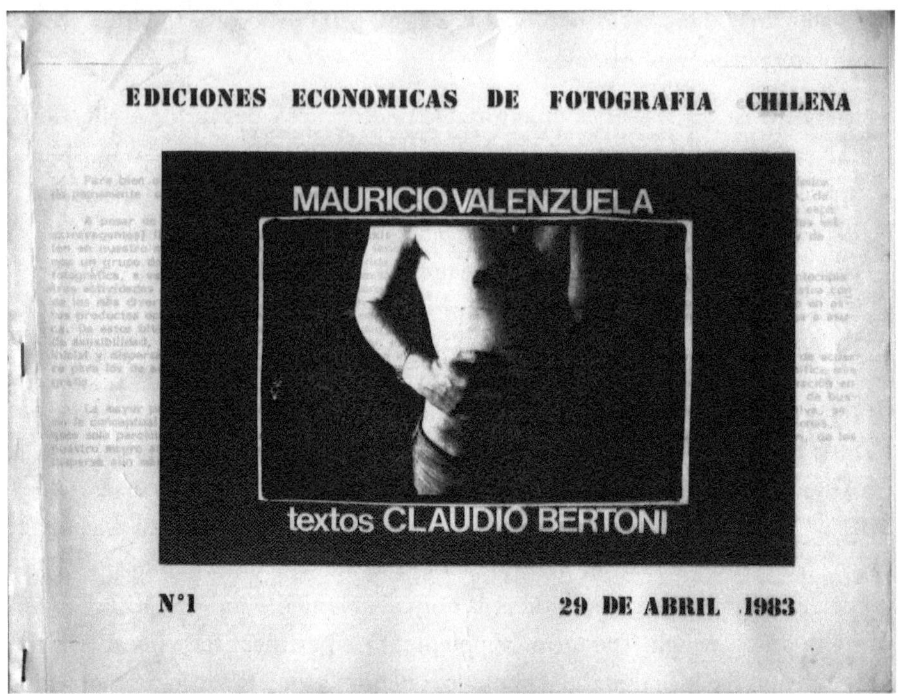

Figure 3.5. Photocopied cover of Mauricio Valenzuela's *Ediciones económicas* vol. 1. Credit: Mauricio Valenzuela. 1983. Black and white. Luis Weinstein's personal archive.

calibrated than the Xerox machine," as Weinstein told me) was not used exclusively to reproduce the photographs published in each issue: it was also used to compose new images.[59] The photocopy, an *artesanía inferior*, encouraged photographers to propose diverse and new forms of composition by integrating different materials (photographs, handwritten and typed texts, corrector fluid or pencil stains, various types of paper, etc.), and writers to rehearse different forms of critical approaches. Each collaborator (Claudio Bertoni, Jaime Gré, Renato Orellana, and Patricio Marchant) approached the photographic works in different ways. Bertoni and Marchant did so from the point of view of poetry without attempting to interpret Valenzuela or Errázuriz's photographs. Gré and Orellana, in turn, approached Weinstein and Errázuriz's photos in dialogue with different photographic theories.

Photographer Mauricio Valenzuela challenged spectators/readers by means of playfulness and textual exploration. This exploration begins on the cover (see fig.

3.5), with a very dark photocopy of a nude torso that could be either masculine or feminine. The photocopy is intriguing, mysterious; it invites us to continue watching. The photocopies reproduced inside seem like little objects suspended in the air: the large white edge that frames them accentuates their condition as image-object. The lightness or faintness of the photocopy is also suggested in the visual content: the perspective and framing of the photocopies favor the air and the sky. Public squares, shadows, traffic signs, cars, men, streets, and buildings are not centered. The framing is unconventional and suggestive; the elements seem to be leaving the frame, as though they were flying, or their view is blocked by something that comes between them and the camera lens, as in the photocopies that frame the Prat Cinema. In the first photocopy, only the top of the building is shown, at the very bottom of the frame (see fig. 3.6). This framing makes the building look almost like a sinking ship. In the second photocopy, the view of the building is completely blocked by a passing bus. These different framings bring attention to the device—the camera—and also to the gaze: from where, how, and how much can I see? I want to see more, but I can't.

Valenzuela plays not only with the framing, but also with the relationship between text and image. A photocopy is framed by a handwritten question: Where is God? The image shows a billboard of the dairy products *La vache qui rit*. Below the photocopy, the handwritten answer: God, I want to take a picture of you. Is God a laughing cow, I wonder, looking at this composition of text and image. Moreover, motivated by the recourse to photocopy, Valenzuela expands the notion of what counts as a "photograph." Four "photographs"—handwritten descriptions—interrupt the visual narrative. These written descriptions shed light on the temporality of the photograph, of what happens and continues happening before and after the moment the shot is taken. These "photographs" depict scenes, situations, or characters that the photographer (if we trust the narrator) was not able to capture for one of several reasons: the camera had no film; the camera did not work (see fig. 3.7); it was a dream; or there was no camera. All of these scenes are labeled "photographs:" "Photo [taken] without a camera;" "Photo [taken] with a broken camera;" "Dreamt photo," and "Filmless Photo." These "photographs," indirectly, nod to precarity: the photographer ran out of film, his camera was not working, or he didn't have a camera. Moreover, this fictional literary practice operates within the performative realm of photography. These written descriptions are as photographic as the other photocopied images in the series. It would be absurd to think of these descriptions as "inferior versions" of a source photograph, not so much because such a photo does not exist (although this, of course, is one of the reasons), but rather because "photography" does not coincide with only one form of being or appearing.[60]

Riobó refers to the inferior craftwork (artesanía) of the *Ediciones económicas*. The manual work implicated in the composition of these photo books—and enabled by the photocopy—is inscribed in the marks and stains that are visible and almost palpable in the copies reproduced in the photocopying machine. It is as if the photographers wanted to make manifest, to inscribe in the photocopied photobook, the processes of edition, writing, montage, and correction. In the flyer announcing a "flash exhibit" and launching of Luis Weinstein's *Ediciones económicas* volume, different layers corresponding to different materials and media are noticeable: handwritten texts over typed text, erasures, stains, and crossouts made with corrector fluid or pencils. Even different layers of paper (a taped photograph over a paper ripped from a notebook) are noticeable. A handwritten text emphasizes the idea of the photocopied photo book as an affordable visual object. On the book cover (see fig. 3.8), the names of Weinstein and the critic who comments on his work (Jaime Gré) are also handwritten over white stains. This text handwritten over correction fluid suggests the stages involved in the composition of the images and of the book—a process that, not unlike the photographer's work in the dark room, involves a series of trial-and-error steps and modifications.

Weinstein's narrative begins with two images taken from a high angle inside Santiago's subway station. This view from above signals the presence of the photographer, his position, and his perspective. His position is significant: from above, the photographer is able to record the presence of an ephemeral pamphlet hooked between the roof rafters, with the word NO (see fig. 3.9). Below the photocopy, a handwritten caption indicates that the photo was taken in September 1980—that is, during the month of the referendum to vote for the new Constitution. The act of inscribing the date of the shot is defiant, as it is the act of including this photocopy at the beginning of the narrative composed by three moments or sequences. In the first part, the camera is so high above the people that men and women appear to be little "subject-points, subject-cysts," as Gré says in his critical text. Photocopies of silhouettes and shadows follow this opening (a recurring theme in Weinstein's work). The narrative ends with a series of photocopies of photos taken in Cartagena, a popular beach town. These last photocopies frame the subjects closely: we see women inside the sea or

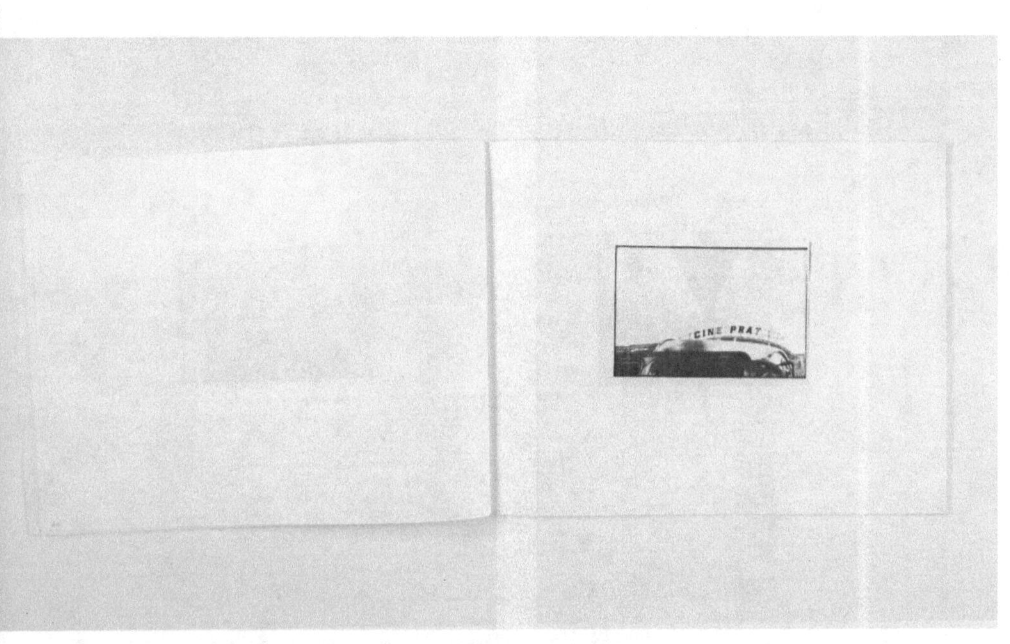

Figure 3.6. Cine Prat, photocopy, in Mauricio Valenzuela's *Ediciones económicas* vol. 1. Credit: Mauricio Valenzuela. 1983. Black and white. Luis Weinstein's personal archive.

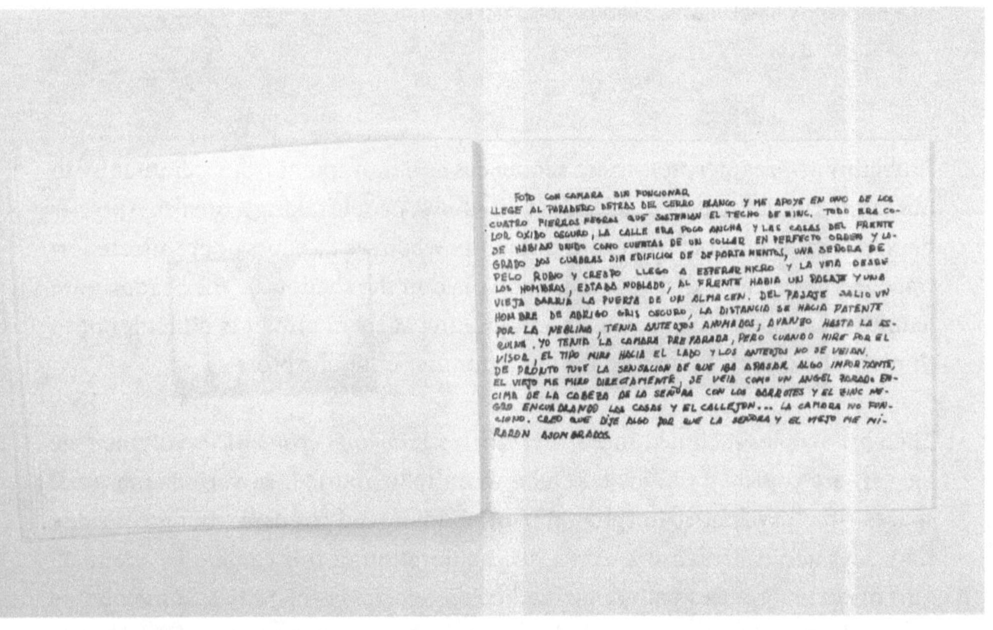

FOTO CON CAMARA SIN FUNCIONAR
LLEGE AL PARADERO DETRAS DEL CERRO BLANCO Y ME APOYE EN UNO DE LOS
CUATRO FIERROS NEGROS QUE SOSTENIAN EL TECHO DE ZINC. TODO ERA CO-
LOR OXIDO OSCURO, LA CALLE ERA POCO ANCHA Y LAS CASAS DEL FRENTE
SE HABIAN UNIDO COMO CUENTAS DE UN COLLAR EN PERFECTO ORDEN Y LA-
GRADO DOS CUADRAS SIN EDIFICIOS DE DEPARTAMENTOS, UNA SEÑORA DE
PELO RUBIO Y CRESPO LLEGO A ESPERAR MICRO Y LA VEIA DESDE
LOS HOMBROS, ESTABA NUBLADO, AL FRENTE HABIA UN PASAJE Y UNA
VIEJA BARRIA LA PUERTA DE UN ALMACEN. DEL PASAJE SALIO UN
HOMBRE DE ABRIGO GRIS OSCURO, LA DISTANCIA SE HACIA PATENTE
POR LA NEBLINA, TENIA ANTEOJOS AHUMADOS; AVANZO HASTA LA ES-
QUINA. YO TENIA LA CAMARA PREPARADA, PERO CUANDO MIRE POR EL
VISOR, EL TIPO MIRO HACIA EL LADO Y LOS ANTEOJOS NO SE VEIAN.
DE PRONTO TUVE LA SENSACION DE QUE IBA A PASAR ALGO IMPORTANTE,
EL VIEJO ME MIRO DIRECTAMENTE, SE VEIA COMO UN ANGEL PARADO EN-
CIMA DE LA CABEZA DE LA SEÑORA CON LOS BARROTES Y EL ZINC NE-
GRO ENCUADRANDO LAS CASAS Y EL CALLEJON... LA CAMARA NO FUN-
CIONO. CREO QUE DIJE ALGO POR QUE LA SEÑORA Y EL VIEJO ME MI-
RARON ASOMBRADOS.

Figure 3.7. Photo taken with a broken camera, photocopy, in Mauricio Valenzuela's *Ediciones económicas* vol. 1. Credit: Mauricio Valenzuela. 1983. Black and white. Luis Weinstein's personal archive.

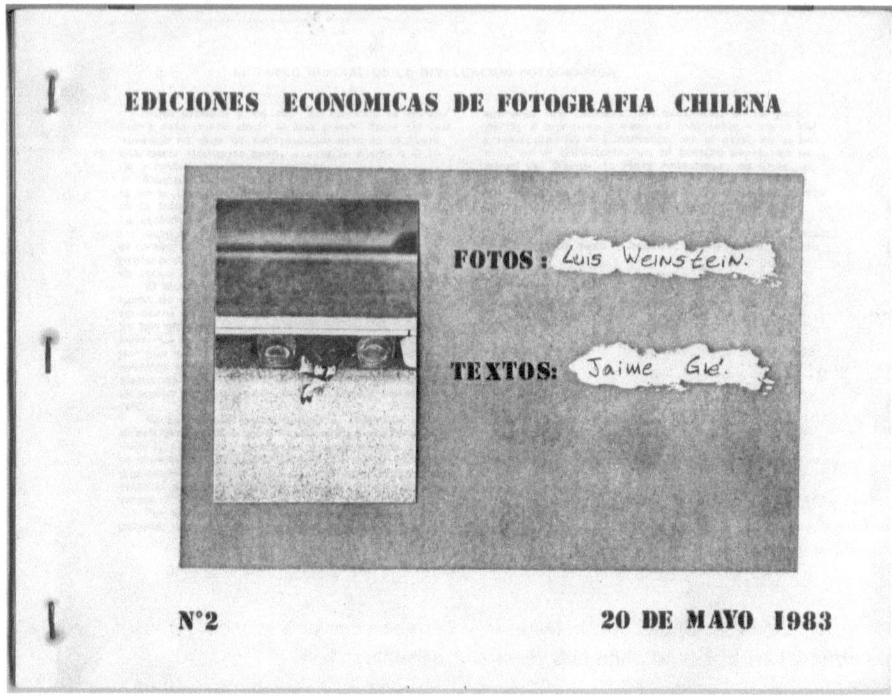

Figure 3.8. Photocopied cover of Luis Weinstein's *Ediciones económicas* vol. 2. Credit: Luis Weinstein. 1983. Black and white. Luis Weinstein's personal archive.

sunbathing. Gré interprets these sequences as a movement from inhumanity to humanity (individuals like little dots, shadows, people taking a break). Another possible reading is that we regain humanity when we face loss or are affected by tragedies such as the disappearances (evoked in the shadows). The shadows are haunting and evocative (see fig. 3.10); looking at them now, it is difficult not to think of the black silhouettes used in a number of public protests.

The photocopies included in Paz Errázuriz's *Ediciones económicas* volume (see fig 3.11) are copies of photos taken between 1980 and 1982 at various marginal spaces—the psychiatric hospital, nursing homes, and circuses—but as Enrique Lihn says about Errázuriz's work, "the exploration of this camera by the margins of society refuses pathologizing."[61] I recognize, in this series, some photos later published in *El infarto del alma* (1990), the first book I saw of Errázuriz's photos, which includes texts by Diamela Eltit. Most photocopies are portraits;

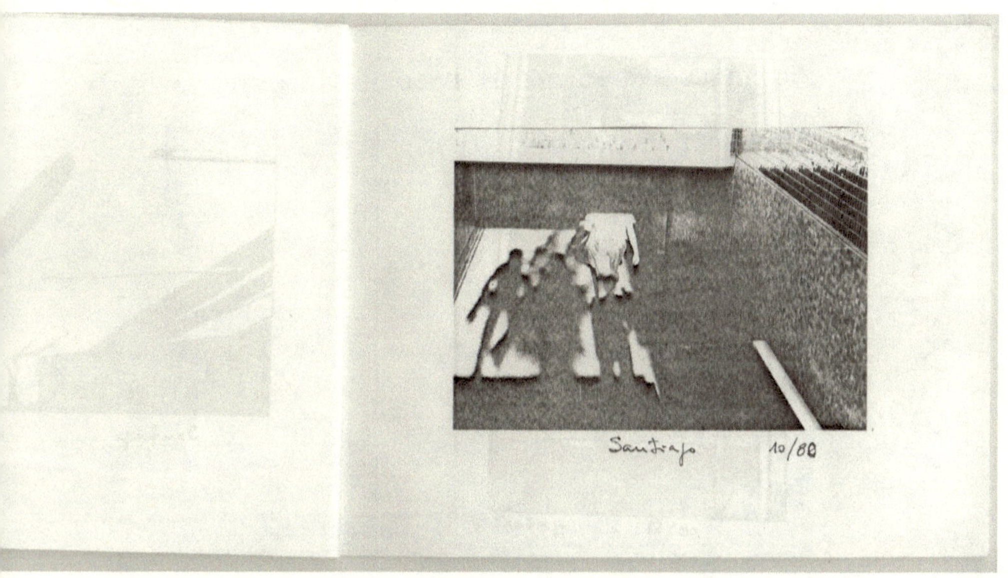

Figure 3.9. NO flyer at subway station, photocopy, in Luis Weinstein's *Ediciones económicas* vol. 2. Credit: Luis Weinstein. 1983. Black and white. Luis Weinstein's personal archive.

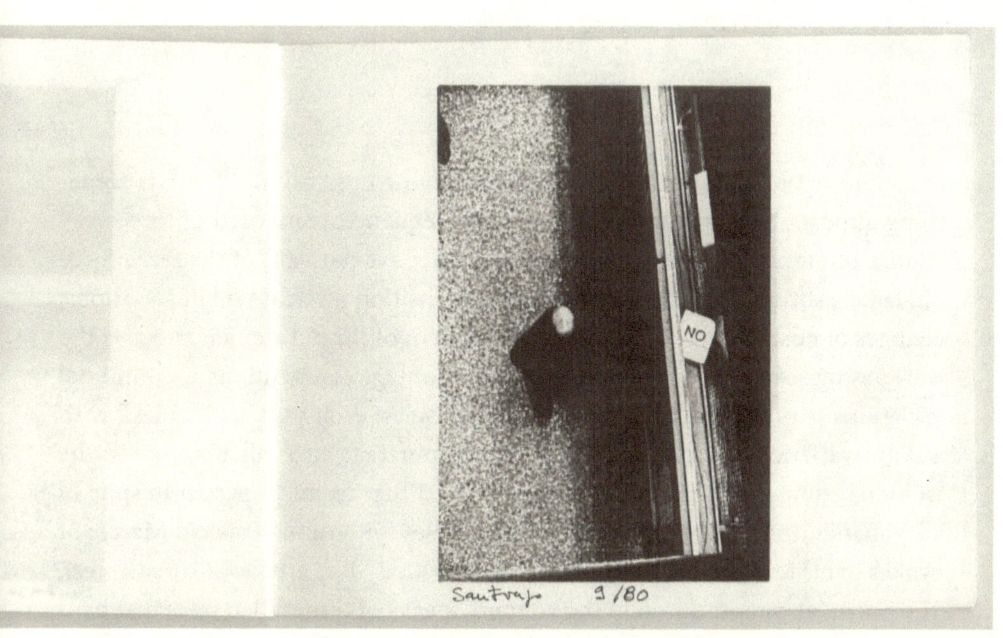

Figure 3.10. Shadows, photocopy, in Luis Weinstein's *Ediciones económicas* vol. 2. Credit: Luis Weinstein. 1983. Black and white. Luis Weinstein's personal archive.

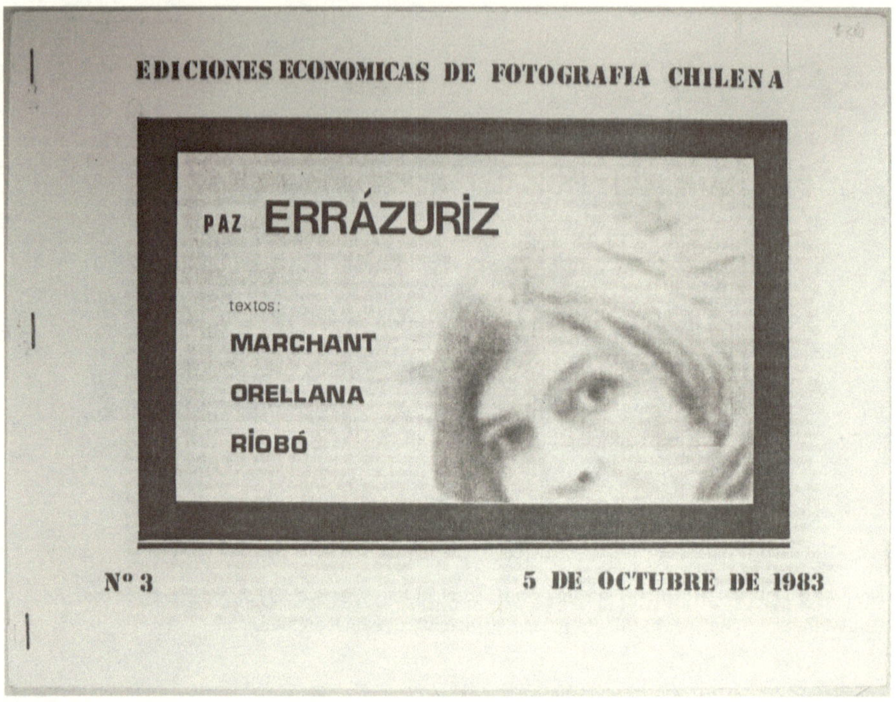

Figure 3.11. Photocopied cover of Paz Errázuriz's *Ediciones económicas* vol. 3. Credit: Paz Errázuriz. 1983. Black and white. Luis Weinstein's personal archive.

the subjects photographed look at the camera or pose calmly. There is something almost cinematic in the introductory sequence, composed of three very similar photocopies. The photocopies are collective portraits of the same three old ladies, sitting together, waiting. The composition inscribes small variations, changes of posture, evoking the slow movement of the old women and also the slow passage of time, the wait. Perhaps, this montage of repetitions and minimal variations is prompted by the use of photocopies: each portrait "copies," with a slight variation, the previous portrait. The portraits also call attention to the women's companionship or friendship, a bond that seems to persist in spite of all—abandonment, poverty, and monotony. Not for nothing Patricio Marchant evokes in his text a poem by Gabriela Mistral titled "Tres árboles" (Three Trees). The poem, also reproduced in the volume, speaks of three fallen trees that have been forgotten by a lumberjack; it goes on to describe how one of the trees extends its limbs—its branches—to another tree to care for it.

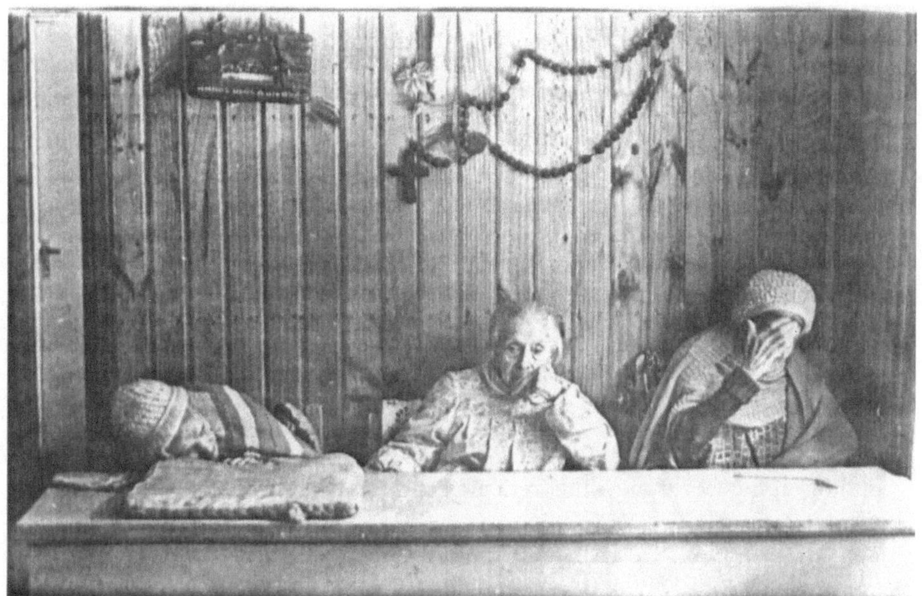

Figure 3.12. Three old ladies at asylum, photocopy, in Paz Errázuriz's *Ediciones económicas* vol. 3. Credit: Paz Errázuriz. 1983. Black and white. Luis Weinstein's personal archive.

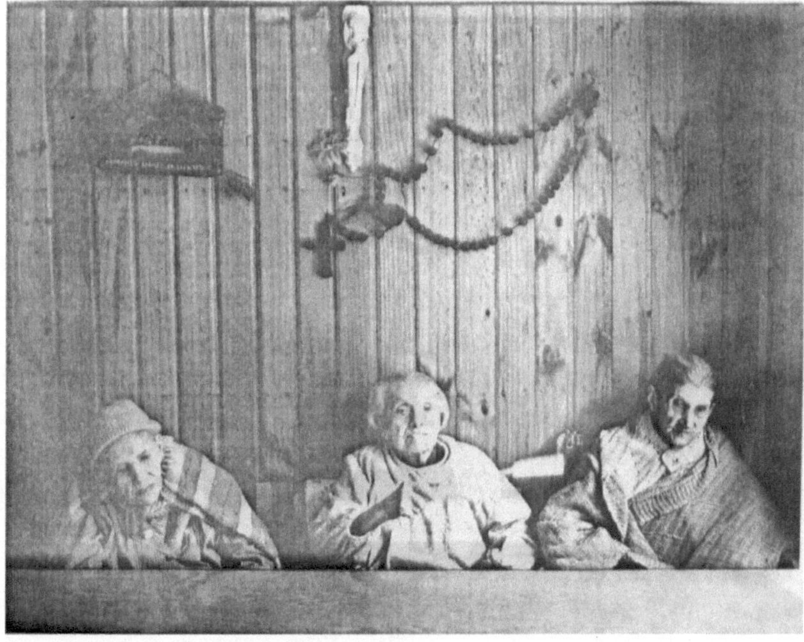

Figure 3.13. Three old ladies at asylum, photocopy, in Paz Errázuriz's *Ediciones económicas* vol. 3. Credit: Paz Errázuriz. 1983. Black and white. Luis Weinstein's personal archive.

Ediciones económicas sought to integrate photographic production with theoretical reflection and to counter the scarcity of photographic publications about Chilean photographers. Riobó also claims in his Presentation that photographic works develop in Chile in a "meager day-to-day [that] makes them vanish and disperses them even more;" he also suggests that conceptual production "remains under the surface and is only partially known [by the public]." At the same time, the photographer underlines that the reflection and writing about the photographic production in the local context, "even if in its initial stages and dispersion, presents the possibility of a new air for those inside and those who are close to photography."[62] I am tempted to suggest that the recourse to photocopy is a sign of this new air. Or, to put it differently, the recourse to photocopy enabled the circulation of "fresh air" in the photographic field: innovative photographic works, new theoretical propositions.

El pan nuestro de cada día (1986)

El pan nuestro de cada día, a documentary photographic essay produced in collaboration by photographers Óscar Navarro, Claudio Pérez, Paulo Slachevsky Chonchol, and Carlos Tobar, aimed to expose and comment on how the implementation of neoliberal economic measures, the military violence, and the police repression affected citizens in their daily lives. Unfortunately, most copies of *El pan nuestro* were stolen and destroyed by CNI agents who broke into the shop where the book recently had been printed and was being stored in preparation for distribution. About a hundred rescued copies circulated scarcely in 1986, *de mano en mano*.[63] Despite its marginality, or, as I want to suggest, precisely because of its marginality, *El pan nuestro* surfaces as an eloquent and relevant example in this context: it is a marginal photographic practice that not only exposes the urgency and the precarity ("the doing and the suffering") which circumscribe the epoch of the dictatorship, but also materializes this precarity. The photos and captions that make up this photographic work formulate statements about the precarious conditions under which people are living, about the state of emergency imposed by the military, and about the role and place of photography within this context.

Urgency and precarity are already evoked in the book's title: "our daily bread" (a common saying and a well-known phrase from the "Our Father" prayer) implies, paradoxically in the Chilean context, the lack of bread, the hunger and scarcity, and the insecurity and violence experienced day after day by thousands of civilians. Hunger and poverty, a sense of exclusion, violent police repression of civilians and photographers, and censorship—all were "daily bread" in the Chile of the dictatorship. The paradox manifest in the title structures the book's composition: the juxtaposition of texts and photos in the spread exposes the contradictions of the economic neoliberal policies implemented by Pinochet and his aides, denounces the violence perpetrated by the military and the police, and uncovers acts of civilian resistance. By means of this juxtaposition of texts and images, *El pan nuestro* reframes or counterframes the triumphalist narrative of Pinochet's regime.

The texts reproduced on each page are not your typical photo captions—I am thinking here of the more traditional captions published along with press or documentary photographs that may indicate the where, when, what, or who in an attempt to constrain, describe, or clarify a photograph's visual content. In *El pan nuestro*, the texts are comments uttered by Pinochet, admirals or policemen, graffiti quotes, excerpts of songs and poems. These quotes do not directly refer to the situation photographed (what Azoulay calls "the photographic event"), nor do they attempt to fix or constrain the photographic content.[64] On the contrary, the quotes open this content up; they invite the reader/spectator herself to establish relations, recontextualize, and signify the photographs. In many instances, this dialectic composition exposes and even derides, not without some humor, the incongruous and shallow rhetoric of the military regime.

The bread evoked in the title—bread that is "ours"—is also represented in one

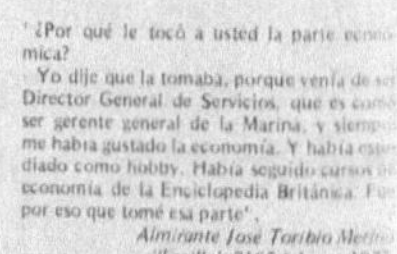
'¿Por qué le tocó a usted la parte econó-
mica?
Yo dije que la tomaba, porque venía de ser
Director General de Servicios, que es como
ser gerente general de la Marina, y siempre
me había gustado la economía. Y había estu-
diado como hobby. Había seguido cursos de
economía de la Enciclopedia Británica. Fue
por eso que tomé esa parte'.
Almirante José Toribio Merino
'Ercilla' 2165 febrero 1977

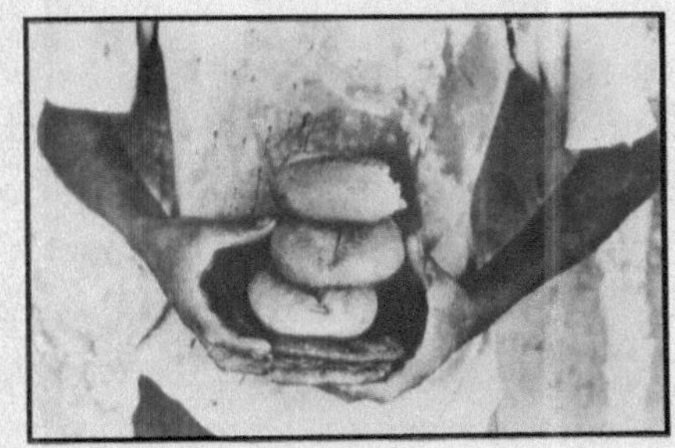

Figure 3.14. *El pan nuestro de cada día* spread, hands holding bread. Credit: Claudio Pérez. 1986. Black and white. Jorge Gronemeyer's personal archive (Taller Gronefot).

of the book's photographs (see fig. 3.14). In the photo, an individual (of whom the viewer sees only the upper extremities, hands, and torso) appears carefully carrying bread—three *marraquetas* and two *hallullas*, typical Chilean breads. The quote reproduced on the page opposing the photo is taken from an interview with Admiral Merino, our photography aficionado and amateur economist:

> —Why were you assigned to the economic sector?
> —I said I'd take it because I had just been General Director of Services, which is like being CEO of the Navy, and I had always liked economics. And I have studied it as a hobby. I followed the economics courses developed by the Encyclopedia Britannica. That's why I took on that role.

Merino says he "took on the role" because he liked it, because he had studied economics as a hobby, as if national economic policies were a matter of role-playing. Merino shares that he "followed courses developed by the Encyclopedia Britannica." (How good of a student could he possibly have been?) Nothing in the photo evokes the idea of abundance. Quite the opposite: scarcity, hunger, and poverty come to mind. This, not only because of the white shirt the individual wears, which appears extremely worn and soiled, but also because of the photograph's main focus, *bread*. These breads orient the photograph as well as my experience as spectator. In other words, these breads orient my gaze at the photograph: the breads appear close up in the center of the frame. Bread matters, the photo seems to be saying; one needs to pay attention to bread, one must not forget one's right to bread, for one must demand one's daily bread.[65] I look at the photo, I read the quote, I come back to the photo, and I wonder: what is the relationship between bread and economy? Bread is a staple in the average working-class Chilean household; it is the chief component of the Chilean diet because it is both cheap and nourishing. The juxtaposition of quote and photo, this counterframing or reframing, seems to be saying: a man who studied economics "as a hobby"—as we have seen, Merino was a man of many hobbies—has been overseeing the country's finances . . . look—here—these are the consequences.[66]

Another photograph depicts four individuals standing behind a fence (at least two other individuals are out of the frame), their faces covered and their hands firmly gripping the bars of the fence (see fig 3.15). The caption accompanying the photo reproduces a promise made by Pinochet: "One in every seven Chileans will have a car; one in every five, a TV set; and one in every seven, a telephone." The position of the individuals in the photograph differs considerably from the triumphant tone and outcome implied in Pinochet's promise. The lack

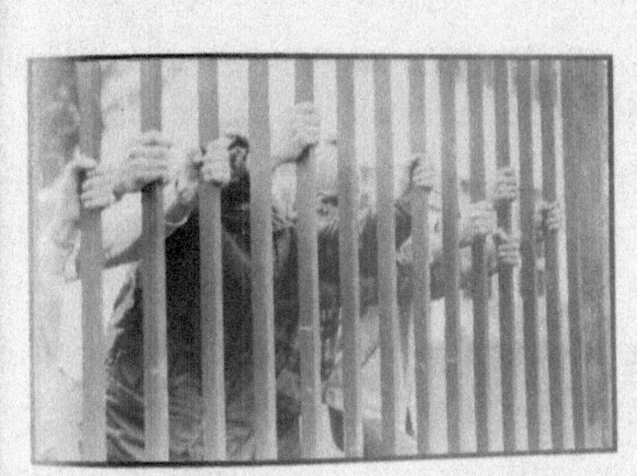

Figure 3.15. *El pan nuestro de cada día* spread, four men standing behind a fence. Credit: Óscar Navarro. 1986. Black and white. Jorge Gronemeyer's personal archive (Taller Gronefot).

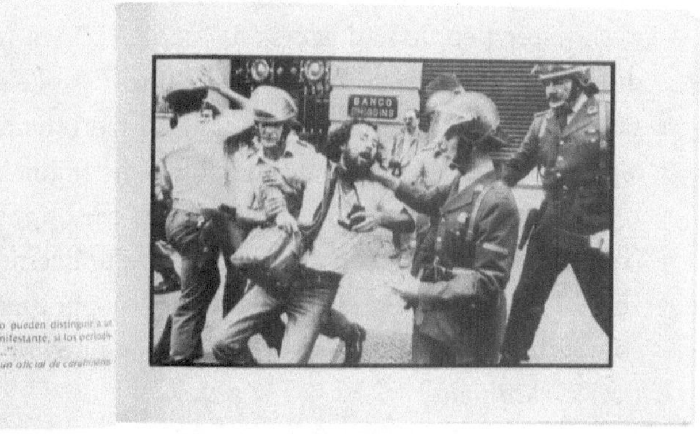

Figure 3.16. *El pan nuestro de cada día* spread, police repression against photographers. Credit: Claudio Pérez. 1986. Black and white. Jorge Gronemeyer's personal archive (Taller Gronefot).

of, let's say, "basic" information—where and when this photograph was taken, the identity of the individuals, the location—allows and invites the spectator (me) to imagine. The subjects' heads are down, as if they were protecting themselves or hiding from someone; perhaps they are trying to escape, preparing to jump to the other side of the fence. Their faces are covered; they don't want to be recognized. I think: imminent danger, urgency, an act of resistance, maybe? The photograph also evokes the idea of exclusion: these individuals are on the "other side" of the fence. If "they" are on the "other side," who is on *this* side of the fence? Or is it, rather, that "we" are on this side of the fence—"we," the collective subject who also lacks bread, "our" bread? Let's think about this "we:" Who is this "we"? Who do these individuals referred to using the pronouns "they" or "we" represent: the majority of Chileans—those excluded from the count (the majority "of every *seven* Chileans . . .")—or the minority (. . . the *one* who will own a car)? The montage of quote and photograph seems to suggest the former, but also, and more importantly, they suggest that there is no "we"—because the "'we' [. . .] is riven from the start:"[67] the photograph exposes a sense of exclusion that is, for a large majority, another "daily bread." The operation is again, then, quite simple: the framing of success is deconstructed, resisted, countered by the photograph. The montage renders visible the incongruity underpinning the new neoliberal model imposed by Pinochet and his aids: one Chilean will own a TV because four shall not; one Chilean will have phone access because six shall not. Within the neoliberal logic, "our daily bread" is not for all to have. Notably, even if Pinochet sought to underline how under Allende's government even *fewer* people had access to "goods" (TVs, telephones, cars), his remarks did not hide this fact: the ratio is telling. I evoke a last reframing about "police rationale" (see fig. 3.16). On one page, I read the following comment uttered by a police officer: "How could the police distinguish a journalist from a protester if journalists don't even wear ties . . ." On the opposite page, I see a photographer (*sans* tie) being attacked and held by two policemen. Needless to say, policemen should never repress either protesters or photographers, but that seems to be something that escapes or is completely beyond the bounds of this police officer's "rationale."

The text reproduced on the back cover of *El pan nuestro* indicates: "Our daily bread is the daily life, an attempt to wake up and come to life, a portrait of the brutality and the humanity which over the last few years we have been feeling and recording. The photograph speaks, it is clear, revealing." The collective subject who makes this statement—"we, photographers"—claims the photograph is a "portrait" of what they—the photographers—have "been feeling and recording." The photographers not only establish a strong linkage between the realm of feelings and the photographic field, but also—indifferent to theoretical debates about the limitations or incapacities of the photographic image (the photo is neither clear nor transparent; the photo is incomplete; the photo is mute or ambiguous, etc.)—suggest that the photograph is not ambiguous. Rather, it is clear, communicative, revealing. However, is *El pan nuestro* so obvious, so blatant in its denunciation that nothing remains to be said about the photos or the book as a whole? I hope that the reading I have performed stands as a testimony to the contrary.

There Is (No) History of Chilean Photography

As I have argued, several photographers and a few critics have insisted on the field's precarious existence, and even on its nonexistence. In this final section, I turn briefly to two critical texts mentioned earlier: Mario Fonseca's "A propósito de la fotografía en Chile" (On Photography in Chile) and Claudia Donoso's "16 años de fotografía en Chile: Memoria de un descontexto" (16 Years of Photography in Chile: Memory of a *Descontexto*). Fonseca curated the photography selection of the exhibition *Chile Vive* held in Madrid in September 1987. He wrote "A propósito" for the exhibition catalogue.[68] Donoso wrote "16 años," for a special issue of *Cuadernos Hispanoamericanos* about Chilean culture under dictatorship. Both texts, then, were written for international (and in the case of Donoso, scholarly) audiences. Like other texts written by photographers throughout this period, both critics built their accounts about the photographic field assisted by such notions as urgency, emergency, precariousness, marginality, disconnection, and discontinuity. At the same time, both claimed that photography had experienced a reemergence of sorts in the eighties despite the precariousness of the cultural field.

In the first lines of his curatorial text, Fonseca declares bluntly: "There is no history, no criticism, no market. Doing photography in Chile today is an adventure, as also is writing this text [. . .] *I rush into writing these lines* so that the thirty-two [photographers] who came and those who didn't can piece together a few strings from the many strings that are loose."[69] In Fonseca's view, the lack of history, criticism, and market has constrained the precarious existence of Chilean photography since the arrival of the daguerreotype in the 1840s. Donoso also underscores "the absence of a market, publishing initiatives—especially of photography books—which could motivate or disseminate authorial expressions, photography criticism, and intersections between photographic works and other cultural systems."[70] Even though photographers did engage in critical discourse—as I discussed earlier—their critical practices were not recognized as "photography criticism" because they were, as Donoso puts it, "absorbed by the contingency."

Both Fonseca and Donoso insist that the "urgency for reporting" bounds the work of a number of photographers during the dictatorship: "we see in this show so many photographers on the front line, risking more than their cameras and a few blows [. . .] while the distant landscapes of their hearts continue waiting, indefinitely," claims Fonseca.[71] Meanwhile, Donoso suggests: "the priority of the immediate reaction before the political violence monopolizes their energies."[72] In both cases, resorting to the present tense is not stylistic, but necessary—what both authors describe is happening: it is in the present. However, the urgency and presentness that circumscribe the photographers' work *also* punctuate the authors' writing. Fonseca not only confesses the urgency of his reflection at the beginning of his text—"I rush into writing these lines"—but also concedes at the end how difficult it is for him to assess a field that is just beginning to take shape (in other words, an *emergent, developing* field): "Chilean photography does not have a background yet, so I am entrusted with providing a generous evaluation."[73] Donoso offers a similar conclusion, although less generous: "As long as books with rigorous editing criteria are not published, the authorial endeavors that have formed the memory of these years will not be known, nor can they be assessed in their true dimension."[74]

This quasi-retrospective view rushes to consider (and assess) a field that is seen as incomplete, imperfect, and amorphous: it lacks a milieu, a background, a context. The quasi-retrospective view seems to imply that sometime in the near or distant future (the present is circumscribed by various emergencies) the field will become autonomous, consolidated. The field's autonomy, moreover, is contingent on (more) authorial views—authorial views that, out of necessity, keep "waiting in the photographers' hearts."[75]

Now, what does the statement "there is no history of Chilean photography" imply? Fonseca later expands on this idea: the photographs "don't convey the perspective of photography as the expression of an author; they are documents."[76] Chilean photography does not have a precise history because photography has been at the service of a separate history—Chilean history. The problem is that photographs have been considered almost exclusively as "documents:" they have been studied, interpreted, and exhibited as archival objects, and incorporated as such into historiography. This statement draws on the aesthetic parameters of art photography criticism: a precise history of photography is, to Fonseca, a history of authors. Yet this seems inadequate; there is no such a thing as a "precise history" of photography.[77] Donoso contends a similar idea. The critic unveils the notion of Chilean photography as the memory of a "decontext," a precarious condition related to limitations and absences. The restrictions imposed by domestic censorship as well as the urgency to denounce violence and repression have hindered the development of the Chilean photographic field, argues Donoso. The notion of "decontext" stresses in this sense the photographic field's marginality with regard to other fields: the photographic field has no background, no referential frameworks, and no traditions to claim for itself; there is also a need for rigorous criticism and publishing initiatives. The quasi-retrospective view insists on this: the development and consolidation of the photographic field have been hindered under military dictatorship, and this is noticeable in the absence of criticism, of publishing support, and of authorial perspectives (with a few exceptions).

Fonseca ends his text acknowledging the following: "we can't fail to mention that contemporary Chilean photography is an emergent movement, constituted as such less than ten years ago, and also that the scarce rigorous criticism from this period has focused on the visual arts (photocopy and video practices, art installations and body art, and more traditional media), where the scene has been much richer in processes and projections."[78] Donoso develops a similar argument regarding the artistic field: "It has been on the margins of the culture linked to the visual arts developed the decade prior to the 80s, where productive processes were registered that creatively and critically considered the Latin American photographic condition."[79] These statements also reproduce concurrent delineations of the cultural field under dictatorship, and this is why I insist on signaling their quasi-retrospective condition. The visual arts scene Fonseca mentions had reached, by 1987, more or less the same age as the professedly "emergent" photographic movement. Donoso, in turn, criticizes the absence of a publishing market as well as the absence of photographic initiatives intersecting with other cultural systems. Two of the photographic initiatives that emerged in this context, the *Ediciones económicas* and the *Anuarios*, are almost dismissed: "Besides editions in photocopy, a couple of *Anuarios* of precarious printing quality, there has been little or nothing."[80] Here surfaces again the quasi-retrospective stance that elucidates this claim: since these critical accounts aim to delineate the potential contours of an otherwise emerging, amorphous, marginal, precarious field, they fail to recognize as eloquent, thriving instances of the photographic field, an array of practices that are also deemed too marginal, too precarious.

"New formations can 'emerge' only when there are frames that establish the possibility of that emergence," suggests Butler.[81] This is precisely what happens with the discursive formulation of the photographic field under dictatorship. In a way, if Fonseca and Donoso could lament the lack of history, of a market, or of criticism, it is because there was already a frame that rendered these lacks visible: the photographic field. Even when they both underscored the shortcomings or "de-contexts" of Chilean photography, they did so considering the photographic activity as a field. Opposing the potential field they both imagine, there stood the real Chilean photographic field under dictatorship: a field circumscribed by its precarious and emergent condition, a field that lacked "precise contours," that developed "randomly" in a "disintegrated context" at the margins of the art field and of criticism. Yet this precarious, marginal, and emergent field thrived and subsisted despite all—despite the economic crisis, the censorship that took on different forms, and the lack of resources.

As I have argued, AFI photographers played a paramount role in this regard. On the one hand, they registered and attempted to visually communicate the contingency and the daily life that surrounded them; on the other, they attempted to stimulate and consolidate the photographic field. The discursive apparatus that grew from their exchanges was nourished by the developing photographic activity and also by the constraints—all kinds—the photographers faced on a daily basis. Reading *Punto de Vista* and the *Anuarios*, I was able to perceive that AFI photographers became editors and critics out of necessity: some of the texts were written in haste; at times, improvisation was part of the method. The reviews proffered and the initiatives put forward were sometimes described as provisional or imperfect, as though they were sketches of the "real" criticism and the "real," "consolidated" field to come. This is one of the effects of writing and reporting "from within," from the contingency: for the synchronous view, everything matters.

The emergent and precarious condition of Chilean photography was not only an issue discussed or touched on by photographers or a few critics in written form; it also motivated and propelled a series of collaborative projects throughout the eighties. If the military dictatorship is considered an "epoch" in the Foucauldian sense, photocopied photo books and seized photo essays surface as eloquent statements, material manifestations of the state of emergency and of the precarity. Without leaving aside the important work of denunciation, the projects I have considered here—the three volumes comprising *Ediciones económicas de fotografía chilena* and *El pan nuestro de cada día*—not only resisted and materialized the precariousness within which they emerged, but also continued consolidating and expanding the field. Besides facilitating the reproduction and dissemination of photographic works in a context that tended to "disperse them and marginalize them," the photocopy allowed the people involved in *Ediciones económicas* (photographers and writers) to explore different forms of composition, montage, and edition in the production of

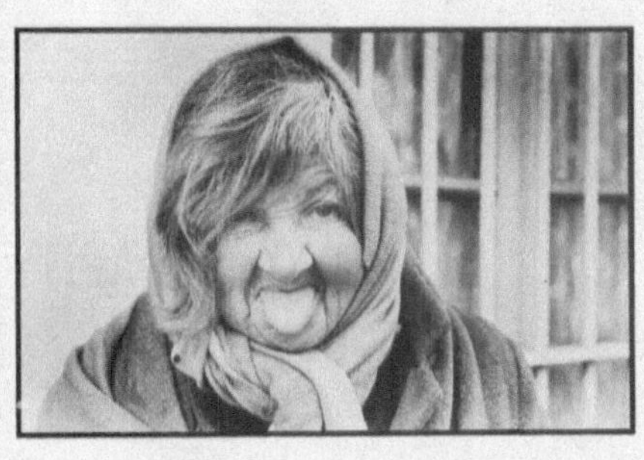

Figure 3.17. *El pan nuestro de cada día* spread. Elderly woman sticking her tongue out. Credit: Óscar Navarro. 1986. Black and white. Jorge Gronemeyer's personal archive (Taller Gronefot).

books of photography. The result of this creative process was deemed and presented as a "precarious object." As I have argued, viewing the photocopy as an "inferior" version of photography—a less serious, ordinary, disposable, transient version—motivated or catalyzed, to some extent, the different textual and visual montages patent in these different photocopied books. In my reading, I underscore the various processes of composition and reproduction, including Valenzuela's "photographs," as statements concerning the photographic field. Meanwhile, the photographers who collaborated in *El pan nuestro* defied the status quo, not only by visually attesting to and documenting the state of emergency, but also by imagining a different state of things. This defying act of photography is manifested in an expressive image depicting an elderly woman sticking her tongue out. Does she defy Merino or Pinochet? That is for us, the spectators, to decide.

4

PHOTOGRAPHY OFF LIMITS

The censored photos, above the chronicle of the protest or its political commentary, are associated symbolically and emotionally with the text not yet well formulated, still oscillating in many aspects, which is the ideology of the opposition. In a way, they anticipate it or, at least, prefigure it.

—Enrique Lihn, "La fotografía: entre la censura y el conformismo"

Even if it appears, at a certain time and place, that an individual or group is capable of destroying the civil contract of photography, along with the citizens of the citizenry of photography, the contract itself surprisingly reclaims its place through the efforts of some of its numerous trustees.

—Ariella Azoulay, *The Civil Contract of Photography*

On Saturday September 8, 1984, the Chief Office of the Emergency Zone in the Metropolitan Region and the Province of San Antonio issued Bando 19 (Edict Number 19), which ordered the magazines *Análisis*, *Apsi*, and *Cauce* and the newspaper *Fortín Mapocho*, all independently printed media opposed to the dictatorship, to restrict "their content to written texts exclusively" and "not to publish images of any kind."[1] The Edict also prohibited any mention of protests on the covers of these publications. From that date onward, the censored media could only "inform [its readers] about the so-called 'protests' in its interior pages." The following week, which marked the eleventh anniversary of the coup d'état, the Journalists Guild inaugurated an unprecedented photographic exhibit.

What was exceptional about this event was not so much its location (this was the first time the Guild held an exhibit on its premises) or its brevity (the photos hung on the walls for less than forty-eight hours) as the nature of the photos exhibited, which were all censored photographs of protests. Besides the concrete objective of showing the censored photos, the exhibit, which was orchestrated in just a couple of days, aimed to convey the Journalists Guild's repudiation of the authoritarian measures taken by the military regime in the name of the state of emergency. Both the ban on publishing images and the creative responses from the censored magazines reveal the key role photography played in the public space of the opposition.

The exhibition at the Journalists Guild was a significant instance of insubordination of photography, but it was not the only one: the civil imagination devised different ways to protest the censorship of the image and condemn the regime's violation of citizens' right to freedom of expression. The prohibited photographs were disseminated through different means. In what could be described as a revealing instance of photography's itinerant condition, the censored photographs traveled from the censored media to other spaces, including an uncensored magazine (*La Bicicleta*); they were also transformed into different visual signs. Because of these displacements, which operated in a supplementary way, the banned photographs kept being viewed, referred to, and discussed, and a different kind of—nonreferential—protest photography emerged. Thus, I shall claim, the ban did not stop photography from being denunciative; it did not stop photography from performing referentially, either. The censored media kept informing their readers and "showing" photographic content by resorting to empty squares and other shapes in lieu of photographs—further proof that truth is never to be located in the photo, that it always lies beyond the frame.

Here, we can begin to elucidate the phrase that gives title to this chapter, "photography off limits." Photographs and photography-derived materials were tactically deployed (fashioned and exhibited) as visual evidence to denounce the crimes and abuses perpetrated by the military regime. The photographs disseminated in the independent media had an undeniable disrupting effect in this regard. The photos that captured the violence and the repression perpetrated by police and military forces and those that registered the visual traces of human rights violations (the discovery of clandestine cemeteries, for instance) had strong documentary force. Given these evidentiary uses, it would not be difficult to claim that the military banned the publication of images in specific independent media because of the photos' capacity to expose what was going on. It could even be argued that the bureaucrats of the military regime were not the only players who understood (and also deployed) news photographs in this way; the photographers and photojournalists who produced the photos, the editors who published them, and the audiences who saw them also understood their potential. Valid though these arguments may be, they do not amount to the claim that photos simply "show" everything there is to see about a particular photographic situation—an episode of military repression, a moment at a massive protest, or any other incident.

In "The Times of the Document," André Rouillé explains that what defines the *modus operandi* of the modern photographic document is the belief that truth is captured and registered by the photo camera. News photos certainly operate under this premise: photography shows, captures, and records.[2] Photographs have permanent or fixed qualities (they are transparent, direct, etc.); photographs are visual evidence; the photographic document is inevitably bound to the truth.[3] Nevertheless, Rouillé reminds us that the photographic document never appears in isolation. It is always inscribed along with other signs and possesses the ability to transit from one space to another. These ideas also apply to news photos, which almost always appear along with written texts of different kinds. While news photos are usually perceived as peripheral content (the written text is the element that normally enjoys prominence), they are not "mere illustrations" of the texts with which they appear. Even though it has been claimed that because of their immediate spatial contexts (captions, written texts, and other visual and verbal cues), the signification of news photographs is more determined than that of other types of images, the news photos possess, like other images, autonomy in relation to their meanings.[4]

Photographs that circulate in the public sphere, such as news photographs, produce their audiences or spectators.[5] These spectators become both the photographs' addressees and the photographs' addressers. As addressers, spectators produce meanings for the photos and disseminate these meanings further.[6] They activate different photographic meanings and readings through their civil intention. The civil intention, as Ariella Azoulay explains, "exists in public, and it is much more difficult to stabilize what is at stake in it just as it is difficult to restrict it or subordinate it to external sources of authority or sovereignty."[7] The civil intention, on which the civil condition depends, consists in "the constant affirmation of the conditions of citizenship and their defense in the face of their takeover or appropriation by any particular group, field, or form of government."[8] Those who enact this constant affirmation do not belong to a homogeneous group. Rather, it is a "heterogeneous collective of individuals" connected through dissent.[9] The citizens of the citizenry of photography enact their citizenship every time they demand the restitution of rights or freedoms that have been suspended or taken away. An effect of the constant affirmation of citizenship enacted by photography's users is that they can formulate and imagine, through photography, that which does not yet exist.

Even if the adjectives traditional and analog are not conveyed explicitly, photography criticism has tended to frame the question of the limits of photography as a problem relative to specific limitations of traditional or analog photography. Also, in what can be described as a rather problematic semantic association, the limits of photography are sometimes assimilated into those of the photographic document, and even to those of documentary photography. These questions surface in quite remarkable ways in the catalogue of an art exhibit curated by Rouillé and held in 1996 at the Museo Nacional de Bellas Artes de Santiago, Chile. Not surprisingly, the exhibit was titled *Los límites de la fotografía* (The Limits of Photography).[10] I begin in the chapter's first section with an examination of the catalogue of this exhibit because it was the texts authored by Rouillé and Nelly Richard that inspired me to think of the limits of photography beyond the field of art in the first place.

As I shall argue, photography does not need the field of visual arts to be transformed into something else or to transgress its assumedly fixed limits. Furthermore, a consideration of the limits of photography under a repressive regime cannot be reduced to a discussion about the technical capacities of the medium (what photography can or cannot do) or about the ways in which visual artists or author photographers explore, interrogate, play with, or transgress photography's (aesthetic, ethic, and material) constraints. With regard to the Chilean case, due to the noteworthy counterinformative labor of the independent press and the key role photography had in this labor, such a consideration must address the authoritarian administrative practices that attempted to suppress the dissemination of news photographs—that is, to set photos off limits—because of their documentary and evidentiary burden, along with the various photographic displacements and transformations devised by the censored media to continue to report, denounce, and protest. This is why in this chapter I turn our attention to the discursive space of news media. I consider the administrative measures that attempted to constrain the independent media outlets that reported on human rights violations, police and military repression, the economic crisis, and the increasing empowerment of the political opposition. The photographic practices I analyze here were formulated in response to a specific limitation. Our focus turns to specifically the censorship imposed on images published in the independent media in 1984. Press photography was the protagonist of this fight for freedom of expression. While the duration of the ban was relatively brief (images were banned for three months), it came to mark a significant chapter in the history of the defense of human rights.

If the limits of photography depend on the interaction between photographs and their many users and visual evidence is constructed according to distinct historical codes of inscription and representation, what happens when news photographs transgress and transform the established codes altogether?[11] Do they continue to operate within the limits of the discursive space of news media? The analysis I develop in the second and third parts of the chapter attempts to answer these questions. Because of the ban, the censored photographs were displaced, relegated to other spaces. And, even more remarkably, they took on new forms. These new, nonphotographic forms (empty frames with captions or doodled signs) continued to operate as though they were photos. These insubordinate acts of photography were the result of the imagination deployed by its users and made possible by the supplementary condition of photography. Both the editors and readers of the censored media reclaimed the civil contract of photography through this photographic practice. The readers understood the important link the editors were establishing between the so-called photos (nonphotographic forms) and other (visual and textual) signs next to which these "insubordinate photos" appeared. The censored media were able to deploy this rhetorical strategy not only because press photographs (at least partially) rely on their framings and contexts to produce and convey meanings, but also because everyday users of photography had already been deploying similar displacements and transformations in the expanding field.

The Limits of Photography (in the Artistic Field)

If a limit involves the existence of at least two entities (one beyond which lies a second), the expression "the limits of photography" suggests not only that photography has limits, but also that something resides beyond them. Not surprisingly, photography's limits have been most consistently considered in light of the artistic practices that broach the medium to explore, reveal, or transgress photography's alleged limits. In Chile, as has been well studied and documented, various visual artists turned to photography or incorporated photographic materials into their practices to question the truth value attributed to the photograph, to denounce the ideologies of representation, and even to problematize the author function or the concept of authorship in the artistic field. Examining these practices, art critics framed or signified photography mainly as a documentary object or practice whose limits were broached and transgressed as this object or practice was incorporated into the artwork or used by visual artists.[12]

If a limit signals a border (and operates as an exclusion), in the exhibition *Los límites de la fotografía*, photography made by (documentary) "photographers" or "photographer-artists" was kept out of the museum, excluded by the limits imposed by André Rouillé, the curator. Photography, according to Rouillé, is inevitably subject to "the imperatives of documentary transparency." The "photographer-artist," for whom photography is both a "job" and an "artistic medium," is "forced to construct an oeuvre at the margins of the document and of communication."[13] Rouillé thus declares: "Excess, audacity, unboundedness, dissolution of formal, traditional boundaries. Photography has taken a radical turn in just over a decade. After having been relegated to practical and utilitarian functions, she has allowed herself to be tempted by art and has thrown herself to experiment, seeking to transgress the old formal limits of the document."[14] What does Rouillé mean by the "old formal limits of the document"? As he explains, the photographic document aspires to refer completely to a thing or reality existing outside of it; the document records the trace of this thing and faithfully reproduces its appearance.[15] If this is the case, then the "old formal limits of the document"—"old" because they have been posited as inherent to the document since the inception of photography—would correspond to qualities that also reproduce the idea of photographic truth: transparency, sharpness, instantaneity, and other elements. In fact, Rouillé refers to these, as well as to other formal and functional attributes of the document (visibility and abundance of details; the faculty of recording, restoring and preserving; permanence) as "formes de la verité."[16] These "forms of the truth" would be determined (and guaranteed) by the indexical quality of the photograph.

In Rouillé's formulation, post-photography marks the moment in which photography is freed from the "servitude of its documentary function," the moment in which "the simple recording of a scene is no longer what matters."[17] It is not surprising that Rouillé refers to the photographic production of the 1990s as post-photography. The formulation of a post-photographic era in the midnineties is part of the post-discourse wave that emerged in that decade—a wave that certainly had an impact on the local Chilean cultural context. Let's not forget that the transition to democracy began in the 1990s, so different debates on and critical approaches to the promises, failures, and "myths," to borrow Tomás Moulián's expression, surrounding the "new" postdictatorial Chile emerged in this decade.[18]

Rouillé defines post-photography as the "space in which new solutions are invented; unheard-of attitudes, unprecedented formulas that open a new field of possibilities, both to art and to photography. The field of the limits of photography."[19] In Rouillé's formulation, the field of the limits of photography extends "beyond" the restrictions and limits imposed by "forms of the truth" and documentary functions. In opposition to the (documentary) "photographer" or the "photographer-artist," Rouillé posits, simply, the artist. Likewise, in opposition to a photographic medium that attempts to detach itself, more or less successfully, from old documentary tenets and forms, Rouillé posits post-photography as follows:

> The process by which photography has evolved from a tool to a contemporary art material corresponds to what I have called 'post-photography' [. . .] We use the tools, but we work with the materials, we experiment, we combine them, we transform them in a thousand ways, *with no more limits than those imposed by technique or aesthetic sense*. Although the material is not a simple inert matter, although it always distrusts the meaning given to it, it is an open element, which is given to a myriad of procedures, without concrete aims, or formal obligations: without limits.[20]

Throughout his career, Rouillé has endeavored not only to elucidate critical notions pertaining to photography (the "photographic document" being a prime example), but also to materialize these ideas in his curatorial work—which highlights and focuses on artistic practices that interrogate and explore allegedly passé ideas about photography and the photographic document.[21] According to the critic-curator, it is in the realm of post-photography that artists "combine, associate, mix, overlap, and juxtapose different negatives, frames, images of all kinds and all sources."[22] Judging by this formulation, which conveys an eminently avant-garde impetus, photography would have been destined "to the same" until the appearance of artists; artists arrive to transgress the limits of a once pure, stable, fixed medium.

Rouillé's presentation also seems to suggest that the problem of the limits of photography would have become visible or an object of consideration in the artistic field first. However, this is an effect of the orientation of a kind of criticism that tends toward certain subject-authors (visual artists and photographers) whose practices might expose and/or exacerbate the limitations of (traditional or documentary) photography, or deconstruct, interrogate or comment on the aesthetic and/or ethical tenets that lie at the core of photographic discourse ("photography is first and foremost a document;" "photography should strive to capture, not to interpret, reality;" etc.). But the medium of photography is not pure, nor has it always remained the same. Photography has been subject to wide-ranging alterations and modifications from very early on and has undergone various changes and transformations in the course of its existence. Regarding the question of the limits of photography, the transformations of greatest interest are not so much those related to technical advances (these changes are better appreciated when considering photography diachronically) as those occurring at a specific time in response to specific situations. These transformations are not necessarily circumscribed to individual artistic practices; rather, they are an effect of the supplementary condition of photography and a result of the imagination deployed by its users.

Richard opens her essay by addressing the problem of these limits first in geocultural terms: Latin America and Europe, the border and the center. In the context of the exhibit, the border or margin is constituted by Chile and Argentina, the countries of origin of the artists displayed; France, here, takes the function of the center. Richard questions the limits of signification and contextualization and warns about the (limited) readings and interpretations the center can make of these works from the "periphery."[23] The center-margin duality implied in the notion of limits in a geocultural sense also surfaces—albeit indirectly—in Richard's description of the cultural field during the dictatorship: in the center, the artistic practices, and at the margins or in the limits of the cultural field, "the practices of the photographers." While not all the works exhibited in *Los límites de la fotografía* were created under dictatorship, this is one of the particular contexts to which Richard refers in her text: "The dictatorial paradigm forced many of the Chilean [artistic] works to reconceptualize the frontiers of an artistic discourse infringed by the confiscation of memory and identity and by the coercive violence of a word fragmented by the Manichean extremism of an exclusive truth."[24] This observation could well have been made regarding the realm of the independent press, which, as we shall see, also had to adapt and alter its practices in order to cope with the coercive violence of the military regime. It is also pertinent to evoke here the limit or border that Richard delineates between two ways of working with photography: "Unlike what happened in the field of visual arts, the lack of connections between personal photography networks and other cultural circuits of critical reflection about the image resulted in a situation whereby the practices of the Chilean photographers tended to refrain from any crossing of platforms and techniques."[25] This explains, as Richard observes, the fact that all the artists showcased (Gonzalo Díaz, Eduardo Vilches, Alicia Villareal, Enrique Zamudio, and Alfredo Jaar) came from the field of visual arts.

As Richard emphasizes, it was in the artistic field that the links between photography, memory, history, mass society, and identity were explored: visual artists proposed ideas about the reproducibility of the mechanical and technical image, and photography was posited as a theoretical object—one which allowed artists to rethink the role of the mechanical image as both social practice and artistic rupture.[26] In Richard's account, photographers and photojournalists stayed out of these debates because their practices "were limited to the primary objectivism of documentary realism (photo-testimony), on the one hand, and a subjectivism aestheticized by the poetic conventionalisms of 'auteur photography,' on the other."[27]

Los límites de la fotografía exhibited individual artistic practices that explored or interrogated different facets or aspects (formal, aesthetic, political, or cultural) of photography. Thus, Rouillé's curatorial selection itself drew a limit, operated by excluding: only post-photographic practices entered the museum, while "simple" or "pure" photographic practices remained outside this domain. I should emphasize that my objection is not that *Los límites de la fotografía* did not include practices from "nonartistic" realms or contexts (any curatorial selection, any act of interpretation or canon operates, one way or another, by exclusion). What I wish to illuminate, rather, is the extent to which Rouillé's and Richard's discursive practices delineate the limits on which their critical approaches are based. Both critics project imaginary limits between, on the one hand, practices that supposedly transgress the boundaries of photography and, on the other, practices that remain confined to repeating the same, circumscribed by the allegedly unchanging limits of the document. For Rouillé, the limits of photography are those of "traditional photography," the "old limits" of the photographic document. For Richard, the limits of photography are those of documentary photography, a practice confined either to denunciation and testimony or to auteur expressionism. In order to show how artistic practices transgress the alleged formal, thematic, or material limits of photography, both critics see the need to present these limits in a disambiguated way, without nuances. In an attempt to differentiate or mark the specificity and exceptionality of the selected artistic practices vis-à-vis the social (quotidian or mass) uses of photography, both Rouillé and Richard obscure the fact that photography has always been open to ambiguity, transformation, and even play.[28] Rouillé formulates the notion of post-photography to mark the moment when photography exceeds or transgresses its ancient limits—the moment when photography supposedly is freed from the formal, thematic, or material obstacles of the document.

Judging from these critical approaches, in order to elucidate the limits of photography, it would suffice to consider those processes, phenomena, and practices that, from within the artistic field, interrogate, explore, or experiment with what is usually defined as photography. Certainly, artistic practices have put forward different ways of approaching photography, continuously shaping the medium. This is not the same as saying that one need only turn to the artistic field to posit the problem of the limits of photography or to consider the transgression or expansion of said limits. The limits of photography are always in flux; they are contingent and dependent on photographs' itinerant condition, as well as on the relationships between the photographs and their publics.[29] This itinerant condition, as we have seen, implies not only that photos can be ripped off from printed pages, archives, or family albums in order to be reproduced, disseminated, or reframed, supplementing previous meanings or even acquiring new ones, but also altered and even transformed into something else: photocopies, textual descriptions of "camera-less" and "film-less" photos, photocopied masks, or other expressions. These transformations reveal photography's performativity and are the materialization of the civil imagination of its users.

Protest Photography, Unbound

Issued in September 1984, Edict Number 19 marked a peak in a growing effort on the part of the dictatorship to silence the independent press. That effort was initiated September 11, 1973, the day of the coup, with the suspension of freedom of speech and of the press. Thereafter, and until March 1978, when the state of emergency was lifted, those rights were curtailed by successive decrees. In 1974, the military instituted the DINACOS, which resorted to all kinds of legal and administrative measures to restrict these rights. For instance, a decree instituted in 1976 ordered that every printed medium looking to be published obtain authorization from DINACOS before going into circulation. Further, starting in

1978, a series of decree-laws introduced "new types of offenses in the Law of the Interior Security of the State, which [increased] the violations because of press laws."[30] Even though the 1980 Constitution guaranteed "the liberty of expressing opinions and [conveying] information, without prior censorship, in any way and by any means," it also specified that guarantee in full of these freedoms would begin only in 1990, and that for the time being they would be circumscribed to the transitory measures stipulated by the state of emergency, also noted in the Constitution. Consequently, the transitory measures left without effect the articles guaranteeing freedom of expression and of the press in accordance with the constitutional text.

With regards to the restriction and control of independent magazines and newspapers, the measures adopted by DINACOS included prepublication censorship at the discretion of the government information office (the most common excuse being that a publication had infringed on the Law of National Security of the State); prohibition of circulation on a regular basis; suspension of information and redaction of specific contents; temporal suspension or requisition of specific issues; legal indictment against the directors of these media; and exhortation to self-censorship.[31] All of these measures sparked criticism and condemnation from the Inter American Press Society.[32] Despite all these restrictions, the independent press media that began circulating in 1976 became the voice of the opposition forces. The magazines *Solidaridad*, *Análisis*, *Hoy*, *Apsi*, and *Cauce* and newspapers *Fortín Mapocho* and *La Época* became effective contra-information and denunciation media; they were also responsible for installing in the public arena the debate about the nonexistence of freedom of the press.[33]

Both Edict Number 19 and the civil responses it unleashed operated according to a substitutive logic. This logic is the effect of the supplementary condition of photography. Let's keep in mind that the supplement not only appears in place of but also adds to. Due to this double act—replacement and expansion—the supplement transforms and alters meaning. Let's first consider the text of the Edict. At first glance, this prohibition is absolute: the censorship applies to images "of any nature." At the same time, we have to consider that the Edict was issued only three days after a two-day massive protest. These *jornadas de protesta* (protest days) ended with ten people shot to death and hundreds injured and arrested in different cities. One of the people killed was La Victoria Parish priest Father André Jarlan, who was shot in his bedroom by *carabineros*.[34] Giving the Edict's timing, it is safe to suggest that DINACOS prohibited the publication of images "of any nature" (including, for instance, comic strips) with the specific objective of impeding the circulation of photos of these protests. The military bureaucracy supplemented, then, a particular kind of image—photos of the protests—with a more comprehensive category—namely, "images." In order to stop the photos of the protests, DINACOS decided to ban *all images*.

Photographers, journalists, graphic reporters, and critics were the first to emphasize this idea. Although the prohibition affected "images of any nature," several voices in the opposition denounced it as a specific form of censorship—that is, one directed largely at photos of the protests. So both the repression that imposed the ban and the different entities that suffered and resisted it focused on "protest photography." The military aimed to deactivate it by banning it; the independent press aimed to reactivate it and keep it in circulation by substituting it and displacing it. A few days after the Edict was issued, a series of censored photographs (all taken during the massive protests of September 4 and 5, 1984) was exhibited in a two-day show. Some weeks later, a shorter selection of photographs taken during the same protests was published in *La Bicicleta*—a magazine that had not previously disseminated this kind of imagery. Moreover, for the entire duration of the prohibition, the censored magazines supplanted—supplemented—the banned images with other forms of representation.

These substitutions ask us to reconsider the concept of "protest photography." What constitutes "protest photography"? Must an act of protest appear on the surface of an image for it to be so considered? Can an image protest without evoking or showing acts of actual protests in its surface? Although the first objective of the Edict was to stop protest photographs, the measure was taken a bit late. By September 8, the day the decree went into effect, *Apsi* already had distributed issue 152, which covered the protests of the previous week. "The protests of September 4 and 5 represented a clear picture [*fotografía*] of these eleven years of military regime," announced the first lines of an Editorial entitled "A once años del once" (Eleven Years after the "Eleventh" [the date of the coup]).[35] This photographic metaphor conveys a particular temporality—a brief and intense protest becomes a clear picture that crystallizes eleven years. It is not so much that the photos of the repression condense on their surfaces the violence exerted by the military during the eleven years it was in power; the idea here, rather, is that the protests themselves become a metaphor, a clear picture of authoritarianism and repression. The photographic metaphor is also telling when considered retrospectively. The same editorial that describes the protests as a "clear picture" and denounces the legal and administrative measures that constantly attacked the press, "the favorite target" of the regime's "politics of repression and exclusion," cannot anticipate (but, how could it?) that, within a matter of days, all the photos taken during these protests would be censored.

Issue 152 of *Apsi* alluded to the September protests both on the cover ("Consequences of the Protests: The Failure of a Heavy Hand") and in the aforementioned Editorial, as well as in an op-ed and a chronicle about the protests entitled "The Protests of September 4 and 5: The Biggest, the Strongest," which was signed by the whole *Apsi* team. This chronicle condemned the "indiscriminate beatings" inflicted on protesters by the police, providing a detailed account of the case of "a young man with an almost emptied eye due to a kick given by a member of the police," and evoked "the surprise" of foreign journalists who, in addition to being sprayed by water-cannon trucks, "witnessed the action of dogs that left—at least—three people injured."[36] The images (without captions) below the chronicle's title documented some of these events: beatings, injuries, and scuffles.

Besides resorting to censorship by administrative and judicial means, the government relentlessly attacked and publicly discredited both the protests and the independent media that reported on them. The text of the Edict alluded to the protests by means of quotation marks and the qualifier "so-called," a gesture that sought to minimize the importance of a series of public acts of resistance that were becoming increasingly frequent and massive. These "so-called protests" (not a minor problem for Pinochet's regime) never appeared framed in positive terms in the media adherent to the regime or on the open TV channels, also controlled by the military.[37] The protests were usually visualized and depicted in these pro-military media outlets as disorganized and violent acts of extremism or as efforts orchestrated by the opposition to destabilize the military regime. Regarding the role of the police or the military forces in the protests, their acts were always justifiable in the eyes of the official media. Government officials also discredited the media that reported on the protests. The then Minister of the Interior Sergio Onofre Jarpa, for instance, claimed that the situation of the "real country is very different from that expressed by independent media because there is abundant progress"; he questioned these media for focusing "only on negative aspects" and, astonishingly, for their proclivity to give "space to people that sometimes don't even have the support of their wives."[38] The Board of Directors of the National Council of Journalists of Chile did not fail to respond to Jarpa's accusations: "The problems Chile faces do exist. They are not created by journalism, as the words of the Minister indicate [. . .] This is to attribute to the media a power that it does not have. And to believe, at the same time, that problems disappear because they are not mentioned."[39]

Implementing prepublication censorship and resorting to misogynous comments aimed at delegitimizing the work of journalists and reporters (many of them women) was not enough to stop the counterinformation labor undertook by independent magazines and newspapers. On the contrary, the coverage of national protests and strikes became a central task of the independent press. Just as the resistance and protests gained space in the streets, so too did their documentation and visual representation in the independent press. Journalist Fernando Paulsen, who worked at the time for *Análisis*, recalls: "Before [1983], our sources were the high spheres of the opposition. Since the protests arose, there was a mix of theory and practice in journalism."[40] The social mobilization that intensified in 1983 not only changed the modus operandi of the independent press, as Paulsen's observation makes clear, but also transformed the political space and the very way of practicing politics.[41]

Before 1983, neither *Apsi* nor *Análisis* had published many photographs. Meanwhile, from 1983 on, photographs of badly injured protesters (and, on occasion, journalists and photographers), of water cannons spraying protesters, of multitudes marching, of villagers performing land seizures, and of businesses closed on strike days or roadblocks in the city's marginal neighborhoods, became more and more recurrent in the independent media. In fact, I would like to posit a visual correlation between the rise of social and political resistance and its concomitant repression in 1983, and the expansion of the photographic surface in the printed pages of the independent media during the same period. As Lorenzo Vilches formulates, the photographic surface refers not to the space that the photo takes up on a particular page, but rather to "the spatial relation between the photo and the page, and between both and the totality of pages" of the magazine or newspaper.[42]

The cover of *Análisis* issue 60 (July–August 1983) is exemplary in this respect. The cover suggests a correlation between protests, repression, and photography while illustrating this connection graphically: under the headline "+ repression + protest," four photographs depicting different instances of protest and repression are mounted (see fig. 4.1). This collage-like montage, in which each image covers some fragment of another, suggests the ideas of accumulation, repetition, and excess: accumulation of rage and repetition and excess of violence and repression. The superposition of images also seems to suggest that no surface is ca-

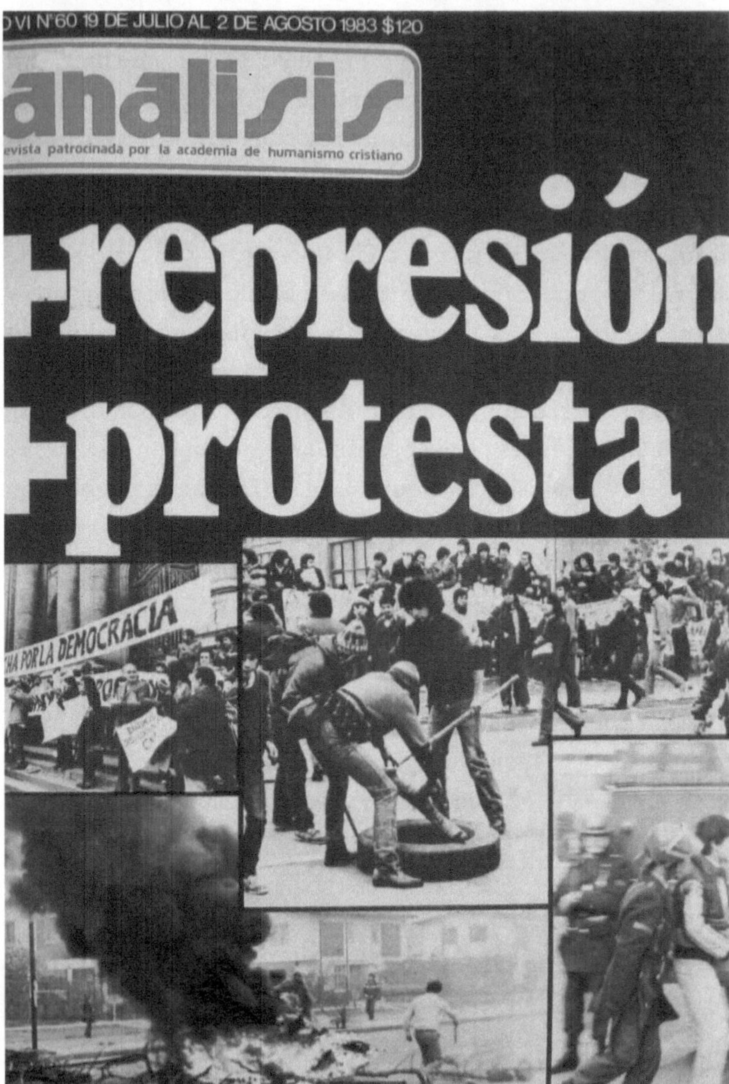

Figure 4.1. "+ Represión + Protesta" cover of *Análisis* 60 (July–August 1983; now defunct). Black and white. Jorge Gronemeyer's personal archive (Taller Gronefot).

pable of containing all of the available images of repression and protest: instead of four, there could have been eight, fifteen, or even twenty photographs. This cover and the overall expansion of the photographic surface in this magazine and others are telling instances of the increasing prominence of press photographs in the independent media.

Pinochet's regime resorted to the transitory measures of the state of emergency to promulgate, in May of 1983, a military edict prohibiting independent media from publishing declarations by leaders of the Central Unitaria de Trabajadores (CUT) (Unitary Central of Workers) and CUT's call for strike. In March 1984, it resorted to similar measures with the promulgation of Edict Number 2, through which *Análisis*, *Cauce*, *Apsi*, and *Hoy* became subject to prepublication censorship. That same March, another Edict mandated that these media were not to highlight "matters, events, or conduct that induce, propitiate, or favor, in any way, alteration of the public order."[43] This was another instance of wholesale censorship. The prohibition aimed not only to curtail freedom of expression but also to suspend media coverage of the events occurring at the time.

In April 1984, *Análisis* conducted a poll about Pinochet that became a cover story. The title read, "Mayoría Absoluta: Que Se Vaya" (By Absolute Majority: Let Him Go). Because of this cover story, Juan Pablo Cárdenas, founder and director of *Análisis*, was apprehended and charged, and DINACOS took the issue out of circulation from the kiosks. *Análisis* challenged this action on the basis of violation of their right to property, an action unprecedented until then. Protesting all these measures (both the prepublication censorship imposed on *Cauce* and Cárdenas's imprisonment, as well as the prohibition on *Apsi* banning it from publishing national news, the censorship of all these publications, and the eight-day delay on the return of confiscated issues of *Cauce* and *Análisis*), journalists chose to mobilize: the Journalists Guild called for an assembly; several journalists organized a march to the public penitentiary where Cárdenas was imprisoned; twenty-three journalists declared a hunger strike in the Association's headquarters. In the midst of all this, the Court of Appeals declared wrongful the prepublication censorship imposed on *Cauce* during the state of emergency. A note published in *Cauce* in May described the court's resolution as "the beginning of the end" of censorship. "The issue that the reader has in her hands has had to undergo pre-publication censorship, we believe, for the very last time," concluded the note.

Also in May, a graphic reportage published in *Análisis* (issue 82) provided information about the violent repression suffered by more than three hundred families during a (frustrated) seizure of land in the municipality of Renca (see fig. 4.2). In the first and last pages of this piece, images and text occupy almost the same amount of the page's surface. Nonetheless, in the central page spread, the photographs themselves, all taken by Kena Lorenzini, construct the narrative: the villagers' arrival with Chilean flags ("symbols of land seizures," accord-

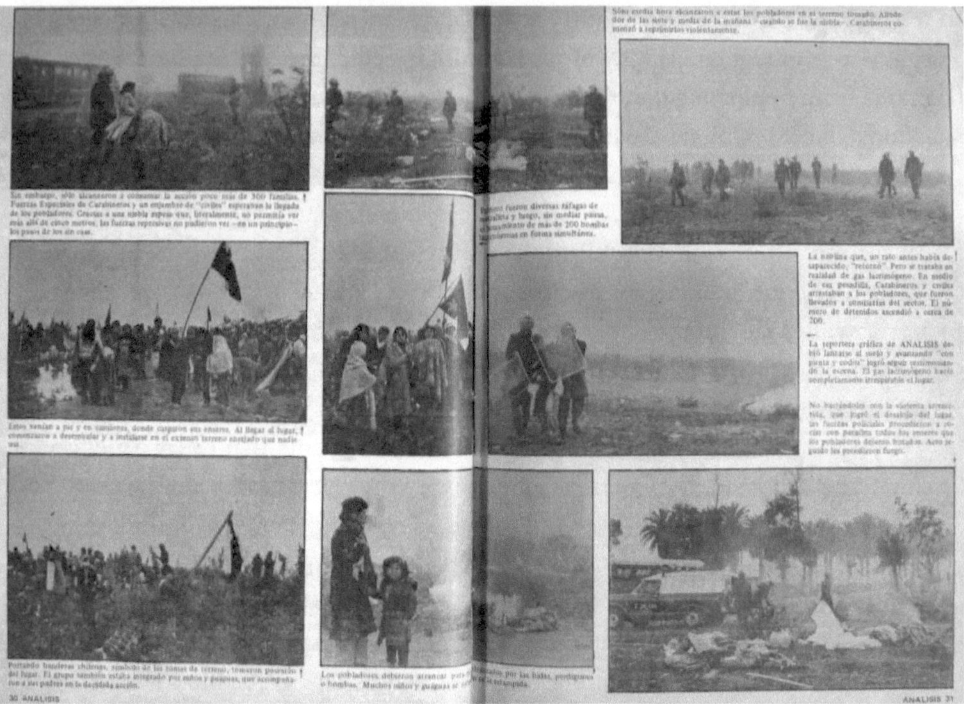

La neblina que, un rato antes había desaparecido, "retornó". Pero se trataba en realidad de gas lacrimógeno. En medio de esa pesadilla, Carabineros y civiles arrastraban a los pobladores, que fueron llevados a comisarías del sector. El número de detenidos ascendió a cerca de 200.

La reportera gráfica de ANALISIS debió lanzarse al suelo y avanzando "con punta y codos" logró seguir testimoniando la escena. El gas lacrimógeno hacía completamente irrespirable el lugar.

30 ANALISIS

ANALISIS 31

Figure 4.2. Photographic reportage of land seizure in Renca, *Análisis* 82 spread (May 1984; now defunct). Credit: Kena Lorenzini. Black and white. Jorge Gronemeyer's personal archive (Taller Gronefot).

ing to the caption), the carrying of personal belongings, clashes between the villagers and police (both in uniform and undercover), the dispersion of villagers by police using teargas, the destruction and burning of the villagers' personal belongings. If the housing and economic crisis propelled the families to occupy and take the land, the urgent nature of the situation propelled the photos to occupy, so to speak, the surface of the page. One of the texts framing the photos underlines the actual physical effort and personal sacrifice made by Lorenzini while taking the photographs: "Our *Análisis* graphic reporter had to drop to the floor and, crawling, managed to continue documenting the scene. Teargas made the place completely un-breathable." This commentary also illustrates the at-times dangerous conditions under which photographers and reporters had to work.

After the court's resolution of May 1984, magazines were permitted to cover land occupations and protests once again, as the graphic reportage I just described illustrates. Nevertheless, and opposing the auspicious forecast of *Cauce*, "the beginning of the end" of censorship did not come. Quite the contrary, DINACOS imposed a ban on images only four months later, in September. And in November, Pinochet proclaimed Law Decree Number 1,217, which altogether banned the publication of *Análisis, Cauce, Apsi, La Bicicleta, Pluma y Pincel,* and *Fortín Mapocho.*[44]

Military Censorship and Civil Responses

Given the comprehensive textual and visual coverage independent magazines had provided of the protests since 1983, why does Edict Number 19 ban images only, without including written texts? Poet Enrique Lihn attempts to provide an answer in a note published in *Cauce*. Arguing against those who claimed that the main objective of the ban on images was to stop the proliferation of political cartoons—which also thrived in these publications—Lihn underlines that the *photographs*, not the cartoons, were "the object of the prohibition." He also underscores that "the graphic reporters are the ones accused of being part of the violence."[45] Even though Lihn does not discard the fact that photographs are "of a faster and easier assimilation [than written texts] for a larger number of recipients," for him, the power of photographs resides in their capacity to convey and express affects and ideas not yet articulated in written form. Photographs are, according to the poet, more effective than written texts not only because they make institutionalized violence blatant and visible, but also (and above all) because they supplement the ideology of the opposition: "the censored photos, above the chronicle of the protest or its political commentary, are associated symbolically and emotionally with the text not yet well formulated, still oscillating in many aspects, which is the ideology of the opposition."[46]

Lihn, an avid reader of Barthes, broaches and questions the common understanding of news photographs as mere illustrations of the written texts with which they appear.[47] He makes sure to remind his readers of this idea: "censored [photographs] are far from simple illustrations of the 'exclusively written texts' about the protest."[48] Photographs touch their publics; they appeal to a system "of empathies and sympathies" which is, ultimately, closer or more immediate to the spectators than the written texts. Needless to say, Lihn's ideas about photography are far more sophisticated than those of the military bureaucracy. For the latter, photographs invariably and truthfully display reality on their surfaces. Since photographs display everything there is to see, in order to conceal reality, it suffices to ban photographs. Such a belief conforms to the regime of truth under which the news reportage operates.

Edict Number 19 was directed toward specific independent media because of their high degree of dissemination. As Matías León Lira explains in his study of *Análisis*, dissemination was key: "The goal was to reach a large number of readers, without caring, in many instances, about the way by which they were accessed."[49] The fact that the magazines were photocopied or that issues circulated from hand to hand was not a problem for their editors.[50] As director of *Análisis* Juan Pablo Cárdenas states, "The printing numbers did not reflect the actual number of readers because a lot of photocopies circulated, a fact that made us all very happy."[51] A significant and daring response to the ban on images was the two-day photo exhibit at the Journalists Guild building, which took place the week following the implementation of Edict Number 19. For two days, the walls of the Journalists Guild building became pages of sort, supplements of the censored pages of *Apsi*, *Cauce*, *Análisis*, and *Fortín Mapocho*. While the Journalists Guild exhibit gave the censored photographs a rather limited exposure, the act of displaying censored photographs became in and of itself an insubordinate gesture. Moreover, the displacement of the photos from the printed page to the building wall enhanced the significance of the photographs. During these two days, the censored protest photographs, and not the protests themselves, became the news.

All the photos exhibited had been taken during the days of national protest. The censored photographs, like so many others taken at previous protests, offered a sharp and unambiguous depiction of the repression. Even though independent magazines had been publishing photos of protests regularly, these photos acquired a special status: they had become "forbidden objects" after the ban. A brief note in *Apsi* highlighted the air of expectation felt outside the Journalists Guild's building and the large number of people waiting in line to see the exhibit.[52] Despite the fact that the "theme" was well known (protests and repression), despite the similarity between these photos and photos previously published, and even despite the rushed planning and execution, the exhibit of censored photographs received more than two thousand people, according to a review published in *Análisis*.[53] The success of the exhibit and the diversity of the public (two elements celebrated in the censored magazines) confirmed it was possible to resist such authoritarian measure. Indeed, the *Apsi* note suggested that the "curiosity of seeing censored photos" was not the only factor that had motivated "dressmakers, students, hairdressers, workers, professionals, housewives, [and] salesmen" to visit the exhibit in downtown Santiago; these people also had attended the exhibit to "demonstrate their repudiation of the restrictive measures."[54] Journalist José Carrasco claimed a similar idea: "the exhibit of protest photographs became [. . .] a space that gathered not only people who, due to their direct relation to journalism, were bound by the fight for the freedom of expression, but also different representative sections of the population that transformed it into a demonstration of popular protest in its own right."[55]

The censored photographs became news, and thus acquired supplementary meanings and interpretations. Not only did they document the repression but also, by making the photographs "uncensored," they defied the ban, allowing spectators to express their repudiation toward the measures adopted by the military. Moreover, they fostered a space to empathize with the victims of the repression. The exhibition itself—the "briefest and most well attended in the country," according to Carrasco—also took on different qualities and attributes: the Journalists Guild's exhibition, by enabling the dissemination and exposure of censored protest photographs, showed that it was possible to counter, even if temporarily and partially, the censorship imposed by Edict Number 19. The event also materialized into a gesture of solidarity with the people affected by the state of emergency, not only the reporters and photographers directly affected by the ban, but also the protesters themselves (some of whom appeared in the censored photographs) and, more generally, all victims of military violence. Meanwhile, the large and diverse crowd of spectators became an eloquent expression of popular dissent, a clear sign of the rejection of censorship. The exhibition of censored protest photographs, organized in just a few days, became thus another instance of protest.

Protest photographs typically appeared alongside chronicles, op-eds, reportages, or other text. These texts oriented and contextualized, to a greater or lesser extent, the meanings of these photographs. At the Journalists Guild exhibition, the photos were exhibited without such texts. Here, Edict Number 19 itself functioned as the most immediate context. The ban both framed and gave meaning to the exhibition. Without chronicles, reportages, or any other kind of text to "frame" the photographs, their expressive traits became stronger. Also, let's not forget that the photos exhibited at the Journalists Guild would have been published in four different publications were it not for the ban. The simultaneous display of dozens of photographs, all mounted directly on the wall (without frames), invited spectators to search for continuities, similarities, and differences among the images. They witnessed, on the one hand, an accumulation of repeated acts of repression, and on the other, gestures of defiance, both of which surely altered the photographs' meanings.

If the brief reviews and commentaries published in the censored magazines made the censored photos "news content," the exhibition made them protagonists of a photographic event. Press photos usually appear reproduced on printed pages; in this case, the photos were printed on photographic paper and hung on walls without captions. Thus, due to the logic of substitution instigated by the ban on images, a particular kind of image (protest photographs) was displaced into a different space, one this kind of photograph does not usually inhabit—the wall. The displacement of protest photographs from the censored magazines to the building walls implied both an aesthetic and a political gesture. For the first time, protest photographs were being exhibited on their own—that is, without visual or textual cues.

The Journalists Guild exhibition was not the only instance of dissemination of censored photographs. *La Bicicleta*, a youth magazine focused mainly on literature and music, also published a selection of these photos in its issue 58 (corresponding to the week of October 23, less than two months after the national protest).[56] As in the exhibit, the photographs were published without captions, but, different from the exhibit, they were here introduced by a brief text that offered a few notions concerning the photographs.[57] Once again, the protest photographs became the news and focus of the story. The brief introduction invited readers to appreciate the photographs displayed as "testimonies of our reality"—that is, it underscored their evidentiary force. Besides offering this basic tenet of the regime of truth under which press photography operates, the editors also attempted a photographic interpretation of their own. They emphasized that photographs were able to fix events on the spectators' retina and refute the reports produced by official media and TV stations. Moreover, they suggested, protest photographs had been censored not because they were testimonies, but because they were *subversive* testimonies: "the image, by showing what happens in the streets, has become subversive [. . .] it denies what the military says." This presentation ended by praising the existence of the "fixed image, transformed in a collective testimony of the times we are living in" and acknowledging "the archives that were opened for us."[58] This final acknowledgment illuminates an aspect of the censored photographs that had not been previously mentioned or considered:

their status as archival objects. In *La Bicicleta*, the documentary force of the uncensored photos is expanded; protest photos are important because of both their evidentiary power *and* their status as archival objects. This implies that they can be recuperated, displaced, and re-utilized.[59] This mobility liberates, so to speak, the photographs from their primary, original context. But more importantly, it reactivates them. It suffices to take them out of the archive, reframe them, and disseminate them. This is precisely what *La Bicicleta* does: it takes the photos out of the archive and reframes or recontextualizes them, thus liberating them, once again, from censorship.

This photographic story published in a teen cultural magazine prolonged the effect of the protest photographs. The story appeared almost seven weeks after the protests of September 4 and 5. Remarkably, even though the ban was still in place, *La Bicicleta* published images taken only on those protest days. In other words, *La Bicicleta* reactivated a specific censored photographic archive. Because of *La Bicicleta*'s target readership, and perhaps also because the photos were being disseminated belatedly—that is, the urgency to denounce the repression had already faded—the photographs selected brought to the fore a different aspect of the protests: the widespread presence of young people at the protests (see fig. 4.3). The selection placed the focus on the energy and liveliness the young protesters brought to the streets during the *jornadas de protesta*. At least six of the fifteen photographs included in the series show groups or multitudes of young people marching and protesting, carrying political signs. One of the photos (by Álvaro Hoppe) depicts a group of students gathered before the main entrance of the campus of the University of Chile School of Law with a large sign reading "MATAR: consigna militar / VIVIR: consigna juvenil" ("TO KILL: military motto / TO LIVE: youth motto"). It is difficult to discern the faces in the photo. The most important element in this image is the site of the protest (the state university) and the message the youth express with their sign.

It wouldn't be a mistake to suggest that more than a few protesters depicted in the photographs were readers of *La Bicicleta*. As protesters, they participated in the event photographed; as readers of the magazines who watched the images many weeks afterward, they also participated in the event of photography. The spectator who returns to *La Bicicleta*'s photographic reportage more than three decades later is also, herself, a participant of this event of photography. Watching these uncensored photographs, these displaced and recuperated archival objects, I cannot fail to notice that two of the policemen portrayed in these photos (one by Miguel Ángel Larrea and the other from *Cauce*'s archive) are *also young*

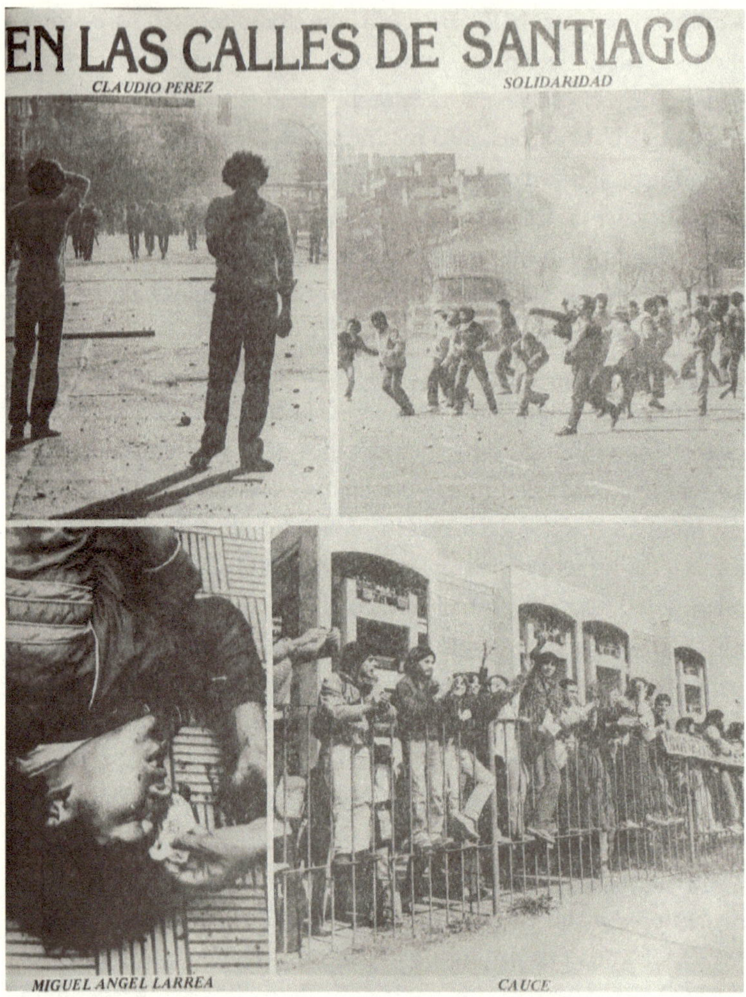
EN LAS CALLES DE SANTIAGO

CLAUDIO PEREZ

SOLIDARIDAD

MIGUEL ANGEL LARREA

CAUCE

Figure 4.3. "Presence of Youth in the Streets of Santiago." *La Bicicleta* 58 spread with photographs not published in other media (October 1984; now defunct). Credits: Claudio Pérez, *Solidaridad*, Miguel Ángel Larrea, and *Cauce*. Black and white. Photograph: Ángeles Donoso Macaya.

people, just like the protesters who flooded Santiago's streets during the national protest days—this is the disciplinary face of the presence of youth in the streets of Santiago.

In *Camera Lucida*, Barthes suggests that "whatever it grants to vision and whatever its manner, a photograph is always invisible: it is not what we see."[60] Paradoxically, the invisibility of the photograph Barthes evokes is dissolved the moment news photos are removed from the photographic surface. Or, to put it differently, the ban on images makes apparent the condition of news photographs as materials objects (see fig. 4.4). This condition, already highlighted in the Journalists Guild exhibit, in which spectators observed the photos pinned to the walls, becomes even more visible, patent, on the photographic surface of the censored media.

Needless to say, censored media were forced to comply with the ban: they

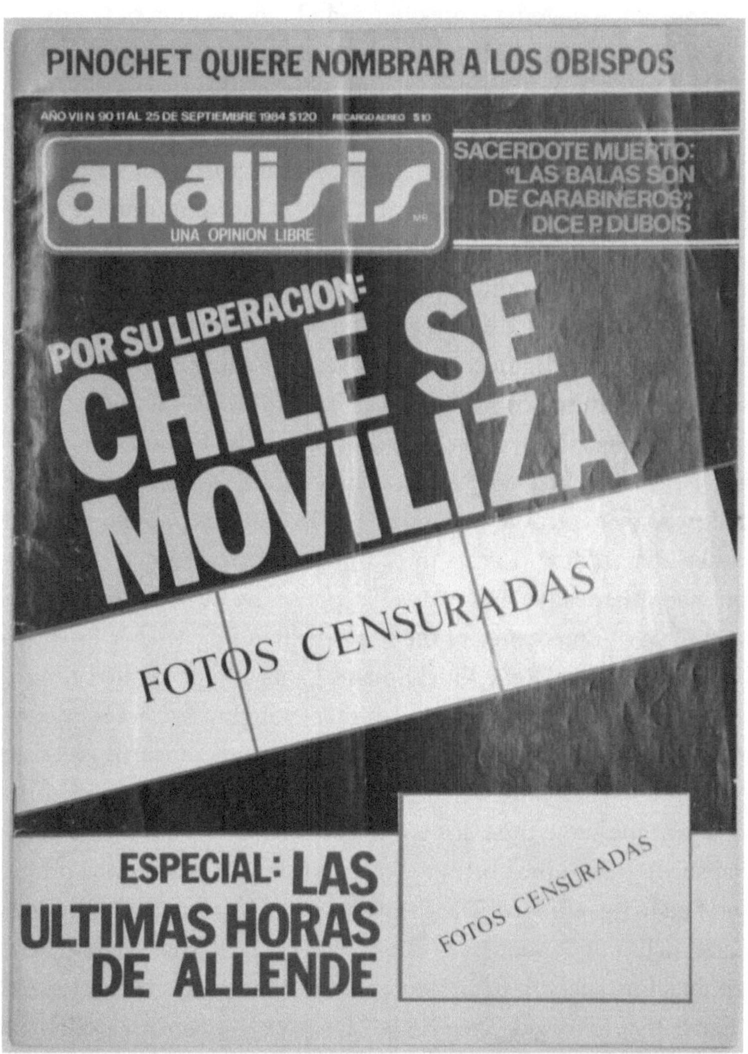

Figure 4.4. Empty frames (censored images), cover of *Análisis* 90 (September 11–25, 1984; now defunct). Color. Luis Weinstein's personal archive.

could not publish any image. Yet, photographs occupy *physical space* on the photographic surface. Therefore, in order to comply with the ban, but above all to sign and denounce the ban, the censored media displayed outlined empty spaces on almost every printed page. The captions and other visual cues invited spectators to see (that is, to imagine) the censored photographs. The word "photograph" began to describe forms or elements that were not, strictly speaking, photos: empty surfaces, sometimes framed in the form of pictures, sometimes intervened with doodles, letters, or signs. This photographic practice achieved different things: it reminded audiences of the ongoing repression and of the violation of their own rights as readers of news media (the ban on images was an attack on the freedom of the press); it also challenged the regime of truth of press photography—that is, the notion that the camera captures and frames the truth and that the photograph shows everything there is to see about an event. More importantly, it ridiculed the ban and eventually rendered it ineffective. Tellingly, this insubordinate act of photography functioned *because* it operated within the limits of the discursive space of news photography. How did this photographic practice of resistance of take form? What did the first (published) censored photo depict?

Because the closing of its edition coincided with the issuing date of the Edict (September 8), *Cauce*'s editorial committee was forced to reduce, at the last minute, all the contents of issue 22 (see fig. 4.5). Protesting the ban on images "of any nature," the editors decided to publish a large white square on the cover of the issue, followed by a caption that read: "His Excellency Captain General Augusto Pinochet Ugarte, now 11 years in command of the country." And under the caption, parenthetically: "His image disappears by express order of the Chief of Zone in State of Emergency of the Metropolitan Region and Province of San Antonio, Major General René Vidal Basauri." This unprecedented gesture exposed the violence and the repression the military sought to conceal by banning the images. Edict Number 19 was an authoritarian (and absurd) measure whose aim was to remove from the visual field *all images* opposing the regime. *Cauce*'s cover page at the same time displayed its compliance with the ban and uncovered its absurdity: even the portrait of the person who ordered the prohibition of images had to be removed. The cover suggested by means of irony, that countless images, including Pinochet's own portrait, would not be seen because of the ban on publishing subversive photographs. This irony also characterized the censored issues that followed. The article "Everyone Demands Freedom of the Press," about the negative response of foreign and national media organizations (even official outlets such as *El Mercurio*) to the ban, was accompanied by

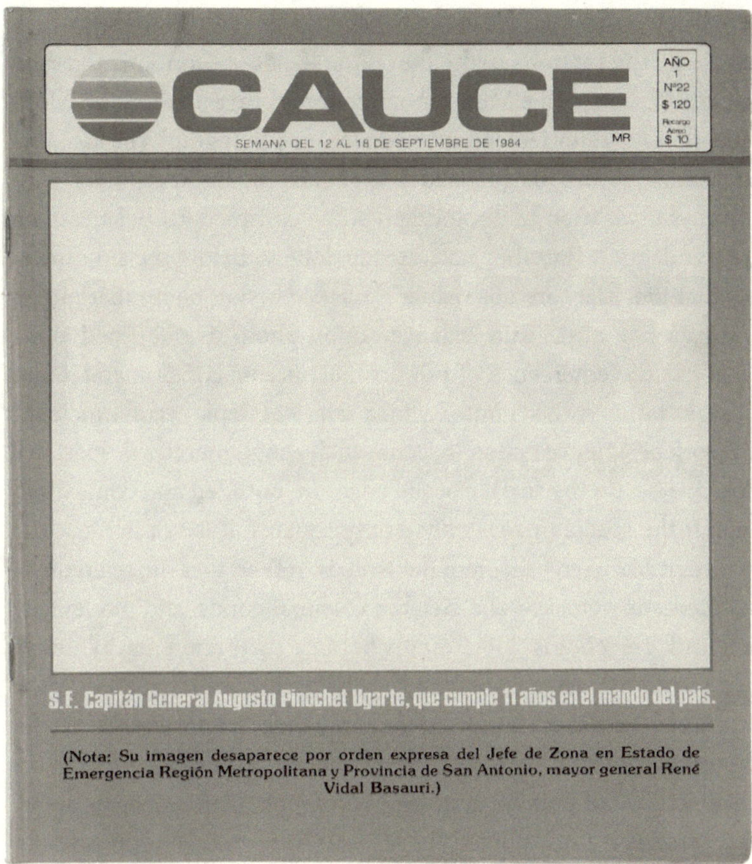

Figure 4.5. Empty square, cover of *Cauce* 22 (September 12–18, 1984; now defunct). Color. Jorge Gronemeyer's personal archive (Taller Gronefot).

a photo whose caption read: "CAUCE exclusive! A photograph of the complete list of freedoms and guarantees granted to the press by the government. Below, to the right, the President's signature." Notice here the way the caption conforms to the rhetoric and formatting of traditional news photo captions, the way it guides the spectator's gaze. Since the photo depicts an implausible object—a list, signed by Pinochet, granting and guarantying freedom of the press—it follows that one doesn't see anything. Another caption announces, "Here we show the tenebrous headquarters of the CNI, but thanks to the providential Edict Number 19, you won't have the chance to see it. You are welcome."

In the Business section of the same issue (24), most captions allude to different facets of the economic crisis. Like the list of freedoms signed by Pinochet, which spectators cannot see, the captions frame the "photos" about economic issues in the following terms: "Escobar [the Minister of Economy] gave a speech on Monday the seventeenth. Our reporters left immediately to photograph the essential goods with a noticeable result: the goods took flight and are imperceptible." "Another disappointment: we tried to photograph some conspicuous businessmen de-dollarizing their debts . . . but they had already done so before the announcement of the devaluation. They are not visible." "Science fiction photo that proves economic groups do not exist." Said "science-fiction photo" is published along with an article about the emergence of powerful economic conglomerates and their interference in politics; the "photo," which *does not* depict economic conglomerates, is a work of "science fiction" because such conglomerates *do* exist. All of these "photos," visible on the surface of the page, are outlined and contextualized by captions. If the spectator sees only empty squares, it is not because the photographic content has been censored: the issue is, rather, that the referents (a list of essential freedoms signed by the dictator, essential goods, and money) are nowhere to be found. The photos "look" empty because their referents do not exist. In this sense, the editors seem to suggest (not without irony) that these "photos" can be considered "visual evidence." At the same time, because of the playful way the photographic content is rendered, these "photos" remind their spectators that truth is never located or pointed at in the photograph. Unfortunately, not all captions are as ingenious as those quoted above—some are quite the opposite. For example, the caption of the only "photo" that appears on the second page of *Cauce* issue 22 states: "Beautiful lady sunbathing on a beach in the south of France, not only 'top-less' but also 'bottom-less,' which you will not be able to see. What a pity." The caption assumes a heterosexual male reader and makes apparent the recalcitrant and naturalized *machismo* that (even today) surfaces in different contexts and scenarios (let's recall that Minister Jarpa condescendingly evoked "the wives" of those who work for independent media to discredit these media).

All the censored media adopt the same strategy—all keep distinguished spaces for the photos—but not all resort to humor or irony in the captions. Some spaces are left blank; others are filled with doodles or signs. *Apsi*, for instance, uses fingerprints to fill most of the empty spaces in its issue 153, a gesture that evokes the linkage between the fingerprint, a trace used as a proof of identity, and the photograph.

Análisis, in turn, prints an entire issue (92) with the motif of traffic signs. Squares are adorned with hand-drawn traffic signs, such as "Do not turn right" and "Stop," which hint at the political situation. The stop sign reproduced on the cover of the magazine is a clear allusion to the protests: *pare* (stop) is here an invitation to join the *paro* (general strike). In another issue of *Análisis*, a large question mark formed by smaller handwritten questions repeated over and over evokes the relatives of the disappeared, who persistently repeated the same questions at rallies and vigils: "Where are they?" "How many are there?" "Who are they?" (see fig. 4.6). *Análisis* does not stop there: the magazine goes so far as

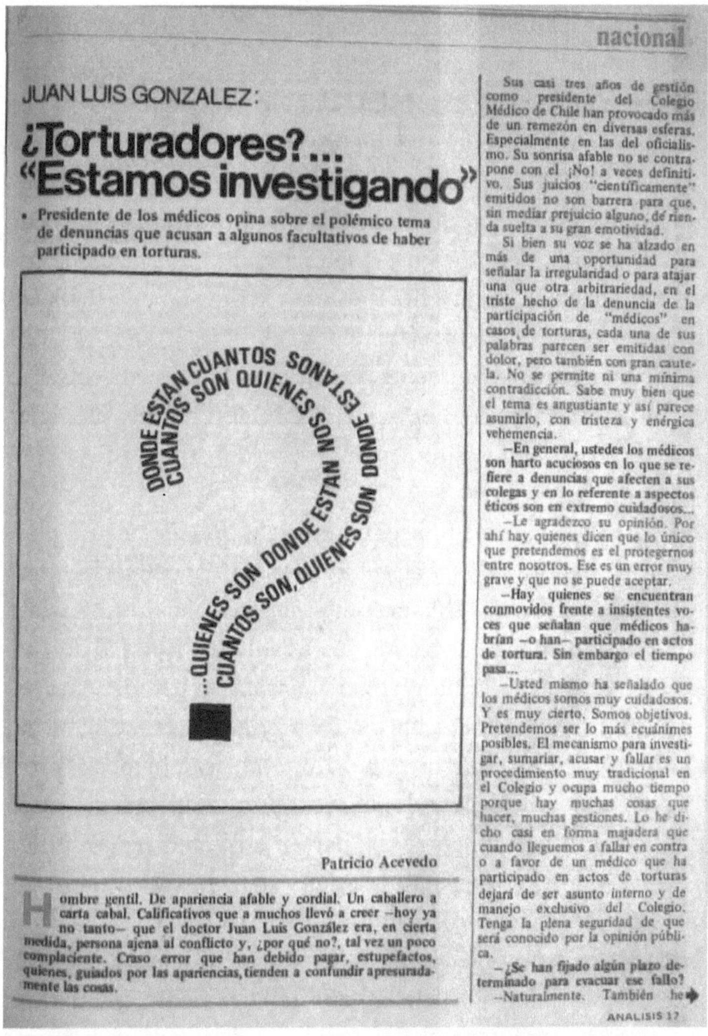

nacional

JUAN LUIS GONZALEZ:

¿Torturadores?... «Estamos investigando»

• **Presidente de los médicos opina sobre el polémico tema de denuncias que acusan a algunos facultativos de haber participado en torturas.**

Patricio Acevedo

Hombre gentil. De apariencia afable y cordial. Un caballero a carta cabal. Calificativos que a muchos llevó a creer –hoy ya no tanto– que el doctor Juan Luis González era, en cierta medida, persona ajena al conflicto y, ¿por qué no?, tal vez un poco complaciente. Craso error que han debido pagar, estupefactos, quienes, guiados por las apariencias, tienden a confundir apresuradamente las cosas.

Sus casi tres años de gestión como presidente del Colegio Médico de Chile han provocado más de un remezón en diversas esferas. Especialmente en las del oficialismo. Su sonrisa afable no se contrapone con el ¡No! a veces definitivo. Sus juicios "científicamente" emitidos no son barrera para que, sin mediar prejuicio alguno, dé rienda suelta a su gran emotividad.

Si bien su voz se ha alzado en más de una oportunidad para señalar la irregularidad o para atajar una que otra arbitrariedad, en el triste hecho de la denuncia de la participación de "médicos" en casos de torturas, cada una de sus palabras parecen ser emitidas con dolor, pero también con gran cautela. No se permite ni una mínima contradicción. Sabe muy bien que el tema es angustiante y así parece asumirlo, con tristeza y enérgica vehemencia.

–En general, ustedes los médicos son harto acuciosos en lo que se refiere a denuncias que afecten a sus colegas y en lo referente a aspectos éticos son en extremo cuidadosos...

–Le agradezco su opinión. Por ahí hay quienes dicen que lo único que pretendemos es el protegernos entre nosotros. Ese es un error muy grave y que no se puede aceptar.

–Hay quienes se encuentran conmovidos frente a insistentes voces que señalan que médicos habrían –o han– participado en actos de tortura. Sin embargo el tiempo pasa...

–Usted mismo ha señalado que los médicos somos muy cuidadosos. Y es muy cierto. Somos objetivos. Pretendemos ser lo más ecuánimes posibles. El mecanismo para investigar, sumariar, acusar y fallar es un procedimiento muy tradicional en el Colegio y ocupa mucho tiempo porque hay muchas cosas que hacer, muchas gestiones. Lo he dicho casi en forma majadera que cuando lleguemos a fallar en contra o a favor de un médico que ha participado en actos de torturas dejará de ser asunto interno y de manejo exclusivo del Colegio. Tenga la plena seguridad de que será conocido por la opinión pública.

–¿Se han fijado algún plazo determinado para evacuar ese fallo?

–Naturalmente. También he ➔

ANALISIS 17

Figure 4.6. Censored images. Question mark made with letters. *Análisis* 92 (October 18–23, 1984; now defunct). Color. Photograph: Ángeles Donoso Macaya.

to publish, in November (issue 93), an actual photograph of the burnt remains of a TIFA (a photo ID for Armed Forces personnel) found in the vicinity of a bombed church, covering the ID picture with the word "censored," and a series of photographs depicting graffiti signs protesting the regime. These more daring gestures can be read as attempts on the part of *Análisis* to defy the ban more directly and test the limits of censorship.

Press photographs are usually taken for granted: they are glanced over rapidly and rarely become the focus of critical consideration. The ban on images had in this sense an *unforeseen* effect (pun intended). Because of the ban, press photographs began to matter even more. I say "even more" because, as a matter of fact, the press photographs already mattered: this fact is asserted both by the increasing prominence of news photographs in the independent media and by efforts on the part of the military regime to suppress them. It is undeniable that press photographs were actually suppressed. These photographs became, in a way, invisible. However, the obligatory invisibility of the photographs enhanced their prominence. As we have seen, they became material to be exhibited and objects to be considered in their own right. The censored media and their fellow media outlets, such as *La Bicicleta*, wrote about the importance of press photographs, underscoring their documentary burden. These media insisted that photos had been banned because they were truthful testimonies of reality, because they contested the lies and misinformation spread by the media adherent to the military.

The ban not only failed to suppress images completely, but also placed photography at the center of ongoing debates about the limits imposed on freedom of speech and freedom of the press. This becomes apparent in the editorials, opinions, and essays denouncing the ban while it was still in effect and also afterward. Journalists, reporters, and photographers insisted on the idea that the ban implied both the prohibition of an informative medium and the silencing of a powerful voice opposing the military regime. Thus, the prominence of press photographs was also revealed in their indirect evocation. In its first censored issue (22), *Cauce* published the full text of the ban in a framed section titled "El miedo a la verdad: Bando No 19 censura voz de la imagen" (The Fear of the Truth: Edict Number 19 Censors the Voice of the Image). Below the text of the ban, the editors ask the following question: "Why censor the image without intermediaries, the most direct form of contact between the reading public and the truth? The voice of the image is what the regime, in its desperation, attempts to silence today."[61] The image without mediators evoked here is not just any image: it is the photograph—more specifically, the news photograph. This substitution circumscribes the meaning of "image" in order to emphasize its efficacy: the image (that is, the photograph) shows and tells ("the image has a voice"), doing so with the truth (the image is direct, independent, and has no mediators). This idea also materializes in the measures implemented by the military bureaucrats (their determination to silence the image was urgent because photographs show and tell the truth). Indeed, despite the manifold forms of censorship DINACOS imposed on the independent press since 1976 on, Edict Number 19 is persistently evoked as the highpoint of the violations of freedom of speech and freedom of the press. For instance, in a document from 1985 that was prepared to serve as reference for a seminar about journalistic practices under authoritarian regimes in the Southern Cone, journalist Fernando Reyes points out: "The prohibition against publishing photographs in a group of magazines was an unexpected and unusual precedent of the repressive forms that announced energetic actions against the alternative system of communication closely inscribed in the process of social mobilization initiated in March of 1983."[62] Meanwhile, in the introduction of *Chile from Within* (1990) (see Epilogue), Marco Antonio De La Parra evokes: "It is not superfluous to remember that in one of the many gyrations of censorship (I do not remember the date; one head cannot hold that many bad memories) opposition magazines were forbidden to print photographs."[63] Even though the ban did not affect only photographs, this is how the prohibition was interpreted then and also *a posteriori*.

Edict Number 19 and the strategies used by the independent media have been evoked by critics and historians to illustrate the repressive mechanisms of the military dictatorship, emphasize the inventiveness of the independent press, and reflect on the effects of censorship in the cultural field.[64] What I have attempted to consider here is the substitutive logic instigated by the ban. While the reason for censoring images may seem evident, the effects of the censorship were not. The ban enhanced the role of press photographs in the discursive field of news media. Because of the supplementary condition of photography, press photography acquired prominence in the debates concerning freedom of expression and freedom of the press: the defense of photography became synonymous with the defense of these freedoms and, more generally, with the defense of democracy. At the end of October, when the editors of the censored media thought the ban was about to end, an article entitled "El triunfo de la imagen" (The Triumph of the Image) appeared in issue 28 of *Cauce*. In the battle between the military bureaucracy and the image, the article suggested, the image would eventually emerge the victor: "The battle against photographs and images of any kind in opposition magazines and newspapers, which the government undertook on September 8 through Edict Number 19, is nearing its end. And everything indicates that the confrontation will be resolved in favor of the image."[65]

There is no doubt that press photographs can serve the interests of the market and the state. However, photography criticism should not focus only on the disciplinary or the propagandistic uses of the documentary image. Because of the civil imagination of photography's many users, not only do photographs acquire different meanings, but they can also become something else altogether. As we have seen, the censored protest photographs were displaced to other spaces and media, a movement that instigated the photographs' recontextualizations and reframings. The recontextualized photos of the protests, taken from the censored media, hung on walls, and reframed in a music and culture magazine, opened themselves to new readings and interpretations.

DINACOS censored images to stop the dissemination of protest photographs, but photography cannot be circumscribed. Indeed, photography can protest in multiple ways. The *exhibition* of "uncensored" photos of the September protests at the Journalists Guild and the *publication* of a selection of these photos in *La Bicicleta*, disseminating efforts, became themselves ways to protest. Likewise, each and every "insubordinate photo" published in the censored media also became an image of protest. Reflecting on the censorship, poet Enrique Lihn claims that photographs are banned not only because they can be read as irrefutable visual proof of the events they depict but also—and above all—because of their potential meanings. These meanings always exceed the visual contents captured by the camera and framed by the photographs and are reactivated each and every time they are seen by spectators. This is why supplementing news texts with demarcated blank or doodled spaces is a photographic practice and an event of photography. As Azoulay argues, "considered as an event, photography invites the gaze to wander beyond what the photograph frames."[66] The military attempted to remove the repression they were exerting as well as the increasing opposition against them. They attempted to do so by displacing the repression and the opposition off the frame, out of the visual field of the printed media. Despite this eminently authoritarian gesture, photography was not placed off limits: photography users, the citizens of the citizenry of photography, kept enacting not only their right to see but also their right to use photography as a tool for liberation. The substitution of all images, including news photos, for other iconic and textual cues was the visual form repression took in the censored media. Censored media began to call "photos" the shapes and volumes that were not, strictly speaking, photographs. The captions and frames that demarcated these new "insubordinate photos" and the visual cues that substituted them made manifest the material effects of the ongoing repression and censorship. Signaling the compulsory removal of images with empty frames made the ban presently visible on the photographic surface. Empty rectangles and squares became a virtual space in which censored media kept expressing their dissent and denouncing the violence. This significant substitution reveals the always-incomplete aspect of the expanding photographic field. Protest photography became an expansive practice, one not defined by referential content.

5

EPILOGUE

A democracy [to-come] must have the structure of a promise—and thus the memory of that which carries the future, the to-come, here and now.

—Jacques Derrida, *Rogues*

For fifteen years the government insisted that the country was in full color. As we can see in these photos, we were dreaming in gray, the color of gunpowder.

—Marco Antonio De La Parra, "Fragments of a Self-Portrait"

The Insubordination of Photography has conceptualized an array of objects as constituents of an expanding field of photography—amended ID photos, reproduced portraits, and the photographic counter-archive they comprised; forensic photographs and documentary films; documentary photography, photojournalism, and precarious photographic publications; photocopied photographs fashioned into masks and photocopied photo books; banned press photographs and censored media. As we have seen, despite having emerged amid a besieged visual field and in a context in which repression was exercised, sometimes secretively and other times in plain sight, in such a way as to make a public spectacle of the military's potential for brutality, the documentary practices of photography challenged and altered the depth of field that the regime attempted to control. These practices were devised to serve different purposes: to make visible and document the crime of forced disappearances; to produce and provide evidence of the repression; to resist and challenge censorship; and to disseminate and consolidate the space of the opposition, among other needs. To keep exposing, denouncing, and challenging the dictatorship, individuals, collectives, and organizations exploited the performative dimension of photography, expanding the medium's limits.

Each chapter has shown distinct instances of this photographic expansion, offering different approaches to the expanding field. Chapter 1 considered the composition and dissemination of the photographic archive of the detained-disappeared: here, the portraits were formulated as the lasting iconic visual rendering—the face—of disappearance; meanwhile, the composition of the portraits' counter-archive was conceptualized as the material consequence of photographic practices devised to secure the visibility of the disappeared in the public space. As we have seen, the portraits, first displayed in public by the relatives of the disappeared, were amended and rephotographed, incorporated into habeas corpus cases filed by the Vicaría, consigned into the photographic archive, and disseminated in the public space by different means. Chapter 2 studied the production and the presentation of the forensic evidence of an emblematic case—Lonquén. As I have shown, the photographs of the furnace and the chimney taken at the site—straightforward images that framed a specific place and the physical evidence found there—soon began to take on supplementary meanings. Besides referring viewers to the site where the heinous crime had been committed, the photos evoked the material aspect of the crime without showing the physical remains. After the obliteration of the mine, they continued to be used to signify disappearance and also to evoke the violence intrinsic to this act of destruction. Chapter 3 investigated the discursive emergence of the photographic field; this phenomenon, as I have argued, was concomitant with the heightening of the economic crisis, the imposition of the state of emergency, and the proliferation of *jornadas de protesta* (protest days). The Independent Photographers Association (AFI), a guild established in 1981 by a group of twenty-nine photographers to protect their work, had a main role in the development of the photographic field. The publications analyzed (*Punto de Vista*, *Anuarios fotográficos*, *Ediciones económicas de la fotografía chilena*, and *El pan nuestro de cada día*), all devised and developed by the photographers amid a context of precariousness and a state of emergency, contributed to the dissemination of Chilean documentary photography and to further developing the photographic field. Finally, I explored in chapter 4 how press photography was transformed into something else in order to challenge and ridicule the censorship imposed by the military dictatorship. The government tried to delimit the photographs published in the opposition media as "off limits," forbidding their circulation in the public space. The censored media (*Análisis*, *Apsi*, *Cauce*, and *Fortín Mapocho*) replied by displaying empty frames and adapting photo captions. These captions, as we have seen, relied on the performative referentiality of the censored photographs—banned from the page, yet framed and evoked as though they were present.

I have approached the civic-military dictatorship period through the expanding photographic field that materialized during those years in order to emphasize the—paradoxically overlooked—political import of photography in the efforts of the opposition. Not only did the practices of photography serve to condemn repression, challenge censorship and official claims that amounted to cover-ups, and disseminate the protest in the public space, but they also played a vital role in the construction of the historical memory of that period. This is why I conclude *The Insubordination of Photography* with a collaborative project that took shape in the final years of the dictatorship, and which had a meaningful, recent iteration. The book *Chile from Within* (New York, 1990), edited by MAGNUM photographer Susan Meiselas in collaboration with a group of AFI photographers, put into circulation abroad a set of documentary photographs taken within Chile. The latest iteration of this project, *Chile desde adentro* (2015), underscored how the circulation, exhibition, and recontextualization of these photographs "within Chile" still enrich debates about historical memory and transitional justice today.

As I shared in the Introduction, a strong affective bond ties me to the photographic practices I have studied here. This connection is multifaceted: I care about these photos as a researcher and as a viewer, as an everyday user of photography, and as someone who was born in Chile during the dictatorship. Several years ago, I bought a used copy of *Chile from Within* I found online. I did not know then who Meiselas was, nor did I understand why or how this astounding book had been edited and published. If, as Sebastián Moreno and the photographers interviewed in *La ciudad de los fotógrafos* state, the story of the AFI was barely remembered and little known in Chile, how does one explain the publication of this book in 1990 in New York? This is how my own sequence of displacements began: the research I started in the United States led me to different archives in Chile, and more importantly, to the photographers themselves, who received me into their homes, showed me their photographic archives, and shared with me meaningful recollections about the many initiatives they organized throughout the eighties—including *Chile from Within*.

Chile from Within

In 1988, Susan Meiselas traveled to Santiago to document the Yes/No referendum that eventually put an end to Pinochet's dictatorship. While in Santiago, Meiselas came into contact with a group of AFI photographers.[1] She spent time with them and had the opportunity to witness the work they had been doing for more than a decade. The idea of editing a book of photographs about life under the dictatorship emerged collectively from their conversations. The product of this collaboration, *Chile from Within*, showcased seventy-five black-and-white photographs taken between 1970 and 1988 by these photographers. With the exception of a few images, *Chile from Within* centered on everyday situations and anonymous individuals in public and private spaces. While the concept "from within," as formulated in the book, did not necessarily undo the binary abroad/within, *Chile from Within* unveiled and disseminated other ways of looking (at) and of documenting conflict. The look from within offered a closer account, in the sense that it was an "intimate" view.[2] In this account, the daily life, the waiting and the wanting, were given as much relevance as—and more visual currency than—more "news-like" events, such as massive protests or instances of police repression. The view from within, which witnessed, accompanied, attended, and waited, was also affected by what it saw. This was revealed in the speed of the takes, the out of focus or partial blur that affected some images, and the close-ups of faces screaming, crying, and singing. Marco Antonio De La Parra evoked the conflicting (at times) affects that traverse the narrative in the introduction he wrote for the book:

> Here are the aunts who gave their jewels for the national reconstruction after the promises of the coup, the aunts who banged their empty pots in opposition to Allende, the aunts who did it against Pinochet, and the aunts who did it on both occasions [. . .] Here are the coffins, the luxury sports cars, the department stores, the credit cards, the soccer headlines, the weddings held in daylight so that the midnight police patrol would not interrupt the reception. Implicit in these photos are the barricades of burning tires, the books slipped by contraband, the photos we did not take: going to work as if nothing, or crying out in a stadium filled with ghosts, visiting a friend held prisoner in an abandoned beach resort, the photos we refused to look at, those we found intolerable to remember [. . .] These photos are a struggle for lucidity, an effort to separate image from

> sentiment, ideas from facts. They were taken against risks made customary, sometimes with confiscated cameras, broken, at times hidden, others surreptitiously from within a crowd, urgently.[3]

As De La Parra's touching account reveals, at the time of publication, *Chile from Within* evoked a present haunted by a traumatic past—despite the hopeful outcome of the plebiscite—and imagined the future as an uncertain time, loomed by the shadows of violence and repression. U.S. critics did not fail to notice the haunting aspect of this book: "many pictures show signs that violence continues. Too many show funerals [. . .] Too many show the wounded, the fights and—most frightening—police carting away the detained. You wonder, will they ever return?"[4] We know that over three thousand didn't.

Chile desde adentro

The Spanish edition of *Chile from Within*, published in Chile in 2015, reactivated debates about pending political reparations and about the historical memory of the dictatorship in the present.[5] The launch of *Chile desde adentro* was accompanied by a traveling exhibition that opened July 21, 2015.[6] The photos displayed at the Gabriela Mistral Cultural Center (GAM) sought not only to shed light on Chile's recent past, but also to offer commentary on its present and future. In this sense, even the chosen exhibition space was significant: the original building where the GAM is housed was built in 1972 during the Unidad Popular government to hold the Third World Conference on Trade and Development of the United Nations (UNCTAD). After the coup, the military junta renamed it and transformed it into its headquarters. The building reopened as a public cultural center only in 2010, during Michelle Bachelet's presidency.[7] One of the photos displayed on the last wall of the exhibit indirectly evoked the GAM's history: the ominous photo, a large close-up of Pinochet's back, was taken by Kena Lorenzini in 1983 inside the same building, when the GAM was called Edificio Diego Portales and housed the Ministry of Defense.

Both *Chile from Within* and *Chile desde adentro* are dedicated to the memory of Christian Montecino and of Rodrigo Rojas De Negri, two photographers killed during the dictatorship. In the introduction to *Chile from Within*, De La Parra suggests that these photos are "our ghosts and our shadows," that "they serve us as memory, evocation, [and] nostalgia," and that because of this, they "will never stop developing."[8] Twenty-five years later, the curator of the exhibition would make a similar claim: "These images talk about a past that remains absolutely present."[9] So present remains the past that the same week the exhibition opened at the GAM, a former conscript linked to the brutal attack that ended Rojas's life in July 1986 and that left student Carmen Gloria Quintana severely injured decided to speak after twenty-nine years of silence. After the revelations of the conscript were made public, the photographers announced an act to commemorate Rojas and the three thousand people who disappeared under the dictatorship. Photographers, relatives, and friends of the victims of the dictatorship, as well as people attending the exhibition, all contributed photos, creating an ephemeral photographic memorial on the exterior walls of the GAM.

In the nearly two months that *Chile desde adentro* was open at the GAM, it attracted more than thirty thousand visitors—including people who participated in or vividly recalled the events photographed, others who were still children during the dictatorship, as I was, and many whose generation came after the plebiscite. The unprecedented success of *Chile desde adentro* (the book sold out very quickly) revealed the keen interest people of different generations had in learning or talking more about the country's recent past. While many viewers didn't have direct recollections of the dictatorship, the exhibition devised different ways to engage the hundreds of visitors who belonged, like myself, to the post-memory generation.[10] Jorge Gronemeyer, curator of the exhibition, made enlarged digital copies of the photographs and printed them in different sizes. The photographers also gave guided tours and visits, which were extremely successful and sought after by audiences of all ages (Paz Errázuriz, for instance, gave one such tour to a group of elementary school children).

In order to emphasize the important role that documentary photographs played in the public space of the opposition, the exhibition tour commenced by showing where and how the photos had circulated during the dictatorship. Several books and magazines published between 1973 and 1990 were showcased in this segment. Some books were exhibited on the walls, while others were projected on a screen. Since the modest platforms in which the photos had been disseminated during the dictatorship were nothing like the large walls of the GAM gallery, the display of these archival objects sought to remind younger audiences that propaganda books, pamphlets, and magazines had been the previous habitat of the large framed photos they were about to see.

In the central gallery, the text of Proclamation Number 7 of the military junta preceded the first set of photographs:

> 1. All persons resisting the new Government should be aware of the consequences. 2. All industries, housing units, and businesses shall cease resistance immediately or the Armed Forces shall proceed with the same energy and decision evident in the attack on La Moneda, the Presidential Palace. 3. The Junta hereby announces that, while having no intention to destroy, if public order is in any way disrupted by disobedience to its decrees, it will not hesitate to act with the same energy and decision which the citizenry has already had the occasion to observe.

The sequence of photographs started with a photo of the destruction of La Moneda (see fig. 5.1). The photo, by Marcelo Montecino, has become an emblematic image of the event. Taken on September 13, after the lift of the curfew, the image centers on a couple in the foreground; behind them, passersby and viewers (mostly men) get a sight of La Moneda in ruins, and only the entrance is seen. While it is not possible to distinguish the facial expressions of the people in the background, one can imagine their reactions: astonishment, worry, incredulity, terror, and perhaps even satisfaction. The contrast between the imposing ruins of La Moneda's entrance in the background and the couple in the foreground is disturbing. The young couple, in each other's arms, is looking away from the destruction in the background. The woman stares directly and intensely at the camera. It is difficult to meet her gaze and hold it.

The photographs that followed were displayed in a single line, as if to suggest a funeral procession. This montage evoked the death of Christian Montecino, brother of Marcelo, who was abducted and shot to death by a firing squad shortly after taking some of the photos displayed here, including one of a group of prisoners at the National Stadium.[11] Looking at this photo on the day I visited the exhibition, I couldn't stop thinking that while Christian Montecino was taking this and other photos inside the stadium (both Christian and Marcelo were able to enter as foreign correspondents), several women waited outside on the street, longingly displaying portraits of their loved ones.

The second wall was devoted to photographs depicting scenes from everyday life: people from affluent neighborhoods and from *tomas*; beauty pageants, communal meals, clashes with police; wedding celebrations, vigils, wakes, and funerals. On a different wall, photographs documenting street protests and demonstrations, which recurred since 1983, were arranged together and reproduced in a smaller size, highlighting the repetitive and recurrent nature of these acts of resistance and repression. This sequence continued with photos

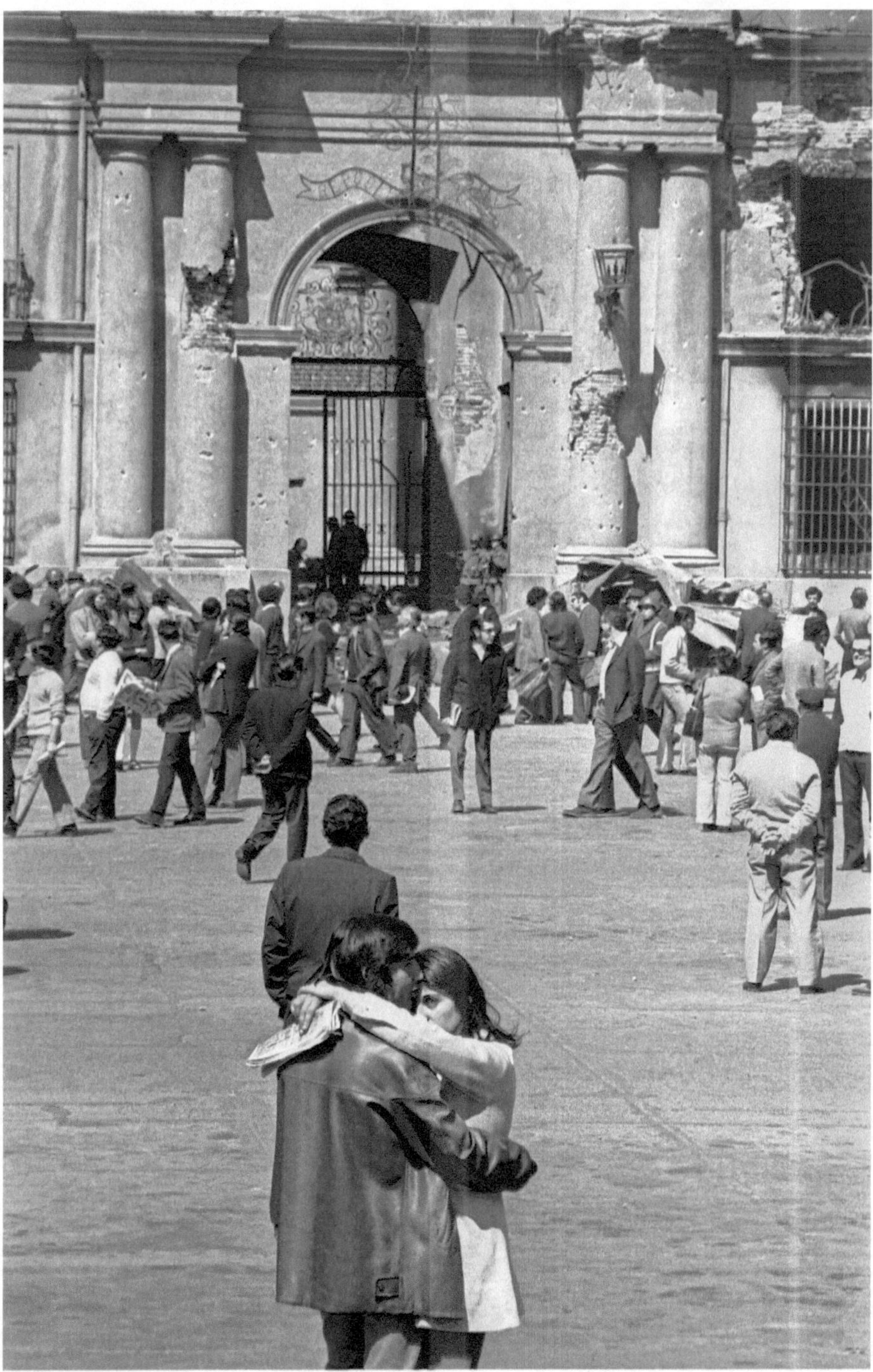

Figure 5.1. Outside La Moneda Palace. September 13, 1973. Credit: Marcelo Montecino. Black and white. Marcelo Montecino's personal archive. (Also reproduced in *Chile desde adentro* [2015]).

of the rallies held before the YES/NO referendum, photos that were displayed alongside others taken after the results were made public and official. However, *Chile desde adentro* did not close with a triumphal vision of the transitional process. Indeed, both *Chile from Within*, published the same year that marked the beginning of the Chilean transition to democracy, and *Chile desde adentro*, published twenty-five years later, insinuate by means of composition and image sequencing the legacies of the dictatorship. These legacies include the hundreds of human-rights violations and disappearances that still remain unresolved; the Chilean Constitution and the neoliberal economic model that frames the health, retirement, and education systems, all implemented under dictatorship; and the all-too-frequent instances of police repression.[12]

The final photograph in the exhibition brought *Chile from Within*'s narrative into the present. This evocative, symbolically loaded photograph, taken in 1985 outside Parque O'Higgins by Héctor López, could have been taken ten years ago, just five years ago, or even today. The photo is split into two halves (see fig. 5.2).

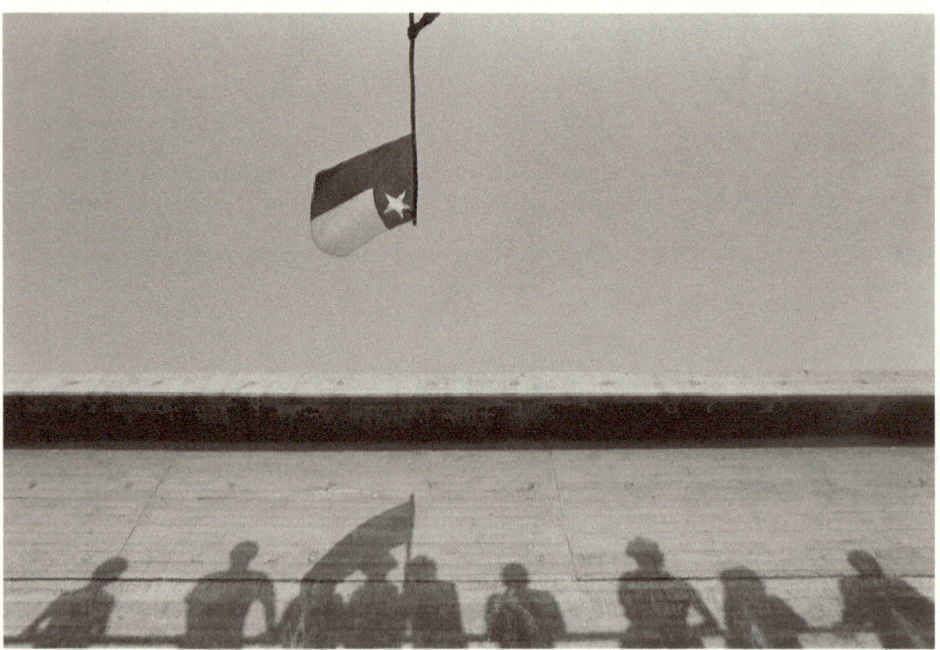

Figure 5.2. Outside O'Higgins Park. 1985. Credit: Héctor López. Reproduced in *Chile from Within* (1990) and in *Chile desde adentro* (2015). Black and white. Jorge Gronemeyer's personal archive (Taller Gronefot).

The top half centers on the Chilean flag, the main national symbol, but turned upside down (its star pointing downward); the lower half frames the shadows of a group of people. One member of this group holds a flag, but it doesn't seem to be the same flag turned upside down in the top half. The image of the flag turned upside down alludes to the ongoing debt, moral and material, of the Chilean state with the families that were victims of state terrorism during the dictatorship. Meanwhile, the photographed shadows continue evoking the persistence of the past in the present.

"[K]nowledge comes only in lightning flashes. The text is the long roll of thunder that follows," writes Walter Benjamin.[13] López's photo offers an evocative take on the idea of democracy as unfulfilled promise.[14] This photo, like so many other documentary images of the period, is one of these lightning flashes, one of countless insubordinate acts of photography. I am tempted to say that a long sequence of lightning flashes, beginning with Lorenzini's "Pico" photograph—also taken, like López's photo, at Parque O'Higgins, at the height of the protests—prompted the long roll of thunder that this book is. Always enlightening the present, these photographic practices shall continue shaping my writing about the expanding field of photography.

NOTES

Introduction: Adjusting the Depth of Field

1. The First National Strike under dictatorship was called by the Confederación de Trabajadores del Cobre (CTC) (Copper Workers Confederation), on May 1, 1983, and took place on May 11, 1983. The CNT was formed shortly after that date.

2. Mönckeberg, "Clamor Popular: Democracia," 17. Unless otherwise indicated, all translations from Spanish are my own.

3. I viewed both photos for the first time in 2010 in Kena Lorenzini's *Fragmento fotográfico: arte, narración y memoria. Chile 1980–1990*, published in 2006.

4. Technically, the depth of field depends on the focal length of the lens, on the camera lens aperture setting (the smaller the aperture setting, the greater the depth of field), and also on the distance between the camera lens and the subject/object photographed. See Gordon Baldwin and Martin Jürgens, *Looking at Photographs*, 28.

5. See Ariella Azoulay, *Civil Imagination: A Political Ontology of Photography*.

6. About the bombardment of La Moneda Palace as a spectacular image produced to be displayed, reframed, and reiterated, see César Barros A., "Declassifying the Archive: The Bombardment of La Moneda Palace and the Political Economy of the Image."

7. *La Tercera* was the only newspaper aligned with the civic-military regime that did not belong to the conglomerate of Agustín Edwards, owner of *El Mercurio*, *La Segunda*, and *Las Últimas Noticias*.

8. As Peter Kornbluh indicates, after the coup, the U.S. government, through the CIA's Santiago Station, kept financing covert propaganda campaigns to popularize the junta's measures: "the CIA continue to covertly underwrite its most important asset, the *El Mercurio* newspaper empire, as it became the leading voice of pro-regime propaganda in Chile, regularly maximizing the military's 'reforms' while minimizing reporting on repression." *The Pinochet File: A Classified Dossier on Atrocity and Accountability*, 215. See also from the same book, 6–7, 91–94; 214–216. See also the documentary film *El diario de Agustín* (2008) by Ignacio Agüero.

9. Tanks had already surrounded La Moneda on the 29th of June 1973, in the failed coup attempt known as the Tanquetazo or Tancazo. See Mónica González, *La conjura. Los mil y un días del golpe*, 183–192.

10. Threatened by the prospect that Salvador Allende would became president in 1964, two years earlier the Kennedy administration (through the CIA) devised and financed a ferocious

propaganda campaign to secure the victory of a different candidate, the Christian Democrat Eduardo Frei Montalva. Millions of U.S. dollars were poured into rightwing media. The intervention was effective: Frei Montalva won the 1964 election by a landslide (he secured 56.1% of the vote). U.S. involvement continued throughout Frei Montalva's term (1964–1970), reaching critical levels during the 1970 presidential elections—which Allende won, despite the intervention—and extreme levels during Allende's interrupted term as president. Besides Kornbluh, see *Covert Action in Chile 1963–1973*, the Staff Report of the Select Committee to Study Governmental Operations with Respect to Intelligence Activities; Stephen G. Rabe, *The Killing Zone: The United States Wages Cold War in Latin America*; Jeffrey Taffet, *Foreign Aid as Foreign Policy: The Alliance for Progress in Latin America*, 67–93.

11. The drafting of this book was a collective effort. Kornbluh indicates, "two CIA collaborators helped the Junta draft a *White Book*." *The Pinochet File*, 215. Meanwhile, Steve J. Stern states, "civilian authors helped craft a coherent narrative to accompany the documents [. . .] among them historian Gonzalo Vial." *Battling for Hearts and Minds: Memory Struggles in Chile, 1973–1998*, 41. The first newspaper to report on Plan Z was a regional newspaper from Concepción, *Crónica*. For a detailed description of the Plan Z revelations and news coverage of the document, see Stern, *Battling for Hearts and Minds*, 41–52.

12. *Libro Blanco*, 3.

13. These and other books are reviewed in Horacio Fernández, editor, *Una revisión al fotolibro chileno*.

14. Quoted in Miguel Ángel Sepúlveda Chávez, "Evolución del discurso anti-resistencia en la dictadura militar chilena," 61.

15. While the authors of *Chile Ayer Hoy* are unknown (the book is unaccredited), there is little doubt that the DINACOS was involved in its production. The DINACOS was in charge of controlling the press, supervised foreign correspondents, and managed the government's propaganda campaigns, both inside and outside the country. The DINACOS operated closely with the Dirección de Inteligencia Nacional (DINA) (Directorate of National Intelligence) and then with its replacement, the Central Nacional de Informaciones (CNI) (National Information Center). *Chile Ayer Hoy* was distributed at different embassies, further indication of DINACOS's authorship.

16. See María Berríos, "Spectres of Counterinsurgency Staged Confrontations and *Montaje* in Authoritarian Chile."

17. About Operación Colombo, see Stern, *Battling for Hearts and Minds*, 100–112.

18. Anyone familiar with Rosalind Krauss's work will recall that she developed the latter concept in the late 1970s. See Rosalind Krauss, "Sculpture in the Expanded Field."

19. Krauss projects the expanded field of sculpture departing from two neutral terms that for her define the modern practice of sculpture: nonarchitecture and nonlandscape, and their respective opposites, architecture and landscape. Krauss's model has instigated several approaches from different fields, particularly those of architecture, cinema, and photography. See, for instance, Spyros Papapetros and Julian Rose, editors, *Retracing the Expanded Field: Encounters between Art and Architecture*; A. L. Rees, David Curtis, Duncan White, and Steven Ball, editors, *Expanded Cinema: Art, Performance, Film*. Regarding photography, see Abigail Solomon-Godeau, *Photography at the Dock*, and George Baker, "Photography's Expanded Field."

20. For Bourdieu, it is everyday users (i.e., not artists, critics, consecrated photographers,

or specialists) who complete—without knowing it—the social foundation of photography. Bourdieu pays special attention to the domestic space, where photography plays a primordial role. See Bourdieu et al., *Photography, a Middle-brow Art.*

21. Olin, *Touching Photographs*, 15.

22. See also Tina M. Campt, *Image Matters: Archive, Photography, and the African Diaspora in Europe.*

23. I am drawing here from Azoulay's ideas about the event of photography. Azoulay argues that the event of photography neither begins nor ends with the printed photograph; she also insists on the idea that photography does not belong to the photographer, the photographed subject, or the spectator. For Azoulay, all those who participate in one way or another in the event of photography, through various practices, are citizens of photography. See Azoulay, *The Civil Contract of Photography*, 85–186.

24. With regards to the relationship between photography and the notions of visible field, visual field, and field of vision, see Azoulay, *The Civil Contract of Photography*, 93–105; Judith Butler, *Frames of War*, 63–100. See also Nicholas Mirzoeff, *The Right to Look: A Counterhistory of Visuality.*

25. Certainly, there are other denotations of the word "field" that are relevant to this study. Field is used to designate different areas of knowledge or activity; field also denotes the battleground and, in the realms of physics and mathematics, the "field of forces and relations" between different elements. The relational aspect involved in these meanings lies at the basis of Pierre Bourdieu's own formulation of the concept. See Bourdieu, *The Field of Cultural Production.*

26. On the issue of heterosexuality as induced behavior, a key reference is the feminist theorist Adrienne Rich. See Adrienne Rich, "Compulsive Heterosexuality and Lesbian Existence."

27. Butler, *The Psychic Life of Power*, 21.

28. Ahmed, *Queer Phenomenology*, 87.

29. The expression "documentary matters" evokes Judith Butler's *Bodies that Matter* and Sara Ahmed's "Orientations Matter." See André Bazin, "The Ontology of the Photographic Image;" John Berger, *Ways of Seeing*; Judith Butler, *Frames of War*; Georges Didi-Huberman, *The Eye of History: When Images Take Positions* and also *Images in Spite of All*; Thomas Keenan and Hito Steyerl, "What Is a Document? An Exchange between Thomas Keenan and Hito Steyerl"; Liam Kennedy, *Afterimages: Photography and U.S. Foreign Policy*; Rosalind Krauss, "Photography's Discursive Spaces: Landscape/View;" Maria Lind and Hito Steyerl, editors, *The Greenroom. Reconsidering the Documentary and Contemporary Art*; Olivier Lugon, *Le Style documentaire. D'August Sander à Walker Evans, 1920–1945*; Susan Meiselas, "Photography, Expanded: Conversation with Chris Boot"; Mary Panzer, editor, *Things as They Are* and her "Introduction," 9–33; Jorge Ribalta, *Universal Archive* and *Public Photographic Spaces*; Martha Rosler, "In, Around, and Afterthoughts (on Documentary Photography)"; Allan Sekula, "Dismantling Modernism, Reinventing Documentary (Notes on the Politics of Representation)"; Susan Sontag, *On Photography*; William Stott, *Documentary Expression and Thirties America*; John Tagg, *The Burden of Representation* and *The Disciplinary Frame*; Alan Trachtenberg, *Classic Essays on Photography.*

30. Mostly Rosler, Sekula, Sontag, Tagg.

31. Lugon, "'Documentary:' Authority and Ambiguities," 29. Lugon places the emergence

of the documentary mode in the 1920s and links it more directly to the artistic field—in particular, French surrealism and the New Objectivity movement in Germany.

32. See Geoffrey Batchen, *Burning with Desire: The Conception of Photography*. See also Allan Sekula, "The Body and the Archive." For a reconsideration of Sekula's genealogy of archival practices, see Deborah Poole, *Vision, Race and Modernity: A Visual Economy of the Andean Image World*, 139–141.

33. For instance: according to Anglo-Saxon and European photography historiography, photographic reportage entered a crisis in the 1960s and '70s. The closing of several magazines dedicated to publishing photographic reportages was due in part to the consolidation of television (news event photographs started to lose value because they were no longer selling like they had before). This narrative does not fit the Chilean case—just another signal pointing to the need to produce other histories of photography. See Jean-Claude Lemagny and Andre Rouillé, editors, *A History of Photography*.

34. Susie Linfield, *The Cruel Radiance*, 3. For a reconsideration of the positions of Sontag and Barthes as viewers of photos of horror, see Azoulay, *The Civil Contract of Photography*, 128–135; Butler, *Frames of War*, 66–72.

35. See Sarah Bassnett, Andrea Noble, and Thy Phu, "Introduction: Cold War Visual Alliances;" Thy Phu, "Vietnamese Photography and the Look of Revolution."

36. Mary Panzer, "Introduction," 27.

37. For a formulation of "iconic photographs," see Robert Hariman and John Louis Lucaites. *No Captions Needed: Iconic Photographs, Public Culture, and Liberal Democracy.*

38. About this photograph, see Rita Ferrer, *¿Quién es el autor de esto? Fotografía y Performance.*

39. Tagg argues that behind the "simple demand" of the documentary mode—"look at the picture"—resided the paternalistic gaze of the New Deal State and the "machinery of staging" put forward by its apparatuses. The "objects" of documentary photography, as the practice flourished under the aegis of Roy Stryker—manager of the Farm Security Administration photographic project—were the dispossessed and the poor. The camera was meant to produce identification with these subjects. See Tagg, *The Disciplinary Frame*, 70–82.

40. See Thomas Keenan and Hito Steyerl, "What Is a Document?"

41. Azoulay, *The Civil Contract of Photography*, 96.

42. Ibid., 97.

43. Richard, *Márgenes e Instituciones*, 38.

44. Justo Pastor Mellado also makes this argument in "La Novela chilena de Mario Fonseca." About the artistic field under dictatorship, see also Pablo Oyarzún, *Arte, visualidad e historia.*

45. Ronald Kay, *Del espacio de acá*, n.p.

46. See José Pablo Concha, "*Del espacio de acá* de Ronald Kay. Una interpretación posible."

47. This critical demarcation generated important critical debates. Federico Galende interviews most of the artists and critics in *Filtraciones I. Conversaciones sobre arte en Chile (de los 60s a los 80s)*. See also Willy Thayer, *El fragmento repetido*, in particular "Vanguardia, dictadura, globalización (La serie de las artes visuales en Chile, 1957–2000)" and "El golpe como consumación de la vanguardia;" Pablo Oyarzún, Nelly Richard, and Claudia Zaldívar, editors, *Arte y política*; see also Nelly Richard, *The Insubordination of Signs*; and Miguel Valderrama, *Modernismos historiográficos.*

48. *Márgenes e Instituciones*, 47–48.

49. Ibid., 46.

50. Ibid., 50.

51. Richard suggests that the practice of the photographers "were limited to the primary objectivism of documentary realism (photo-testimony), on the one hand, and a subjectivism aestheticized by the poetic conventionalisms of 'auteur photography,' on the other." Richard, "Bordes, límites, fronteras," 7. I comment further on this idea in chapter 4.

52. Richard, *The Insubordination of Signs*, 4. Emphasis in the original.

53. Ibid., 5. Emphasis added.

54. Ibid., 4–5.

55. Ibid., 7.

56. Ibid., 18.

57. Ibid., 18.

58. Díaz seems to suggest, paradoxically, a reverse operation to that described by Richard: it is not the art practice that renders photography reflexive, but rather photography that enables the artwork's reflexivity in working with and through historical memory. Díaz's text is reproduced in the last page of the exhibition catalogue. See Justo Pastor Mellado, *Sueños Privados, Ritos Públicos.* About Díaz's *Lonquén 10 años*, see Pablo Oyarzún, "Estética de la sed: *Lonquén 10 años*, diez años después;" Rodrigo Zúñiga, "Posdictadura y conmoción del secreto (*Lonquén 10 años*, de Gonzalo Díaz y la escenografía trizada de la Transición)."

59. Richard, *The Insubordination of Signs*, 5.

60. Ibid., 1.

61. Hirsch's work has been central to my understanding and formulation of the linkage between photography, memory acts, and imagination. Hirsch has emphasized on numerous occasions the vital mediating role of photographs and the importance of imagination, creation, and projection in the connection between the "postmemory generation" and past events. See, in particular, *The Generation of Postmemory: Visual Culture after the Holocaust* and *Family Frames: Photography, Narrative and Postmemory.*

62. Ahmed, *Queer Phenomenology*, 14. Emphasis added.

63. Ibid.

64. Eduardo Cadava eloquently argues in *Words of Light* that the mode of inscription of history itself belongs to the order of photography.

65. Says Ahmed: "The lines that allow us to find our way, those that are 'in front' of us, also make certain things, and not others, available. What is available is what might reside as a point on this line. When we follow specific lines, some things become reachable and others remain or even become out of reach. Such exclusions—the constitution of a field of unreachable objects—are the indirect consequence of following lines that are before us: we do not have to consciously exclude those things that are 'not in line.' The direction we take excludes things for us, before we even get there." *Queer Phenomenology*, 14–15.

66. As the government treatment and initial reaction to the murder of the Mapuche *comunero* Camilo Catrillanca by special police forces in December 2018 shows, cover-ups have not stopped. In the documentary *Newen Mapuche* (2011), filmmaker Elena Varela tells a related story, instigated by the murder of Alex Lemun in 2002 by police (Lemun was seventeen years old). Varela tells this story and her own ordeal after being arrested by police and framed as a con-

spirator of a possible Mapuche attack. The police raided Valera's house and confiscated the film footage; Varela was released shortly after. *Newen Mapuche* recreates part of these experiences.

67. See Maurizio Ferraris, *Documentality: Why It Is Necessary to Leave Traces*; Lisa Gitelman, *Paper Knowledge: Toward a Media History of Documents.*

68. Stern, *Battling for Hearts and Minds*, 239.

69. The full name of this organization was Comité de Cooperación para la Paz en Chile (Committee of Cooperation for Peace in Chile). The Comité had the protection of the Archdiocese of Santiago and was also supported by the World Council of Churches.

70. The Agrupación started with twenty members in late 1974 and grew to 323 members by the end of 1975. See Cynthia G. Brown, *The Vicaría de la Solidaridad in Chile*, 7.

71. When the Comité began to file legal suits on behalf of detainees, many of its personnel received threats. In October 1975, Lutheran bishop Helmut Frenz (the Comité co-president) was not allowed to return to Chile, and in November two lawyers and three priests, all members of the Comité, were arrested. Moreover, Pinochet sent a letter to Archbishop Raúl Silva Henríquez saying the Comité Pro Paz was a Marxist-Leninist instrument and that it created problems for regular citizens who wanted to live in peace. Brown, *The Vicaría de la Solidaridad in Chile*, 8. For a history of the Comité and the Vicaría, see also Eugenio Ahumada et al. *Chile: La memoria prohibida*; Stern, *Battling for Hearts and Minds*, 113–130.

72. The report *The Vicaría de la Solidaridad in Chile* was written by Cynthia G. Brown, Associate Director of Americas Watch.

73. International Commission of Jurists, *Chile: A Time of Reckoning. Human Rights and the Judiciary*, 62.

74. Purísima Elena Muñoz is interviewed in Ignacio Agüero's documentary, *No Olvidar* (Not to Forget).

75. Thomas Keenan and Hito Steyerl, "What Is a Document?" 64.

76. The Central Nacional de Informaciones (CNI) (National Information Center) was the secret intelligence police force that operated between 1977 and 1990. The CNI continued with the labors of persecution, abduction, murder, and disappearance of civilians after the DINA was dissolved, due to the pressure exerted by the government of the United States as a result of the murder of Orlando Letelier in Washington—a crime orchestrated by the DINA in conjunction with the CIA in 1976. About Leterlier's murder, see Stern, *Battling for Hearts and Minds*, 106–107 and Naomi Klein, *The Shock Doctrine*, 121–123.

77. *Análisis*, *Hoy*, *Apsi* (acronym for *Agencia Periodística de Servicios Informativos*, News Agency of Information Services), and *Cauce*, were current events magazines. *Análisis* was founded by Juan Pablo Cárdenas and sponsored by the Catholic Church; *Hoy* was founded by Emilio Filippi, former editor of *Ercilla* magazine. The newspaper *Fortín Mapocho*, founded in 1947, was suppressed on September 11, 1973, and reestablished in 1984. Other publications that were also part of the independent media were Vicaría's *Solidaridad*, established in 1976; the cultural magazine *La Bicicleta*, established in 1978; the cultural magazine *Pluma y Pincel*, founded in 1982; and the newspaper *La Época*, founded in 1987. The independent press, unlike newspapers such as *El Mercurio* and its affiliates, or *La Tercera*, did not receive any form of state subsidies or support. Because of its ecclesiastical sponsorship, *Solidaridad* was the only publication not subjected to the control of DINACOS. See Fernando Reyes Matta, Jorge Andrés Richards, and Juan Pablo Cárdenas, *Periodismo independiente ¿Mito o realidad?*

78. Editora Nacional Gabriela Mistral operated until 1976 and became a key tool for spread-

ing anti-Marxist sentiment and propaganda. See Isabel Jara Hinojosa, "Editora Nacional Gabriela Mistral y clases sociales: indicio del neoliberalismo en la retórica de la dictadura chilena."

79. See the review of *Chile Ayer Hoy* by Jorge Gronemeyer in Fernández, editor, *Una revisión al fotolibro chileno*, 142.

Chapter 1. Persistence of the Portrait

1. Unless otherwise indicated, all translations from Spanish are my own. Ana González was a human-rights activist, and member of the Agrupación de Familiares de Detenidos Desaparecidos (AFDD) (Association of Family Members of the Detained-Disappeared) since 1976. She was the wife of Manuel Recabarren Rojas, mother of Luis Recabarren González and Manuel Recabarren González, and mother-in-law of Nalvia Mena Alvarado—all of whom are detained-disappeared. González passed away on October 26, 2018. The passage quoted in the epigraph is from González's interview with Sebastián Moreno in the documentary *La ciudad de los fotógrafos*.

2. The *Report of the Chilean National Commission on Truth and Reconciliation* states that the National Stadium "became by far the largest detention site in this region with more than seven thousand detainees by September 22 according to the International Red Cross. Between two and three hundred of these were foreigners from a variety of nations. [. . .] People from all over Santiago, who had been arrested in many different circumstances, were transferred there" (182). However, as Pascale Bonnefoy Miralles emphasizes in *Terrorismo de Estadio* (2016), giving an exact total number of the detainees who remained in the National Stadium is impossible. The official figure that the military junta gave at the time was seven thousand prisoners, and a list published in 2000 by former director of the DINA Manuel Contreras indicates that there were nine thousand detainees (2). Meanwhile, Bonnefoy Miralles indicates that former detainees agree that the total number of prisoners may have been easily double that—about twenty thousand. As for the people executed at the stadium, Bonnefoy Miralles records forty-five executions (four more executions than those documented in the *Report of the Chilean National Commission*), but again, she stresses that this figure does not include the dozens of victims who were executed and then made disappeared (their bodies thrown in common graves, the Mapocho River, etc.). Carmen Luz Parot's 2003 documentary *Estadio Nacional* also sheds light on the story of this emblematic sports center turned concentration camp. Parot interviews thirty-five survivors on camera and tours the stadium with some of them.

3. Sebastián Moreno and Claudia Barril's documentary *Habeas Corpus* (2015) includes archival audiovisual footage and photographs not previously seen, taken both inside and outside the National Stadium. A particularly moving sequence shows the moment at which dozens of prisoners are released from the stadium. Some women with children in their arms run both excitedly and in tears to greet and hug their loved ones who are leaving the stadium in an orderly line, while other women walk in circles, desperately looking for their loved ones among the released.

4. See Leiva Quijada, *Luis Navarro: La potencia de la memoria*, 15–16.

5. Exonerated artists and professors from the Faculty of Arts of the University of Chile, where Luz Donoso had been a professor and Hernán Parada a student, formed the TAV in 1974. The TAV received the support of the Archbishop of Santiago, and the embassies of

France and England, among other institutions. Paulina Varas tells the story and comments on the work and actions organized by this collaborative workshop in her book *Luz Donoso. El arte y la acción en el presente*, a moving study of Luz Donoso's noteworthy documentary work (108–124).

6. As Ann Laura Stoler argues in "On Archiving as Dissensus," "That of which the act of 'countering' consists is neither self-evident nor a decided affair. To seek the inverse of what an institutional or colonial state archive demands is not enough: 'to counter' can take on multiple forms" (46). My reading of the work done by the Vicaría as a form of counter-archival practice follows closely the ideas developed by Stoler and also by Ariella Azoulay in "Archive."

7. The audiovisual archive of artistic interventions and public demonstrations is extensive and continues to be studied. In my interviews with Luis Navarro (July 10, 2016; October 3, 2018; November 4, 2018; December 17, 2018) and Helen Hughes (August 20, 2018; December 22, 2018), the photographers recalled different occasions on which members of the Agrupación had notified them in advance of where and when a particular demonstration was going to take place, so they could be there on time with their cameras ready to document the action. Regarding the artistic field, there exists extensive documentation about the collective CADA (see, for instance, Robert Neustadt, *CADA día: la creación de un arte social*; Nelly Richard, *Márgenes e Instituciones*). Luz Donoso, moreover, documented numerous artistic interventions—including Parada's actions with the mask—and public demonstrations organized by the Agrupación. Varas includes these actions in her book. See Varas, *Luz Donoso*, 124–138 and 188–191.

8. The word "evident" comes from the Latin *evidens*, which refers to something obvious to the eye or mind.

9. Gilles Deleuze explores (and defamiliarizes) the surface in *Francis Bacon*. Giuliana Bruno, reading Deleuze, reminds us that "surface matters," beginning with "the surface as it contains the face. We rarely think about this, but the face is our primary form of communication and also contains the traces of our life history. It is a drawing of what we live through, a map of our own history." See Giuliana Bruno by Sarah Oppenheimer (Interview).

10. In the second part of this chapter, I will comment on some of the formulations by Nelly Richard, Andrea Noble, Diana Taylor, and others.

11. Benjamin, "The Work of Art in the Age of Its Technological Reproducibility: Third Version," 258.

12. Benjamin, "Little History of Photography," 514.

13. For instance: "No matter how artful the photographer, no matter how carefully posed his subject, the beholder feels an irresistible urge to search such a picture for the tiny spark of contingency, of the here and now, with which reality has (so to speak) seared the subject, to find the inconspicuous spot where in the immediacy of that long-forgotten moment the future nests so eloquently that we, looking back, may rediscover it." "Little History of Photography," 510.

14. Benjamin offered different formulations for the concept of the aura. One of the most elucidating ones appears in "The Work of Art" essay, where he defines the aura (in a footnote) as "the unique apparition of a distance, however near it might be," and adds, "the *essentially* distant is the unapproachable." See Benjamin, "The Work of Art in the Age of Its Technological Reproducibility: Third Version," f11, 272.

15. Benjamin, "Little History of Photography," 518.

16. Ibid., 517.

17. Sekula, "The Body and the Archive," 17.

18. Ibid., 30.

19. Deborah Poole, *Vision, Race, and Modernity*, 140. While the topics studied by Poole do not bear a direct relation to the topics I explore in the present book, her important (and right on point) criticism of Sekula's genealogy must be emphasized. Poole urges us to consider more critically the erasure of the colonial visual archive from traditional histories of photography.

20. Noble, "Travelling Theories of Family Photography and the Material Culture of Human Rights in Latin America," 51, 44. Noble follows here Hirsch's formulations regarding the family snapshot, a highly coded and conventional artifact.

21. Noble, "Travelling Theories," 44.

22. Da Silva Catela, "Lo invisible revelado. El uso de fotografías como (re)presentación de la desaparición de personas en Argentina," 337.

23. Gabriel Gatti considers the paradoxical figure of the detained-disappeared from a sociological perspective in the Argentinean and Uruguayan context in *Surviving Forced Disappearance in Argentina and Uruguay: Identity and Meaning*. See also Vikki Bell, "On Fernando's Photograph: The Biopolitics of *Aparición* in Contemporary Argentina;" Jean-Louis Déotte, "El arte en la época de la desaparición;" Macarena Gómez-Barris, *Where Memory Dwells: Culture and State Violence in Chile*; Andrea Noble, "Travelling Theories;" Nelly Richard, "Imagen, recuerdo y borraduras;" Ludmila Da Silva Catela, "Lo invisible revelado;" Diana Taylor, *Disappearing Acts*.

24. Taylor, *Disappearing Acts*, 140. Emphasis in the original.

25. Ibid., 142.

26. See Introduction.

27. Déotte, "El arte en la época de la desaparición," 156.

28. Ibid.

29. Barthes, *Camera Lucida*, 80.

30. Regarding the influence of theoretical formulations about photography in the Chilean artistic field, see Idelber Avelar, "La escena de Avanzada. Photography and Writing in Post-coup Chile—A Conversation with Nelly Richard." For a contextualization of *CAL*, see Nicolás Raveau, *Revista CAL, una historia*.

31. Richard, "Imagen-recuerdo y borraduras," 166. Emphasis added.

32. On this issue, see also Luis Ignacio García and Ana Longoni, "Imágenes invisibles. Acerca de las fotos de desaparecidos."

33. Kerry Bystrom, "Memoria, fotografía y legibilidad en las obras de Marcelo Brodsky y León Ferrari," 318, 320. According to Bystrom, "from the moment these [photos] are taken as indisputable evidence and as emotional connections with the disappeared—and because, in this sense, they have been so successful that they tend to carry a 'pre-packaged' political meaning—there is a danger that, rather than encouraging an interaction with the past, they will make it more difficult" (318).

34. By December 1975, "The Pro Peace committee had filed 2,342 habeas corpus petitions—only 3 received judicial acceptance—and had knowledge of 920 persons long arrested and disappeared but about whom state authorities disavowed knowledge." Stern, *Battling for Hearts and Minds*, 104.

35. The passage quoted is from Egaña Barahona's interview with Sebastián Moreno and Claudia Barril in the documentary *Habeas Corpus* (2015).

36. Newsstands did not sell *Solidaridad*. It was distributed through subscription, churches, trade unions, universities, neighborhood organizations, and parishes in many poor communities all over the country.

37. Luis Navarro started to work at the Vicaría in 1976. At the beginning, he worked designing informative contents. Since he usually carried his camera when visiting through the parishes, they invited him to also work as a photographer for the magazine. His photographs began to appear in number six of the magazine. See Gonzalo Leiva Quijada, *Luis Navarro*, 13.

38. Gonzalo Torres, Jorge Rojas, and Washington Apablaza designed these publications; Navarro and Hughes provided feedback and ideas. Hughes, interviews, October 20, 2018; December 22, 2018; Navarro, interviews, October 3, 2018; November 4, 2018; December 17, 2018. See also Consuelo Pérez Mendoza, *Los protagonistas de la prensa alternativa: Vicaría de la Solidaridad y Fundación de Ayuda Social de las Iglesias Cristianas*; Stern, *Battling for Hearts and Minds*, 115–122.

39. Helen Hughes, interviews, August 20, 2018; December 22, 2018.

40. *Report of the Chilean National Commission on Truth and Reconciliation*, 8.

41. Ibid.

42. Ibid.

43. The passage quoted is from Contreras's interview in Moreno and Barril's documentary *Habeas Corpus*, which centers on the archival and legal work done by the Vicaría (several people who worked there are interviewed on camera). Emphasis added.

44. *Habeas Corpus* includes archival footage in which Vicaría workers are seen checking information in *la sábana*.

45. About the Vicaría's documentation and archival work, see also Stern, *Battling for Hearts and Minds*, 154–155 and 393–395.

46. Navarro, interview, July 10, 2016.

47. The Cuatro Álamos Detention Center was part of the Tres Álamos Detainee Camp. The former was clandestine, administered by the DINA, while the latter was considered public and was under the charge of the Carabineros de Chile. Cuatro Álamos and Tres Alamos functioned from 1974 to 1977. Mardones, Figueroa, Zuleta, Drouillas, and De la Fuente were freed in June of 1977. Jorge Troncoso became a disappeared person.

48. See Jacques Derrida, "The Deaths of Roland Barthes," 53–54.

49. Cadava and Cortés-Rocca, "Notes on Love and Photography," 8. Cadava and Cortés-Rocca offer here an evocative reading of Barthes's essay. Jacques Rancière offers a somewhat different reading of Barthes's essay in *The Emancipated Spectator*. He proposes that we concentrate on the different indeterminations present in the image. These indeterminations—the interplay of given visual elements and selected temporal issues, attitudes, different positions of the subject in the frame, etc.—constitute the pensiveness of the image. The philosopher defines this notion as "an effect of circulation, between the subject, the photographer and us, of the intentional and the unintentional, the known and the unknown, the expressed and the unexpressed, the present and the past" (114–115).

50. The concept of habeas corpus is a legal recourse, defined in the *Merriam-Webster* dictionary as a "a writ for inquiring into the lawfulness of the restraint of a person who is

imprisoned or detained in another's custody" and as "the right of a citizen to obtain a writ of habeas corpus as a protection against illegal imprisonment."

51. Navarro, interview, July 10, 2016.

52. Precht, "Introducción," 10. Emphasis added.

53. My formulation of the "photo-copy" is inspired by ideas put forward by Jacques Derrida in *Paper-Machine*: "So there's what we normally use, following the 'usual' name, *papier-machine,* to the letter, in the strict or the literal sense: the form of a *matter, the sheet* designed as the *backing or medium* for a *typewriter's* writing, and also now for the printing, reproduction, and archiving of the products of so many word-processing machines, and the like. This then is what becomes a figure here, what a rhetorician would also call a 'locus'" (1).

54. Derrida, *Archive Fever*, 17.

55. Stoler, "On Archiving as Dissensus," 47.

56. Precht, *¿Dónde están?* Vol. I, 10–12.

57. Ibid.

58. Ferraris, *¿Dónde están?* Vol. 5, 6.

59. Azoulay, "Archive," n.p.

60. See Introduction.

61. Camilo D. Trumper explores some of these ephemeral practices of protests in his book *Ephemeral Histories. Public Art, Politics, and the Struggle for the Streets in Chile.*

62. Varas, *Luz Donoso*, 196.

63. Ibid.

64. Donoso et al., "Acciones de Apoyo," 4.

65. Donoso had used the portrait of Valdenegro previously. These actions were also made in collaboration with Parada. For "Delito persistente" (Persistent Crime), the artists produced a big banner with Valdenegro's portrait and the legal definition of "delito persistente," which they had cropped from a newspaper. They used the banner in several demonstrations organized by the Agrupación in 1979. See Varas, *Luz Donoso*, 172–177.

66. Nelly Richard points out this dialectic between visibility and invisibility in her reading of the action. See Richard, "Imagen, recuerdo y borraduras," 68–69. For more on this action, see also Varas, *Luz Donoso*, 183.

67. Quoted in Varas, *Luz Donoso*, 183.

68. Cadava and Cortés-Rocca, "Notes on Love and Photography," 7.

69. See Varas, *Luz Donoso*, 185.

70. Quoted in Varas, *Luz Donoso*, 126. About the different stages of "Obrabierta A," see Varas, *Luz Donoso*, 124–137.

71. Hernán Parada, e-mail message to author, December 11, 2018. Located in Santiago's General Cemetery in Chile, Patio 29 is the largest mass grave used by the military during the dictatorship. There, the military secretly buried hundreds of political prisoners anonymously.

72. Taylor refers to this phenomenon as "percepticide": "The triumph of the atrocity was that it forced people to look away [. . .] spectacles of violence rendered the population silent, deaf, and blind." *Disappearing Acts*, 122–123.

73. We know of the content of this performance thanks to the audio recording made by Luz Donoso.

74. See Peggy Phelan, "Haunted Stages: Performance and the Photographic Effect."

75. Barthes, *Camera Lucida*, 12.

76. Cadava, *Words of Light*, 113.

77. Thayer, "El xenotafio de luz," 173.

78. Didi-Huberman, *Images in Spite of All*, 120.

79. Hirsch, "The Generation of Postmemory," 115.

80. Hernán Parada, e-mail message to author, May 19, 2015.

81. Diana Taylor, *The Archive and the Repertoire*, 178. Taylor's claim that the photos of the detainees were purged from official archives should be reconsidered. Víctor Basterra's *Testimonio sobre el Centro Clandestino de Detención de la ESMA* (Testimony about ESMA's Clandestine Detention Center), published in 1984, proves the widespread use of photographic archives inside clandestine detention centers. For more on Basterra's testimony and ESMA's photographic archive, see Luis Ignacio García and Ana Longoni, "Imágenes invisibles. Acerca de las fotos de desaparecidos;" see also Claudia Feld, "La imagen que muestra el secreto. Alice Domon y Léonie Duquet fotografiadas en la ESMA."

82. Noble, "Travelling Theories of Family Photography and the Material Culture of Human Rights in Latin America," 46.

Chapter 2. Forensic Matter

1. Eugenio Ahumada et al., editors, *Chile: La memoria prohibida*, vol. 3, 145. The old man's name was Inocencio de los Ángeles, but Vicaría staff would continue to call him "el viejo."

2. Ibid., 146.

3. The Lonquén case is well documented. My account in this chapter is based on Ahumada et al., editors, *Chile: La memoria prohibida*, vol. 1, 213–219, 229–234, and vol. 3, 145–158; Máximo Pacheco, *Lonquén*; *Solidaridad* 62 (1st half, January 1979), *Solidaridad* 65 (2nd half, February 1979), *Solidaridad* 66 (1st half, March 1979), *Solidaridad* 73 (1st half, July 1979), and *Solidaridad*, "Separata" 33 "Lonquén: Chile estremecido" (September 1979); Fundación Documentación y Archivo de la Vicaría de la Solidaridad, Arzobispado de Santiago, Recortes, 6.9.2 (Caso Lonquén); Patricia Verdugo and Claudio Orrego V., *Detenidos-Desaparecidos: Una herida abierta*; and *Informe de la Comisión Nacional de Verdad y Reconciliación*, vol. 1; Steve J. Stern, *Battling for Hearts and Minds*, 155–167; I am also grateful to photographers Luis Navarro and Helen Hughes and attorney Genaro Arriagada for answering my questions.

4. Stern, *Battling for Hearts and Minds*, 156.

5. Ibid., 157.

6. Máximo Pacheco, *Lonquén*, 9.

7. Ibid.

8. Bórquez quoted in Ahumada et al., editors, *Chile: La memoria prohibida*, vol. 3, 153.

9. On November 7, 1975, Sergio Diez, the United Nations Chilean delegate, declared before the Third Commission of the UN General Assembly that Sergio Miguel Maureira Muñoz "did not have legal existence." He also declared "dead" seven of the fourteen other men previously claimed as disappeared, based on information provided by lists of the Medical Legal Institute: Enrique Astudillo Alvarez, date of death October 7, 1973; Nelson Hernández Flores, date of death October 11, 1973; Oscar Humberto Hernández Flores, date of death October 9, 1973; José Manuel Herrera Villegas, date of death October 6, 1973; José Manuel Maureira Muñoz, date of death October 11, 1973; Rodolfo Antonio Maureira Muñoz, date of death October 15,

1973; Segundo Armando Maureira Muñoz, date of death October 15, 1973. See International Commission of Jurists, *Chile: A Time of Reckoning. Human Rights and the Judiciary.*

10. Stern, *Battling for Hearts and Minds*, 157.

11. Ibid.

12. Hughes is not mentioned by name in any of the sources I consulted. An article published in *Qué Pasa* (2nd half, December 1978) indicates that an "American photographer" was present during the visit on November 30.

13. According to Ariella Azoulay, "Every image, including images whose contents are explicitly political, also exists on the aesthetic plane. It is necessary to understand the aesthetic dimension of the image and its manner of affecting our senses." Azoulay, *Civil Imagination*, 52.

14. Thomas Keenan and Eyal Weizman, *Mengele's Skull. The Advent of Forensic Aesthetics*, 24. Emphasis in the original.

15. See, for instance, Ximena A. Moors, "Para una arqueología del testimonio: el rol de la Iglesia Católica en una producción textual (1973–1991)"; Pablo Oyarzún, "Estética de la sed: *Lonquén 10 años*, diez años después."

16. See, for instance, Stern, *Battling for Hearts and Minds*, 137–195.

17. See Molly Nesbit's "The Use of History," a compelling study of the cultural and historical specificity of photographic documents vis-à-vis Eugene Atget's documentary work. See also Annelise Riles, editor, *Documents: Artifacts of Modern Knowledge*; Diane Dufour, editor, *Images of Conviction: The Construction of Visual Evidence.*

18. Lisa Gitelman notes that reproduction is one clear way that documents are affirmed as such. *Paper Knowledge*, 1.

19. This famous formulation is derived from Charles S. Peirce's writings on the sign. In the late nineteenth century, Peirce divided signs into icons, indexes, and symbols. Peirce argued that in the same way that smoke or ashes are physically connected to a fire—since they indicate the fire's prior existence—a photograph is also physically connected to its referent. It is a physical trace of the object regardless of the photograph's likeness to it. See Charles Peirce, "What Is a Sign?" in *The Collected Papers of Charles Peirce* v. 2.

20. For a discussion of the history of photographic evidence, see Jennifer L. Mnookin's "The Image of Truth: Photographic Evidence and the Power of Analogy."

21. Jennifer L. Mnookin, "The Image of Truth: Photographic Evidence and the Power of Analogy," 13.

22. Vincent Lavoie, "Displaying Forensic Pictures in Court: Photography as Visual Argument," 88.

23. Suzanne Briet, "What Is Documentation?" 10.

24. See Gitelman, *Paper Knowledge*, 2; Riles, "Introduction: In Response," 29.

25. Thomas Keenan and Hito Steyerl, "What Is a Document?" 62.

26. Ibid., 60.

27. Ibid.

28. Ibid., 61.

29. Keenan and Weizman, *Mengele's Skull*, 28.

30. Ibid., 29.

31. Alejandro González's deposition, Lonquén Case File, folio 5017.

32. Ibid.

33. Helen Hughes's deposition, Lonquén Case File, folio 5019.

34. Luis Navarro's deposition, Lonquén Case File, folio 5202.

35. Luis Navarro, interview, October 3, 2018.

36. Declaration reproduced in Pacheco, *Lonquén*, 27.

37. Ibid.

38. Ibid., 29.

39. Ibid., 72.

40. Ibid., 75.

41. Ibid., 168. Emphasis added. Navarro worked with one camera only—he didn't have a second camera. It is not clear to me why the subcomisiaries would have lied about the photographic equipment. Perhaps to imply how prepared this "professional photographer" was.

42. Pacheco, *Lonquén*, 169. The deputy commissioners indicate that they were not called on Monday, but that when they arrived on Tuesday, they saw again Navarro and the other members of the Vicaría. By then, they were able to identify Navarro by name: "On December 5 and 6, 1978, the Investigators verified at the Site of the Incident, the presence of the staff of the Vicaría, recognizing MARIO, HECTOR, and LUCHO, the photographer who until the 6th was [devoted to the task of] taking photographs of the remains of corpses, clothes, etc., extracted [from the oven]." Pacheco, *Lonquén*, 173.

43. Luis Navarro's deposition, Lonquén Case File, folio 5203.

44. Abraham Santibañez, "Testimonio de un visitante," 13. In Fundación Documentación y Archivo de la Vicaría de la Solidaridad, Recortes, 6.9.2 (Caso Lonquén).

45. Keenan and Weizman, *Mengele's Skull*, 15.

46. Pacheco, *Lonquén*, 72.

47. *El Mercurio*, December 10, 1978. In Fundación, Recortes, 6.9.2 (Caso Lonquén).

48. See also Stern, *Battling for Hearts and Minds*, 158–167.

49. The news published in *El Mercurio* on December 8 even resorted to "scientific" racist vocabulary to keep spreading misinformation: "'Among the cadavers, one of them presents negroid [*sic*] features,' said a person who was present at the time of the exhumation." *El Mercurio*, December 8, 1978. In Fundación, Recortes, 6.9.2 (Caso Lonquén).

50. Stern observes, "damage control in the officialist media resembled that exerted in the Letelier affair: reports that suggested the government's good-faith commitment to proper legal procedure, and commentary and innuendo that discredited the bearers of scandal." Stern, *Battling for Hearts and Minds*, 165.

51. Pacheco, *Lonquén*, 206.

52. *Hoy*, "Identificación positiva," (February 1979): 12–13. In Fundación, Recortes, 6.9.2 (Caso Lonquén).

53. Quoted in Pacheco, *Lonquén*, 37.

54. *La Tercera*, January 25, 1979. In Fundación, Recortes, 6.9.2 (Caso Lonquén).

55. Ibid.

56. *Hoy*, "Identificación positiva" (February 1979): 12–13. In Fundación, Recortes, 6.9.2 (Caso Lonquén).

57. Eduardo Cadava, "Lapsus Imaginis: The Image of Ruins," 41.

58. Georges Didi-Huberman, *Images in Spite of All*, 33.

59. Ibid.

60. Ibid. Emphasis in the original. Didi-Huberman claims that the different manipulations and alterations undergone by the four photographs taken in Auschwitz by members

of the Sonderkommando in August of 1944 had the objective of making the images more "informative" or "presentable"—that is, to make a specific idea of the horror coincide with the inexact contingency these documents depicted.

61. I asked colleagues and friends what they thought the image depicted. These are some of their answers. One friend asked me if it was an echography.

62. Abraham Santibañez, "Testimonio de un visitante," *Hoy* (December 1978): 13. In Fundación, Recortes, 6.9.2 (Caso Lonquén).

63. Cadava, "*Lapsus Imaginis*: The Image of Ruins," 36.

64. Let's remember the importance of the function of repetition in Freud—the traumatic event cannot be simply incorporated, it can only be repeated—it must be repeated. In a commentary on one of Freud's cases in *The Interpretation of Dreams*—the one about the father who dreams of his son telling him, "Father, can't you see that I am burning?"—Lacan wonders if perhaps the dream is not in essence an act of homage to that lost reality, a reality that cannot reproduce except by repeating itself in a never successful awaking. See Jacques Lacan, *The Four Fundamental Concepts of Psychoanalysis*, 57–60.

65. Pacheco, *Lonquén*, 10. Emphasis added.

66. Ibid., n.p.

67. Ibid., n.p. Emphasis added.

68. Ibid., 10.

69. Ibid.

70. *La Segunda*, "Agotado," March 31, 1981. In Fundación, Recortes, 6.9.2 (Caso Lonquén).

71. Genaro Arriagada, e-mail communication with the author, November 26, 2018. Arriagada was one of Editorial Aconcagua's directors.

72. Diane Dufour, "Introduction," 5.

73. Keenan and Weizman, *Mengele's Skull*, 28.

74. Ibid., 23.

75. The mass at Recoleta Fransciscana church, where the bodies were supposed to be received, was scheduled for 3 p.m. Monsignor Jorge Hourton broke the horrible news—that the bodies would not arrive—at 4:30 p.m. Stern, *Battling for Hearts and Minds*, 163.

76. Ibid., 159.

77. Ibid., 167.

78. Ignacio Agüero, "No Olvidar de Ignacio Agüero." About Agüero's documentary work, see Valeria De los Ríos and Catalina Donoso, *El cine de Ignacio Agüero: El documental como la lectura de un espacio*.

79. Agüero's *No Olvidar* and Moreno's *La ciudad de los fotógrafos* are almost thirty years apart. And yet, the documentary echoes of Lonquén continue to resonate. In 2011, the series "The Archives of the Cardinal" premiered on TVN (the Chilean National Television). The series was based on the most important legal cases brought forward to the justice by the Vicaría. The first chapter, centered on Lonquén, reenacts the moment of the finding of the human remains inside the ovens and acknowledges the documentary weight of the photographs in the Lonquén case. In one important sequence, the character that plays the Vicaría photographer appears taking photos of the remains found inside the oven. Moreno and Barril's *Habeas Corpus* also revisit the Lonquén Case File.

80. In 2010, thirteen bodies were identified and properly buried (of the fifteen victims, Manuel Navarro and Óscar Hernández still need to be identified).

81. In 2014, the Minister of the Court of Appeals of San Miguel indicted seven policemen (retired) for the crimes of qualified kidnapping and simple kidnapping; in 2016 these men were sentenced and convicted for these crimes; in 2018, the Supreme Court upheld this sentence in a split decision.

82. This was one of the many photos taken during the first *romería* held at the Lonquén ovens. Many photographers took pictures during these processions. Indeed, Helen Hughes, who also worked for the Vicaría, took one photo that became iconic.

83. Cadava, "*Lapsus Imaginis*: The Image of Ruins," 38. Here, Cadava is paraphrasing a fragment of the Convolut N of Benjamin's *The Arcades Project*: "For the historical index of the images not only says that they belong to a particular time; it says, above all, that they attain to legibility only at a particular time." Walter Benjamin, *The Arcades Project* [N3,1], 462.

84. Jacques Derrida, *Rogues*, xii.

85. Ibid. The passage from the *Metamorphoses* to which Derrida is referring here says, "'Is anyone here? and 'Here'! cried Echo back. Amazed, Narcissus looks around in all directions and with a loud voice cries 'Come!'; and 'Come!' she calls him calling." Quoted in Derrida, *Rogues*, 162.

86. Ibid., xii.

Chapter 3. Emergence of a Field

1. See Gonzalo Leiva Quijada, *AFI: Multitudes en sombras*, 39–49.

2. See Gonzalo de la Maza and Mario Garcés, *La explosión de las mayorías: Protesta Nacional 1983–1984*, 14; see also J. Samuel Valenzuela, "La Constitución de 1980 y el Inicio de la Redemocratización en Chile."

3. de la Maza and Garcés, *La explosión*, 10. Unless otherwise indicated, all translations from Spanish are my own. See also Eugenio Ahumada et al., *Chile: La memoria prohibida*, v. 3, 458.

4. The Ecumenical *Te Deum* is a liturgy held annually in Chile on the 18th of September to celebrate national holidays. The *Te Deum* of March 11 was therefore a special *Te Deum*, celebrated to consecrate the beginning of the new Constitution.

5. Navarro, interviews, November 4, 2018, and December 17, 2018.

6. The CNI knew who Navarro was from his work as a photographic expert in Lonquén. Like other Vicaría personnel, Navarro had been constantly harassed since 1978. He had been receiving calls at home, and people had followed him. Navarro, interviews, November 4, 2018, and December 17, 2018. See also Cynthia Brown, *The Vicaría de la Solidaridad in Chile*, 35–42.

7. "11 de marzo: garantías suspendidas."

8. Gilles Deleuze, "Foucault. Les formations historiques. Cours de Gilles Deleuze. Anné universitaire 1985–1986." The translation from French is mine.

9. My reading here draws both from Jacques Derrida's formulation of the trace (its nonoriginality, iterability, and its supplementarity) in his *Of Grammatology*, 80–81, 171–178, 264–278, and from Michel Foucault's methodology in his *The Archeology of Knowledge*.

10. Cf. Leiva Quijada, *AFI: Multitudes en sombras*, 53, where the critic underscores that Navarro's arrest was the most urgent or prominent cause, but that AFI's formation was due to an array of factors.

11. Photographer Paz Errázuriz underscores the AFI's importance as a legitimizing in-

stance. In her interview with Sebastián Moreno in *La ciudad de los fotógrafos*, she claims that the AFI allowed her and others to identify as photographers for the first time: "the most beautiful thing about this recovery is recognizing oneself [. . .], giving oneself the credit [. . .], becoming a photographer. I think a lot of us started using the name [photographer] thanks to the AFI. In a way, daring to name oneself, to call oneself a photographer."

12. Deleuze, "Foucault. Les formations historiques."

13. Deleuze describes this *on dit* as a "deep anonymous murmur." See Deleuze, *Foucault*, 7.

14. It is perhaps useful to recall here the triangulation between subject, discourse, and historical convergence described by Butler as follows: "When and if subversion or resistance becomes possible, it does so not because I am a sovereign subject, but because a certain historical convergence of norms at the site of my embodied personhood opens up possibilities for action." "Performativity, Precarity, and Sexual Politics," xi–xii.

15. *Fotogente* was published between 1980 and 1981 by the School of Art Photography of Chile and was directed by photographer Hernán Soza.

16. Merino, "Carta," 2.

17. Claudia Donoso, "16 años de fotografía en Chile: Memoria de un descontexto," 30.

18. Felipe Riobó, "Fotografía chilena: proyecto actual, proyecto posible," 8.

19. Jorge Ianiszewski, "Editorial," 2.

20. *13 Fotógrafos AFI*, catalogue exhibit.

21. See Agamben, "The State of Emergency."

22. Butler, *Frames of War*, 29. See also Butler, "Demonstrating Precarity."

23. See Introduction.

24. Gonzalo Leiva Quijada's *AFI: Multitudes en sombras* also underscores this.

25. AFI photographers, "Ausencia de la crítica: un comentario," 5.

26. Most of the photography exhibitions were held at the Chilean British Institute of Culture's Sala Edwards, the Chilean French Institute, the Goethe Institute, the Mapocho Cultural Center, and the galleries Época and Sur.

27. Sontag's text (translated by Adriana Valdés) had begun circulating in 1979 in the magazine *CAL*.

28. For a critique of Sontag's formulations and a reappraisal of the photographs of horror, see Susie Linfield, *The Cruel Radiance*. See also Butler, *Frames of War*, 63–100.

29. AFI photographers, "Agencias AFI," 4.

30. Quoted in Gonzalo Leiva Quijada, *AFI: Multitudes en sombras*, 94.

31. Weinstein, "Editorial," 2.

32. Ibid.

33. Repression against photographers continued throughout the eighties. On November 19, 1984, photographers Kena Lorenzini and Constanza Peña were arrested after an event held by the Sebastián Acevedo Movement against Torture. They were released two days later after suffering violence and cruelty. Photographers Jaime Robothan, Claudio Pérez, and Óscar Navarro were arrested in December 1985 during a Human Rights Day demonstration. One of the most extreme cases of violence occurred on July 2, 1986, when the young photographer Rodrigo Rojas Denegri (also an AFI member) and student Carmen Gloria Quintana were arrested by a military patrol while participating in a demonstration. They were doused with gasoline and burned alive. Rojas Denegri succumbed to his fatal injuries four days later; Quintana survived only after undergoing numerous surgical procedures.

34. One of the most critical moments regarding censorship was the establishment of Edict Number 19 on September 4, 1984, whereby the Chilean Ministry of Defense prohibited the publication of "any kind of graphic image" in the magazines *Apsi*, *Análisis*, *Cauce*, and in the newspaper *Fortín Mapocho* (see chapter 4).

35. "Editorial," n.p.

36. Cf. Gonzalo Leiva Quijada, where the scholar emphasizes the "diachronic jump" of four years between the publications of the fifth issue—which appeared in January 1984—and the sixth issue of December 1987. While one could establish a correspondence between a period marked by successive states of siege, censorship, and repression against the resistance, on the one hand, and the discontinuity of *Punto de Vista*, on the other, the "diachronic jump" suggested by Leiva Quijada is not accurate: it disregards the edition published in August 1985. By ignoring this unnumbered edition and suggesting instead the idea of a coherent "evolution" from newsletter to magazine, Leiva Quijada replicates the idea of a heroic, coherent subject. See *AFI: multitudes en sombras*, 89–90.

37. Loreto Guerrero was in charge of the design of *Presencia del hombre*; Ricardo Astorga coordinated the edition and Gracia Aguilar the composition.

38. The noun "man" stands here for the whole of "humanity" and supplants the more controversial (because it is ideologically charged) "people," but knowing this does not make the word choice less regrettable. The title also evokes the famous 1955 itinerant photo exhibition *The Family of Man*, conceived by Edward Steichen at the MoMA. This exhibit, in turn, inspired a Chilean version, which was curated by photographer Antonio Quintana in 1960 and was titled *El rostro de Chile*.

39. *Presencia del hombre*, Editorial, n.p. To confuse the censors even more, AFI photographers asked a group of regional artists and anthropologists based in Temuco, Agrupación Cultural Puliwen-Antu (Puliwen-Antu Cultural Association) to appear as editors of *Presencia del hombre*. Weinstein, e-mail message to author, July 10, 2012.

40. This kind of categorization (this photograph is political; this photograph is not) falls under what Azoulay calls "the political judgement of taste." See Azoulay, *Civil Imagination*, 29–124.

41. As we shall see, silouettes and shadows also appear in both Mauricio Valenzuela's and Luis Weinstein's *Ediciones económicas*.

42. About the metonymic force of photography, see Derrida, "The Deaths of Roland Barthes," 58–59.

43. This precarious corpus is also presented to its potential audience as inevitably incomplete: "The problems facing any artistic publication, even more if it is the first of its kind, did not allow us to further expand the universe of exhibitors."

44. *Presencia del hombre*, Editorial, n.p.

45. I am also evoking here Agamben's reading of Benjamin: "Repetition restores the possibility of what was, renders it possible anew; it's almost a paradox. To repeat something is to make it possible anew. Here lies the proximity of repetition and memory. Memory cannot give us back what was, as such: that would be hell. Instead, memory restores possibility of the past." Agamben, "Difference and Repetition," 315–316.

46. *Presencia del hombre*, Editorial, n.p.

47. For Derrida, the iterations of the sign are different because the sign exists each time in a different context; meanwhile, iterations become recognizable as iterations *because* they repeat

(this repetition, however, is not "of the same," because there is no "same"—only iterations). See *Of Grammatology*, 227; see also "Signature Event Context."

48. AFI photographers, Introducción, *Segundo Anuario*, 5.

49. In 1985, for example, José Luis Granesse compiled *Fotografia chilena contemporánea* (Contemporary Chilean Photography), a volume encompassing various styles and modes of representation, from documentary to fashion photography. It is also worth mentioning one of the first scholarly works about the history of photography, Hernán Rodríguez Villegas's "Historia de la fotografía en Chile: registro de daguerrotipistas, fotógrafos, reporteros gráficos y camarógrafos," published in 1986 in *Boletín de la Academia de Historia.*

50. See also Leiva Quijada, *AFI: Multitudes en sombras*, 83. Leiva Quijada speculates that the copies were probably sold by the printshop as recycled paper.

51. For a history of the Chicago Boys, including an in-depth analysis of their disastrous policies, see Naomi Klein's excellent *The Shock Doctrine*, 91–176. Klein remarks that the full document, printed at the presses of *El Mercurio* newspaper on the day of the coup, was distributed to General Officers of the Armed Forces on September 12, 1973 (92).

52. *El ladrillo*, 15. The complete title of this document read *"El ladrillo:" Bases de la política económica del gobierno militar chileno* (The Brick: Foundations for the Chilean Military Government's Economic Policy). In *Speculative Fictions*, Alessandro Fornazzari suggests that while "El Ladrillo," in and of itself, "is an unremarkable economic text [. . .] it does reveal fundamental elements of the Chilean neoliberal project" (52). Klein also notes the striking resemblance between *El ladrillo* and Milton Friedman's *Capital and Freedom.*

53. Most of the enterprises and industries taken over by the state under the Unidad Popular government were privatized (all but the copper industry); the lands redistributed under the agrarian reform, a process that had begun with Jorge Alessandri in 1960, were restored to their former owners; previous labor measures designed to protect workers' labor rights were eliminated. Additionally, in 1979, a new Labor Plan came into effect created by then Minister of Labor and Pensions José Piñera (also considered a Chicago Boy, even though he had studied at Harvard). Piñera's Labor Plan dismantled all the entitlements gained by the labor unions and popular movements under previous governments; pension funds and preventive health were also privatized. In 1980, the year of the pension reform, a new system of retirement management (AFP, the Administrator of Retirement Funds), overseen by private entities, was implemented; in 1983 the Institutions for Preventive Health (ISAPRE) system came into effect; this privatized health insurance system is still in force in Chile. See David Harvey, *A Brief History of Neoliberalism*; Naomi Klein, *The Shock Doctrine.*

54. Klein, *The Shock Doctrine*, 104.

55. In Horacio Fernández's words, "Riobó [. . .] managed [. . .] to reach the degree zero of the photobook." *The Latin American Photobook*, 146. See also Ángeles Donoso Macaya, "Ediciones económicas de la fotografía chilena" in *Una revisión del fotolibro chileno.*

56. Riobó insists on the *Ediciones's* affordability: "The *Ediciones* were cheap, really cheap. They were so cheap that I could have financed some with no effort because in two or three days you would recoup your initial 'investment.'" Riobó, e-mail message to author, July 3, 2015.

57. Riobó, "Presentación," in Mauricio Valenzuela, *Ediciones económicas* vol. 1, n.p.

58. According to Errázuriz: "We tried to adjust the quality of the photographic copies in order to improve the quality of the photocopies [. . .] There were good photographs that

could not be used for the affordable editions because we couldn't work with good copies." Quoted in Horacio Fernández, *The Latin American Photobook*, 146.

59. Luis Weinstein, e-mail message to author, May 12, 2015.

60. See Eduardo Cadava, "The Itinerant Languages of Photography," 24.

61. Quoted in Paz Errázuriz, *FotoNo*, 83. See also Paz Errázuriz, *La manzana de Adán*; Paz Errázuriz and Diamela Eltit, *El infarto del alma*; Nelly Richard, *Paz Errázuriz and Lotty Rosenfeld: Poetics of Dissent*.

62. Riobó, "Presentación," in Mauricio Valenzuela, *Ediciones económicas* vol. 1 (April 1983).

63. In the exhibition catalogue of *Urbes Mutantes: Latin American Photography 1944–2013* (co-curated by Alexis Fabry and María Will), the authors indicate *El pan nuestro* "was censored as soon as it was published, and the agents of the National Department of Publications [*sic*] took the time to suppress, page by page, content deemed subversive. Because of this, in all of the copies, the book spine was disproportionate in relation to the number of pages" (174). This account is somewhat innaccurate: photographer Claudio Pérez told me that *El pan nuestro* had been stolen by CNI agents (not by the National Department of Publications, an agency that did not exist; the authors probably meant the DINACOS, the National Department of Communications). Fortunately, the photographers who collaborated on this book took approximately one hundred copies from the shop a few days before the break-in occurred. The copy Alexis Fabry saw was a shorter version—not because of censorship, but because of authorial decision. Pérez himself created this new version of *El pan nuestro*, showcasing only photos he had taken. It was Pérez's doing, rather than the military's, that explains the missing pages from the copy Fabry saw. Claudio Pérez, e-mail message to author, August 25, 2016.

64. Azoulay distinguishes the photographic event from the event of photography. See Azoulay, *Civil Imagination*, 26–27.

65. In saying the bread *orients* the photograph and the bread *matters*, I draw from Ahmed's "Orientations Matter." See also Ahmed, *Queer Phenomenology*.

66. The precarious milieu revealed by *El pan nuestro* was widely addressed by an array of social and artistic practices throughout this period. It suffices to recall one prominent example from the artistic field. In 1979, the Colectivo de Acciones de Arte (Collective of Art Actions) (CADA) initiated four simultaneous actions titled *Para no morir de hambre en el arte* ("So as not to die of hunger in art" or "For not dying of starvation in art"), each of which had milk as its main focus. See Robert Neustadt, *CADA día: la creación de un arte social*; Nelly Richard, *Márgenes e Instituciones*, 63–74.

67. See Butler, *Frames of War*, 14.

68. Organized by the Ministry of Culture, the Community of Madrid, the Institute of IberoAmerican Cooperation, and the Fine Arts Circle (among other institutions), *Chile Vive* (Chile Lives) showcased painting, sculpture, photography and architecture; press samples and literary works; music, theater, and poetry performances; video projections; a selection of the work made by the Vicaría in defense of human rights; plus additional talks and debates.

69. Fonseca, "A propósito," 33. Emphasis added.

70. Donoso, "16 años," 32.

71. Fonseca, "A propósito," 37.

72. Donoso, "16 años," 31.

73. Fonseca, "A propósito," 38.

74. Donoso, "16 años," 32.

75. Donoso, in fact, underscores the authorial utopia implied in AFI's name—she assimilates the notion of "independent photographer" to that of "author."

76. Fonseca, "A propósito," 33.

77. See John Tagg, *Grounds of Dispute*, 75. About the different histories of photography, see Ariella Azoulay, *The Civil Contract of Photography*; Geoffrey Batchen, *Burning with Desire: The Conception of Photography*; Régis Durand, *Le temps de l'image: essai sur les conditions d'une histoire des formes photographiques*; Deborah Poole, *Vision, Race, and Modernity*.

78. Fonseca, "A propósito," 38.

79. Donoso, "16 años," 32.

80. Ibid.

81. Butler, *Frames of War*, 139.

Chapter 4. Photography Off Limits

1. An edict issued a few days earlier had already censored a number of radio stations. The information services of Cooperativa, Chilena, Voz de la Costa (Osorno), El Sembrador (Chillán), and Presidente Ibáñez (Punta Arenas) were forced to shut down during two days of national protests (September 4 and 5, 1984).

2. In *Another Way of Telling*, John Berger and Joan Mohr also question the tendency to fix—the "people say"—the truth status of the photograph in absolute terms. A photograph of a volcano does not belong to the same order of truth as a photo of a man crying, the authors tell us: "if no theoretical distinction has been made between the photograph as scientific evidence and the photograph as a means of communication, *this has been not so much an oversight as a proposal*. The proposal was (and is) that when something is visible, it is a fact, and that facts contain the only truth" (100; emphasis in the original). See also Sekula, "Dismantling Modernism, Reinventing Documentary (Notes on the Politics of Representation)" and Martha Rosler, "In, Around, and Afterthoughts (on Documentary Photography)."

3. Rouillé, "The Times of the Document," 9.

4. See Lorenzo Vilches, *Teoría de la imagen periodística*. Vilches notes photographs are not "indifferent to the spatial context" of the medium that contains them. Besides the graphic and linguistic elements that contextualize the photos on the printed page and the channel that disseminates them, the journalistic genres and the thematic areas also give the photos meaning. See also Barthes, "The Photographic Message."

5. See Thierry Gervais, editor, *The "Public" Life of Photographs*.

6. Azoulay, *The Civil Contract of Photography*, 14.

7. Azoulay, *Civil Imagination*, 104. As Azoulay suggests in the passage quoted as epigraph, the civil contract always reclaims its place "through the efforts of its numerous trustees." See Azoulay, *The Civil Contract of Photography*, 127.

8. Ibid., 105.

9. Ibid., 106.

10. This international exhibit gathered artists from France, Chile, and Argentina. The show was inaugurated on March 13, 1996, in Santiago and opened in Buenos Aires, Argentina, on May 2.

11. On photographic evidence see Diane Dufour, editor, *Images of Conviction: The Con-*

struction of Visual Evidence; Thomas Keenan and Eyal Weizman, *Mengele's Skull: The Advent of Forensic Aesthetics*; Jennifer L. Mnookin, "The Image of Truth: Photographic Evidence and the Power of Analogy." On the semiotics of news photography, see Vilches, *Teoría de la imagen periodística*.

12. See Introduction.

13. Rouillé, "Los límites de la fotografía," 5. Unless otherwise indicated, all translations from Spanish are my own.

14. Ibid.

15. Rouillé, *La photographie*, 73.

16. Ibid., 117.

17. Rouillé, "Los límites," 5.

18. See Tomás Moulián, *Chile actual: Anatomía de un mito*.

19. Rouillé, "Los límites," 5.

20. Ibid. Emphasis added.

21. I make this clarification because Rouillé formulated some of the ideas quoted here after 1996 (*La photographie* was published in 2005, and "The Times of the Document" was published in 2013). I quote from these later publications because they expand on ideas introduced by the critic in his 1996 curatorial text.

22. Rouillé, "Los límites," 5.

23. Richard, "Bordes, límites, fronteras," 6.

24. Ibid., 7.

25. Ibid.

26. Ibid., 8.

27. Ibid.

28. See Foucault, "Photogenic Painting," 83–84. See also Cadava, "The Itinerant Languages of Photography," 24–25.

29. See Eduardo Cadava and Gabriela Nouizelles, editors, *The Itinerant Languages of Photography*.

30. Human Rights Watch, *Los límites de la tolerancia*, 92.

31. See Jorge Mera and Carlos Ruiz, "Notas sobre la libertad de prensa, censura y política en Chile." The authors argue that even though freedom of expression, information, and social communication was severely restricted and repression was "brutal and direct" (176) in the context of the dictatorship, a detailed revision of these rights during the republican era demonstrates that they have always been restricted, precisely because they were never conceived as rights but as freedoms and "the social and economic conditions that would allow for the exercise of these freedoms by every social sector are not assured" (181) in the 1980 Constitution.

32. The ways in which the military dictatorship repressed Chilean independent media have been widely documented. See the 1985 report produced by the Inter American Commission on Human Rights; see also Human Rights Watch, *Los límites de la tolerancia*; Fernando Reyes Matta and Jorge Andrés Richards, *Periodismo independiente ¿Mito o realidad?*; Claudio Durán, Fernando Reyes Matta, and Carlos Ruiz, *La prensa: del autoritarismo a la libertad*, 127–142 and 175–206; María Olivia Mönckeberg, *Los magnates de la prensa*; Colegio de Periodistas de Chile, *Las Batallas por la libertad de expresión (1979–1986)*.

33. To learn about these publications, see Consuelo Pérez Mendoza, *Los protagonistas de la prensa alternativa*; Matías León Lira, *El periodismo que no calló: Historia de la revista* Análisis

(1977/1993); Emilio Filippi, *Libertad de pensar, libertad de decir* and, by the same author, *La fuerza de la verdad*; Fernando Ossandón and Sandra Rojas, *El primer impacto*, a study about newspapers *Fortín Mapocho* and *La Época*; Stern, *Battling for Hearts and Minds*, 297–329.

34. During these protests, army lieutenant and regional chief of the CNI Copiapó Julio Briones Rayo was also killed. He was dressed as a civilian and mingled with the students, according to a note published in *Apsi* 152.

35. Sergio Marras, "A once años del once," 1.

36. Equipo *Apsi*, "Protesta 4 y 5 de septiembre: La más grande, la más fuerte," 7–8.

37. The first independent audiovisual informative production, *Teleanálisis*, appeared in 1984. See Mönckeberg, *Los magnates de la prensa*, 40–43.

38. Quoted in Colegio de Periodistas de Chile, *Las batallas*, 113.

39. Ibid., 114.

40. Quoted in León Lira, *El periodismo que no calló*, 57.

41. As historian Alfredo Jiognant Rondón argues, the political and social transformations that occurred during the early eighties are posited in several historiographical accounts as "concomitant with the passage from a de facto regime to an institutionalized political system" (22). According to these views, one of the clearest signs of these transformations would have been the nomination, in 1983, of Sergio Onofre Jarpa, a renowned right-wing politician (and not a member of the military), as Minister of the Interior. Jarpa himself boasted of the so-called aperture Chile experimented during his tenure, which made possible, for example, the appearance of *Cauce* in November of 1983. Nevertheless, this was also a period marked by recurring social protests and heavy military repression. This is why it is questionable to attribute the social changes and political transformations to the legal measures adopted by the military.

42. Vilches, *Teoría de la imagen periodística*, 54.

43. Quoted in Human Rights Watch, *Los límites de la tolerancia*, 92–93.

44. The State of Siege of November 1984 remained in effect for more than seven months.

45. Lihn, "La fotografía: entre la censura y el conformismo," 40. In Lihn's edited volume, *Textos sobre Arte*, editors Adriana Valdés and Ana María Risco include a text entitled "Sobre la fotografía: el reportaje gráfico y las fotos censuradas." A note by the editors indicates: "Unpublished article, presumably written in 1984. The original text does not seem definitive and has some ambiguities in its writing. That is why it includes more revisions by the editors than other texts in this volume." There must be some kind of confusion, because this allegedly unpublished text was published in October 1984 in *Cauce*—precisely in one of the censored issues—and it is entitled "La fotografía: entre la censura y el conformismo." To avoid adding to this confusion, I quote the 1984 text published in *Cauce*.

46. Lihn, "La fotografía: entre la censura y el conformismo," 41.

47. See Barthes, *Image-Music-Text*, particularly "The Photographic Message" and "Rhetoric of the Image."

48. Lihn, "La fotografía: entre la censura y el conformismo," 41.

49. León Lira, *El periodismo*, 43.

50. Regarding readership numbers, Stern offers the following estimates: "For *Solidaridad*, which circulated in community contexts of loans and shared readings, 150,000 (the low end of the 150,000–200,000 estimate of the Vicaría); for all others, 150,000, or two readers per copy sold." Stern, *Battling for Hearts and Minds*, 463. Note that Stern acknowledges using a conservative methodology in his estimation of these figures.

51. Quoted in León Lira, *El periodismo*, 43. Fernando Reyes also refers to the use of photocopiers as a factor that increased the readership numbers and circulation of these publications. See Reyes, "Periodismo independiente alternativo en Chile," 26.

52. "Fotos Des-Censuradas," 2.

53. José Carrasco Tapia, "La prensa de nuevo en la mira," 10. Renowned journalist and international editor of *Análisis* José Carrasco Tapia was one of the thousands of victims of the dictatorship. On September 8, 1986, he was abducted by CNI agents; a few hours later, his body was found near the General Cemetery in Santiago, with thirteen bullet holes.

54. "Fotos Des-Censuradas," 2.

55. Carrasco Tapia, "La prensa de nuevo en la mira," 10.

56. The temporary use of pages from fellow media due to censorship was a recurring practice in the independent press. For example, in June 1979, *Hoy* was censored for two months for publishing interviews with Clodomiro Almeyda and Carlos Altamirano. *Análisis*, despite having published texts by José Miguel Insunza and Luis Corvalán, was not subject to this restrictive measure, as it was still sponsored then by the Academia de Humanismo Cristiano. During these two months, *Análisis* gave a number of pages to *Hoy* journalists so they could publish their work. See León Lira, *El periodismo*, 31.

57. The photos credited their authors' names (in the case of freelance photographers) or the name of the magazine that provided the photos from their archives.

58. "Presencia de jóvenes," 14.

59. As Thomas Keenan argues, all photographs have this decontextualizing and deappropriating efficacy. See Keenan, "I Decided to Take a Look, Again," 78.

60. Barthes, *Camera Lucida*, 6.

61. "El miedo a la verdad," 27.

62. Reyes, "Periodismo independiente," 14–15.

63. De La Parra, "Fragments of a Self-Portrait," 15.

64. See, for instance, Stern, *Battling for Hearts and Minds*; Claudia Donoso, "16 años de fotografía en Chile."

65. "El triunfo de la imagen," 55.

66. Azoulay, *Civil Imagination*, 107.

Chapter 5. Epilogue

1. The photographers who participated in *Chile from Within* were Paz Errázuriz, Alejandro Hoppe, Álvaro Hoppe, Helen Hughes, Jorge Ianiszewski, Héctor López, Kena Lorenzini, Juan Domingo Marinello, Christian Montecino, Marcelo Montecino, Óscar Navarro, Claudio Pérez, Luis Poirot, Paulo Slachevsky, Luis Weinstein, and Óscar Wittke.

2. See Lee E. Douglas, editor, "Fragments from a conversation: Making of this book. Spring/Summer, 1989. Exchanges between Susan and Chilean photographers: Alejandro, Álvaro, Claudio, Héctor, Helen, Marcelo, Óscar, and Paz."

3. Marco Antonio De La Parra, "Fragments of a Self-Portrait," 13.

4. Susan Freudenheim, "Chilean Photos, Folk art, Document Rage, Passion." In the *Tribune*, San Diego, Friday, September 22, 1989, C-1. Filed in Meiselas's *Chile from Within* project archive.

5. There is a prior electronic version of *Chile from Within* in Spanish; in 2013, Susan Meise-

las, Luis Weinstein, Helen Hughes, and Lee E. Douglas co-produced a bilingual e-book edition entitled *Chile from Within / Chile desde dentro.*

6. The traveling exhibition of *Chile from Within* opened at the Mandeville Gallery at University of California, San Diego, in September 1989.

7. In 1989, the space became a venue for conventions and meetings while still housing the Ministry of Defense. A fire that destroyed part of the building in 2006 prompted the government of Bachelet to reconstruct and transform the building into a public cultural center.

8. Marco Antonio De La Parra, "Fragments of a Self-Portrait," 13, 15.

9. Rodrigo Rojas was brutally beaten and burned alive by a troop of military police during a street demonstration on July 2, 1986. The ex-conscript's statements confirmed the direct responsibility of retired high-ranking military officers in Rojas's death and exposed the subsequent cover-up of the crime by top military officials. Furthermore, the ex-conscript's statements coincided with the declassification of U.S. Department of State documents that also confirmed the cover-up (the National Security Archive at The George Washington University declassified these documents on July 31, 2015). About the attack, see Patricia Verdugo, *Rodrigo y Carmen Gloria: Quemados vivos.*

10. See Hirsch, *Family Frames: Photography, Narrative, and Postmemory.*

11. Christian Montecino was detained on October 16, 1973, shortly after the National Stadium photographic assignment. Ulterior investigations determined he was abducted and executed by mistake. See Gonzalo Leiva Quijada, *AFI: Multitudes en sombras*, 40.

12. In 2016, Amnesty International published a report entitled '*I didn't know there were two kinds of justice:' Military Jurisdiction and Police Brutality in Chile.*

13. Benjamin, *The Arcades Project*, 456.

14. I am evoking here Derrida's formulation of a democracy to come that has the structure of a promise. See Derrida, *Rogues*, 85–86.

WORKS CITED

Agamben, Giorgio. "The State of Emergency." *Generation Online*, www.generation-online.org/p/fpagambenschmitt.htm. Accessed 22 April 2019.

———. "Difference and Repetition: On Guy Debord's Films," in *Guy Debord and the Situationist International*, edited by Tom McDonough, translated by Brian Holmes, 313–319. Cambridge: MIT Press, 2002.

Agrupación Cultural Puliwen-Antu. *Presencia del hombre: Primer Anuario fotográfico chileno*. Santiago: Gráfica Siglo XXI, 1981.

Agüero, Ignacio. "No Olvidar de Ignacio Agüero." *Cine Chileno Wordpress*, www.cinechileno.wordpress.com/2009/01/03/no-olvidar-de-ignacio-aguero. Accessed 22 April 2019.

———, dir. *No Olvidar*; Ignacio Agüero y Grupo Memoria, 1982.

———, dir. *El diario de Agustín*; Ignacio Agüero & Asociados, Amazonía Films, 2008.

Ahmed, Sarah. *Queer Phenomenology: Orientations, Objects, Others*. Durham, NC: Duke University Press, 2006.

———. "Orientations Matter," in *New Materialism*, edited by Diana Coole and Samantha Frost, 234–257. Durham, NC: Duke University Press, 2017.

Ahumada, Eugenio, et al. *Chile: La memoria prohibida*. 3 vols. Santiago: Pehuén, 1989.

Amnesty International. "'I didn't know there were two kinds of justice': Military Jurisdiction and Police Brutality in Chile," London: Amnesty International Publications, 2016. Amnesty.org, www.amnesty.org/en/documents/amr22/3209/2016/en. Accessed 22 April 2019.

Apsi. "Fotos Des-Censuradas." October 1 to October 14, 1984.

Asociación de Fotógrafos Independientes (AFI). *Segundo Anuario Fotográfico Chileno*. Toronto. Instituto Chileno Canadiense de Cultura, 1982.

Avelar, Ibelber. "La escena de Avanzada. Photography and Writing in Postcoup Chile—A Conversation with Nelly Richard," in *Photography and Writing in Latin America: Double Exposures*, edited by Marcy E. Schwartz and Mary Beth Tierney-Tello, 259–270. Albuquerque: University of New Mexico Press, 2006.

Azoulay, Ariella. *The Civil Contract of Photography*. Translated by Rela Mazali and Ruvik Danieli. New York: Zone Books, 2008.

———. *Civil Imagination: A Political Ontology of Photography*. Translated by Louise Bethehem. London: Verso, 2012.

———. "Archive," translated by Tal Haran, in *Political Concepts: A Critical Lexicon*, www.politicalconcepts.org/issue1/archive. Accessed 22 April 2019.

Baker, George. “Photography’s Expanded Field.” *October* 114 (Fall 2005): 120–140.

Baldwin, Gordon, and Martin Jürgens. *Looking at Photographs: A Guide to Technical Terms.* Revised Edition. Los Angeles: J. Paul Getty Museum, 2009.

Barad, Karen. “Posthumanist Performativity: Toward an Understanding of How Matter Comes to Matter.” *Signs* 28, No. 3 (Spring 2003): 801–831.

Barril, Claudia, and Sebastián Moreno, dirs. *Habeas Corpus.* Películas del Pez, 2015.

Barros A., César. “Declassifying the Archive. The Bombardment of La Moneda Palace and the Political Economy of the Image,” in *Technology, Literature, and Digital Culture in Latin America: Mediatized Sensibilities in a Globalized Era,* edited by Matthew Bush and Tania Gentic, 127–145. New York: Routledge, 2014.

Barthes, Roland. *Camera Lucida.* Translated by Richard Howard. New York: Hill and Wang, 2010.

———. *Image-Music-Text.* Translated by Stephen Heath. New York: Hill & Wang, 1978.

Bassnett, Sarah, Andrea Noble, and Thy Phu. “Introduction: Cold War Visual Alliances.” *Visual Studies* 30, No. 2 (2015): 119–121.

Basterra, Víctor. *Testimonio sobre el Centro Clandestino de Detención de la ESMA.* Buenos Aires: CELS, 1984.

Batchen, Geoffrey. *Burning with Desire: The Conception of Photography.* Cambridge: MIT Press, 1997.

Bazin, André. “The Ontology of the Photographic Image.” Translated by Hugh Gray. *Film Quarterly* 13, No. 4 (1960): 4–9.

Bell, Vikki. “On Fernando’s Photograph: The Biopolitics of *Aparición* in Contemporary Argentina.” *Theory, Culture & Society* 27, No. 4 (2010): 69–89.

Benjamin, Walter. *The Arcades Project.* Translated by Howard Eiland and Kevin McLaughlin. Cambridge, MA: Harvard University Press, 2003.

———. “Little History of Photography,” in *Selected Writings, Volume 2, 1931–1934,* edited by Howard Eiland and Michael W. Jennings, translated by Rodney Livingstone et al., 507–530. Cambridge, MA: Harvard University Press, 1999.

———. “Central Park,” in *Selected Writings, Volume 4, 1938–1940,* edited by Howard Eiland and Michael W. Jennings, translated by Edmund Jephcott et al., 161–199. Cambridge, MA: Harvard University Press.

———. “The Work of Art in the Age of Its Technological Reproducibility: Third Version,” in *Selected Writings, Volume 4, 1938–1940,* edited by Howard Eiland and Michael W. Jennings, translated by Edmund Jephcott et al., 251–283. Cambridge, MA: Harvard University Press.

Benovsky, Jiri. “The Limits of Photography.” *International Journal of Philosophical Studies* 22, No. 5 (2014): 716–733.

Berger, John. *Ways of Seeing.* London: Penguin, 1973.

Berger, John, and Jean Mohr. *Another Way of Telling.* New York: Vintage, 1995.

Berríos, María. “Spectres of Counterinsurgency: Staged Confrontations and *Montaje* in Authoritarian Chile,” in *Contested Histories from El Complejo,* edited by Hans Carlsson, Claudia del Fierro, and Julia Willén, 35–49. Malmö, Göteborg, and Santiago: Julia Willén, 2017.

La Bicicleta. “Presencia de jóvenes.” October 23, 1984.

Blejmar, Jordana, Natalia Fortuny, and Luis Ignacio García, editors. *Instantáneas de la memoria. Fotografía y dictadura en Argentina y América Latina.* Buenos Aires: Libraria, 2013.

Bonnefoy Miralles, Pascale. *Terrorismo de Estadio. Prisioneros de guerra en un campo de Deportes*. Santiago: Editorial Latinoamericana, 2016.

Bourdieu, Pierre. *The Field of Cultural Production*. Edited by Randal Johnson. New York: Columbia University Press, 1993.

———, et al. *Photography, a Middle-brow Art*. Translated by Shaun Whiteside. Palo Alto, CA: Stanford University Press, 1990.

Briet, Suzanne. *What Is Documentation?* Translated and edited by Ronald E. Day and Laurent Martinet with Hermina G. B. Anghelescu. Toronto: Scarecrow Press, 2006.

Brown, Cynthia G. *The Vicaría de la Solidaridad in Chile*. New York: The Americas Watch Committee, 1987.

Bruno, Giuliana. "Interview." Interview by Sarah Oppenheimer. *Bomb Magazine* 128 (Summer 2014), Bomb online, www.bombmagazine.org/article/10056/giuliana-bruno. Accessed 22 April 2019.

Butler, Judith. *The Psychic Life of Power: Theories of Subjection*. Palo Alto, CA: Stanford University Press, 1997.

———. *Frames of War: When Is Life Grievable?* London: Verso, 2009.

———. *Bodies that Matter: On the Discursive Limits of Sex*. New York: Routledge, 2011.

———. "Performativity, Precariety and Sexual Politics." *AIBR, Revista de Antropología Iberoamericana* 4, No. 3 (2009): i–xiii.

———. "Demonstrating Precarity: Vulnerability, Embodiment, and Resistance." Interview by Arne de Boever. *Los Angeles Review of Books*, March 23, 2015, www.lareviewofbooks.org/av/demonstrating-precarity-vulnerability-embodiment-resistance. Accessed 22 April 2019.

Bystrom, Kerry. "Memoria, fotografía y legibilidad en las obras de Marcelo Brodsky y León Ferrari," in Feld and Stites Mor, 315–337.

Cadava, Eduardo. *Words of Light: Theses on the Photography of History*. Princeton, NJ: Princeton University Press, 1998.

———. "'*Lapsus Imaginis*': The Image in Ruins." *October* 96 (Spring 2001): 35–60.

———. "The Itinerant Languages of Photography," in Cadava and Nouzeilles, 24–37.

Cadava, Eduardo, and Paola Cortés-Rocca. "Notes on Love and Photography." *October* 166 (Spring 2006): 3–34.

Cadava, Eduardo, and Gabriela Nouzeilles, editors. *The Itinerant Languages of Photography*. New Haven, CT: Yale University Press, 2014.

———. "Introduction," in Cadava and Nouzeilles, 17–23.

Campt, Tina. *Image Matters*. Durham, NC: Duke University Press, 2013.

Carrasco Tapia, José. "La prensa de Nuevo en la mira." *Análisis*, September 24 to October 8, 1984.

Cauce. "Ofensiva militar contra la prensa." September 12 to September 18, 1984.

Cauce. "El triunfo de la imagen." October 23 to October 29, 1984.

Colegio de Periodistas de Chile, A.G. *Las Batallas por la libertad de expresión (1979–1986)*. Santiago: Colegio de Periodistas de Chile, 1986.

Coleman, Kevin. *A Camera in the Garden of Eden*. Austin: University of Texas Press, 2016.

Comité Editorial. "Introducción," in *Segundo Anuario Fotográfico Chileno*. Toronto: Instituto Chileno-Canadiense de Cultura y AFI, 1982, 5.

Concha, José Pablo. "*Del espacio de acá*, de Ronald Kay: una interpretación posible." *Aisthesis* 35 (2002): 101–105.

Constitución Política de la República de Chile de 1980, www.camara.cl/camara/media/docs/constitucion_politica.pdf. Accessed 22 April 2019.

Da Silva Catela, Ludmila, "Lo invisible revelado. El uso de fotografías como (re) presentación de la desaparición de personas en Argentina," in Feld and Stites Mor, 337–361.

De Castro, Sergio. *El ladrillo: bases de la política económica del gobierno militar chileno.* Santiago: Centro de Estudios Públicos, 1992.

De La Maza, Gonzalo, and Mario Garcés. *La explosión de las mayorías: Protesta Nacional 1983–1984.* Santiago: Educación y Comunicación, 1985.

De La Parra, Marco Antonio. "Fragments of a Self-Portrait," in *Chile from Within*, edited by Susan Meiselas, translated by Marcelo Montealegre, 13–15. New York: W.W. Norton & Company, 1990.

De Los Ríos, Valeria. *Fantasmas artificiales. Cine y fotografía en la obra de Enrique Lihn.* Santiago de Chile: Hueders, 2015

De Los Ríos, Valeria, and Catalina Donoso. *El cine de Ignacio Agüero. El documental como la lectura de un espacio.* Santiago: Cuarto Propio, 2015.

Deleuze, Gilles. *Francis Bacon: The Logic of Sensation.* Translated by Daniel W. Smith. Minneapolis: University of Minnesota Press, 2005.

———. "Foucault—Les formations historiques. Année universitaire 1985–1986. Cours de Gilles Deleuze." Transcription: Annabelle Dufourcq (with the assistance of College of Liberal Arts, Purdue University), www2.univ-paris8.fr/deleuze/article.php3?id_article=403. Accessed 22 April 2019.

———. *Foucault.* Translated by Sean Hand. Minneapolis: University of Minnesota Press, 1988.

Déotte, Jean-Louis. "El arte en la época de la desaparición," in *Políticas y estéticas de la memoria*, edited by Nelly Richard, 149–161.

Derrida, Jacques. "Signature Event Context." *Limited, Inc.* Translated by Samuel Weber and Jeffrey Mehlman, 1–23. Evanston, IL: Northwestern University Press, 1988.

———. "Structure, Sign, and Play in the Discourse of the Human Sciences," in *A Postmodern Reader*, edited by Joseph Natoli and Linda Hutcheon, translated by Richard Macksey, 223–242. Albany: State University of New York Press, 1993.

———. "The Deaths of Roland Barthes," in *The Work of Mourning*, edited and translated by Pascale-Anne Brault and Michael Naas, 34–67. Chicago: University of Chicago Press, 2001.

———. *Archive Fever: A Freudian Impression.* Translated by Eric Prenowitz. Chicago: University of Chicago Press, 1998.

———. *Paper-Machine.* Translated by Rachel Bowlby. Palo Alto, CA: Stanford University Press, 2005.

———. *Rogues. Two Essays on Reason.* Translated by Pascale-Anne Brault and Michael Naas. Palo Alto, CA: Stanford University Press, 2005.

———. *Of Grammatology.* 40th Anniversary Edition. Translated by Gayatri Chakravorty Spivak. Baltimore, MD: Johns Hopkins University Press, 2016.

Didi-Huberman, Georges. *Images in Spite of All.* Translated by Shane B. Lillis. Chicago: University of Chicago Press, 2012.

———. *The Eye of History: When Images Take Positions.* Translated by Shane B. Lillis. Minneapolis: University of Minnesota Press, 2018.

Donoso, Claudia. "16 años de fotografía en Chile: Memoria de un descontexto." *Revista de Crítica Cultural* 2 (November 1990): 28–32.

Donoso Macaya, Ángeles. "Arte, documento y fotografía: Prolegómenos para una reformulación del campo fotográfico en Chile (1977–1998)." *Aisthesis* 52, No. 2 (December 2012): 407–424.

———. "Re-pensar la memoria fotográfica. Desplazamientos e irrupciones del retrato fotográfico durante la dictadura militar en Chile," in *Des/memorias: culturas y prácticas mnemónicas en América Latina y el Caribe*, edited by Adriana López Labourdette, Silvia Spitta, and Valeria Wagner, 33–57. Barcelona: Linkgua Ediciones, 2016.

———. "Ediciones económicas de la fotografía chilena," in *Una revisión al fotolibro Chileno*, edited by Horacio Fernández, 210. Santiago: Fundación Sud Fotográfica, 2018.

Douglas, Lee E., editor. "Fragments from a Conversation: Making of This Book. Spring/Summer, 1989. Exchanges between Susan and Chilean Photographers: Alejandro, Álvaro, Claudio, Héctor, Helen, Marcelo, Óscar, and Paz," in *Chile from Within* IBook, edited by Susan Meiselas. New York: MAPP, 2013.

Dufour, Diane, editor. *Images of Conviction. The Construction of Visual Evidence*. Paris: Le Bal/Editions Xavier Barral, 2015.

Durán, Claudio, Fernando Reyes Matta, and Carlos Ruiz, editors. *La prensa: del autoritarismo a la libertad*. Santiago: Centro de Estudios de la Realidad Contemporánea e Instituto Latinoamericano de Estudios Transnacionales (ILET), 1986.

Durand, Régis. *Le temps de l'image: essai sur les conditions d'une histoire des formes photographiques*. Paris: Editions de La Différence, 1995.

Errázuriz, Paz. *FotoNo*. Santiago: Consejo Nacional de la Cultura y las Artes Gobierno de Chile, 2012.

———. *La manzana de Adán*. Santiago: Zona, 1990.

Errázuriz, Paz, and Diamela Eltit. *El infarto del Alma*. Santiago: Francisco Zegers, 1994.

Fabry, Alexis, and María Will. *Urbes Mutantes: Latin American Photography 1944–2013*. Mexico City/Paris: RM/Toluca Editions, 2013.

Feld, Claudia. "La imagen que muestra el secreto. Alice Domon y Léonie Duquet fotografiadas en la ESMA," in Blejmar, Fortuny, and García, 45–67.

———. "Fotografía, desaparición y memoria: fotos tomadas en la ESMA durante su funcionamiento como centro clandestino de detención." *Nuevo Mundo/Mundos Nuevos*, 1 (2014): 1–22.

Feld, Claudia, and Jessica Stites Mor, editors. *El pasado que miramos. Memoria e imagen ante la historia reciente*. Buenos Aires: Paidós, 2009.

Fernández, Horacio, editor. *The Latin American Photobook*. New York: Aperture, 2011.

Ferraris, Maurizio. *Documentality. Why It Is Necessary to Leave Traces*. Translated by Richard Davies. New York: Fordham University Press, 2012.

Ferrer, Rita. *¿Quién es el autor de esto? Fotografía y Performance*. Santiago: Ocho Libros, 2010.

Filippi, Emilio. *Libertad de pensar, libertad de decir*. Santiago: Cisec, 1979.

———. *La fuerza de la verdad*. Santiago: Araucaria, 1983.

Flusser, Vilém. *Towards a Philosophy of Photography*. Translated by Anthony Matthews. London: Reaktion Books, 2000.

Fonseca, Mario. "A propósito de la fotografía en Chile," in *Chile Vive. Muestra de Arte y Cultura*. 33–40. Madrid: Ministerio de Cultura de España, 1987.

Fornazzari, Alessandro. *Speculative Fictions*. Durham, NC: Duke University Press, 2011.

Foster, Hal. *The Return of the Real*. Cambridge: MIT Press, 1996.

Foucault, Michel. "Photogenic Painting," translated by Dafydd Roberts, in *Gérard Fromanger: Photogenic Painting*, series editor Sarah Wilson, 81–106. London: Black Dog, 1999.

———. *The Archeology of Knowledge: And the Discourse of Language*. Translated by A. M. Sheridan Smith. New York: Vintage, 1982.

Freud, Sigmund. *The Interpretation of Dreams*. Translated by James Strachey. New York: Basic Books, 2010.

Galende, Federico. *Filtraciones I. Conversaciones sobre arte en Chile (de los 60's a los 80's)*. Santiago: Universidad ARCIS, 2007.

García, Luis Ignacio, and Ana Longoni. "Imágenes invisibles. Acerca de las fotos de Desaparecidos," in Blejmar, Fortuny, and García, 25–44.

Gatti, Gabriel. *Surviving Forced Disappearance in Argentina and Uruguay: Identity and Meaning*. New York: Palgrave Macmillan, 2014.

Gervais, Thierry, editor. *The "Public" Life of Photographs*. Cambridge: MIT Press /Ryerson Image Centre Book Series, 2016.

Gitelman, Lisa. *Paper Knowledge. Toward a Media History of Documents*. Durham, NC: Duke University Press, 2014.

Gómez-Barris, Macarena. *Where Memory Dwells: Culture and State Violence in Chile*. Oakland: University of California Press, 2008.

González, Mónica. *La conjura. Los mil y un días del golpe*. Santiago: Universidad Diego Portales/Catalonia, 2012.

Granesse, José Luis, editor. *Fotografía chilena contemporánea*. Santiago: Kodak Chilena, 1985.

Gronemeyer, Jorge, "Chile Ayer Hoy," in *Una revisión al fotolibro Chileno*, edited by Horacio Fernández, 142. Santiago: Fundación Sud Fotográfica, 2018.

Hariman, Robert, and John Louis Lucaites. *No Captions Needed: Iconic Photographs, Public Culture, and Liberal Democracy*. Chicago: University of Chicago Press, 2011.

Harvey, David. *A Brief History of Neoliberalism*. Oxford: Oxford University Press, 2005.

Hirsch, Marianne. *Family Frames: Photography, Narrative and Postmemory*. Scotts Valley: CreateSpace Independent Publishing Platform, 2012.

———. *The Generation of Postmemory: Writing and Visual Culture after the Holocaust*. New York: Columbia University Press, 2012.

———. "The Generation of Postmemory." *Poetics Today* 29, No. 1 (Spring 2008): 103–128.

Human Rights Watch. *Los límites de la tolerancia: Libertad de expresión y debate público en Chile*. Santiago: LOM, 1998.

Ianiszewski, Jorge. "Editorial." *Punto de Vista*, October, 1982.

Inter-American Commission on Human Rights. "Report on The Situation of Human Rights in Chile." 9 September 1985, www.cidh.org/countryrep/Chile85eng/TOC.htm. Accessed 22 April 2019.

International Commission of Jurists. *Chile: A Time of Reckoning. Human Rights and the Judiciary*, www.icj.org/wp-content/uploads/1992/01/Chile-time-of-reckoning-thematic-report-1992-eng.pdf. Accessed 22 April 2019.

Jara Hinojosa, Isabel. "Editora Nacional Gabriela Mistral y clases sociales: indicio del neoliberalismo en la retórica de la dictadura chilena." *Historia* 48, No. 2 (July–December 2015): 505–535.

Joignant, Alfredo. *El gesto y la palabra. Ritos políticos y representaciones de la construcción democrática en Chile*. Santiago: LOM/ARCIS, 1998.

Kay, Ronald. *Del espacio de acá. Señales para una mirada americana.* Santiago: Metales Pesados, 2005.

Keenan, Thomas. "I Decided to Take a Look, Again," in Cadava and Nouzeilles, 78–83.

Keenan, Thomas, and Eyal Weizman. *Mengele's Skull: The Advent of Forensics Aesthetics.* New York: Sternberg Press, 2012.

Keenan, Thomas, and Hito Steyerl. "What Is a Document? An Exchange between Thomas Keenan and Hito Steyerl." *Aperture Magazine* 214 (Spring 2014): 58–64.

Kennedy, Liam. *Afterimages: Photography and U.S. Foreign Policy.* Chicago: University of Chicago Press, 2016.

Klein, Naomi. *The Shock Doctrine: The Rise of Disaster Capitalism.* New York: Picador, 2008.

Kornbluh, Peter. *The Pinochet File: A Classified Dossier on Atrocity and Accountability.* New York/London: The New Press, 2013.

Krauss, Rosalind. "Sculpture in the Expanded Field." *October* 8 (Spring 1979): 30–44.

———. *The Originality of the Avant-Garde and Other Modernist Myths.* Cambridge: MIT Press, 1986.

———. *Le photographique: Pour un théorie des Écarts.* Translated by Marc Bloch and Ann Hindry. Paris: Éditions Macula, 1990.

Lacan, Jacques. *The Seminar of Jacques Lacan: The Four Fundamental Concepts of Psychoanalysis, Book XI,* edited by Jacques-Alain Miller, translated by Alan Sheridan. New York: W.W. Norton & Company, 1998.

Lavoie, Vincent. "Displaying Forensic Pictures in Court: Photographs as Visual Argument," in *The "Public" Life of Photographs,* edited by Thierry Gervais, 75–95. Cambridge, MA: MIT Press/Ryerson Image Centre Book Series, 2016.

Lazzara, Michael. *Chile in Transition: The Poetics and Politics of Memory.* Gainesville: University Press of Florida, 2011.

Leiva Quijada, Gonzalo. *AFI: Multitudes en sombras.* Santiago: Ocho Libros, 2008.

———. *Luis Navarro: La potencia de la memoria.* Santiago: Gobierno de Chile/Fondart, 2004.

Lemagny, Jean-Claude, and Andre Rouillé. *A History of Photography.* Cambridge: Cambridge University Press, 1987.

León Lira, Matías. *El periodismo que no calló. Historia de la revista Análisis (1977/1993).* Santiago: La Nación Domingo, 2005.

Libro Blanco del Cambio de Gobierno en Chile. Santiago: Editorial Lord Cochrane, 1973.

Lihn, Enrique. "La fotografía: entre la censura y el conformismo," *Cauce,* October 16 to October 22, 1984.

———. *Textos sobre arte,* edited by Adriana Valdés y Ana María Risco. Santiago: Universidad Diego Portales, 2008.

Lind, Maria, and Hito Steyerl, editors. *The Greenroom. Reconsidering the Documentary and Contemporary Art #1,* New York: Sternberg Press, 2008.

Linfield, Susie. *The Cruel Radiance. Photography and Political Violence.* Chicago: University of Chicago Press, 2011.

Lorenzini, Kena. *Fragmento fotográfico: arte, narración y memoria. Chile 1980–1990.* Santiago: Ocho Libros, 2006.

Lugon, Olivier. "'Documentary': Authority and Ambiguities," in Lind and Steyerl, 28–37.

———. *Le Style documentaire. D'August Sander à Walker Evans, 1920–1945.* Paris: Éditions Macula, 2001.

Marras, Sergio. "A 11 años del once." *Apsi*, September 10 to September 23, 1984.

Meiselas, Susan. "Photography, Expanded: Conversation with Chris Boot," *Aperture Magazine*, aperture.org/blog/photography-expanded-conversation-chris-boot. Accessed 22 April 2019.

———, editor. *Chile from Within*. New York: W.W Norton, 1990.

———, editor. *Chile from Within* IBook. New York: MAPP, 2013.

Mellado, Justo Pastor. "La novela chilena de Mario Fonseca," in *Fotografía: 1986–1995. Mario Fonseca Velasco.* n.p. Santiago: Museo Nacional de Bellas Artes, 1996.

———. *Sueños Privados, Ritos Públicos. En ocasión de la muestra* LONQUÉN 10 AÑOS *de Gonzalo Díaz que se realiza en Galería OJO DE BUEY.* Santiago: Ediciones de la Cortina de Humo, 1989.

Memoria Viva. "Lonquén," in Desaparecidos/Casos/Lonquén, www.memoriaviva.com/Desaparecidos/lonquen.htm. Accessed 22 April 2019.

Mera, Jorge, and Carlos Ruiz. "Notas sobre la libertad de prensa, censura y política en Chile," in Durán, Reyes Matta, and Ruiz, 175–206.

Merino, José Toribio. "Carta" *Fotogente* N°2 (1980).

Merriam-Webster Dictionary, www.merriam-webster.com. Accessed 22 April 2019.

Mirzoeff, Nicholas. *The Right to Look: A Counterhistory of Visuality*. Durham, NC: Duke University Press, 2011.

Mnookin, Jennifer L. "The Image of Truth: Photographic Evidence and the Power of Analogy," in *Images of Conviction: The Construction of Visual Evidence*, edited by Diane Dufour, 9–15. Paris: Éditions Xavier Barral, 2015.

Mönckeberg, María Olivia. *Los magnates de la prensa*. Santiago: Debate, 2009.

———. "Clamor Popular: Democracia," *Análisis* 81, May 8 to May 22, 1984.

Moors, Ximena A. "Para una arqueología del testimonio: el rol de la Iglesia Católica en una producción textual (1973–1991)." *Revista Iberoamericana* LX, No. 168–169 (July–December 1994): 1161–1176.

Moreno, Sebastián, dir. *La ciudad de los fotógrafos*; Películas del Pez/Zoofilms, 2006.

Moulián, Tomás. *Chile Actual. Anatomía de un mito*. Santiago: LOM/ARCIS, 1997.

Navarro, Arturo. "El sistema de prensa bajo el régimen militar (1973–1986)," in Durán, Reyes Matta, and Ruiz, 127–142.

Nesbit, Molly. "The Use of History." *Art in America* 74 (February 1986): 72–83.

Neustadt, Robert. *CADA día: la creación de un arte social*. Santiago: Cuarto Propio, 2001.

Olin, Margaret. *Touching Photographs*. Chicago: University of Chicago Press, 2012.

Ossandón, Fernando, and Sandra Rojas. *La* Época *y Fortín Mapocho. El primer impacto*. Santiago: ECO-CEDAL, 1989.

Oyarzún, Pablo. "Arte en Chile de veinte, treinta años," in *Arte, Visualidad e Historia*. Santiago: Ediciones La Blanca Montaña, 2000, 1–31.

———. "Estética de la sed: *Lonquén 10 años*, diez años después." *Revista Iberoamericana* LXIX, no 202 (January–March 2003): 85–94.

Oyarzún, Pablo, Nelly Richard, and Claudia Zaldívar, editors. *Arte y política*. Santiago: Universidad ARCIS/Universidad de Chile/Consejo Nacional de la Cultura y las Artes, 2005.

Oxford Dictionaries, www.oxforddictionaries.com. Accessed 22 April 2019.

Pacheco, Máximo. *Lonquén*. Santiago: Comisión Chilena de Derechos Humanos /Editorial Aconcagua, 1983.

Panzer, Mary, editor. *Things as They Are*. New York: Aperture, 2005.

Papapetros, Spyros, and Julian Rose, editors, *Retracing the Expanded Field: Encounters between Art and Architecture*. Cambridge: MIT Press, 2014.

Parot, Carmen Luz, dir. *Estadio Nacional*; Ford Foundation/Corfo, 2003.

Peirce, Charles S. *The Collected Papers of Charles Peirce* v. 2, edited by Charles Hartshorne and Paul Weiss. Cambridge, MA: Harvard University Press, 1932.

Pérez Mendoza, Consuelo. *Los protagonistas de la prensa alternativa: Vicaría de la Solidaridad y Fundación de Ayuda Social de las Iglesias Cristianas*. Santiago: Fundación Archivo Vicaría, 1997.

Phelan, Peggy. "Haunted Stages: Performance and the Photographic Effect," in *Haunted: Contemporary Photography / Video / Performance*, edited by Jennifer Blessing, 50–63. New York: The Solomon R. Guggenheim Foundation, 2010.

Phu, Thy. "Vietnamese Photography and the Look of Revolution," in *Photography and the Optical Unconscious*, edited by Shawn Michelle Smith and Sharon Sliwinski, 286–320. Durham, NC: Duke University Press, 2017.

Poole, Deborah. *Vision, Race, and Modernity: A Visual Economy of the Andean Image World*. Princeton, NJ: Princeton University Press, 1997.

Precht, Cristián. "Introducción," in *¿Dónde están?* Vol. I, 9–11. Santiago: Vicaría de la Solidaridad, 1978.

Punto de Vista. "Agencias AFI." October, 1981.

Punto de Vista. "Ausencia de la crítica: un comentario." December 1982—January 1983.

Punto de Vista. "Editorial." August, 1985.

Rabe, Stephen G. *The Killing Zone: The United States Wages Cold War in Latin America*. Cambridge: Oxford University Press, 2012.

Rancière, Jacques. *The Future of the Image*. Translated by Gregory Elliott. New York: Verso, 2009.

———. *The Emancipated Spectator*. Translated by Gregory Elliott. New York: Verso, 2011.

Rees, A. L., David Curtis, Duncan White, and Steven Ball, editors, *Expanded Cinema: Art, Performance, Film*. London: Tate Modern, 2011.

Report of the Chilean National Commission on Truth and Reconciliation, www.usip.org/sites/default/files/resources/collections/truth_commissions/Chile90-Report/Chile90-Report.pdf. Accessed 22 April 2019.

Reyes Matta, Fernando, Jorge Andrés Richards, and Juan Pablo Cárdenas, editors. *Periodismo independiente* ¿Mito *o realidad?: debates sobre militancia, profesionalismo, democracia y verdad con los directores de las revistas prohibidas y censuradas en Chile bajo el Estado de Sitio*. Santiago: Instituto Latinoamericano de Estudios Transnacionales, 1986.

Ribalta, Jorge. *Universal Archive. The Condition of the Document and the Modern Photographic Utopia*. Barcelona: Museu d'Art Contemporani de Barcelona, 2008.

———. *Public Photographic Spaces: Propaganda Exhibitions from Pressa to The Family of Man, 1928–55*. Barcelona: Museu D'Art Contemporani de Barcelona, 2009.

Rich, Adrienne. "Compulsive Heterosexuality and Lesbian Existence." *Journal of Women's History* 15, No. 3 (Autumn 2003): 11–48.

Richard, Nelly. "Bordes, límites, fronteras," in *Los límites de la fotografía*, edited by André Rouillé, 6–7. Paris: AFAA, 1996.

———. *Residuos y Metáforas. Ensayos de crítica cultural sobre el Chile de la transición*. Santiago: Cuarto Propio, 1998.

———, editor. *Políticas y estéticas de la memoria*. Santiago: Cuarto Propio, 2000.

———. "Imagen-recuerdo y borraduras," in *Políticas y estéticas de la memoria*, edited by Nelly Richard, 165–172.

Richard, Nelly, and Alberto Moreiras. *Pensar en/la Postdictadura*. Santiago: Cuarto Propio, 2001.

———. *The Insubordination of Signs: Political Change, Cultural Transformation, and Poetics of the Crisis*. Translated by Alice A. Nelson and Silvia R. Tandeciarz. Durham, NC: Duke UP, 2004.

———. *Márgenes e Instituciones. Arte en Chile desde 1973*. Santiago: Metales Pesados, 2014.

———. *Paz Errázuriz and Lotty Rosenfeld: Poetics of Dissent*. Barcelona: Ediciones Polígrafa, 2016.

Riles, Annelise, editor. *Documents: Artifacts of Modern Knowledge*. Cambridge: MIT Press, 2006.

Riobó, Felipe. "Fotografía chilena: proyecto actual, proyecto possible." *Punto de Vista*, June–July, 1983.

———. "Presentación" in *Ediciones Económicas: Mauricio Valenzuela*. vol. 1 (April 1983).

Rodríguez Villegas, Hernán. "Historia de la fotografía en Chile: registro de daguerrotipos, fotógrafos, reporteros gráficos y camarógrafos" *Boletín de la Academia de Historia* 96 (1985): 189–340.

Rosler, Martha. "In, Around, and Afterthoughts (On Documentary Photography)," in *The Contest of Meaning: Critical Histories of Photography*, edited by Richard Bolton, 303–340. Cambridge, MA: MIT Press, 1990.

Rouillé, André. *Los límites de la fotografía*. Paris: AFAA, 1996.

———. *La photographie. Entre document et art contemporain*. Paris: Éditions Gallimard, 2005.

———. "The Times of the Document," in *Slow Motion, A Cámara Lenta, Volume* 5, edited by André Rouillé, Elena Foster, and Marta Gili, 9–12. Madrid: Ivorypress, 2013.

Santibáñez, Abraham. "Testimonio de un visitante." *Hoy*, December, 1978.

Sekula, Alan. "Dismantling Modernism, Reinventing Documentary (Notes on the Politics of Representation." *The Massachusetts Review* 19, No. 4 (Winter, 1978): 859–883.

———. "The Body and the Archive" *October* 39 (Winter 1986): 3–64.

Sepúlveda Chávez, Miguel Ángel. "Evolución del discurso anti-resistencia en la dictadura militar chilena." *Religación: Revista de Ciencias Sociales y Humanidades* 1, No. 3 (2016): 55–75.

Solomon-Godeau, Abigail. *Photography at the Dock*. Minneapolis: University of Minnesota Press, 1994.

Solidaridad. "11 de marzo: garantías suspendidas." March 1981.

Sontag, Susan. *On Photography*. New York: Picador, 2001.

Staff Report of the Select Committee to Study Governmental Operations with Respect to Intelligence Activities, *Covert Action in Chile 1963–1973*, www.intelligence.senate.gov/sites/default/files/94chile.pdf. Accessed 22 April 2019.

Stern, Steve J. *Battling for Hearts and Minds: Memory Struggles in Chile, 1973–1998*. Durham, NC: Duke University Press, 2006.

Stoler, Ann Laura. "On Archiving as Dissensus." *Comparative Studies of South Asia, Africa and the Middle East* 38, No. 1 (2018): 43–56.

Stott, William *Documentary Expression and Thirties America*. Oxford/NewYork: Oxford University Press, 1973.

Taffet, Jeffrey. *Foreign Aid as Foreign Policy: The Alliance for Progress in Latin America*. London: Routledge, 2007.

Tagg, John. *Grounds of Dispute*. Minneapolis: University of Minnesota Press, 1992.

———. *The Disciplinary Frame. Photographic Truths and the Capture of Meaning*. Minneapolis: University of Minnesota Press, 2008.

Taylor, Diana. *Disappearing Acts: Spectacles of Gender and Nationalism in Argentina's "Dirty War."* Durham, NC: Duke UP, 1997.

———. *The Archive and the Repertoire. Performing Cultural Memory in the Americas*. Durham, NC: Duke University Press, 2003.

Thayer, Willy. *El fragmento repetido*. Santiago: Metales Pesados, 2006.

———. "El xenotafio de luz," in *Políticas y estéticas de la memoria*, edited by Nelly Richard, 173–174.

Trachtenberg, Alan. *Classic Essays on Photography*. Sedgwick: Leete's Island Books, 1980.

Trumper, Camilo D. *Ephemeral Histories: Public Art, Politics, and the Struggles for the Street in Chile*. Oakland: University of California Press, 2016.

Valderrama, Miguel. *Modernismos historiográficos. Modernismos historiográficos. Artes Visuales, postdictadura, vanguardias*. Santiago de Chile: Palinodia, 2008.

Valenzuela, J. Samuel. "La Constitución de 1980 y el inicio de la Redemocratización en Chile." *The Helen Kellogg Institute for International Studies, Working Paper* 242 (September 1997), kellogg.nd.edu/sites/default/files/old_files/documents/242_0.pdf. Accessed 22 April 2019.

Varas, Paulina. *Luz Donoso. El arte y la acción en el presente*. Santiago: Ocho Libros, 2018.

———. *Una acción hecha por otro es una obra de Luz Donoso*, www.lascondes.cl/resources/descargas/cultura/catalogos/una_accion_hecha_por_otro.pdf. Accessed 22 April 2019.

Varela López, Elena, dir. *Newen Mapuche*; Ojofilm, 2011.

Verdugo, Patricia. *Rodrigo y Carmen Gloria: Quemados vivos*. Santiago: Catalonia, 2015.

Verdugo, Patricia, and Claudio Orrego V. *Detenidos desaparecidos: Una herida abierta*. Santiago: Aconcagua, 1980.

Vicaría de la Solidaridad *¿Dónde están?* 7 v. Santiago: Vicaría de la Solidaridad, 1978.

Vilches, Lorenzo. *Teoría de la imagen periodística*. Barcelona: Paidós, 1993.

Weinstein, Luis. "Editorial." *Punto de Vista*, December 1982–January 1983.

———. "Editorial." *Punto de Vista*, June–July 1983.

Williams, Raymond. *Marxism and Literature*. Oxford: Oxford University Press, 1978.

Zúñiga, Rodrigo. "Posdictadura y conmoción del secreto (*Lonquén 10 años*, de Gonzalo Díaz y la escenografía trizada de la Transición)," in *Arte y Política*, edited by Pablo Oyarzún, Nelly Richard, and Claudia Zaldívar, 27–32. Santiago: Universidad ARCIS/Universidad de Chile/Consejo Nacional de la Cultura y las Artes, 2005.

Index

ÁNGELES DONOSO MACAYA is professor of Spanish at the Borough of Manhattan Community College/CUNY and professor of Latin American Culture and Visual Studies at The Graduate Center/CUNY. She is coeditor of *Latinas/os on the East Coast: A Critical Reader.*

Reframing Media, Technology, and Culture in Latin/o America

EDITED BY HÉCTOR FERNÁNDEZ L'HOESTE AND JUAN CARLOS RODRÍGUEZ

Reframing Media, Technology, and Culture in Latin/o America explores how Latin American and Latino audiovisual (film, television, digital), musical (radio, recordings, live performances, dancing), and graphic (comics, photography, advertising) cultural practices reframe and reconfigure social, economic, and political discourses at a local, national, and global level. In addition, it looks at how information networks reshape public and private policies, and the enactment of new identities in civil society. The series also covers how different technologies have allowed and continue to allow for the construction of new ethnic spaces. It not only contemplates the interaction between new and old technologies but also how the development of brand-new technologies redefines cultural production.

Telling Migrant Stories: Latin American Diaspora in Documentary Film, edited by Esteban E. Loustaunau and Lauren E. Shaw (2018; paperback edition, 2021)

Mestizo Modernity: Race, Technology, and the Body in Postrevolutionary Mexico, by David S. Dalton (2018; first paperback edition, 2021)

The Insubordination of Photography: Documentary Practices under Chile's Dictatorship, by Ángeles Donoso Macaya (2020; first paperback edition, 2023)

Digital Humanities in Latin America, edited by Héctor Fernández L'Hoeste and Juan Carlos Rodríguez (2020)

Pablo Escobar and Colombian Narcoculture, by Aldona Bialowas Pobutsky (2020)

The New Brazilian Mediascape: Television Production in the Digital Streaming Age, by Eli Lee Carter (2020)

Univision, Telemundo, and the Rise of Spanish-Language Television in the United States, by Craig Allen (2020)

Cuba's Digital Revolution: Citizen Innovation and State Policy, edited by Ted A. Henken and Sara Garcia Santamaria (2021; first paperback edition, 2022)

Afro-Latinx Digital Connections, edited by Eduard Arriaga and Andrés Villar (2021)

The Lost Cinema of Mexico: From Lucha Libre to Cine Familiar and Other Churros, edited by Olivia Cosentino and Brian Price (2022)

Neo-Authoritarian Masculinity in Brazilian Crime Film, by Jeremy Lehnen (2022)

www.ingramcontent.com/pod-product-compliance
Lightning Source LLC
LaVergne TN
LVHW091121080826
845145LV00008B/2005
* 9 7 8 1 6 8 3 4 0 3 5 4 8 *